Pioneers

Larry Allen Denham

iUniverse, Inc.
New York Bloomington

Pioneers

iUniverse books may be ordered through booksellers or by contacting:

iUniverse
1663 Liberty Drive
Bloomington, IN 47403
www.iuniverse.com
1-800-Authors (1-800-288-4677)

ISBN: 978-1-4401-9935-6 (sc)
ISBN: 978-1-4401-9936-3 (ebook)

Printed in the United States of America

iUniverse rev. date: 12/10/2009

ONE

▼

IT WAS A bittersweet feeling, no matter how he looked at it. Although he had had the satisfaction of winning the individual all-around several times in his career, the thought of his team falling just short of its goal, a victory at the National Team Invitational, was enough to remind Patrick that his job was far from finished. Even though he had become what some would call the best gymnast to ever come out of the Pioneer Gymnastics club, Patrick Goodman knew that there was still one more hill to climb, a national team championship. Even though their latest failed attempt was more than four months ago, the sting was still as sharp as if the meet had been just last night. The pain that he felt was no secret. Everyone on the team felt it. Patrick, AJ, Dallas, and the rest of the team had come up though the same system and shared the same dream. His dream. Coach Lowery's dream. This dream of winning the NTIs had actually become more than a dream. It had become an obsession. Which was more important, individual success or team success? It was all pretty much the same when Patrick thought about it. If all of the individuals within the team excelled, wouldn't the team excel as well? And, so what if the team fails, as long as they did their best, right? Nope, it still leaves an empty spot in the stomach, regardless of individual effort and success. It would mean so much. After all, not any team in Tennessee, much less his little town just outside Knoxville, had ever brought home a team championship.

Just the thought of coming so close made Patrick ill. Then, he thought about all the time he had put into this sport, and what time he had left to accomplish what he so desperately wanted. Not just for his coach, but also for himself. Patrick had been there with Coach Lowery through the tough times when he was one of the only guys on team. And now they finally had a team that was almost big enough, and almost good good enough to contend. Clubs in the bigger cities, with more people to draw from, could hand pick their talent, and could always count on having a large team. The Pioneer teams had always been small. Although Patrick often wondered what it would be like to train with the powerhouse programs up North and out West, he was content with the sense of family that came with training in a smaller gym and the benefit of not having to compete for the coach's attention. Time was running out for Patrick. This would be his last season as a Pioneer. After all, gymnasts graduate, and then some continue in college, while others just sort of fade away. And it's not like awesome gymnasts are growing on trees to fill in the rest of the puzzle. In the big towns you can almost always count on somebody moving into town from somewhere who has done some gymnastics, but it's really not likely to happen this far away from everything.

Although Patrick would be starting his senior year at Kennedy High in just two weeks, he had been much too busy training to look at colleges. Not that Patrick was the only senior, because he was one of four on the team. The difference was that the others already had plans: AJ was going to work full time with his dad; Mackee was mulling over two schools, each of which wanted him to compete rings; and Dallas was headed for the Ivy League.

For Patrick, it was different. He needed gymnastics. A scholarship in gymnastics was about the only way he was going to get to college, and he was counting on it. For years, he had fallen asleep with mental images of performing difficult routines effortlessly and dominating awards ceremonies with his teammates. He couldn't picture himself not doing gymnastics. But, with the dwindling number of college gymnastics programs, and with it the dwindling number of scholarships available, combined with not already being on the short lists of those schools, Patrick knew the likelihood of being recruited was becoming more and more remote. Sure, it would be nice to have Dallas's money and be able to pick and choose, but unless there was a school willing to take a chance on a country boy from east Tenneessee, Patrick had very few options, and none of them involved gymnastics.

Patrick felt ill again.

Training had become as much a habit as eating or brushing his teeth. He had turned it into a ritual. He would show up at the gym about a half hour early, tape his wrists, stretch, and swing a little—to get the kinks out. As the other guys arrived, he would make sure they warmed up properly, without cheating, and that everyone was ready for first event when Coach came out of his office, usually about twenty minutes into workout.

Today, however, something seemed different, and not just to Patrick. The other guys had the same eerie feeling that something was not normal.

Warm-up was just about finished when it started—a rumbling that felt somewhere between a freight train and an earthquake. As it neared, the disturbance identified itself. It was a combination of a motorcycle motor grumbling and Heavy Metal turned up so it could be heard over the motor's roar. Then, just as the rumbling sounded as though it would come through the gym wall, it stopped. The teammates looked at each other, then to Patrick, hoping he had a clue, but he was just as confused. Just as Dallas started to open his mouth, most likely with some wisecrack, Coach Lowery's door opened. Walking out with their mentor was an unfamiliar character. He looked like a lot of things, but "gymnast" was not on the list. From the looks of his over-the-calf leather motorcycle boots, tattered jeans, and black leather jacket, which were complemented by his long blonde hair and the crucifix in his left ear, the team knew this guy was in the wrong building.

"Gentlemen, I'd like you to meet Chris McClure, your new teammate. He just moved here from California," Coach Lowery said.

Any one of them could've been knocked over with a feather. Then, as though he had been nominated as team spokesman, Patrick spoke up, his voice almost cracking.

"Hi … uh … Chris, I'm Patrick … uh, Goodman. Um … welcome to Pioneer Gymnastics."

"Uh, thanks, Patrick, was it? You can just call me Slash," Chris answered as he peered over the top of his dark sunglasses and shook Patrick's hand.

Six jaws dropped, and twelve eyes bugged out. Patrick shook his hand out of reflex while his brain tried to process how this guy could possibly be a gymnast.

"You mind if I have my hand back, Pat?" Chris said, puffing out his chest and casting a stern gaze at the group.

"Oh, sorry, sorry," Patrick apologized.

"Dudes, I'm just kidding. Relax. Just call me Chris." Chris broke character and tried to lighten the mood.

That was enough to break the ice. As everyone relaxed, each team member introduced himself.

Dallas was first. "How ya doin', Chris? I'm David Dallas, but everybody just calls me Dallas."

"Great to meet ya, David," Chris said, almost sarcastically.

"*Dallas*," replied Dallas, as his smile turned to a half sneer.

"Sorry … Dallas," Chris returned, only half serious.

With each introduction, the guys tried to make Chris feel a little more comfortable with his new surroundings.

"Don't let these jerks get you down. They're always brutal on the fresh meat," came a small, nearly cracking voice from his left. Chris turned to see the smallest of his new teammates. Joey Johnson was every bit of five feet three inches tall with reddish hair and blue eyes. He looked like a model for a Norman Rockwell painting.

"Stick with me, Chris, I'll show you how to deal with these jokers. By the way, my name is Joey." Everyone chuckled at Joey's display of machismo. Then, it was time to get back to work.

"So, Chris, are you ready to work out?" asked Patrick.

"Can't today. Didn't bring my stuff. Just wanted to drop in and find out the schedule. I'll check you guys tomorrow. Take it easy." And with that, Chris thanked his new coach and turned to leave. Within moments, the roar of a motorcycle and the wail of Metalica punctuated his exit. Each Pioneer stared at each other until the tornado that carried in their newest member was nothing more than a distant hum.

"Well, you don't see too many guys like that around Knoxville," offered Ty. Being the only black gymnast on the team, and a Michigan transplant, Ty Street knew the feeling of not immediately fitting in.

"Listen, fellas," said Coach. "Do your best to help him fit in."

"I'll betcha things won't get dull around here for a while," said Mackee as he strapped on his high bar grips.

"Yeah, but I was kinda getting used to dull," said Patrick. Even though the thought of another teammate was exciting to everyone, Patrick could feel that this new gymnast would disrupt the daily routine he had become accustom to.

"If you ask me, I think the guy's a veg between the ears," said Dallas.

Coach Lowery yelled for everyone to get to work, and in the hours that passed, everyone's thoughts turned more toward gymnastics and away from the dark, radical stranger that would soon turn their lives upside down.

T W O

▼

WEDNESDAY WORKOUTS WERE usually pretty mundane. Hit a few routines on each event, try to make some progress on a new skill or combination, do strength conditioning, and go home. Today, however, everyone's mind was on the new guy from California. It was thirty minutes into workout when the first mention of Chris was made.

"Are you sure he knew what time workout started, Patrick?" Joey asked.

Patrick opened his mouth, but before words could come out, Dallas added his two cents.

"Yeah, I'm sure he knows," Dallas interjected, still sore from his verbal confrontation of a day ago. "He's probably at home sleeping off a hangover. I wouldn't count on this guy for anything special. I kinda hope the jerk doesn't even show."

"Lighten up, Dallas. You're gonna break into hives!" exclaimed Ty, who knew a case of overreaction when he saw one.

Just then, the already familiar din that preceded Chris's entrance a day ago could be heard in the distance and growing louder.

"Well then, I hope he can train with a headache," remarked Joey sarcastically.

A few minutes later, the locker room door burst open and into the gym walked, in no apparent hurry, the seventeen-year-old upstart from Riverside, California. His appearance was more that of a punk rocker than of a gymnast. He was wearing a tank top three sizes too large with holes in it, as though he had just lost a knife fight. His shorts, which at some point were probably blue, were a dingy grayish white from excessive wear and tons of gymnastics chalk. His grips and other gear were in a brown paper lunch bag.

He was met halfway by Coach Lowery, who also was a little anxious.

"You *do* know that practice started at five, don't you, Chris?" came the obvious question in a half inquisitive, half ticked-off tone.

"Yeah, Coach, I know. I'm sorry. Couldn't be avoided, but I promise it won't happen again," replied Chris in an apologetic tone that did not fit his appearance.

"Well, see that it doesn't. I try to run things pretty close to schedule, and you've already missed warm-up. Get stretched, and join the guys back on rings."

Having said his piece, Coach Lowery turned and started across the floor exercise carpet toward the team, which had already started warm up swings on rings. About halfway across the floor, he heard the sound of running behind him. As he turned, Chris, like a ragging bull, was charging across the forty-by-forty-foot spring floor. Having tucked his bag under his shirt, he began back handspringing across the floor faster than any one of them had ever seen. Just as it looked as though he would tumble out of control, off the floor, and into harm's way, he blocked the floor hard with his feet, redirecting him fifteen feet straight up, with no sign of rotating to his feet. Then, at the peak of his flight, he tucked into a tiny ball, rotated to upside down, and kicked out at vertical, only to drop like a cat onto his feet. Without breaking stride, Chris bolted toward the rest of the team to take his place in line, yelling at Coach over his shoulder and pulling his long hair back into a ponytail as he ran. "I think I'm warmed up now!"

"I can already tell—that son of a gun is gonna be the death of me," Coach Lowery said under his breath, and he continued across the floor to join the rest of the team. "Okay, Chris, let's start with just some basic swing to get the old body warmed up."

Chris jumped up on the rings. His first swing was anything but basic. Each swing moved effortlessly from handstand to handstand, arms locked, each body position perfect.

That's the most fantastic swing I have ever seen, thought Coach. After ten perfect lock-arm giant swings in each direction, Chris dismounted with a full-twisting double back with a stuck landing.

"Basic swing, eh, Chris?" prodded his new coach.

"Yeah, pretty much," answered Chris in a nonchalant toss back.

"Basic show-off, if you ask me," Dallas whispered to AJ.

"Basic excellence, if you ask me," returned AJ, "Why don't you keep an eye on this guy? You might accidentally learn something."

"Chris, that was awesome," said Joey, nearly falling off the platform he was using to get to the rings.

"Thanks, little guy," said Chris. Joey hopped up on the rings to take his turn. From his swings, Chris could tell that, although Joey was not quite the caliber of the rest of the team, he had strengths and potential yet to be realized.

"That was pretty nice, Chris," Coach Lowery commented. "Let's see if your skills match your swing."

"Sure thing, Coach."

With each member's turn, the difficulty increased. The difference being Chris's turns started out far better than everyone else's and got better from there, distancing himself from the level of the rest of the team. With each turn, it was hard not to wonder where this level of gymnastics had been hiding. Coach Lowery and the team thought they had seen the best the country had to offer, but this was a level none of them had seen before.

As the team finished its swing workout on Rings, the guys switched to strength parts and combinations.

"Hey, Chris, check this out," said Mackee, by far the best ring man in the gym—in the state, for that matter. He hopped up on the rings, and executed, from a dead hang, a straight-arm backward roll to an iron cross with a ninety-degree bend at the hips. After a three-second hold, Mackee pressed down harder with his hands, slowly rose to a momentary L support, opened his hips to a straight body support, and continued to roll forward while pressing, with a straight body, to a rock-solid handstand.

"Very good, Mackee. What do you do for an encore?" said Chris. Mackee swung from the handstand to a double-twisting, layout double back, stuck.

Everyone's eyes panned over to an applauding, smiling Chris. Sure that Chris had found his match, everyone else smiled, too.

Without a word, Chris chalked his hands, spit on his grips, and approached the rings. Blowing out a breath, Chris jumped to grab the rings. His first strength skill, a butterfly cross, was enough to show that there was no contest. The butterfly is best described as a straight-armed pull from a dead hang to an iron cross. Without so much as a tight upper lip, he continued to press upward while rotating forward until he was in a horizontal cross, also known as a Maltese. After a three-second hold, and the first signs of sweat beginning to show, he pressed down on the rings and rotated his body forward and upward until he arrived at an upside-down, or inverted, cross. He held the position for about four seconds and then finished his press upward into a motionless handstand. Chris gasped for a breath. Then, before everyone else had a chance to catch his own breath, he dismounted with an almost effortless triple back, stuck.

As if his landing were a cue, everyone burst into applause at the most incredible strength set they had ever witnessed. Although also impressed, Dallas kept his emotion in check and offered only slight acknowledgement. "Not bad, Slash."

Mackee summed everything up as he shook Chris's hand, "Not bad? Holy crap! Man, that was unbelievable. I mean, that was unbe-frigging-lievable!"

Patrick joined in the congratulations. "Man, that was pure, unadulterated fantastic. I hope you're not a one-event gymnast."

"To be honest," replied Chris, "rings isn't even my favorite event."

"You don't say," retorted Patrick. "I say, let's see what you're made of." And with that, the workout continued with Chris showing the rest of the team what *real* gymnastics was about. As each gymnast showed off his favorite skill, Chris seemed to have the ability to take that skill and make it better. If Ty landed a huge Tsukahara vault, Chris would do the same vault and add a full twist. Dallas showed a strong double back off of Parallel Bars and Chris would do it in piked position. The rest of the team either tried to keep up or conceded to Chris's mastery of the sport and chose simply to watch in awe.

After the workout, Chris headed for the locker room.

"Wait a minute, Chris!" exclaimed Patrick. "We're not quite finished. We haven't done the Pioneer Circle."

"What the hell is a Pioneer Circle?" came the obvious question.

"Come here. We'll show you," said Ty. Everyone formed a circle in the middle of the spring floor.

"Just do what we do," said AJ.

Then everyone yelled..

"Pioneers!" And everyone did a backflip. Chris was only a beat behind and quickly did his back tuck.

"That's cool, guys, I'll see ya." Then, Patrick added, "No, no, no, man. We don't stop yet!"

"Yeah, man. You gotta pop until you drop!" quipped Joey.

"You mean flip to the last man?" asked Chris.

"Yep, 'til there's just one man standin'," answered Dallas.

And with that, they flipped, each time the entire team yelling the name of the gymnastics club that they had all sweat blood for and would gladly do again. Each flip brought them all closer to exhaustion. First Joey, then AJ, then Dallas. Then Mackee dropped out with a loud thud and a curse word, leaving Ty, Patrick, and the newcomer. Although they were out of the running, the fallen comrades were not out of the game. With each flip, they yelled with the combatants, and each cheered his favorite. Then, Ty dropped out, leaving the team captain and the radical upstart. Five, ten, fifteen more flips went by, each using the other's fatigue to fuel his desire to continue. After forty-seven backflips, both were visibly drained. Chris could see that Patrick was tiring, although he knew that he, himself would not last much longer. While they gasped for breath, Chris took it upon himself to get into Patrick's head. "Hey ... Patrick," he said with a gasp, "had enough?"

"Man … I'm … just warmin' … up," was Patrick's breathless reply. Although he, too, was ready to drop, Patrick wasn't about to let a newcomer best him just by suggestion.

"All right then. … Loser buys burgers and fries … okay?"

"Okay … you're on."

With the bet in place, everyone yelled, "Pioneers!" and the feud continued.

Then Patrick faltered, stumbling and nearly touching his knee to the floor.

"You're … gettin' old … dude," snickered Chris.

"We'll see, blowhard," came Patrick's retort.

On the next flip, both gymnasts nearly fell to their knees, but after a few stagger steps, both remained alive. But, eventually, one had to fall. And fall he did. With a thud that shook the gym, Chris couldn't even get his feet around to the floor as his last flip landed him squarely on his knees. It didn't take long for Patrick to follow once he saw his adversary lying in a crumpled heap on the floor next to him.

With every ounce of energy he could muster, Patrick crawled to the mess of flesh that was Chris. In almost a whisper, he said, "I like my burger medium rare."

"Right … you drive?" managed Chris, his head still buried in the floor exercise carpet.

"I'll drive."

"Man, I hope every workout isn't like this," gasped Chris.

Joey reached down to help Chris to his knees and said, "Only most," not passing up the chance to get in a jab on the newcomer.

The rest of the team helped Chris and Patrick to their feet. Workout, the first of many for Chris as a Pioneer, was finally over.

The boulevard in Knoxville that almost every teenager frequented was not unlike the cruising strips of every other small town in the country. A ritual unto itself, teens cruised up and down the same three miles of road, turning around in the Tastee-Freez parking lot at one end and at the Quik Sak on the other end, honking their horns at the same fellow cruisers that they'd honked at since they started driving, only occasionally stopping to actually involve themselves in conversation longer than the duration of a red light.

"Thanks for dinner," Patrick said to Chris as he negotiated his '67 Mustang convertible through the snarled traffic.

"Don't mention it. You earned it." said Chris, "Sweet ride, plowboy. If you don't have an outside job, how do you afford this? Did your folks give it to you?"

"Kinda, my dad restores cars as a hobby. This was my 17th birthday present."

"Excellent. So you should be set for college then."

"Well, not exactly. There's not enough vintage cars out there that need a serious makeover to make his hobby lucrative, and my dad doesn't pull down a lot where he works, so I'm likely on my own as fall as school goes."

"Don't worry. With your talent you should have no trouble finding a school to give you a ride. Hey," said Chris, changing the subject, "speaking of ride, how does anyone get anywhere in this mess?"

"*When* you get there is not the point, but *how* you get there. In our case, we're getting there with class and in style," returned Patrick.

"And just where might that be?"

"Who knows? Who cares? We'll know as soon as we get there."

"Get where?" prodded Chris.

"Wherever," was Patrick's nonanswer.

"Geez, what a waste of time. There's a ton of things I'd rather do than waste my gasoline trying to wade through these zit-faced rednecks!" remarked Chris with a bite in his voice.

"Like what? Get wasted with a bunch of burnouts and watch the plaster drip off of the ceiling?"

"No, that's not my idea of being productive, either," said Chris, defending himself. "What makes you think that that's the way I would kill time?"

"Well, you are from California, right? The land of free love, free spirits, and free drugs, and all that," came the stereotypical response of anyone east of the Mississippi.

"Wow, like, you must have studied really, really hard on your recent history, dude," Chris said, mocking a surfer accent. "Like, totally gnarly, dude."

Then, he broke out of his accent, saying, "Listen, you boneheads can think what you want, but not every Japanese tourist carries a dozen cameras, and not every Californian has scorched their brain for the sake of the artificial rush!" barked Chris.

"Sorry, man. Don't take it so personal. Just remember, not everybody in the South is a redneck, either."

"Right. Point taken," returned Chris, sounding a little apologetic.

Chris looked around at the typical, mid-America, small town architecture. "Say, what do you guys do for fun around here?"

Patrick paused with a puzzled look on his face, then turned to Chris and replied, "We're doin' it."

"This is it? In all this, the best you guys can come up with is polluting the air while you *almost* move through this stupid mess?"

"What'd you expect? Remember, we're just a bunch of barefoot hillbillies. Shucks, it don't get no better'n this," said Patrick in his best hick imitation. After a pause, both laughed at the fools they had both made of themselves.

"But seriously, Patrick, you're better than this. After all, you're a gymnast, for cryin' out loud. You put your butt on the line every time you work out or compete. Doesn't that give you a rush?"

"I've never looked at gymnastics as a source for a rush. I've always enjoyed the progression and the process of learning. You know, tryin', failin', tryin' again. I guess I never thought about needing to feel a rush," concluded Patrick.

"Let me see if I got this right. You like doing drill after drill, slow, prodding progression, until all doubt, danger, and risk are gone before going to the next step?"

"I know it doesn't sound exciting, but it suits me just fine," Patrick said a little testily, tightening his grip on the steering wheel.

"Yeah, but it's boring beyond belief! How the crap do you find enough time to learn all you have to learn to be your best? After all, we all only have a small window of time to get as far as we can in this sport before age says, 'Sorry, pal, you're done.'"

"Yeah, well, it's worked for me, okay? I've been to NTIs, and I've beat some pretty good guys in my time." Patrick was getting defensive.

"Big deal! I've done all that and a bag of chips, but I can't see how you'll ever get to know how good you can ever be without pushin' it to the edge every time!"

"Well, maybe pushing the edge isn't for everyone."

"Wow, plowboy, you're missing the best part of gymnastics. Picture this: you're poised on the high bar just before you're about to try the hairiest skill you can think of … let's say a Def, you know, a full-and-a-half-twisting Geinger."

Patrick imagined the extremely difficult flyaway-twist-regrasp and shuddered in spite of himself.

"You fight with your insides whether or not you should try at all, then you commit!" Chris became more excited as he continued, Patrick just continued to sweat.

"You cast to your handstand, and before you know it, you're swinging giants. With each swing, your heart pounds so hard, it feels like it's gonna jump right out of your chest. You're almost hyperventilating as you get closer and closer to the point of no return. Then it happens. You tap your final swing and then, the release. Your body skies like it's a mile above the bar. Everything has gone silent except for the sound of your own breath and the pounding in your chest, and everything is moving in slow motion.

"It feels like you're never gonna finish twisting, much less catch the bar. Then, just like you imagined it in your dreams a thousand times, there it is. The bar draws closer, and you extend your arms toward it. And as your hands make contact, everything explodes. Teammates cheer, coaches clutch at their hearts, cheerleaders throw their clothes at you, and you can't wait to get off the bar so you can celebrate. And, as your feet hit the floor, you go nuts as you break into a cold sweat, and you can't believe what you just did. Man, they haven't found a drug that will reproduce that feeling. When they do, I'll be a junkie for life!"

While Chris relished the feelings he had just described, Patrick puffed out a sigh of relief and unclenched his fists and his butt cheeks.

The next few miles went by without a word. Chris had become almost impatient about something and looked at his watch.

"Hey, plowboy, are we about done playing with the teenyboppers here?"

"Sure, I guess so. What did you have in mind?" Patrick answered nonchalantly, hiding a slight twinge of nerves, wondering what this crazy Californian was about to propose.

"I wanted to give you an idea what a rush is all about," said Chris, confirming Patrick's fears.

"Great. Okay, where to?" he responded, not about to give Chris a reason to add "sissy" to the already-annoying "plowboy" title.

"Well, take me back to the gym so I can get my bike, and you can just follow me."

"Sure," said Patrick as he looked for a place to turn around. "You know, this cruising stuff is a gigantic pain in the ass when you really want to get somewhere."

"You don't say," quipped Chris as Patrick squealed the tires on his Mustang. Before long, they were headed back to the gym.

As a native of the area, Patrick thought he had been down every dirt road and back street in the county, but the road Chris was leading him down was new to him. They had traveled well over fifteen miles outside of town when Chris pulled his Kawasaki 1100 into an overgrown field dimly lit by the distant farmhouses. Then, Chris stopped, as though he knew exactly where he was. Patrick pulled up alongside Chris's bike. Chris pulled off his helmet.

"From here, we walk," he said.

Patrick parked his Mustang, hopped out, and quickly caught up to Chris, who had not bothered to wait for him.

"Where'd you find this happenin' place?" popped Patrick.

"I live about two miles that way with my mom," Chris answered as he pointed back over to his right.

"Where's your dad?" marked Patrick, as he tried to make conversation.

"Oh, he left my mom when I was real young." Chris never broke stride.

"Do you ever see him?" questioned Patrick, realizing that he was treading on thin ice.

"No," retorted Chris with a bite in his voice, "not since he left."

"You mean he's never seen you do gymnastics?"

"Nope. He's never seen me do anything," answered Chris dryly.

"Think he cares?"

"Who knows?"

"So, why come to Knoxville?"

"This is where my mom is from. She had always intended to come back someday. Dad had never intended to come back," answered Chris. Then, a few steps later, he stopped. "We're here."

"We're where?" asked Patrick.

"This is my place. This is where I come to deal with everything and forget whatever." Chris had led Patrick to a set of railroad tracks. "I've only been in this town for two weeks. This seems to be the only place to get away from everyone."

As they walked along, they shared views on varied topics from grades to girls. Then, Chris interrupted. "My watch doesn't have a light. Can you see what time it is?"

"11:35. Why do you ask?"

The reason became apparent as a light appeared in the distance.

"Ah, here she comes."

"What, the train?" asked Patrick.

"Yeah. When it goes buy, I yell at the top of my lungs to help clean out my muddled thoughts."

"Shouldn't we get off the tracks?"

"Not yet. That train is still a few miles off," answered Chris, his voice becoming more sullen and monotone. "You know, plowboy, everyone has to have a code to live by."

"What do you mean?"

"Well, you kinda have to follow a certain way of living, a reference point by which you make decisions in your life," said Chris, waxing philosophic.

The train was closing the gap between itself and the young men. Patrick was starting to feel uneasy.

"I think it would be a good decision to get off these tracks."

"Naw, there's still plenty of time."

"Not for this guy. Kill yourself if you want to. I'm getting off." Patrick stepped off the track but continued to walk alongside it, trying to coax Chris to follow him.

"My code is very simple … "

The train came closer.

"Chris, get off the track!"

"If you can't take a punch, don't start a fight."

The train was almost upon him.

"Chris, get your ass off the track!"

"Don't fire a gun if you can't take getting shot."

The engineer could see Chris and blew the whistle.

"Damn it, Chris, get off the track!"

Chris stopped and looked right at Patrick and he yelled at the top of his lungs,

"And you can't walk out on the gymnastics floor to try to be the best if you can't accept the possibility of the worst!"

Chris's last words came with the train a mere ten feet away. Patrick screamed, "Chriiis!"

Chris had disappeared.

All Patrick could do was wait as the train raged by. Car after car went by. Patrick looked under the wheels to the other side of the track. There was no sign of Chris.

Thirty seconds went by. Then forty-five. Then a minute, then two. Finally, after what seemed like an eternity, the end of the train rushed by. No sooner than the caboose passed did Patrick leap over the tracks to search for his foolish friend. And there he was, sitting next to a tree, arms resting on his knees as he played with a weed he had pulled from the ground in front of him.

"Did you hear me yell?" Chris inquired nonchalantly.

"You yell? Did you hear me screaming my lungs out? I thought that train had you carried halfway to Chattanooga by now! Are you trying to kill yourself?" Patrick screamed in panic as he had nearly lost control of his bodily functions.

"Pretty good rush, eh? Sure beats cruisin' the old boulevard, don't it," Chris answered with a snicker.

A silence fell over the two as Patrick caught his breath and wiped a cold sweat from his brow. Finally, he broke the silence.

"Don't you ever think about injury? I mean serious injury, or even death?"

"Sure I do," answered Chris as he rose to his feet. "Every time I watch you swing high bar."

"You know, Chris, you're gonna kill yourself."

"Yeah, I know. But when?"

Without another word, the two walked back to their separate vehicles and went their separate ways.

THREE

▼

SATURDAY WAS CHRIS'S first day off from the gym. He had procrastinated long enough and it was time to get some needed shopping done. New shoes, a couple of shirts, and a pair of jeans were all on his list, as were the essentials: deodorant, cologne, and, of course, some new music. The obvious place to get everything was the mall. But Chris hated malls. To him, they were on about the same level as cruising: nothing but a bunch of brainwashed zombie consumers, walking free in a post-modern prison. Just a quick in and out, and he'd have what he needed without anyone he knew seeing him.

Chris filled his shopping list and was headed for the door, apparently unseen, when he realized that between him and the exit doors was the greatest obstacle he had ever faced. Time and time again, he had challenged this awesome foe, but never had he ever overcome the power of the … food court. He had forgotten that he passed it when he came in, but he wasn't hungry then.

Have these mall designers no mercy? he thought. Oh well, I'll just hold my breath and concentrate on the exit doors. I'll make it this time.

But just as his hand touched the glass door to leave, the smell of pizza smacked him square in the face, just as it had in the past. Boy, I'm hungry, he thought. Well, maybe just a couple slices, and I'll be on my way.

Not one to pass up a meal, Chris walked into Pizza Roma, sat down, and once again, admitted defeat. "I've got to go on a diet," he told himself.

After a few minutes of studying the menu, he could sense the presence of someone next to him. But, he shook it off and began to give his order.

"I'll have a couple of—" he began before his eyes veered off of his menu and lost his train of thought when he saw her. His jaw dropped. From the floor up, tan, muscular calves, smooth, strong thighs, and then the drab uniform of a pizza shop waitress, which still had difficulty hiding the awesome figure of the best-looking girl he had ever seen. Long blonde hair, green eyes, and a tan that could rival any native Californian.

"You were saying, sir, a couple of. … ?" said the strange beauty in a voice that made it even more difficult for Chris to remember what he had come to order.

"A couple … " he said, staring at her chest. "Oh yeah, uh, a couple slices of pepperoni, mushroom and double cheese," he continued, trying to sound as though he had never lost his composure.

"Okay, that's a double order pep, mush and heavy cheese. Would you like anything else, sir?"

Chris's brain thought of many things. Unfortunately, none of them were on the menu.

"Uh, yeah, bring me a large diet soda."

"Coming right up." Chris watched as she walked away and disappeared behind the counter. His head fell into his propped hands. *Geez, what a babe,* he thought. He closed his eyes and tried to recall her face. Just as her image filled his head, the table shook and likewise shook Chris out of his daydream.

"Joey. What are you doing here?"

"Hey, Chris. You here scoping the action?" came the high, squeaky voice of his young, redheaded teammate.

"Naw, man. I'm just here to wolf some pizza, head back to my crib, and crash," replied Chris, as cool as he could be. "What are you doin' here, runt? Your mama bring you up here to keep you out of her hair?"

"Smart, motorhead. Naw, this is a part of my daily routine," snapped Joey.

"Your routine? You mean you make it a habit to hang out at this consumer's nightmare?"

"No, man. It's one of my stops in my fifty-mile conditioning circuit."

"Conditioning circuit?"

"Yeah, I do it every day," Joey continued. "See, I live exactly thirteen miles from here. Every morning, I'm up at four thirty. I ride my ten-speed from my house to here. Then, I get off my bike, run around the mall three times. That's two miles. Then I ride to school, another ten miles. That makes twenty-five miles in all."

"Then after school?" asked Chris.

"Right. I just go back in reverse."

"Why do you do this to yourself, Joey?"

"Well, it's like this. I'm at a disadvantage. I really don't have much gymnastics talent. You've no doubt noticed. You guys either way outdistance me on talent or, by being older than me, have more experience. I figure I can't control factors like talent and experience, so I do the one thing that I can control."

"And that is … ?"

"Condition my butt off. It's gotta pay off someday," concluded Joey, as though he were presenting a legal case.

"But why do you keep doing the gymnastics if everybody's got this advantage over you?"

"Simple, my friend," answered the youngest Pioneer confidently. "I'm gonna be the best someday. You'll see."

Chris realized that this was a man with a mission.

"I like you, runt. You got guts. Not much brains, and not a whole lot of talent, but you do have guts."

"Thank you, I think." Both chuckled.

Before the laughter subsided, Chris's pizza arrived. And before he knew it, he again was caught in a puppy love gaze as his eyes stayed with the young vixen until she had once again disappeared into the kitchen.

"Earth to Slash, come in, Slash. You're way out of control. You're about to crash-land. Abort! Abort!" teased Joey.

"Huh? Oh, I'm sorry, guy. It's just that honey that took my order is driving me nuts."

"Your waitress? What? Are you kidding? Forget about her, man. She's bad news."

"Yeah, right, runt. What do you know about women? You probably haven't been beyond hand-holding, and *you* are gonna tell me about women?" quipped Chris, trying to put Joey on edge and draw the attention away from the fact that he was crazy about this stranger.

"Okay, you think I don't know women? All right, I bet you ten bucks if you ask her for her number, she'll smack your face."

"What? Slap my face for asking her number? Okay, zit face, you're about to lose two fin."

Chris told one of the other waitresses that he needed to see his waitress. As she came out with a puzzled look on her face, as though she had done something wrong, Joey reached over and grabbed a slice of Chris's pizza.

"I'm sorry, sir, did I forget something?" she inquired

"Yes," replied Chris, a glint in his eye as he glanced at Joey. "You forgot to leave me your number."

Surprised, the waitress drew back her right hand, and before Chris could react, she smacked him so hard that he nearly fell out of his chair. She then turned and stormed back to the kitchen.

Chris gathered his wits and looked at Joey, who hadn't even paused from eating his pizza.

"How'd you know she'd do that?" Chris pleaded as he rubbed his stinging cheek.

Slyly, Joey answered, "Easy. She's my sister, Haley. I'll take my money in small bills, thank you. Hey, you gonna eat that other slice?"

"Why, you son of a b——" Chris said, realizing that he had been had. He tore off after the little con man, spilling the remainder of his diet cola on the floor and sending the other slice of pizza face down to the tiled surface. But before Chris could catch him, Joey was out the door, on his bike, and gone. Chris just stopped and stared, wiping soda off of his pants.

"Hey, kid," came a deep voice from behind him, "you are gonna pay for this pizza, right?"

Chris muttered some curse words under his breath, then turned around and dug into his pocket for money to cover the pizza he didn't even get a chance to eat.

"I really hate malls," he said.

Mondays are a lousy way to start a week, thought Chris. He felt there needed to be a new day of the week between Sunday and Monday called Restday. Afterall, one can't be expected to bounce right back into the grind after having two perfectly good weekend days to trash your body.

But, this Monday was different for Chris. Although he was in no particular hurry to get to the gym—in fact, he was already a half hour late, as usual—he was looking forward to training. He had been wandering around in a daze for the past few days, by and large because of the cute blonde he could not get off his mind. His cheek still stung from the cold right she laid on him two days earlier. Today was not exactly a rock-and-roll kind of day, so the radio on his bike was turned off the whole ride—for the first time since he bought his bike three years ago.

As he walked into the gym, the team was already at pommel horse. Everyone was at the chalk bucket except for Dallas, who was taking his turn. All the guys were laughing, and as Chris drew closer, he heard the source of their mirth.

"And then, I scarfed his pizza and said, 'I'll take my ten in small bills!' Ha, ha, ha … " Everyone laughed, including Dallas, who had lost control, smacked the horse with his legs, and fell to the floor, still laughing. No one had noticed that Chris had come into the gym. Mackee was the first to see him, and he cleared his throat loudly.

One by one, everybody stopped laughing, except for Joey. He was still laughing, with his back to the object of his folly. Then, Joey's laughter started to subside when he noticed that everybody else had assumed a straight face.

Joey's face went from hysterical to terrified. "He's right behind me, isn't he?" Five faces turned to stone and nodded in unison.

"Is he ... smiling?" Joey said nervously as, again in sync, five heads twisted side to side without emotion.

Joey winced as he realized that he was about to face the music and, likely, be beaten to a pulp. "Hi, Chris, ol' buddy. How's it goin', dude?" he said without turning around.

Just as Chris was about to grab Joey by the shoulder, he himself was spun around.

"Why are you late again, McClure? It better be good," said Coach Lowery in a lather.

"Hey, Coach. I'm really sorry. I meant to call, honest. I had to ... uh ... drop my mom off at the hairdresser. I had no control," Chris said, alibiing as fast as he could. This gave Joey the opportunity to get away and postpone the inevitable trashing he would eventually have to take.

"Fine, McClure, but I'm afraid you won't slide this time. Give me a hundred push-ups, then join the rest."

With a glare to his sullen teammates, Chris dropped to the floor and began his penance. The teammates looked at each other, then went back to work.

By the time Chris finished, the team was finishing with pommel horse. "What now, Coach?" he said.

"Well, AJ, Dallas, and Mackee are finished on pommels. You can join the guys on high bar. I'll be sending the others over when they're finished."

While putting on grips, AJ seized the opportunity to dig at Chris.

"So, Chris, sounds like Johnson and his sister scammed you pretty good! Heh, heh."

"Yeah, I guess I got caught with my pants down," answered Chris, trying to brush it off.

"Yeah, I heard that's not the only thing that was hangin' out, you limpweed," said Dallas with a bite in his voice, still trying to get Chris back for their opening confrontation a week ago.

"Hey, why don't you just bite my shorts, David?" came the return from Chris.

Dallas turned in a huff and headed for the water fountain for a drink.

"Don't mind him, Chris," said Mackee. "Dallas has always had a short fuse."

"Not nearly as short as his life span if he doesn't drop the subject," threatened Chris.

No one for a moment thought he was bluffing.

One by one, the rest of the team finished their first events and were joining the others on High Bar. After a couple of swings, Chris headed toward the water fountain. Partly because he was thirsty but mostly to get away from Dallas, who had continued to get on his nerves. There, between him and the water fountain, was Joey, waiting to take his final turn. There was nobody around him, and it looked to be the perfect opportunity to deal with him without interference.

"Hey, Joey," said Chris, chilling the blood in Joey's veins as he knew it was time for life as he knew it to end. "I want to talk to you."

"Look, guys! Looks like Chris is gonna nail Joey!" exclaimed Ty.

"I'll show that bastard," said Dallas as he started to bolt across the gym.

"Man, that was a pretty funny bit Saturday. Hey, what are you—" before Chris could get out another word, he was once again grabbed at the shoulder and spun around, this time by Dallas.

"Stay away from him, you son of a bitch. Pick on somebody your own size," threatened Dallas.

"What the hell's your problem, dick brain?"

"You, you slime!" retorted Dallas as he shoved Chris in the chest with both hands full force, only to have his action made moot as Chris barely moved. Dallas stepped back, stunned.

"I tried to avoid this, David." With a swift right cross, Chris immediately put Dallas on the ground, obviously in pain and disoriented.

That's just about the time Coach Lowery got to the scene of the crime. "That's it, McClure! Get your stuff, and get your sleazy hide out of my gym! I don't condone fighting!"

"No way, Coach. It was Dallas who started the whole thing!" yelled Joey.

"Uh-uh, Coach," said Dallas, trying to defend himself. "This bastard was about to nail Joey for the whitewashin' he took at the mall Saturday."

"No, he wasn't. You've been lookin' for a reason to scrap with Chris from the minute he first stepped in the door. Besides, who named you my guardian angel, David? I think I can handle my own problems, thank you."

"Yeah, he could probably kick your butt easier than I did," joined Chris.

"All right, guys," interrupted Coach Lowery, "we get enough injuries around here without you guys trying to do each other in. Dallas, McClure, you guys just bought double conditioning for the whole team." The team responded with a collective groan. "Next time, take it outside. You guys don't have to like each other, but you do have to work with each other if the team is to succeed. So, everybody, break it up, and get back to work."

As they headed back to the high bar, Joey caught up to Chris.

"Hey, man, sorry I got you into trouble," Joey said apologetically.

"Don't sweat it, runt. Trouble has a way of following me, anyway. Hey, you busy after workout?" said Chris.

"Me? Naw, why?"

"You want to go get a burger or somethin'?" asked Chris.

"Sure thing! Great!" said Joey as though he had just been invited to the White House by the president himself.

"Chris," approached AJ "Good shot, man. I've been wantin' to do that for the past three years!"

Chris chuckled and went back to work.

Not one to let someone else do his work for him, Chris decided to do triple conditioning instead of the double conditioning ordered by Coach Lowery. This left him the only one remaining after the rest of the team had gone home, except for Joey, who was always the last one in the gym. "I'm gonna be the best someday, you'll see," was the phrase that went through Chris's head as he watched Joey push himself through another strength set on rings.

"You're not finished yet, McClure?" said Coach as he walked up to Chris, who was on his last set of swinging dips on the parallel bars.

"You know, Coach. Gotta stay ahead of the Joneses," was the tart reply as he dropped off the bars.

"You know, McClure, I'd rather have ten of him than ten of anyone else," said Coach as he watched Joey, who had moved to the wall bar to do leg lifts. "In all my years of gymnastics, as an athlete and coach, I've never seen anyone with as much drive and determination as Joey Johnson."

"Yeah, he works his butt off," said Chris.

"What's his motivation, you think? He knows he's not very gifted, he's always behind everybody else, and he's always the last one to pick up a new skill," Coach was visibly puzzled.

"The reason is simple, Coach. He's gonna be the best someday. He told me himself."

"Boy, that kid is a dreamer. I wonder when he'll ever wake up," said Coach with a snicker.

"Or when he'll wake everybody else up," quipped Chris. Then, Chris seized the opportunity to probe his coach's brain.

"Hey, Coach, what's the big deal with the NTIs? I know it's a big deal, but these guys always seem worked up about it."

"The National Team Invitational? Well, as you probably know, it's the biggest meet of the year. It started about fifteen years ago in St. Louis. It rotates cities every year. In fact, next year, it's scheduled for Los Angeles. Every six-man team worth anything comes out. I'd say there were an easy twenty, twenty-five teams competing in the meet back when I competed. It was phenomenal. People cheering like it's the Super Bowl. The best gymnastics teams in the country were there, everyone you've ever heard of, all competing to be the best team in the country. Everybody competes on Saturday. Then, Sunday night is finals. The top six teams compete head-to-head. Six years ago, one of the superchannels bought the television rights. They've been televised ever since."

"Have you ever won?" Chris had just asked the million-dollar question.

"No," was the reply as Coach's head dropped a little and his tone changed from excited to sullen. "Almost did, once. I was a senior, like yourself, and top man on our team. I was ranked in the country, too. Had a dogfight on my hands with the reigning national champion, Chuck Chambers. Going to our last event, our team was three-tenths of a point ahead of the other five, but I was six-tenths behind Chuck for the all-around. I was planning on using a new dismount in my floor routine, a full-twisting double back. I had been doing them for quite a while but had never used it as a dismount because it uses so much energy at the end of a routine," Coach paused, rubbed his eyes, and continued.

"My coach knew how bad I wanted to win the all-around, to finally beat Chuck. But, he also knew the chance we had at bringing back a national team title to Tennessee for the first time. He came up to me right before my last routine—in this case it just happened to be floor—and he said, 'Be conservative. Don't dismount with the full-in. Dismount easy, with a layout double twist. We can win this thing!' But I had my mind set on other things, namely winning the all-around. I knew that dismounting with an easy double twist would not have the difficulty I would need to catch Chuck. My set started perfect, probably the best floor routine I had ever put together. I stuck my mount, a double layout. My second pass and side pass were effortless. I had no form breaks, and my handstands were rock solid. It wasn't until I was standing there getting ready for my last pass that it hit me. It wasn't just about me. My teammates were counting on me to help them win, as well. Should I water back my dismount and waste the best routine of my life to ensure a team victory? Or should I go for the full-in to win the all-around?"

He started to chuckle. "That must have been the longest pause in gymnastics history," he continued as his face returned to sullen. "My rationale was simple. If I stick my full-in, not only do I win the all-around, but we also win the team award."

"So, what happened?" Chris was on the edge of his seat, which happened to be a folded mat.

"Well, needless to say, I didn't quite make it," he concluded.

"Tell him, Coach," came the voice of a fatigued Joey Johnson as he approached the two, having finished his conditioning. "Tell him how you under-rotated so bad that you barely got your feet under you," Joey prodded.

"Pretty nasty, what I can remember of it," Coach continued. "Woke up the next day in the hospital. I got my feet under me, but they folded up. Compound fracture of the right tibia, severely sprained left ankle."

"And a concussion from his head colliding with his right kneecap," Joey finished the story which had become difficult for Coach. "We get to hear this story every year. That's why we're obsessed with winning the NTIs"

"And, you haven't won it since then?" asked Chris.

"Nope," was Coach's return. "Been close twice. Trouble is, I can never put together six really good gymnasts to take to the meet. Patrick's freshman year was the closest. Placed three gymnasts in the top ten, but just didn't have the depth to keep up with the other teams."

"Are you guys pretty close to being finished? I'd like to get something to eat tonight," remarked Joey.

"Yeah, I'm finished," answered Coach. "Anything else you want to know, Chris?"

"Not now. Thanks, Coach," replied Chris as he gathered his grips and paper bag and made his start with Joey toward the locker room.

"See ya tomorrow, Coach," both gymnasts chimed.

"See you tomorrow, boys."

Then, the gym was once again empty.

"Didn't your mama teach you that it's not polite to stare?" said Chris as he jammed a large bite of his hamburger into his face.

Joey paused, as if he were formulating a response. "I just can't figure you out, Slash."

"*Chris*, please," he corrected. "What do you mean?"

"Well, you're this lone wolf kinda guy, but you turn around and ask me out for a burger. I don't get it," probed Joey.

"Just wanted company is all. Don't make such a big deal over it," said Chris, brushing aside Joey's question.

"Why are you like that? Why do you always have to come off like this man with a mission, 'get out of my way, let me do it myself' attitude? Looks to me like you're tryin' to prove something to somebody," Joey said, pushing for a suitable answer.

"Not that it's any of your business," replied the Californian as he crammed a handful of ketchup drenched fries into his mouth, "but I guess it has something to do with my folks. For the first year after my old man split, my mom had this 'how can we go on without him' attitude. And, it was hard for my mom to have confidence in me. I guess it might have had something to do with the fact that I was a rotten kid. I was always either in trouble or looking for it. Once my family fell apart, I reassessed my life, and ever since, I guess I've been trying to show them and the rest of the world that I'm not quite as bad as they thought."

"Well, that answers that question. Now, for the money, why did you bring me out to Burger Boy's?" asked the redhead.

"Tell me about your sister," answered Chris.

"So, that's it. You just want to use me to get to Haley. Nice try, Slash. Find another girl. You don't want to get involved with her. She hates gymnasts."

"She hates gymnasts? Why?" probed Chris.

"She used to date one."

"Who?"

"Patrick Goodman."

"Plowboy? You gotta be kiddin' me. How long ago?" asked Chris.

"They dated for about two years. Broke up just last spring," returned Joey. "I guess they were incompatible."

"Do you know why they broke up?"

"Not exactly," Joey continued, "but I do know that it had something to do with gymnastics."

Chris came to the conclusion that the cause had more to do with Patrick than it did with gymnastics. Chris figured he could probably work around that.

"Joey," he said, "I want you to help me get to know your sister."

"No way, Slash!" was his reply.

"I'll do your conditioning tomorrow."

"Uh-uh. I'm not gonna sell out my sister."

"I'll do your conditioning for a week and pay you twenty dollars," was the next offer.

Joey stood firm. "No, sir. No way. There's no way I'm gonna let you anywhere near my sister. Not for any amount of money!"

Chris thought. Then, in a sly voice, came his next offer. "I'll teach you to ride my motorcycle."

"She works out a the fitness center on Tuesdays, Thursdays, and Sunday mornings and works at Pizza Roma on Mondays, Wednesdays, Fridays, and Saturdays," Joey had given in. "but you didn't hear it from me."

"Of course not," Chris soaked in the information and formulated a plan.

"Thanks, runt. I knew I could count on you."

"No problem. Where's your bike?" asked the sibling traitor.

"Right outside."

The two finished their meals and left the fast-food restaurant, both wearing big smiles.

FOUR

▼

CHRIS HAD GOTTEN used to sleeping in. After all, wasn't that what weekends were for? Predawn awakening and Chris were just not made for each other. So, why was he doing it, getting out of bed before any other life-form? Certainly, no girl is worth this much effort, he thought to himself as the spray of cold water spilled out of the showerhead to chill and shock his slow-moving body.

If there was one good aspect to such an early rising, it was the experience of riding his Kawasaki at dawn. Seeing the sun rise over the Smoky Mountains and feeling the morning cool breeze had made the struggle of getting up worth the agony. I should do this more often, he thought.

He got to the fitness center just before seven. Upon entering, he noticed that the architecture of the facility would make one believe that this was an expensive way to spend one's free time.

Joey had given Chris his sister's routine, and Chris did not want to miss his first opportunity at a "chance" encounter. According to Joey, Haley started her five-mile jog around the indoor track at seven thirty. At 7:25, Chris started jogging. Like clockwork, she walked in five minutes later, did a light warm-up, then started to jog. Chris positioned himself halfway around the track from Haley then gradually sped up. Before she had finished her second lap, he was right on her tail. Savoring the moment, Chris carried out the next stage of his strategy. Almost running on her heels, he called to her, "Passing." As a reflex, Haley moved to the right to allow the runner by. Chris made sure to pass her at a rate slow enough so she could recognize him but fast enough so it didn't look as though he were slowing down. As he passed, he turned his head slightly to the right and said, "Thank you."

Haley looked at the fellow runner and noticed that she had never seen this stranger at the track before, but he so looked familiar. She didn't realize this was the guy she had slapped just four days earlier.

As she labored to recall how she knew him, Chris continued to put distance between them until he was a quarter lap in front of her. Aggravated by her inability to recall the stranger, she decided to use a more straightforward method. Increasing her speed, but not so fast as to make it look deliberate, she caught up to Chris over two laps. She would have caught up to him sooner, but, unbeknownst to her, Chris had seen her accelerate from the corner of his eye and increased his speed slightly just to see her work a little harder.

When she caught up to him, she signaled her pass, "Passing."

Chris moved to the right, and Haley began her pass. Once they were side by side, Haley slowed her run to the same pace as Chris'. She had to know who this was. She started the conversation.

"Kind of new here, aren't you?"

"Is that a line?" returned Chris, almost sarcastically.

"Not exactly. I've just never seen you here before. Are you a new member?" she asked.

"Well, kinda. I've been a member since I moved here a few weeks ago."

"Why is it I've never seen you before?" she inquired as they maintained their pace.

"I usually workout on Mondays and Fridays, but I missed yesterday," he lied.

"Oh. Well, my name is Haley Johnson. Nice to meet you," she said offering her right hand.

"Hi, I'm Chris, Chris McClure. Nice to meet you, too."

The name sounded familiar, but she still could not figure out who he was. She probed for more information,

"You said you just moved here. Where are you from?"

"A little town called Riverside, California," answered Chris, not volunteering too much information.

"California? How did you find Knoxville from California?" she continued the inquest.

"Well, my mother asked for and got a transfer within the company she works for. This is her hometown."

"So, how do you like Knoxville so far?" Haley now was going from inquisitive to hospitable.

"Kinda slow, if you ask me. I'm kinda used to a little more hustle and bustle, if you know what I mean."

"What's wrong with slow? It's less stressful here," she defended her lifestyle as her voice became more defensive.

"Nothing is wrong with slow," he said, "unless, of course, you want to get somewhere. In California, anything you want to do, you can do it without having to go all over the country to find it. It's all right there—dancing, movies, ball games, concerts—"

"Street gangs, muggings, prostitutes, perverts. I've heard about your fast-paced California," Haley interjected. "If you ask me, it's not worth it."

"Have you ever been there?" he asked defensively.

"No, but I read the papers, I watch the news. They don't paint a very rosy picture," she retorted.

"That's not their job. You don't sell newspapers or win TV ratings with pictures of normal homes in normal neighborhoods, not unlike yours," said Chris. *Touché*, he thought.

"How would you know where I live?" she was now back into her prying mode.

"I don't," he said, trying to cover his obvious blunder. Of course, he knew what her neighborhood looked like. He had given Joey a ride home the night before. She had still been at work. He had made the same comment to Joey about the similarities between California and Tennessee suburban neighborhoods. He continued to cover. "I just assumed that most neighborhoods were similar to the one I grew up in."

Then it hit her. "Wait a minute," she said coming to a complete stop. "My brother said he had a new teammate from California."

Chris had been made. He tried to cover his tracks. "Is your brother Joey Johnson?"

"Are you a gymnast?" she continued. "Hold it. Now I know where I've seen you before! You made a pass at me at the mall Saturday. You were sitting with Joey! I smacked you in the face!" Suddenly, it had all come back, and she had realized that this was a scam. "Get away from me, you pervert!" And, she picked up her pace to put distance between her and her adversary.

"Wait a minute, Haley," he called as he accelerate to match her pace. "You don't understand. I just want to talk to you."

"Is that why you made that smart remark at the mall to get my number? So we can 'talk?' I wonder what Patrick has told you about me," she retaliated, turning his words around to fit her purpose.

"Listen, when I saw you on Saturday, I had no idea who you were. I had no idea that you were Joey's sister, and I certainly had no idea that you used to date Patrick," he said, speeding up to close the gap.

"Well then, how did you know that we used to date?" she said, breathing heavier as she tried to increase her pace.

"Joey told me last night after workout." He was only a few steps behind now.

"You already tried to fool me today. How can I believe you now?" she said as she put on a burst of speed. Haley was ten steps ahead when fatigue set in. Both she and Chris slowed to a stop. Still several steps apart, both sought support for their exhausted bodies. Haley leaned against the outside wall, and Chris collapsed against the same wall with his back, sliding down slowly until he was seated. After several gasps for oxygen, he answered her request.

"You don't have to believe me. You don't have to believe anything. In fact, all you have to do is say the word, and you'll never hear from me again," he had made his final stand.

Silence. Then, realizing the effort that must have gone into the great charade, she decided to give him the benefit of the doubt.

"You thirsty?" she said.

"Thought you'd never ask," he replied, obviously exhausted.

Haley took a deep breath, blew it out, and walked over to Chris, helping him to his feet.

"For a gymnast, your cardio fitness really sucks!" She helped him walk out the door.

"Yeah, getting healthy is gonna kill me."

For the next week, as soon as workouts were over, Chris would bolt from the gym to go see Haley. Thus far, Joey was the only Pioneer to know that Chris was seeing his big sister. Because he had his mind on either his gymnastics or Haley, Chris was beginning to spend less time working with the other guys. Primarily, he would train on his own in silence, get his work done, then leave.

"Chris sure is acting weird," said Ty as Chris disappeared through the locker room door after Saturday's workout.

"Wonder where he's headed in such a big hurry?" added AJ

"Probably goin' out to rob a liquor store," surmised Dallas.

Patrick added his two cents. "No, I bet Chris has probably found him a little hillbilly girl and is too ashamed to tell us."

Knowing how close Patrick was to the truth, Joey, who had been laughing at Dallas's answer, quickly drew quiet and finished his conditioning. This did not go unnoticed by Patrick.

FIVE

▼

MOST FIRST DATES are pretty tame, Haley thought. See a movie, eat dinner at someplace impressive, but not too expensive, and have me home right on time. Haley had had several first dates, but she hoped that her first date with Chris would not be quite so predictable. They had been seeing each other for a week, but between Chris's workouts and Haley's job, they had not actually been out on a date. Plus, there was the small fact that he hadn't asked her out yet.

Not wanting to disturb her at work, he waited until nine fifteen to show up at Pizza Roma.

"It's about time you got here. This place has been dead for an hour," she said, sounding like a mother who had been waiting up for a child who had missed his curfew.

"Well, I'd hate for your boss to get mad at me for hangin' around while you're working," said Chris, defending himself.

"You're very thoughtful, but my boss left two hours ago. He left me to close up." At this time, she planted the seed. "You know, Chris, we've been seeing each other for almost a week now. And I know between your training and my job, we haven't really been able to spend much time together."

"Okay, I'll bite. What's your point?" replied Chris.

"Well, in all this time, you have yet to actually ask me on a date."

Chris knew he had to think fast. As they say, hell hath no fury like a woman without a date.

"You know ... we've both been busy, and ... uh ... school starts tomorrow. And, heck, I don't know, Haley. I just haven't gotten around to it. It's no big deal." Chris could have said anything but that.

"No big deal, eh?" she said, enraged. "I guess if I'm no big deal, I'll just have to find someone else—"

"No, no, no. You know what I meant," Chris defended himself. "We've been together every night this week, but we both get finished so late. There hasn't been time for a real date."

"So, when do we get one?" She had him trapped.

"I don't know. What do you have in mind?"

She didn't hesitate. "I'll pick you up at your house at six thirty tomorrow morning, okay?"

"Six thirty? What about your training at the fitness center?" he asked.

"Don't worry, we'll get our exercise in the morning," she replied. "You'd better go home and get some sleep. Be ready when I get there."

"Sure you don't want to go hang out or something?"

"Nope, we've got a big day tomorrow. You better get some rest."

As the gate to Pizza Roma slammed down and he and Haley went their separate ways, Chris thought to himself, Did I just get asked out on a date by someone who just yelled at me for not asking her? And, I didn't like the way she used the word "we" when she referred to getting exercise. I sure hope I didn't bite off more than I can chew.

Realizing he didn't have the answers, Chris sped up on his motorcycle and headed home.

The plan was fairly simple. Wake up at six fifteen, splash his face, brush his teeth, get dressed, and be waiting on his doorstep when she arrived. However, hitting the snooze button on the alarm twice put his schedule off a bit. He was still asleep when Haley's Suzuki Sidekick pulled up to the house. The sound of her pulling in the driveway made him groggy, but before he could gather his senses, she laid on the horn. This brought Chris to his feet in one big hurry. No time for pleasantries. Just throw on some clothes, splash the face, and go.

Chris came out the door with his shirt open, his fly down, and his tennis shoes in his hands. Haley laughed. She waited until he was seated in her car to tell him, "Your clothes are all wrong." She pushed him back out of he car and aimed him back toward his house. "Go back and put on some jeans, maybe a flannel shirt, and some shoes you don't mind tearing up, preferably some hiking shoes. And don't forget socks!" she screamed as Chris disappeared into his house.

Ten minutes later, Chris appeared, dressed correctly but still about three cups of coffee away from being awake. No sooner had he crawled into the passenger's seat, Haley threw it into reverse, backed out of the driveway, and they were off.

"Don't suppose you had a chance to eat today." she said, already knowing the response.

"Uh, no. Um, I didn't have time," he said, still trying to find consciousness.

"Here," she said as she pulled a box from behind his seat. "Eat a couple of these."

Chris looked into the box of wheat doughnuts and bran muffins. He scrounged around until he found a muffin that looked like it had some kind of fruit in it.

After ten miles and four muffins, Chris was finally awake.

"So, what's on the agenda for today?" was the question he had had on his mind for the past ten hours.

"Oh, you know, a little of this, a little of that," came the nonanswer.

"Oh, okay. Well, will you let me know when we stop doing 'this' and start doing 'that?'" came Chris's typical smart-mouthed response.

"Oh, you'll know the difference," was Haley's response as she was headed for the foot of the Great Smoky Mountains.

Chris had figured out, he thought, what the day would consist of. A leisurely walk in the wilderness, a picnic lunch in a meadow, spend some time looking at a waterfall. Wonderful, right off a Hallmark card.

Haley pulled into a parking lot at the foot of a mammoth mountain. "Okay, we're here." She parked her Sidekick, and they began to unpack.

From the back of her Sidekick, she pulled out two very large backpacks.

"Here, this one's yours." She gave the bigger of the two to Chris.

"Why do I get the big one?" he asked, only half kidding.

"Genetics," she teased.

"No, really, what have you got in these, bricks?" He noticed that the backpacks contained more than just a picnic lunch.

"Well," she said as she threw hers on with no effort, adjusting the straps for a better fit, "it's a long way up. We've got food for later. Plus, there's a couple sweaters. It gets chilly at night."

"Just how long does it take to get where we're going?" he said.

"Oh, just a few hours, but we'll be up there for a while. Then, there's the climb down. This will be a full day. We'd better get started." And the two started their trek up the mountain, Haley leading and Chris behind, still juggling his backpack, trying to adjust it to the least amount of encumberment.

It was easy to see that Chris had never undertaken such an activity as mountain climbing. He walked into trees, tripped over roots, and kept stepping in things he should've tried to avoid. After three miles, he had worked out most of the kinks and was able to keep pace with his counterpart.

They were three-and-a-half hours into their journey when Chris decided to throw gallantry out the window and plead like a four-year-old on family vacation.

"Are we there yet? My feet are getting a little tired."

Haley chuckled at his dismay. "You're soft, McClure. We're still about an hour away, but there's a clearing up ahead. We can stop and rest, I mean, get a snack, there."

A hundred yards ahead, they came to a ridge. It looked like a popular spot, with cut logs for chairs and a trash can. Once they got to the clearing, Chris looked out at a most amazing panorama he had ever seen. Until now, all he had seen were the trees around him and the ground beneath his every step.

"This is awesome!" he said with a gasp. "You come here often?"

"Once in a while, when I need to think. This is a special place. This is, however, the first time I've brought someone with me," she replied.

"You mean you never brought Patrick up here?"

"He never was interested in doing anything like this. Ever since I've known him, he's been obsessed with his gymnastics and has never taken the time to discover that there are other things in life besides the gym."

"You know, that reminds me. Why is it that everyone on the team is so obsessed with the NTIs? It's just one meet in a whole season. I can understand Coach Lowery's reasons, but I don't follow why the team is just as wrapped up."

"I'm probably not the one you should be asking," she said, "but having dealt with Joey and Patrick, I do have a pretty good idea. It all has to do with payback."

"Payback?"

"Yes. See, when you win a medal or trophy, you know it's not just you. It's you, your coach, your teammates. Everyone is partly responsible for your victory, but when the meet is over, you're the one carrying home the hardware. When the team wins, there's always a trophy symbolizing the accomplishment. And that trophy goes to the gym. It's a way for the team to show its appreciation for what the gym has done for them. That's what being a Pioneer is all about."

Chris sat and thought about Haley's insight as he stared out at the view before him. Meanwhile, Haley had gotten up and replaced her backpack to her shoulders. "Come on, Chris, we still have a ways to go."

"You're telling me," he said, referring to more than just the hike. Chris put his backpack on and quickly caught up to the enchanting blonde who had just given him a new perspective on life.

"So you think Knoxville is slow by California standards?" she said, setting Chris up.

"Well, maybe slow is not the word. More like … tame," came the response from the brash young man.

"Tame? How so?" she replied, sarcastically.

"I don't know exactly. I guess it has something to do with the pace of the people and the slow southern drawl," he concluded, finishing his sentence with a hillbilly accent.

"Tell you what. If you still think that Knoxville is slow, tame, or whatever after the next ten minutes, I'll buy you dinner for the next month, okay?" she exclaimed as she made the final push over the top of the mountain they had spent the last four hours climbing.

Chris, five steps behind, responded to her challenge. "Okay, but remember, we're going by my barome … ter … " his words trailed off as he topped the mountain, only to find the source of Haley's confidence. Hang gliders pushing off the edge of a cliff at a rate of one every minute. "Holy crud. You do this stuff?" he said with almost no voice.

"Yeah. Neat, ain't it? I've been teaching hang gliding for three years in my off time," replied Haley, giggling at the sight of Chris's jaw hanging open almost as wide as his eyes. "I have my own kite, but I didn't want to give away what we were going to do by carrying a couple of twelve-foot poles in my backpack."

"'We?' Whatchu mean 'we,'?" mocked Chris at the thought of participating in such an activity.

"Of course 'we.' You're not scared, are you, Chris?" she said, prodding him to reveal any trace of fear.

"Who, me? I'm not scared," he said, trying to mask his true feelings. "I just have a small problem with slamming into the ground at a high rate of speed."

"Why? You do it every day at gymnastics practice." she reasoned.

"Yeah, but that's dropping from twelve feet, not twelve hundred!"

"What's the difference? Besides, it's not the drop that kills you. It's that sudden stop!" she joked.

"Listen, Haley, I'd really love to do this, but I have no idea how to steer one of those things."

"Don't worry," she said, "you don't have to. We'll fly tandem, in a trainer." Haley removed her backpack as she approached the object of discussion, a hang glider with two slings. "See, this kite is made for two people, an instructor, me, and a pupil, you. It'll be fun. You'll see."

Chris was beginning to see that there was no way of talking his way out of flying off the side of a perfectly good mountain.

No sooner did Chris have his backpack off did Haley start fitting him into the harness, all the while giving him instructions on the finer points of hang gliding. "All you have to do is hang on. I'll do all the work. Just keep your body tight and move as I do. Who knows, McClure, you may just like this stuff."

The last items to go on were the helmet and goggles. By this time, they were standing at the end of the jump point. "Just run with me and jump. I'll do the rest," she said.

And with that, they were signaled by the monitor to start their run. And run they did. With each step, the pitch in Chris's panicked cry rose until they pushed off the longest step in his life.

"AAAiieeee!!" Chris screamed as they pushed off.

"Geez, McClure, you sound like a little girl!" snickered Haley.

Then everything went quiet.

For the first few seconds, all Chris could do was look around him at the most awesome sight in his life. In front of him was thebeautiful scene he had seen from the ledge, but this time was much different. Instead of having his field of vision blocked by trees and mountain, there was nothing but an unobstructed view of natural beauty. It was breathtaking. From that moment, he forgot all about his initial fear.

The first, and only, scary moment came with the first turn. Haley, who was on the left, leaned to her left and pulled the metal bar to the right, causing the glider to bank sharply into a left turn.

"Whoa! What are you doin'?" Chris cried.

Haley waited until she was finished with the turn before returning a reply. "Sorry to startle you, but that's how you turn this thing." Before she had finished her response, the flight had returned to its previously easygoing manner. But now, the view was different. Instead of the familiar scene from the mountain, the view was of the mountain itself. Chris didn't realize that the mountain that they had spent most of their day scaling was quite so big. This is great, he thought.

They had only been aloft five minutes. Chris was getting into the ride and the view, both of which Haley was offering in abundance. With large sweeping turns and graceful plunges and rises, she provided an experience that was both exciting and beautiful. Then she asked him, "Would you like to try?"

"Who, me? I'd probably get us killed," was his response.

"No, you won't. Here, it's easy. Just pull to the opposite side you want to turn, pull back to go down, push forward to go up. If you mess up, I'll take over."

Reluctantly, Chris took over. At first, he kept everything on an even keel, making only very subtle turns. After five minutes, he began to feel control, increasing the size of his turns and becoming a little more aggressive on rising and descending. With each new movement, Chris's adrenaline surged. "Wow, this is great!" he exclaimed, without reservation.

They remained aloft for hours. As the sun was getting closer to the horizon, Chris relinquished control of the glider to Haley to bring it in for a landing. Haley set the colorful kite in a field a scant fifty yards from the space where she had left her car. No sooner had they hit the ground did the first exclamation come from Chris.

"Wow, what a rush!"

"I kinda thought you'd like it. Now, let's see if we can pack this kite and get it back up to the top of the mountain before dark."

"You mean we have to carry this thing back up that mountain?" Chris exclaimed.

"Naw. We'll drive it up in the Sidekick."

"You mean we could've driven up there instead of wasting our morning climbing that rock?"

"Do you consider what we did this morning a waste of time?" she inquired.

"Well, no. Now that I think about it, that climb was actually pretty cool."

"All right, then, let's get to work."

Within moments, the two disassembled the glider, folding the nylon wing and stowing the poles that served as the ribs into the small vehicle. They were halfway up the mountain before either said a word. Then, Haley opened the conversation. "So, McClure, still find Knoxville slow?"

"This was a definite improvement. I think I could get to like you, I mean *it*, here."

"I see what you mean," replied Haley, catching the blunder in Chris's comment but agreeing none the less.

Once the glider was returned to storage, the two started down the mountain. "Hungry?" asked Chris.

"Famished."

"Dinner's on me," offered the Californian.

"No way, city boy, this is my date. I'll buy. You can buy when you set up the date."

"Fair enough."

And, from then until they returned to town, Chris talked nonstop about the incredible experience he had just had.

After dinner, the two decided to call it a night. They next day was the start of a new, and the final, high school year, for Haley and Chris. Haley pulled up to the curb outside Chris's house. Both were quiet, as neither wanted to start what, for every teenage couple, was the most awkward of all conversations, the "good night" talk.

"Well, thanks for a fantastic day, Haley."

"It's my pleasure any time I can educate poor old city boys like yourself in the ways of good old country fun," she chuckled. Once again, silence fell over the two as they tried to find comfortable words to tell their feelings.

"You know, you really knocked my socks off today. I mean, nobody has ever made me feel what I felt today—helpless and safe at the same time. I … I think I could … really … "

The two closed in as their eyes locked, each making sure that they shared the same idea.

"Yeah, Chris … I know … what you … mean … "

In an instant, contact. Their entire bodies tingled with life and emotion as their lips met. Then, they embraced, arms encircling, pulling each other tighter. Then, Chris pulled away. Haley's face turned from passionate to furiously curious.

"What's the matter, Chris? I thought … you … " she inquired frantically.

"No, no … it's not you. It's me, Haley … I'm sorry. Hey, maybe I'll see you tomorrow, okay?"

"Chris, what's the matter?" she cried as he started walking toward his front door. No answer. Haley jumped out of the car and raced across his lawn to cut him off before reaching the door.

"Listen, you, I went to a lot of trouble to make today special. If this is it, tell me now or I'll knock you on your ass as sure as I'm standing here."

Suddenly, the memory of being knocked out of his chair at the mall raced through his mind. "Look, Haley, I had a great time. Everything was wonderful. And you are by far the greatest girl I've ever gone out with, but there are things about me you don't know, and it's probably best you don't get too close to me. I really like you a lot, a whole lot, and that scares me. I'd really like to just slow things down right now. Maybe later, when we know each other a little better, we can pick up the pace."

"What, are you scared?"

"No, it's not that at all. Well, maybe a little, but … "

"Patrick," she exclaimed. "It's Patrick, isn't it? You know that Patrick and I used to date, and you don't want to deal with that."

"No, it has nothing to do with Patrick. If that's all it was, I wouldn't think twice about going out with you," he answered.

"Then, what is it? Tell me, Chris. I want to know!"

"I'm not so sure you would if you did."

"Try me."

After careful consideration, Chris decided that if he was planning any extended relationship with Haley, he needed to be honest with her from the start. He could only hope that his secret would be safe with her.

"When do you have to be home?" he asked.

"I don't have to be home for another hour."

"Come on in. Brace yourself," he said, and the two went inside his house.

When Haley emerged two hours later, she was sullen but otherwise satisfied with what she was told. Chris got a kiss on the cheek from his new friend. Moments later, she drove away.

SIX

▼

THE COMPETITIVE SEASON was just around the corner. Practices had started to shift emphasis from skills and combinations of skills to the composition of routines. The feelings and personalities of the gymnasts were also changing. Tension was starting to build as the first meet came closer. This year seemed different, and it was becoming easy to see why. The Pioneer team was becoming a contender; all of the guys could feel it. This was the first season that Pioneer would have a full team and, counting Joey, one to spare. Joey was the safety valve, and he knew that although he could be called on to count in the team score, with six powerful teammates, he would be nothing more than the second-string quarterback whose team won the Super Bowl. He would get to share the victory or shoulder the defeat, just like the guys that actually competed. He could deal with that.

All the guys were showing the nerves that come with the knowledge of a possible national team championship and that each one of them would be ultimately responsible for the outcome of the season. One stupid mistake, one break in concentration, one dumb injury, and the best possible chance to be on top would be shattered like all the years before. The mood of workouts became sullen. Each gymnast enveloped in his own personal vision quest. The only one making any noise at all was Chris. He treated every workout like every one before. To watch the workouts, it was easy to see why. No one who ever went through Pioneer was anything like Chris. He never missed. If Coach Lowery demanded ten hit routines, he would hit ten in a row, sometimes doing back-to-back sets without getting off the equipment. The other guys had become somewhat jealous of his uncanny ability to hit routines. This, combined with the added pressure of the upcoming season, created a very tense personal atmosphere as well.

Chris had just hit his fifth consecutive high bar routine. The rest had only seven among them, Patrick having accounted for four of them. Although no one could deny the fact that Chris was easily the best gymnast they had ever seen, this knowledge did very little to prevent animosity from stirring within his teammates. Of course, Dallas was the first to make his frustrations known.

"Hey, Crash, you ever think about maybe missing a set just to let us peons know that you're really just as mortal as we are?" said Dallas with a bite in his voice.

"Heck, Dallas, I figure you guys need to see what you could do if you work as much as you talk." This did nothing to ease matters.

Basically, the problems were simple. Chris was ready to compete. In fact, he probably could've been competition-ready when he walked into the gym for the first time two months ago. The real problem was the rest of the team. While most of the guys were having trouble hitting routines, the ones who could hit with any degree of consistency were incomplete in some necessary requirements or were lacking difficulty in their routines required to be competitive at the national level. It was not uncommon for guys like Patrick to start the season with routines short of the necessary value to be competitive and later add some difficulty as the season goes on. Chris could see the shortcomings of the team, but most of their egos would not accept his comic, sometimes terse, remarks as constructive criticism. Rather, they thought that Chris was merely gloating about his own perfection.

Patrick had just finished his high bar routine, hitting his fifth out of eight. Chris thought he would throw a comment to help. "Hey, plowboy, you know you're gonna be about three-tenths short of your competition with that set."

"Well, for your information, when I clean this routine up, I'll be three-tenths ahead," he replied.

"No, I'm talking after you clean it up. You're still gonna be short."

"How do you figure?"

"Man, you're gonna be goin' up against the best guys in the country this year, all you guys. If you expect to be competitive with the guys from Texas and Arizona, not to mention the guys up north, from Ohio, Michigan, and Pennsylvania, you're gonna have to beef up your routines with more difficulty."

Dallas came to Patrick's aid. "Yeah, right. Everybody knows that good routines with great form will beat great routines with poor form."

"That's true, David, but who said that that's your competition?" returned Chris. "Right now, with perfect execution, Patrick's high bar routine will only score about a 9.3, at best. You go up against the guys from Clinton

Gymnastics out in Arizona—they go four men deep with routines with twice the difficulty, perfect execution, and ungodly form. These guys score 9.5 on a bad day."

"You know, you guys, he has a good point," Patrick added. "We have been kinda lazy. I mean, compared to last season, we really haven't added much new to our sets."

"Yeah, but that's 'cause we did so good with the routines last year," said Mackee.

"But we're gonna have to get a lot better to keep up with the rest of the guys in the country," added Joey.

"That's easy for you to say, shrimp." attacked Dallas. "You have yet to count in a team score. You're the one who needs to beef up his routines just to catch up with us."

Chris immediately rallied behind Joey. "You know, Dallas, it's bogus remarks like that that come back to haunt you."

Ty joined the chorus. "That's right, Dallas. Besides, Joey made a very good point. If you're not moving forward, you're moving backward."

AJ dropped off the bar to add his portion. "Yeah, Dallas, like my dad says, 'If you're not preparing to win, you're preparing to lose.' I never knew what he meant, until now."

Everyone looked at each other, then Patrick conceded the point. "Okay, Chris, let's assume that you're right. What exactly do you propose for us to do to add difficulty to routines we can't even hit yet?"

"Well, first of all," Chris took a breath before hopping up on the bar to take his turn, "I don't think your not hitting routines is a problem," he said almost incoherently as he had started swinging around the bar. "You guys haven't made hitting routines important enough yet. When you do, hitting will not be a problem." Chris continued to do his routine as he carried on the conversation.

"What do you suggest adding to my routine?" asked Patrick.

"Well," returned Chris, pausing to finish his sixth consecutive hit routine with a full-twisting double somersault in layout position. "You could try twisting your Geinger," he said upon landing.

"What? Are you crazy? I only hit about 60 percent of them now, and you want me to add a twist? You gotta be crazy!"

"No, man, *you've* got to be crazy!" barked Chris, getting into Patrick's face. "That's the only way you're gonna get what it's gonna take to beat your competition. Your competition is crazy. You can count on it. I know them. You're gonna see a guy from Austin named Danny Diego who will not only show you what a twisting Geinger looks like, but he'll show you two more D releases and a double-twisting double layout. And, he does not miss. Then, when you go up north, you'll see Marty Reynolds, who is also certifiable. He likes to find the craziest moves, and he does them all, and with no form breaks." Chris finished removing his grips and stowed them with the rest of his gear in his paper bag and started toward the part of the gym where he would start his conditioning.

"I'll see you guys at the Pioneer Circle when you finish." He turned as he left, "Yeah, plowboy, *you* gotta be crazy." Chris left the group to start his conditioning, having finished his event work.

Patrick looked at each of his teammates, then stared at the high bar, the source of his anguish, and just shook his head.

"Forget Chris, Patrick," came the consoling voice of Dallas. "Our sets will score just fine, you'll see."

"Shut up, Dallas. He's right, and you know it."

SEVEN

▼

SCHOOL IS GREAT; it's just all the work involved that makes it so terrible, Chris thought. He had been working on the same physics problem for an hour and a half with no luck. If all I had to do in life was gymnastics, I'd get by fine. Besides, when am I gonna use this stuff in the real world? He thought. He stared at the phone, wondering whether he should call for help. No, that's a sign of weakness. Besides, the best student in his class probably would not want to talk to me anyway. At last he gave in. His heart pounded louder with the push of each button on the telephone. The phone rang several times without answer. Maybe no one is home, he thought. Just as he had given up and started to hang up the receiver, the click of someone on the other end picking up stopped his motion, and he drew his phone to his ear.

"Hello?"

"Haley?"

"Speaking. Chris?"

"Yeah. Hi, how ya doin'?"

"Fine. Just fine. How are you?"

"I'm dyin'."

"You're what?" she said in a panic.

"No, no, nothing serious. I'm just dyin' in physics class. I've been working on this homework for forever, and I'm just lost."

"Well, for someone whose entire life is defying physical principles, that doesn't surprise me a bit. What part is giving you the most trouble?"

"The part right after the teacher says, 'Open your books.'" He laughed.

"Sounds like you need help," she surmised.

"Any chance we can get together and work on this problem?" he asked. "I'd ... I'd really like to see you."

"I've missed you, too. Do you want to meet at the library?"

"That will be just fine. Do you want to go get something to eat later?"

"Sure, that'll be fun. See you in a half?"

"At the card file."

"See you in a bit."

"Bye." Both hung up. Both breathed a sigh of relief.

Haley arrived early by about five minutes. She had been waiting fifteen minutes when Chris arrived.

"Sorry I'm late. I had no idea where the library was! I just rode around until I found it. I actually passed it once, not knowing what it was!"

"It's good to see you, too, Chris," she said, noting his less than graceful entrance. Once Chris realized his blunder, both laughed and then embraced.

"I missed you so much," he said.

"Me, too," she returned. "Now, let's get you through these physics problems so we can get out of here."

"Why don't we just blow off the physics and get out of here?"

"No way. You fail physics, and you won't be academically eligible to compete."

With that, the two disappeared into a deep section of the library where they could talk about physics, among other things.

Two hours later, they emerged from the library, laughing, arm in arm. Chris had conveniently parked his motorcycle next to Haley's car. After a couple of words, they agreed where to go for food and left for a nice Italian restaurant.

The food was delicious and the conversation lively until the subject of their relationship came up. Neither wanted to take the lead. Haley was the first to break the silence.

"You know, Chris," she said, "we really don't have to struggle with this. I think whatever the problem, we can work it out."

"Oh, you do, do you? What if something happens to me and we can never be together again? Then what?" he returned.

"Well, I guess I'll cross that bridge when I come to it. If nothing else, at least we will have had our time together," she replied.

"And you can rest easy with that?" he questioned.

"Yes."

"Well, what about me? I've never been comfortable with relationships."

"I'm sure I can help you over that one," she said confidently.

"Well, okay then. I guess we can give it a try," he conceded.

With those words, they took each other's hand and smiled. Once the check was paid, the time had come to say good-bye.

"Well, I'm kinda glad you're lousy at physics."

"I'm kinda glad that you've been patient with me."

"It takes a special guy to jump off the side of a perfectly good mountain with someone he barely knows. I think you're worth the wait. Besides, if you'll just relax, you might get to like this relationship stuff." Haley, having made her point, left Chris no room for argument.

Chris looked deep into her eyes, searching for approval. I could die in those eyes, he thought. He drew her closer until their bodies entangled in a mutual embrace. Then, he kissed her. Their electricity could have lit up a city block. This time, there would be no pushing away. Realizing that they were standing on a busy sidewalk in downtown Knoxville, they slowly moved away from their embrace.

"I'd better get home. It is a school night," she said.

"Right. I'll give you a call, okay?"

"Sure, anytime," she responded. They went their separate ways with their thoughts on the other.

Outside her house, Haley could hear the phone ringing inside. She burst through the door and picked up the receiver.

"Hello?" she said.

"Hey," came the familiar voice of the brash young man she had just left. "Just wanted to make sure you haven't changed your mind. About us, I mean."

Haley chuckled before returning her answer to the silly question, "Of course I haven't changed my mind. I think you are a great guy, and I'm looking forward to spending a lot of time with you."

"You're sure?"

"Of course I'm sure! Now, say good night, and put that paranoid brain of yours to bed and get some sleep."

"Okay, if you say so. Oh, Haley?"

"Yes, Chris."

"You're the greatest!"

"Say good night, Chris."

"Good night, Chris!" he said, mocking her request.

Haley hung up the phone, laughing to think that this macho, antisocial example of counterculture was making a fool of himself for a girl.

Before she could finish her thought, the phone rang again. What has gotten into this guy? she thought. She answered the phone with a flip remark prepared for her new beau. "Chris, haven't you had enou—"

"Chris?" came the different, but familiar, voice.

"Patrick! Why are you calling me so late?"

"I've been trying to reach you all afternoon! You've either been gone or the line is busy. Where have you been?"

"I've been out, if it's any of your business."

"It is my business. I had heard that Chris McClure has been after you, and I wanted to warn you about him, but I guess I'm a little late."

"First of all, Mr. Goodman," came the voice of an obviously enraged young lady, "for your information, Chris has not been after me. If anything, I've been after him. Second, he happens to be a perfect gentleman. Third, what's it to you? You haven't given me a second thought since we broke up over six months ago. Why the sudden interest?"

"Well, I heard that McClure was after you, and I just thought—"

"You just thought that you would warn me about him," she interrupted. "Well, thanks for the warning. I know who to stay away from now."

"Haley, don't take this the wrong way. I just wanted to protect you."

"From what? As far as I'm concerned, it's you and Dallas I need to stay away from. Did Joey put you up to this?"

"Heck, no. Joey looks up to McClure like he's some kind of god or something."

"Well, at least he doesn't make snap character judgments. You guys could learn something from Chris."

"Yeah, like how to snake a teammate's girlfriend."

"Ex-girlfriend, you mean," she corrected. "Listen, Patrick, thank you for trying, but I'm a big girl. Don't worry about me. I can take care of myself."

"Hey, green eyes, I'm sorry if I ruffled your feathers," he apologized sincerely. "If you really like this guy, I'm not gonna cause a problem. But, if he hurts you, so help me—"

"If he hurts me, Patrick, you'll be the first guy I call, honest."

"Okay. I guess I better let you go. I've made enough of an ass of myself for one night," he said.

"Oh, you didn't really make much of an ass of yourself. Besides, it's kind of flattering to think that you want to protect me. I feel like a princess with two avenging knights."

"Good night, Haley."

"Good night, Patrick. Take care of yourself."

Haley hung up the phone, for she hoped the last time that night, thinking back on how boring she had expected the evening to be when all she had to do was some chemistry homework. She chuckled once more and got ready for bed.

EIGHT

▼

THE PUSH HAD begun. Although the first meet of the season was still a week away, the team still had quite a ways to go before it could become a national contender, but the plan was in place. Banners that read "All the Way to LA" and "Go Pioneers" adorned the gym. The first couple of meets are traditionally used to work out the kinks and get the body accustomed to competition again. Coach Lowery had a different idea. This year, he wanted to show the state, the region, and the whole country that his Pioneers were going to show the way from wire to wire. The mood in the gym had gone from tense to focused. Each gymnast had developed his own tunnel vision. What two weeks ago were labored, half routines were now becoming polished. And, the personal tensions between team members were kept out of the gym.

Chris was showing no sign of nervousness. He trained with perfect execution and world-class difficulty. His teammates could only stare at him in awe. In the three months that he had been a Pioneer, no one could recall him missing a single skill or falling during a routine.

"This guy can't be for real," Dallas said to Patrick under his breath. "Surely, the pressure of competition will get to him sooner or later. He'll crack, you'll see."

"I certainly hope you're wrong, Dallas," returned Patrick. "As much as you and I hate to admit it, we really need this guy."

"How can you say that, man? After all, isn't he the guy that took your girl?"

"Why don't you find something more constructive to do with that overworked imagination, Dallas? You're really starting to become a pain. Haley has the right to see whoever she wants. I can't help it if she's lost her sense of taste." Patrick had appeased Dallas, but like everyone else, he himself was caught between hating the Californian for being what he was and admiring him for the magic he could do with his gymnastics.

The trip to Atlanta served many purposes. It gave the guys time to go over the routines that they would be competing the next day. Those who chose not to think about routines could catch up on homework they had put off in order to put in a few more hours of training that week. Most of all, the trip was boring. Between tension and anticipation, nobody really wanted to be cooped up in a van with these guys for three minutes, let alone three hours.

Arriving at the Quality Lodge at ten-thirty didn't leave much time for getting comfortable before going to bed. Coach had called for a team meeting in his room at 10:45. Once everyone arrived in Coach Lowery's room, he closed the door to address his charges.

"Men, this is the first competition of the season. This meet in no way will tell whose going to be on top at the end of the season, but I want every spectator and every competitor to leave the arena tomorrow having a pretty good idea who will. In this room, we have the potential for winning it all this year. We've been close before, but we've never been this deep. We've been good before, but never this good. The only thing that will keep us from winning every meet between here and the national championships is the attitude that you carry into each meet. I know that this is the first meet of the season, and we can expect to see a lot of bugs in the routines. This is everybody's first meet of the season. The guys from Memphis, Birmingham, Jackson, Mississippi, and, yes, even the guys from Atlanta, are competing here for their first meet of the season as well. Although we are competing for a team award this meet, I want you to focus internally for this meet. I want you to support your teammates, but, more importantly, I want you to concentrate on your own routines. Analyze, scrutinize, and dissect your routines. Everyone should not only come away from this competition feeling that he should've done better, I want you to know what you have to do to become better, and that's what I will expect to see from you from here on out. What it will take to get to Los Angeles at the end of the season begins with what we do here. Does everybody understand?"

A collective "Yes, sir" was offered up by the travel-weary athletes.

"Okay, room assignments," Coach said as a mumble began to swell. Coach was notorious for rooming guys together that would not have chosen to otherwise.

"AJ, you're with Ty. Patrick, you got Mackee. Dallas, you, Chris, and Joey are together. Joey, you got the rollaway."

"Why do I get the rollaway, Coach?" Joey pleaded. "McClure is the rookie. I have seniority!"

"Yeah, Johnson, but you're a freshman, and McClure's a senior. Sorry, Charlie," came the response from the Pioneer mentor.

"Hey, Coach, any way I can swap out with somebody?" asked Dallas. "I'm … uh … allergic to McClure's cologne!"

"No way, Dallas. Just stay away from him. You'll get over it. Okay, men, let's get right to bed. We've got to be in the gym at eight tomorrow morning. Lights-out at eleven thirty. Anyone still up and around at 11:31 is scratched from the meet. Any questions?"

With heads shaking side to side, the guys headed for their rooms. As Patrick passed Dallas, he whispered into Dallas's ear, "I'll swap rooms with you right after lights-out."

"Okay, you got it," came the reply.

Once everybody got settled in, Joey noticed that Dallas was not getting ready for bed. "You going somewhere, Dallas?"

"Yeah, he's swapping rooms with some poor slob. Seems Dallas doesn't want to share our company, squirt," replied Chris.

"*Your* company, Crash," Dallas said. "I'm not crazy about training in the same gym as you, much less sleep in the same room."

"Man, what is your problem?" asked Joey. "You have been a royal pain in the butt ever since Chris got here. He hasn't done a thing to you."

"He ain't us, Joey. He's Californian. He doesn't care about us. All he cares about is himself. He rides that motorcycle around, actin' like a big shot. Look at him. He's been in Tennessee for three months, and he still looks like a hood—goofy hairdo, earring, weird clothes. He's just not one of us!"

"Seems to me you might be sounding just a little jealous, Dallas," quipped Joey. "I seem to recall your blond locks cut into one of those "skate or die" hairdos last summer when I first came to Pioneer. You looked pretty radical yourself."

"Yeah, but that didn't change what's inside," Dallas tried to defend himself. "I still say he ain't us. He's not a Pioneer."

"Yeah, right. I also seem to recall several times that I've caught you staring, like all of us, at Chris, with your jaw hanging open, when he does the crazy skills he does. And, didn't I see you tryin' a couple of Chris's parallel bar combinations last week? Sounds to me like somebody you'd like to imitate, not insult."

"Johnson, why don't you just keep your ideas to yourself," remarked Dallas as he gathered his stuff at bolted out the door.

"Golly, I didn't mean to chase him off," said Joey.

"You didn't, squirt," said Chris, laughing. "He had an arrangement to swap out with Patrick."

"Yeah, but Coach said—"

Just then, the door opened up and Patrick hurried into the room. "What Coach said is one thing. What we actually do is another. What he don't know won't hurt him," said Patrick, checking to make sure that the switch had not been detected.

"If he don't find out, nobody gets in trouble, right, Joey?" added Chris.

"Uh, right, Chris," said a confused Joey. "By the way, Patrick, why did you want to swap out with Dallas, anyway?"

"I think it has something to do with your sister, squirt," surmised Chris. "You might want to be somewhere else."

"No way, dudes. I'm the one who hooked both of you guys up with Haley. I think I have a vested interest in this conversation!"

"I don't care if he stays, if you don't," said Patrick.

"After the way he just stuck up for me with Dallas, I'd be a fool to send him out now," said Chris.

"Well, I just wanted to know what your intentions were with Haley," asked Patrick.

"My intentions?" asked Chris.

"Yeah, like, are you gonna get serious with her, or what?" said Patrick, inquisitively.

"To be honest, I have no *intentions*," Chris said, making quotation marks with his fingers. "We're just kind of enjoying each other's company. If she decides that she wants to get more serious, well, that's up to her."

"I just want to be sure that she doesn't get hurt."

"Like the way you hurt her?" added Joey.

"What do you mean, like I hurt her?"

"After all, you're the one who talked Haley out of teaching hang gliding. You thought she would get hurt."

"I didn't like her doing that. That's dangerous stuff. She could get killed," Patrick returned.

"Yeah," added Chris, "but you can get killed doing gymnastics, too."

"That's different," replied Patrick.

"To whom?" inquired Chris.

For a moment, Patrick pondered the thought. Realizing that he may have made a mistake, he conceded. "Okay, so I did some dumb things, subjecting Haley to my stupid double standards. That doesn't give you the right to do the same, McClure."

"Wouldn't think of it, plowboy. Heck, if you want me to stay away from her, just say the word. But I'll tell you this, I'm not the only one who created this situation. It takes two to tango. If you're not careful, you'll have one pissed-off little girl on your hands."

"Naw, you don't have to break up with her. Just promise me you won't screw up like I did."

"Consider it done, plowboy," answered Chris.

"That's it? No fireworks? No punches?" asked a disappointed Joey.

"Sorry to disappoint you, squirt," said Chris.

"Yeah, not every fight has to end with a haymaker," added Patrick.

"Man, you guys are boring. I was expecting big-time wrestling, not an after-school special!"

"Hey, you guys, lights out!" came the voice outside the door.

"Uh-oh, you guys. That was Coach. We'd better get to sleep," said Joey.

"Yeah, good idea, squirt. Hey, good luck tomorrow, you guys," said Patrick.

Chris killed the final light, and the room grew dark. Joey lay awake for hours thinking about the competition. Patrick was also restless as he struggled with gymnastics, Haley, and his future. Chris, on the other hand, was out as soon as his head hit the pillow.

Six o'clock came very early for Chris. Joey and Patrick had already taken their showers when Chris started dragging himself out of bed. Still wrapped in the sheet, Chris stumbled into the bathroom.

"Let's go, McClure," said Patrick. "We're supposed to be at breakfast in ten minutes."

"You guys go on without me. I'll be there in a minute," came the response from their slow-to-rise teammate, who sounded like his vocal chords were being raked across a washboard. "Let me get a quick shower, and I'll meet you guys downstairs."

Chris arrived at the breakfast table just as the remainder of the team was finishing the last of their meals.

"Sorry I'm late, Coach, but—"

"Save it, McClure. I think you're gonna be late for your own funeral," said Coach Lowery. "You've missed breakfast."

"That's okay. I never eat breakfast, anyway," Chris turned to the waitress as she was clearing away some of breakfast dishes. "Uh, miss? Could you bring me a cup of coffee, please?"

"Is that all you're going to have?" asked Mackee.

"Trust me, this is all I need," came the response.

As was the case with most invitationals, this competition was in the gymnasium of a local college. Although media coverage was normally reserved for national championship competitions at the end of the season, there were several representatives of the gymnastics magazines and other sports publications and a dozen or so photographers. The hosts of the competition,

Firestorm Gymnastics, had done quite a bit of hype to promote this preseason event.

The Pioneers were not the first to arrive. In fact, the majority of the competitors were already stretching out on the floor exercise carpet.

"Nice crowd," remarked Chris. "Are all meets here in the South always this big?"

"Nah," said Patrick, "everyone just likes to come to Atlanta to compete. But, it does seem to be a bit bigger that usual. I wonder why."

"I think I see the reason why," said Chris, as he elbowed Patrick. "Look over there by rings. See the guy stretching his shoulders out?"

"Yeah. What about him?"

"That's who I was telling you about. That's Danny Diego!"

"From Austin?" said Joey.

"That's what the man said, shrimp," answered Mackee.

"Cripes!" exclaimed Ty. "There's a dozen of 'em!" referring to Danny's teammates.

"Yep," returned Chris, "and they all look like they mean business." Chris looked around at his teammates, all with their jaws hanging wide open and their eyes glazed over. "When you guys roll your tongues back into your mouths, I'll meet you over at floor." Chris headed for an empty spot on which to stretch as his dumbfounded teammates followed slowly behind.

As the team sat down, Joey noticed that Danny was headed their way.

"Hey, Chris, Danny Diego's comin' this way!"

Danny, a native of Austin, was a handsome example of an athlete. His five-foot-nine-inch frame was packed with muscle, and his face had the smile of a movie star.

"Geez, they'll let anything into these meets!" Danny said, extending his hand for Chris to shake. "Well, now I know why the media circus is here. What are you doing this far east of the Rockies, anyway, McClure?"

"My mom and I moved to Knoxville back in August," answered the Californian.

"I don't think Tennessee will ever be the same again," added Patrick as a cue for Chris to make some introductions.

"Oh, I'm sorry, guys. Danny, let me introduce you to my new teammates." Chris introduced the Pioneers in the order in which they were sprawled on the floor exercise carpet. "This is AJ, Mackee, Ty, Dallas, Joey, and this is our team captain, Patrick Goodman."

"Hey guys, nice to meet ya. Goodman. Goodman? Yeah, I remember you. You won the meet in Tucson last year, right?" said Danny.

"Yeah. You were there?"

"Only as a spectator. I rolled my ankle pretty good in warm-ups, and I had to scratch. You looked good, though."

"Thanks. That was my best meet of the season. We've heard a lot about you, too. Chris says you're tough to beat."

"I'm tough to beat? This guy is the man to beat," said Danny, motioning to Chris. "This guy beat me three out of four times last year!"

"Yeah, but I bet you're the reason all the press and photographers are here," said Chris.

"No way, man. It's all of us. Marty Reynolds is here from Lake Erie, Dustin Hathaway is here from Minnesota. Heck, fifteen of the top twenty are here!"

"Man, didn't anyone tell these guys that this a preseason invitational?" added Patrick.

"This is gonna be interesting," said Chris.

"Interesting? I think it's gonna be chaotic!" returned Patrick.

"Hey, guys. Let's have some fun," said Danny as he turned to join his teammates before the start of timed warm-ups. Before getting too far away, he turned back. "Hey, Chris, pizza to the top?"

"Pizza to the top, Danny."

Patrick turned to Chris. "Pizza to the top?"

"Yeah," answered Chris, "whoever finishes lower buys the pizza for the guy who finishes ahead."

"How many pizzas have you had to buy, Chris?" asked Joey.

"Only one. National championships last year. The turkey beat me by two-tenths of a point. Caused me to take second."

"You were second in the country last year?" asked Joey in amazement.

"Yeah, but nobody remembers second place, do they, squirt?" Everyone turned to look at Patrick.

"What?" said Patrick, acknowledging the stares of his teammates.

"It's time to get crazy, my friend," responded Chris.

Then a voice came over the loud speaker, "Gentlemen, report to your first timed warm-up event, and begin warm-up."

"Let's go, guys," said Coach Lowery as he returned from the coaches meeting. "We start on Rings."

"Oh, great," said Patrick. "Austin and Lake Erie start on Rings."

"Now, this is what I call interesting," said Chris as the guys hustled to Rings, putting on their grips as fast as they could in line so as not to miss their turn.

The first guys up in warm-up were the guys from Austin. It was all the Pioneers could do to keep from staring at the awesome display presented by the Texans. Chris realized that his teammates were drifting into another world, watching the best gymnastics that they had ever seen before. "Hey, you guys!" said Chris, waiting until he had everyone's attention before going on. "Stay focused. Remember, intimidation is a two-way street. If you don't act impressed, they become the ones asking themselves questions. Stay sharp!"

It soon became obvious that the organizers of the meet had stacked the deck, putting the three best teams in one squad. One by one, the Pioneers warmed up their events, trying hard not to look overwhelmed at the display of talent. Although Chris was, for the most part, as cocky as usual, acting weird when they got to high bar warm-ups.

"What do ya say, fellers?" Chris barked at the gathering of gymnasts as he was the first to mount the bar. "Let's have some fun?" And with that, Chris began cranking giants, faster and faster. After several very fast giants, Chris did a blind turn to front giants without losing speed, punctuating the turn with a "Yeeeeee-haaaaaw!" Then, with a big arch over the bar, Chris tapped his swing through the bottom to release the bar and soar to twenty feet above the dismount mat, doing two front flips, half-twisting the second, only to land effortlessly on the dismount mat. Without acknowledging the burst of applause and whistles coming from his teammates, Chris walked by Patrick on his way to the end of the line.

"That's what I mean by crazy, Patrick. Now whose jaws are hanging open?" Patrick looked around, and sure enough, all the guys in the group, in fact, every guy in the gym, were standing with their mouths wide open and their eyes fixed on Chris as he blew the chalk off of his grips. Patrick looked at Chris. Chris gave him a wink and a smile, which caused Patrick to chuckle before he jumped up on the bar for his turn, and it suddenly made sense. It's just another meet.

The remainder of warm-up was pretty tame, considering the level of the gymnasts, with the exception of Chris, who with each turn became crazier and cockier, not at all the way he trained. At home, Chris was very matter-of-fact about his gymnastics, but something about competition brought out the animal in him.

"You look surprised, Goodman," said a voice from behind. Patrick turned to see Danny Diego.

"Yeah, just a little, maybe," came the response from the Tennessean as he watched his Californian teammate do five front flips in a row on the floor exercise mat. "Believe it or not, this is not what he looks like training back at the gym."

"Yeah, I know. As long as I've known him, he's been like this. I think it's part of the psych job he does on the other guys. I've been watching this clown for six years. He'll be the best this sport has ever seen, if he lives."

Patrick understood Danny's comment and silently agreed. It was easy to see how Chris's difficult skills would also put him at a higher risk. Both shuddered at the possible outcome of an errant turn.

"Any way, have a good meet, Patrick."

"You, too, Danny," replied Patrick as the two resumed their warm-up.

Once warm-ups had concluded, the gymnasts prepared for the march-in. Dallas walked up to Patrick. "Look, man," he said, pointing to Chris, who was balled up with his head between his knees. "I told you he would crack when competition hits. Look at him. He used up all his juice showing off in warm-ups," concluded Dallas.

"I don't know, man," returned Patrick. "I think he still has a second wind he hasn't let out yet."

But, Patrick took it upon himself to make sure that Chris was really okay. He sat down beside Chris. "Hey, man. You alright?"

Chris raised his head. "Oh, sure, plowboy. I'm just goin' through routines in my head."

"Oh, I get it. You're visualizing the routine that you've done hundreds of times to make sure you don't leave anything out, right?"

"Actually, I'm making 'em up as I go!" Chris replied as he smiled and got up to get in line for march-in.

The march-in music sounded more like the theme song for a heavy metal rockfest than it did the beginning of a sporting event, which suited Chris just fine. The teams were marched in one by one to a crowd of just a little under five thousand spectators.

During the introductions, the reason became clear for the coincidence of so much talent in a preseason competition. "Ladies and gentlemen, Firestorm Gymnastics presents the Firestorm Invitational. Within these walls are assembled some of our country's best gymnasts!" It was obvious that the meet promoter had worked hard to get some of the best gyms in the country to come to their meet. The announcer sounded like a circus sideshow barker as he announced each team and highlighted the star gymnast from each team.

"From Austin, Texas, Texas Star Gymnastics featuring your national all-around champion, Dannyyyyy Dieegooo!" The crowd was being whipped into a fever pitch as each team got more and more hype from the announcer. Then came the introduction for Pioneer. "And returning for the seventh straight year, from Knoxville, Tennessee, Pioneer Gymnastics with their newest addition from Riverside, California, your national championship all-around runner-up, Chriiis McCluuuure!" Patrick's heart dropped into the pit of his stomach. For the first time, he realized that he was no longer the leader of his beloved Pioneers. An upstart who had still to learn about the meaning of the word *team* had become—for the time being, anyway—the favored Pioneer.

For the Pioneers, the meet got off to a shaky start. Pommel Horse, the team's least favorite, was the first event, and it set the tone for the remainder of the competition. Joey, being seventh man on the team, would lead off for the team on each event. Patrick and Chris would switch off anchoring the six events. Joey got the Pioneers off to a good start, hitting a solid routine. Although he could make his routines without falling, Joey still had a way to go before he would have the difficulty to compete against the big guys. As he sat down, Chris patted him on the back. "Way to start us off, squirt!" When the 8.2 was flashed, it did very little to convince Joey of that fact. Ty had a fall early in his routine, which lead to more problems, but he was able to manage an 8.35. Dallas, AJ, and Mackee each had a fall in their routines, and they scored 8.5, 8.25, and 8.3, respectively.

"Geez, I hit my set and still can't outscore these losers with falls!" said Joey.

"Don't worry, squirt," said Chris as he got chalk for his routine. "Your time is coming, and, believe me, it's not very far off!" Chris's words did very little to console the pride of his comrade.

Next came Patrick. His routine was typical for his ability. Straightforward, fulfilling the requirements of basic difficulty without anything chancy that might bring a deduction. He dismounted with a very clean flair to handstand, full pirouette to the other end, to a stuck landing.

"Good set, plowboy. You should do well with that," remarked Chris.

"Thanks. I hope it scores well."

"Don't be too optimistic. You still lack some heavy-duty bonus."

"You really know how to cheer a guy up, don't you, McClure?" came the remark from Dallas.

"He's right, Dallas," said Patrick. "I'm still short about half a point in difficulty."

The score was posted. 9.25. "See?" said Patrick, "Another half point and I would be the guy the announcer would be screaming over." Suddenly, everyone realized how much being left out of the opening ceremony had hurt Patrick.

Now it was Chris's turn.

"You guys ready for some fun?" Chris said to his downtrodden teammates.

Chris saluted the judge, and from his opening sequence of skills, it was easy to see that there would be a judges conference after the routine. From his mount to his dismount, Chris did skills no one had seen before, ones that most gymnasts have only dreamed about. Chris spent the first twenty seconds of his routine without using the pommels; circling, turning, and traveling on only the leather. Then, he did several skills on just one pommel. Seven, eight, nine hand placements on one pommel, each handplacement increasing the difficulty of his routine. Then, he quickly moved to the other pommel with another complex combination. Once finished with his pommel work, Chris slowed down just enough to fulfill his scissor requirement before breaking into Thomas flair circles that popped into and out of handstands. Then, with a travel to the end, Chris flaired once again to handstand only to pirouette from end to end without touching the middle, hopping a half turn, and landing on his feet to a stuck landing. The crowd exploded. When the score of 9.75 came up, after a lengthy judges conference, the crowd booed its disapproval.

"Eh, that's about all it was worth," said Chris, not showing much feeling either way.

"Holy crud, McClure," said Patrick. "I'd give my left nut for a 9.75!"

"Some day, you may have to, plowboy," replied Chris.

Once the Pioneers finished their routines on pommel horse, it was time for the boys of Texas Star Gymnastics to compete. Chris's routine was a difficult act to follow, it appeared, as the first three gymnasts for Texas had four falls between them. It became apparent that Chris's ploy to be the intimidator instead of the intimidated had worked for now. The fourth routine for the Austin team had more of the style described to the Pioneers weeks earlier by Chris. It was a difficult routine with only the slightest suggestion of a form break. It scored a 9.45.

Patrick sat, dazed, knowing that the best gymnasts were yet to come. Just then, Chris, who had been paying no attention at all to pommel horse, nudged Patrick.

"Plowboy, quick, check out pipe. Marty Reynolds is up! Just watch!"

Patrick glanced at the high bar in time to see the junior from Lake Erie mount. By the time his routine was finished, Marty had done more than twenty skills, including four consecutive release moves that made every heart in the arena jump into their throats. Then, he dismounted with a flawless double-twisting, double layout flyaway with a small step on the landing. His score was 9.75.

"You weren't kidding when you said he was crazy, Chris," said Patrick.

"Yep, he's mad as a hatter, God love him!" returned Chris, almost reverently.

Once the thunder of applause subsided, it was time for Danny to mount the horse as the final competitor of the first rotation. Everything that Chris had told his team about this senior from the Lone Star State proved itself true as they watched an immaculate routine with no form breaks. His dismount, like many of the day, swung into a beautiful handstand pirouette before dropping lightly to the floor with a stuck landing. Score—9.85

Chris leaned to Patrick. "He's done that same routine for two years. I think he has it just about right."

"Uh-huh," returned Patrick, his jaw hanging wide open in disbelief.

Once the opening event jitters were out of the way, the remainder of the competition was fairly predictable. The lower guys in the order hit or missed average routines, getting mediocre scores, only to set up the anchors of their teams, who would dazzle the crowd with breathtaking difficulty and stuck landings.

When the competition was over, the Pioneers had no reason to hang their heads. Mackee managed a 9.1 for fifth place on Rings, Ty and AJ tied for sixth on Vault with 9.45, and Dallas had an impressive score of 9.5 on Parallel Bars, which was good enough for fourth. Patrick managed two bronze medals on Floor and Rings. Chris, through his flamboyance and style, had given everyone a lesson in preseason gymnastics, winning Floor, Rings, and Parallel Bars, as well as winning the all-around with a score of 58.35, three-tenths of a point ahead of Danny, who finished second all-around and first on Pommel Horse and Vault. Patrick had finished out of medals in the all-around with a seventh place score of 55.45. The team as a whole fared well, with third place, 1.3 points away from second place Lake Erie and a full seven points behind Texas Star, who walked away with twenty-one medals in all and a combined team score of 333.50.

It was hard to tell from the bus ride home whether the team had won or lost the meet. Dallas was blaming everything—from the lighting in the gym to the lousy judging—for what was, in his opinion, unfair scores, and Patrick was deep in thought about his performance and what he could do to improve his scores. Coach Lowery was going over the results of the meet to help determine the direction of the workouts until the next meet, while the rest of the team had put the meet behind them. Ty and AJ were working on a new rap Ty had heard on the radio. Mackee was giving Joey some new ideas about conditioning for rings. And Chris, the one who had reason to be most jubilant, had turned inside himself, listening to Metalica on his headset.

Just as Chris was about to fall asleep, he was jolted to consciousness by Joey.

"Hey, Chris, you sleepin'?"

"Not now, thanks," returned Chris as he stretched and removed the headset from his ears. "What's up?"

"Look at Patrick. He looks like he just lost his best friend."

Chris looked a few seats ahead to see the disenchanted young man staring out the bus window.

"Yeah, squirt, I see what you mean. I think what you see there is a guy who is struggling with the fact that his best is not gonna cut it," surmised Chris.

"Wow. Is there something we can do?"

"Yep, I've already thought about it. This week we start Operation Plowboy."

"Cool."

NINE

▼

"Where's McClure?" came the all too familiar barking of Coach Lowery as he stepped from his office door at the beginning of Monday's workout.

"I think he had to stay behind after chemistry class, Coach," said Patrick.

"Why, the next time he's late for workout, I'll—" before Coach Lowery could finish his sentence, the Californian burst through the locker room, tucking in his shirt.

"Sorry I'm late, Coach. Ms. Ballard kept me after chemistry."

"You know, McClure, I don't think you've been on time for a single workout since you joined the team. I wish that just once, you'd show up on time," said Coach.

"Gee, Coach, sounds to me like I've given you a reason to get up every morning. Besides, I sure wouldn't want to give you a heart attack!" returned Chris as he hustled over to join the others in warm-up.

"Kid, if I was gonna have a heart attack, you've already given me a zillion reasons to have one by now."

"Well, I'll see if I can't give you a few more today. How's that?"

"That's what I was afraid you'd say," said Coach as he hung his head before heading toward his charges.

The team had gathered in the middle of the floor exercise to stretch.

"Gentlemen," said Coach, drawing the attention of his gymnasts, "third place team is nothing to sneeze at. However, if we plan on contending for national championships, we have got a ton of work to do."

"We could've beat Lake Erie if Johnson had more difficulty in his routines!" Dallas blasted.

"I guess your four falls had nothing to do with it," answered Joey in self-defense.

"Yeah, Dallas," added Mackee, "if I remember right, Joey hit all six events."

"That's right, Dallas," added Ty. "As a matter of fact, didn't he beat you on Vault?"

"All right, guys, break it up," Coach interrupted before the shouting became a riot. "Nobody on this team is in a position to throw stones."

"Except for Chris," Joey jumped in. "He hit all six and won the meet!"

"Oh yes, McClure," said Coach. "Those were some, uh, *different* routines you did this weekend. You want to tell me why you are the only guy who felt he had creative license over his routines this weekend? Why didn't you compete the sets you've been training in the gym?"

"Sorry, Coach. Just wanted to have some fun."

"You have fun on your own time, McClure. Your goofing off could have cost you the meet, if not serious injury."

"Sorry, Coach. I'll think twice next time."

As Coach Lowery went on to explain the reasons for the Pioneers' shortcomings at the previous meet and his solution to the problem, Joey leaned over to Patrick and whispered, "Chris said he'd think twice, but I noticed he didn't say it wouldn't happen again." Patrick snickered.

As workout concluded, the boys went there separate ways. Joey got on his bicycle to do his evening training, Patrick was off to the library to do research on a paper, the rest of the guys went home to their studies, and Chris was off to see Haley at the mall.

Haley had been working hard and was soon to be off work when Chris came in.

"Hey, babe," she said. "I'll be done in a bit. What can I get you?"

"Just a mineral water, thanks," he replied as he sat down at a table near the entrance.

Haley brought out the beverage and gave Chris a puzzled look. "Why are you sitting here by the entrance instead of over here in my section?"

"Joey comes by this door during his training, right?"

"Sure, but why?" she inquired.

"I want to be sure to catch him," said Chris.

"Why couldn't you talk to him at the gym?"

"Cause Patrick was there," he returned without taking his eyes off of the mall entrance.

"Patrick? What does Patrick have to do with—"

"There he is!" and Chris bolted for the door.

Before Haley could sort her thoughts, Chris was walking back to his table with Joey in tow. Actually, in a semi-headlock. Chris planted Joey in the chair opposite his.

"Haley, get this guy something to drink," said Chris.

Haley returned with Joey's soda, and Chris motioned for her to sit. "Okay, this is the first official meeting of Operation Plowboy. Together, the three of us have to come up with a way to help Patrick get over this gigantic fear factor he has."

"Fear factor? Patrick? No way. You guys can count me out!" demanded Haley.

"Haley, no! I need you. Nobody knows Patrick as well as you," said Chris.

"I've tried already, remember? If he won't go hang gliding on a trainer, I doubt that you'll be able to change his attitude about much."

"Maybe hang gliding was a little too traumatic, or he didn't want to show fear in front of you, or who knows what? After all, you can't expect your average joe to volunteer to go over Niagara Falls in a barrel without a little resistance."

"Wait, that's it! A waterfall!" jumped Joey.

"What are you babbling about, squirt?" said Chris.

"I have an idea that just might work," said Joey. And the three of them began to speak in whispers as if plotting to overthrow a government.

Saturdays are normally reserved for uninterrupted sleep. Instead of counting sheep, the aspiring gymnast goes through every routine, seeing it as perfect, from whatever vantage point looks best. Then as he falls into slumber, the dream continues, just as it has night after night since the first time his hands touched chalk. He sees himself doing impossible skills with simplistic ease to the maddening roar of an appreciative audience. And finally, he stands on the top position of the awards podium, and the loudspeaker roars as he is presented with the gold medal. "Ladies and gentlemen, the world champion, Patrick—"

"Goodman! Get up!" came a voice he was not used to hearing in the morning. Patrick's eyes wearily opened to see the faces of Chris, Joey, and Haley standing before him.

"What the … ? What are you guys doin' here?" he asked groggily.

"You're traveling through another dimension," said Chris, standing erect, hands clasped in front of him, in his best Rod Serling impression.

"A dimension not only of sight and sound, but of mind," added Joey, mimicking Chris's voice and posture.

"A journey to a wondrous land whose boundaries are that of the imagination," added Haley, quite out of her normal character, mimicking the other two.

"The signpost up ahead, the Twilight Zone," finished Chris before breaking character and grabbing Patrick's covers. "Come on, plowboy, it's time to get your lousy butt out of bed."

"Holy cow, you guys! I'm still in my underwear!" Patrick pleaded.

"That's okay, Patrick. We've all seen you in your underwear before. We're not impressed," quipped Haley.

With that, Joey went to Patrick's chest of drawers and started throwing clothes around until he found the appropriate attire for the day's activities.

"Hey, shrimp!" Patrick yelled, trying to gather enough of his blanket to cover himself. "Quit throwing my clothes around, or I'll pound you!"

"In your underwear, plowboy? How inappropriate. I don't think you're in much of a position to do much of anything," replied Chris, pulling Patrick's feet from under him and then sitting on his chest.

"Here, these clothes will do just fine," said Haley, selecting a pair of denim shorts and a tank top.

"What's this all about?" pleaded Patrick.

"Patrick, ol' buddy. We've decided to spend our Saturday with you," said Chris.

"Why me?"

"Holy smoke, Patrick. Why not you?" added Joey.

"Good point, Joey," added Haley. "Patrickins," Haley changed to a baby voice, "don't you want to spend one wittle Saturday havin' oodles and boodles of fun wif Joey, Kwissy, and wittle Haywee?"

"Not exactly," came the return as Patrick scrambled to gather his clothes.

"That's really too bad, plowboy," added Chris, "'cause we're gonna have fun today, whether you like it or not. And since we're gonna insist—"

"You mean *force*."

"Whatever, *take* you with us, you might as well try to have a good time."

"I bet I don't have much say in this, do I?" asked Patrick, by now dressed by force.

"Nope," said the chorus.

"Well, I guess I'll try to have fun."

"You've made a wise decision, my friend," said Chris as he put his arm around Patrick and the four headed out to Haley's car. The top was down, and a cooler was wedged between the back two seats, behind which were several bundles. Chris motioned for Patrick to get in back with Joey.

"I don't suppose you guys are gonna tell me where we're going?" said Patrick, sensing a conspiracy.

"Nowhere in particular, old pal," returned Chris in a disarming tone as he got behind the wheel. "Is there somewhere you'd like to go?"

"Yeah, back to bed. You guys woke me out of an excellent dream!"

"Whoever she is, she can't be half as attractive as the three of us," quipped Haley, sitting next to Chris in the front passenger's seat.

"Don't bet on it."

"Yeah, dude," added Joey, "and sleeping would be the worst on such a beauty day."

"And what could be better than spending such a wonderful day with your very best pals in the world?" concluded Chris.

"Maybe so, but I still get the feeling that something fishy is going on."

"Why, Patrick?" exclaimed Haley. "What is so wrong with us not wanting to waste this perfect day? Why, I'm insulted that you would think that the three of us would have something other than the most honorable intentions for our good friend, Patrick Goodman."

"Not to worry, my friend," said Chris. "Haley has packed a fantastic picnic lunch, Joey and I have selected some juicy tunes for the ride, and the cooler behind you is fully stocked with sodas. You need only sit back, dig the ride, and try to have some degree of fun, that is if that's not too much trouble."

"Uh, no, uh, I guess I can enjoy this for a while, that is if I have no choice," concluded Patrick.

"None whatsoever," said Chris, looking at Patrick through the rearview mirror. With that, Chris turned up the radio, hit the gas, and pointed the small compact convertible toward the mountains. Three faces smiled with anticipation, and one was twisted in confusion.

Very little was said during the forty-five-minute drive. Not that much of anything else could've been heard over the sound of the wind, the roar of the radio, and Chris's off-key singing. Patrick broke the silence. "I know you guys don't plan on telling me where we're going, but are you gonna tell me when we get there?"

"Oh sure, Patrick," said Haley.

"Well then, will you tell me if we're getting close?"

"Oh, we're more than close, plowboy," added Chris. "We're here!" Chris pulled into a gravel parking lot, grown over with weeds.

"What's here?" inquired Patrick.

"Nothing," said Joey. "We just can't take the car from here."

"You mean we're walking? How far?"

"Not far," said Haley, "two and a half, three miles maybe. Patrick, be a dear and grab one of these." Haley then handed Patrick a fully loaded backpack.

"What the heck have you guys been plotting?" asked Patrick, donning his pack, then helping Haley with hers.

"Man, there's this excellent spot for a picnic back here," said Joey, grabbing a backpack for himself and stuffing it with a few extra sodas.

"Yeah," added Chris, "and if you don't quit acting like the FBI, we're not going to let you come back with us the next time."

The foursome headed into the mountains. Patrick noticed a sign on the side of the path,

Abram's Falls 2.5 Miles

The first part of the journey passed rather quickly, but after the first mile, the signs of a mountain climb with backpacks began to show as Joey started to fall behind.

"Tell you what, guys," said Chris, noticing Joey's fatigue, "how about we rest here for a minute."

"Fine with me," said Joey, catching up to the group, removing his pack, and sitting down.

The four sat in a clearing, each pulling a drink from their packs. Once everyone had a chance to catch their breath, Patrick decided to make polite conversation. "Say, Chris, what would you have done if you weren't doing gymnastics?"

"Wow, you mean here in Knoxville, or anywhere?"

"Anywhere. What would you be doing instead?"

"That's a tough one," said Chris, replacing his backpack, cueing the others to do the same. "I guess I would join the circus."

"The circus?" said Joey. "Why the circus?"

"I don't know. I guess because of the rush. I can't think of anything else I would do."

"Because you'd still get to do the same hairy skills that you do in gymnastics?" guessed Haley.

"No, probably because that's the only other activity that allows you to risk your life in front of a crowd," surmised Patrick, sarcastically.

"You might have something there, plowboy," agreed Chris. "What would you be doing if there was no gymnastics?"

"I don't know. Probably a team sport, like baseball or football."

"I think whatever you'd have chosen, you would've excelled," complimented Chris.

"Why, thank you, Chris. That was very nice of you to say. I don't think I have ever heard such kind words—"

"Okay, I take it all back. You'd make a lousy football player."

"Gee, do you think so?" asked Patrick.

"Just drop it, okay?"

"Golly, what makes you think that Patrick would've made for a good football player, Chris?" asked Joey.

"Well, he has the physique. He has the thought process of a good quarterback. We all know the quality of his athleticism. And the big thing— there's a reduced element of fear."

"What's that supposed to mean?" Patrick jumped in to defend the final statement from the Californian.

"No offense, plowboy, but you have the physical ability to succeed at whatever you want to do. It's the psychological barriers you have problems with," answered Chris.

"Just because I don't feel like risking my life day in and day out, like you do, does not mean that I have psychological problems!"

"I think the fact that you consider difficult skills as a threat to your life suggests some kind of mental block," added Haley.

"Oh, I get it. This is why you brought me out here, to rake me across the coals?"

"Hey, Patrick," Joey jumped in, "don't climb all over them. After all, you brought up the subject!"

Chris stood up, readjusting his pack. "I think it's time we pushed on."

After lengthy stares, everyone replaced their packs, and Chris and Haley led the trek onward. Chris looked back to see Patrick bringing up the rear with his head down in deep reflection. Chris then looked at Haley and gave her a wink.

The remainder of the walk was in silence. Chris didn't speak for fear of upsetting Patrick. Haley tried not to be partial to the situation. Joey's attention was diverted to the water they were walking by. And, Patrick trying to figure out why he was invited on this trip, anyway.

As they approached their destination, the party could hear the roar of water from the waterfall. Soon, they could see the mist rising just beyond the edge, where the rush of water stopped. Then, they found themselves at their destination, Abram's Falls. The route that they had taken brought them in to the top of the falls, looking out at a large reservoir some fifty feet below. The group made its way to a point about halfway down, to a natural break that was commonly used as a picnic area.

"So, this is what you brought me out here for?" exclaimed a cynical Patrick.

"Yeah, isn't it awesome!" said Joey, almost yelling over the roar of the falls.

"We felt that we, including you, needed a break from the daily grind of gymnastics to appreciate nature," added Chris, his arms outstretched.

"Well, for once, I think you made the right decision. Good job," concluded Patrick.

"Why thank you, plowboy," Chris took his bow.

Finally, as the four broke out the food and picnic supplies, the mood swung from tense to lighthearted as they simply enjoyed each other's company.

After a hearty lunch of fried chicken with all the trimmings and Haley's own fudge nut brownies, the group rested for a moment to let the food digest. The rest period was short, however. Chris stood up and made his intentions known. "I feel like going for a swim. Anyone want to join me?"

"Count me in," said Haley.

"You guys can't go anywhere without me," added Joey.

"All right, you guys win. I'll come, too." Patrick made it unanimous.

As the other three headed out from the site, Patrick noticed that they were headed up the rock face, not down toward the bottom.

"Hey, where are you guys goin'?"

"We're going back up to the top to wade in the current of the rapids!" answered Joey.

"You guys could get carried over the side!" warned Patrick.

"Not if you're careful. Besides, the boulders will keep you from going over," added Haley.

Almost reassured, Patrick followed the others to the top of the falls. There, the four waded into the rapids. After a few minutes, Patrick figured that, once again, he had overreacted, his fear of the worst-case scenario getting the best of him.

Chris decided it was time to have a little fun. Walking out of the water, Chris approached a log that extended out over the falls.

"Hey, guys! Who's up for jumping off with me?" Chris announced.

"McClure! Get back from there! You want to get yourself killed!?" yelled Patrick some several yards away.

"Don't be silly, Patrick," said Haley. "This is one of the favorite diving spots in the Smokys. I'll be right there, Chris."

"Joey, surely you're not going along with this?" pleaded Patrick to the youngest member of the party.

"I don't know, man. I've never done it before, but I've heard that it's great. Let's go watch." The two then waded to the shore and walked closer to the log to get a better view of the log and the drop into the pool of water below.

Chris was first, walking out to the edge of the long since fallen tree that extended some twenty feet over the edge of the falls.

"Bye, guys," And with that announcement, Chris jumped out another ten feet to drop and quickly disappear into the dark water, only to resurface seconds later, throwing his hair back and screaming a tribal war chant. "Wooooooweeeee! What a rush!" he exclaimed.

"See, Patrick?" said Haley. "There's really nothing to worry about! Come on out!"

"No thanks. You guys go ahead and risk your lives. Joey and I will stay right here."

"Whatchu mean 'we,' paleface?" exclaimed Joey, who had made the decision to join his sister and other pal. "I'm goin' in, too!" Joey started his walk out toward the log.

"I'll see you guys later," said Haley as she turned and jumped, holding her nose. It took less time for her to reappear at the surface, but her scream of triumph was every bit as loud as Chris's had been.

"Yeeeeeoooww!" she exclaimed.

Then, Chris, who had covered half of the rocky face to take his second attempt, answered Haley's call with his own modified Tarzan yell.

"Man, this is great!" exclaimed Joey, now halfway out on the log. "You really ought to try this, Patrick, just once."

"No thanks, little guy. I prefer to keep all my body parts together and intact."

"Okay, suit yourself, but this is really safe stuff. Take this log for instance," Joey began to jump and turn on the log. "It's really quite stable ..."

"Joey, cut that out!" exclaimed Patrick, becoming more concerned that Joey might get hurt.

"Oh, don't worry, Patrick. I'm completely in ... control ... whoa ... whoa ... Patriiick!" Joey had hit a slick spot on the log and stumbled, falling backward off the side of the log, flipping out of control and hitting the water head first.

"Joey!" screamed Patrick as he rushed out on the log too late to see exactly where he went in. "Chris! Haley! Joey fell in! He may be hurt!" Patrick noticed that both Chris and Haley were in the middle of their climb and couldn't possibly reach him in time. Without further hesitation, Patrick forgot about his fear and dove into the water. He looked and looked with no sign of the freshman. He gasped for air and submerged several times until he was exhausted. Soon, all there was to do was swim ashore and hope that Joey would surface in time for artificial respiration to save him. Patrick looked up to see two bodies hit the water. Finally, Chris and Haley had joined him in the search. It's about time, he thought. But, something was peculiar about the pair. They emerged from the water with no look of concern on their faces.

"You okay?" asked Haley.

"What do you mean am I okay? You just lost your brother. Are you okay?" came the delirious return.

"Oh, I didn't lose anybody. And, neither did you."

"What? What do you mean? I saw Joey hit the water! He never came back up!"

"Yes, he did. You just didn't see him," added Chris.

"What?"

"Yeah. Joey, you can come out now!"

Out from under the waterfall came the fifteen-year-old, swimming to shore.

"Joey! You're alive! But, the fall … and … I saw you go under!"

"Sorry to do that to you, buddy," said Joey.

"He's been pulling that stunt on his friends since he was twelve," explained Haley.

"See, I act like I've fallen into the water and then swim around and come up under the waterfall."

"But why?" pleaded Patrick.

"Motivation, plowboy," added Chris. "We just wanted to see just how much you would need to be motivated into action in a less than desirable situation."

"You mean you guys planned this whole stunt?"

"Yes, for your own good," said Haley.

"What good?"

"Think about it, plowboy. You want to be the best gymnast in the country. This little demonstration just goes to show that those barriers that stand in your way, you've placed them there yourself," concluded Chris.

"And you think shock therapy is what I need?"

"Nope, just opening your eyes," said Chris. "Just remember, if you want it bad enough, fear is an afterthought."

"I can't believe you guys went to all this trouble just to screw me over! And you were all in it together!" Patrick screamed.

"It was for your own good, Patrick," said Haley.

"Who the hell elected you guys to decide what's good for me?"

"We just thought—" said Chris.

"No, you didn't think. You didn't think at all, except how to make me look like a horse's ass!"

"You didn't look like a horse's ass, or anyone else's ass, for that matter," said Chris.

"Quit tryin' to be so damned funny. Someone could've gotten hurt! Especially me! I've had enough of this. I'm outta here!" Patrick started back up the side of the waterfall to gather his things.

"Wow, I think the plan backfired," said Joey.

"Naw," answered Chris, "he just needs to cool off."

"I hope you're right," added Haley.

"Come on, you guys," said Joey, shaking off the water, "let's go home."

"Good idea," added Chris. "I think we gave Patrick plenty to think about."

Patrick's head hung low as he climbed the rocky face, confused as to whether he should be furious or thankful to his friends for the effort they had gone through to help him see his problem.

The three followed Patrick back up the side of the falls, cleaned up their picnic site, donned their backpacks, and headed for home.

TEN

▼

IN THE DAYS that passed since the incident at Abram's Falls, Patrick had become very sullen. No one knew if his disposition stemmed from his anger with the three who perpetrated the stunt that tricked him into risking his life or from the fact that the experience had caused him to finally come face to face with the greatest pitfall in his quest for perfection—his own fear.

Patrick's attitude had spilled over to his training. Whereas once Patrick was a happy–go–lucky team captain, always with a kind word and friendly advice for his teammates, now he had become introverted and quiet, focusing solely on his own training and removing himself from the rest of the team.

Patrick's attitude had not gone unnoticed. Chris and Joey knew to keep their distance, but the other guys were curious as to why their captain had become so secluded.

"Hey y'all, what's gotten into Patrick?" asked AJ

"Let's just say Patrick is searching for himself," said Chris.

"All right, what did you guys do to him?" asked Ty.

"We kinda pulled Joey's pratfall joke at Abram's Falls," replied Chris.

"And you guys tricked Patrick into jumpin' off the log?" surmised Dallas.

"Yep," added Joey.

"You guys are real jerks, McClure!" Mackee jumped in. "It's a wonder he didn't go into shock!"

"Give it a rest, Mackee. Goodman is a big boy. He can handle himself. He's just having a tough time dealing with the fact that he has a gigantic fear problem," answered Chris.

"I wonder if he's the one with the problem!" Mackee stormed away from the group.

The workout had not been a particularly good one. Everyone had a difficult time maintaining concentration, with thoughts of concern for Patrick and the pressure of the upcoming meet in Michigan. Everyone was relieved to be finished with the workout and glad to be conditioning, where they could work out some frustration. Mackee had just finished his rings strength and noticed Patrick by himself working dips on parallel bars. He decided to let Patrick know that he still had a friend.

"Hey, Patrick," said Mackee, trying to break him from his doldrums, "how's it going, buddy."

"Not bad. How 'bout yourself?" came the cold return.

"Not too bad, thanks. Hey, Jeanie and I are gonna go see a movie and get some pizza tomorrow night. You want to join us?"

Without looking into Mackee's eyes, Patrick's monotone response came. "No thanks, bud. I think I'm gonna try catch up on some studying."

"Aw, come on. Tomorrow is Friday. Nobody studies on Friday. Besides, Jeanie's sister, Missy, is going with us, and she needs a date to keep from feeling like a third wheel. You know how much you've wanted me to set up a date between you two. Well, here's your chance."

"Yeah, I know, but I'm really not much in the mood for socializing, Mack. Thanks anyway, bud," Patrick said, feeling sorry for himself.

"Well, you have my number. Give me a call if you change your mind."

"Sure thing," Patrick said, and he went back into his own little world as Mackee left for the locker room.

Soon, everyone had gone into the locker room except for Patrick. He was still conditioning, hoping that the strain on his body and the impending exhaustion would help relieve him of the even greater pain he was feeling inside.

Dip after dip, Patrick continued to push his body harder. Just ten more, he thought as the oxygen debt increased and he could feel the lactic acid building in his arms. Soon the pH factor in his bloodstream rose and pain gave way to cramps. Still, he continued. With each dip came increasing pain, making each additional dip more difficult. Finally, he reached a point where he was frozen in mid-dip. Too weak to finish but too stubborn to drop, Patrick shook with the strain of struggle. His face, already drenched with sweat, had gone through every color in the rainbow and even created a few. Finally with a primeval scream, Patrick locked his elbows, successfully finishing the dip. Finally, a small victory, he thought as he took a few seconds in support on the bars, then cranked out ten more dips before collapsing, clutching his aching arms, laughing and crying at the same time as he came to rest on the mat.

As his normal color returned to his face and his breathing returned to normal, Patrick stared at the gym ceiling and began to really understand what it was that he was trying to do. It had come to him that his anger and attitude had replaced the tunnel vision he had for becoming a national champion.

In an instant, it all came back to him: the hunger for perfection, the desire to be the best, the drive and sheer determination that had gotten him to this point. In that instant, he knew what he had to do—take his gymnastics to another level. And, he knew he would have to take his training to another level as well.

Patrick picked himself up from the mat and walked to the water fountain, where he got a quick drink and headed toward the high bar. His face was stone cold as he put on his grips, looking at the bar as if to stare down the inanimate apparatus. I am much bigger than this skill, he thought. I just have to approach this the same way I've learned everything else. I just have to take one step at a time.

Patrick hopped up on the bar and began swinging giants. The first step, he thought, is to do a Geinger very high to make sure I have time enough to add a full twist. He then kicked his legs up, as if to hit the ceiling, and released the bar. His body rose higher and higher as he rotated backward and turned his chest toward the bar, maintaining eye contact with the bar. At the peak of his flight, his body was upright, his feet easily two feet above the bar. All that was left was to drop about six feet and catch the bar. Piece of cake, he thought. After he caught the bar, Patrick hopped down to get more chalk.

"Nice Geinger, Goodman, but you know the rules about training alone!" came the voice of Coach Lowery as he emerged from his office.

"Thanks, Coach. Yeah, I know the rules, but I just gotta get over this block. And besides, I knew you were still here," said the Kennedy High senior with a voice of confidence and calm. "Just one more turn, and I'll be outta here."

"Okay, Pat, but hit or miss, this is your last turn. I've got to get home sometime tonight."

Patrick turned his attention toward the matter at hand. As he stuck his hands in the chalk bucket, he went through the visualization of the skill he was going to attempt. He could see every aspect as though he were looking at high-speed film in slow motion from every different angle. Each visualization ending with a successful catch. Then, the time came to stop envisioning his new skill and make the attempt.

"Don't forget to spot the bar before you twist, Pat," came his coach's comment.

"Right, Coach," responded Patrick, more out of reflex that confirmation. Patrick had already gone through every step in his mind. Any outside coaching would merely be a distraction.

Patrick jumped from the spotting platform beside the high bar, mounted over a seven-foot-deep foam safety pit, and began to swing. At first, his swings were small, back and forth, as he went through the skill in his head one more time. Then with a hard exhale, Patrick started to pick up his swing to giant circles. As the time came closer to the release, Patrick's swing increased speed in time with his accelerating heart rate. His breathing became shallow, and he had blocked out all sound except for the pounding of his heart. Then came time for the release. As he let go of the bar, his body seemed to rise for an eternity. Patrick rotated and turned just as he had hundreds of times before. Then, as his body became upright and he spotted the bar, the time had come to take his eyes off of the bar to add the full twist. Patrick turned his head and wrapped his arms in tight to make his body twist. Then, he opened from the twist, expecting to see the bar in front of him, but the bar was nowhere to be found.

"Aaah!" yelled Patrick as he instinctively assumed a fetal position and protected his head with both arms, waiting for the impact of his body crashing to earth.

"Patrick! Are you okay!?" came the cry from Coach Lowery as he rushed to the side of the pit.

Patrick opened his eyes to darkness all around him. "I'm dead! I'm dead!" he shouted.

"No, you're not, Goodman. You're just stuck in the pit!" said Coach to a pair of legs sticking up out of the loose foam.

Patrick regained his composure, righted himself, and crawled out, nursing a sore neck and a wounded pride.

"You sure you're alright, Pat?" asked coach.

"Yeah," answered Patrick, still rubbing his neck. "I just got lost."

"You were actually very close, Patrick. You just over-rotated a little bit. It'll get there," said Coach in a comforting voice. "What you just did took a lot of balls."

"Yeah, and I nearly lost 'em up there. I think I'll try that again in a couple of years."

"Well, Patrick, there's a fine line between courage and stupidity. If you analyzed the skill and followed logical progression, then approached it much in the—"

"Thanks, Coach, I feel much better now," interrupted Patrick, not wanting to hear his coach give the same lecture he had given himself for so many years. "I need to get back up and try it again. I gotta have this trick!" He climbed to the top of the platform for another turn, battling between his fear and his desire.

"Hold on, cowboy. I don't think you get the point. You're all caught up in the idea that you have to be something other than what you are to be a great gymnast. You are still a great contributor whether you can do these hairy skills or not."

"But, I don't just want to be a contributor. I want to be a champion!" shouted Patrick.

"Well, you can't get it all in one day. You've not been yourself lately, Patrick. Why don't you give your brain and your body a break. Take in a movie, raise a little hell, or just vegetate this weekend. The next meet isn't for two weeks. It won't hurt you to ease up this weekend. You can't train constantly. Your body will break down without proper rest. Take it easy this weekend."

"Maybe you're right, Coach."

"I know I'm right. Besides, you don't want to peak too early, Patrick." Coach Lowery put his arm around Patrick and walked him to the locker room. "It'll be there when you need it, Patrick."

"I sure hope you're right, Coach." Conceeding that it would come another day, Patrick jumped down from the platform and started removing his grips.

A long hot shower gave Patrick time to think about what he had done. Over and over, he saw himself do the skill, each time missing the bar, just as he did in workout, but an eerie calm came over him. Although his first attempt was unsuccessful as far as catching the full-twisting Geinger, he did go for it. Patrick rinsed the soap off of his head, and a smile came to his face as the words formed in his brain: I did it!

ELEVEN

▼

"Ouch!" screamed Patrick, more from frustration than from pain.

"Patrick! Are you okay, dear?" called Patrick's mother from downstairs.

"Yeah, I'm fine, Mom. I just cut myself shaving—again!" Patrick's nervousness was beginning to show as this was his third cut. He was beginning to wonder if he had made the right choice taking Mackee up on his offer to double-date.

"Hey, Pat," called his father from the living room, "why don't you just use my electric razor. We haven't paid the deductible on the medical insurance yet! Har, har, har!"

"Very funny, Pop." Patrick looked into the mirror at his face, which was quickly beginning to resemble a battlefield of blood and toilet tissue. I gotta be nuts. he thought. I can't believe I'm this nervous about a stupid date. Then again, this is the first date I've been on since breaking up with Haley. A guy gets out of circulation for a few months, and he forgets how to act. And this is no ordinary date. I've been trying to get Mackee to set me up with Missy for six months now. I sure hope I don't look like a clod. I already look like I've been in a knife fight.

Patrick's thoughts were interrupted by the sound of a car horn.

"Patrick! Mackee's here!" called his mom.

"Hey, dude! Let's get a move on!" yelled Patrick's longtime teammate.

"Keep your shirt on, Mack. I'll be right down!" Patrick grimaced as he tore the tissue off of his face, crossed himself, then splashed on cologne and held back the scream that would normally follow the burning sensation of alcohol on an open wound.

Patrick bounded down the stairs, throwing on his jacket.

"Bye, Mom," he said as he gave his mother a peck on the cheek on his way out the door. "I'll be home early."

"Have fun, son," she answered.

Patrick hoped into the passenger's side of Mackee's '66 Chevy Impala Super Sport.

"Yeah, we're gonna have fun, dude," said Mackee as he descended into the driver's seat and began to pull away.

"What's that supposed to mean?" asked Patrick.

"Just that. Have fun. Face it, dude, every since McClure came to town, you've been a real wet blanket. You used to be such a fun guy, but now you are so bent on being the best that you've put aside the best part of you. Gymnastics used to be fun. A challenge, sure, but a challenge that you used to make fun. Now, you seem to be on some kind of vision quest, and everything has become so serious that no one wants to be around you in the gym anymore for fear that you're gonna bite their head off!"

"It's not that bad."

"Trust me, it's that bad," returned Mackee. "But listen, dude. We're gonna forget all that nonsense for one night, and you're gonna enjoy yourself, whether you like it or not!"

"Last time someone said that to me, I wound up at the bottom of Abram's Falls looking for a corpse and scared out of my gourd!"

"Don't worry, I don't think Missy has any plans of testing your courage tonight, pal. Chivalry? Yes. Courage? Probably not."

As the two set off to pick up their dates, Mackee's thoughts turn to Jeanie, while Patrick's thoughts turned to Mackee's comments about his attitude, which, in turn, turned his thoughts to where they normally were, on gymnastics.

Mackee turned his car into the drive, then turned to Patrick.

"Listen, Patrick, we're havin' fun tonight. No talk about McClure, gymnastics, none of that stuff, okay?"

"Sure, Mack," answered Patrick with a puzzled look on his face. It hadn't occurred to him before, but Patrick got the point that most of his conversations seemed to gravitate toward gymnastics.

Before the two reached the front door, the girls came out. Jeanie, the older of the two, prodded her younger sister through the door as if it were more of a getaway than a date.

"Bye, Mom. Bye, Dad. See y'all later," said Jeanie, cutting off the last word with the sound of the door closing. "Let's go, you guys, before my mom and dad catch us!"

"Why? What's the problem?" asked Mackee as they headed for the car.

"Oh, no real problem. It's just that since they found out that Patrick was going with us, they haven't shut up about wanting to meet the famous Patrick

Goodman. And, if I know my parents, there's no way we could've gotten out of there tonight."

"Certainly, you're not serious?" asked Patrick.

"Yeah," added Missy. "Since they saw you win regionals last year, you've become a real celebrity around our house. By the way, my name is Missy."

"Oh, yeah, how stupid of me," admitted Mackee, forgetting his manners. "Patrick Goodman, I'd like you to meet Missy Woods."

"Pleased to meet you, Missy. I've seen you around school. I'm glad we've finally had a chance to meet," remarked Patrick politely.

"Actually, we have meet once before," said Missy with her head tilted slightly downward and her long brown hair covering most of her face. She lifted her head to look at Patrick. "I met you in Nashville last year when I came with Jeanie to watch Mackee compete. You were awesome!"

"That's right! I remember now. You two sat right behind our bench."

"Let's get out of here, you guys, before Patrick's head gets too big to fit in the car," said Mackee as the group climbed into the car, Mackee and Jeanie in the front, Missy and Patrick in the back.

This might just turn out all right, Patrick thought.

"So, Patrick," asked Missy, "do you think you'll win nationals this year?"

Patrick looked up to see Mackee's eyes peering at him in the rearview mirror.

"I … uh … don't know, Missy. I really haven't given it much thought," answered Patrick, lying through his teeth while politely trying to avoid the subject. That thought had been the only thing on his mind for the past two years.

"But you must admit, you've got a pretty good chance!" she returned. Mackee's glare shifted from a defenseless Patrick to Jeanie.

"Leave the poor guy alone, Missy," said the older sister. "You sound like a reporter!"

"I was just trying to make conversation, thank you very much!" returned Missy, defending herself.

"Girls, girls, girls! This is no way to conduct ourselves," Mackee broke in. "Let's just try to find something else to talk about besides gymnastics."

"That's a good idea, Mackee," said Jeanie. "I'm sure there's something."

Unable to think of a suitable substitute topic, the group remained silent until they arrived at the theater.

After the movie, the four emerged from the theater laughing.

"I must admit that was an interesting choice of movies, Mack," said Patrick.

"Yeah," added Missy, "anyone can go see a coming-of-age film or a slasher film or a comedy."

"But, only you could find a comedy about a coming-of-age ax murderer!" exclaimed Jeanie.

"I do my best," answered Mackee. "Besides, the only other stuff showing is garbage. That is, of course, unless you like guys running around in spandex costumes trying to save the world from evildoers in darker spandex costumes."

"I'm getting kinda hungry. Where are we going for food?" asked Patrick.

"Leave it to a man to worry about food right after a bloody slasher movie," answered Jeanie.

"It's just that the sight of all that raw meat made me hungry for steak!" joked Patrick.

"That's been cut with a chainsaw?" inquired Missy. All laughed.

"Actually, I thought I would leave it up to the group. Majority rules. What would you guys like?"

"Pizza," said Missy.

"Italian," said Jeanie.

"Steak," said Patrick.

"And, since I'm in the mood for a hamburger, I'm glad I made reservations at the Japanese steak house." The group piled into the car and headed for the restaurant of nobody's choice.

The foursome entered the restaurant still laughing at jokes Mackee and Patrick made about the movie. They were quickly seated around one corner of the hibachi table. Just as they placed their order, Jeanie noticed a familiar couple entering the restaurant. She nudged Mackee. Patrick noticed and turned to look over his shoulder to see what Jeanie had noticed—Chris and Haley taking their seats at a table across the room.

"Hey, Patrick, we can go somewhere else if you'd like," said Mackee.

"Naw, I'm okay."

"Why?" asked Missy. "What's the problem?"

"Well, that's Haley Johnson over there with Chris McClure, the new guy on the gymnastics team. Haley used to be Patrick's girlfriend," said Jeanie.

"And, the fact that the two of them and Haley's brother just played a bogus trick on Patrick doesn't help things," added Mackee.

"Patrick, if you want to leave, we can go somewhere else, really," Jeanie reassured him.

"No, no, don't worry about me. I'm fine," said Patrick. Although his words tried to console his friends, he knew that they didn't believe him.

"I'll be right back." Patrick made his way over to their table.

"Well, I guess they'll let anybody in this place," said Patrick, catching his friends off guard.

"Plowboy! Good to see ya, pal."

"Hello, Patrick. It's good to see you," Haley added.

"Same here," answered Patrick, turning an empty chair around and taking a seat. "What brings you guys out here?"

"Well, you gotta eat sometime, dude. But we should be asking you the same question. What brings you here?" quizzed Chris.

"Mackee, Jeanie, her sister, and I went to see a movie."

"Missy Woods? Are you dating Missy Woods, Patrick?" inquired Haley.

"Well, I wouldn't go that far. This is the first time we've been out. In fact, I just met her officially tonight."

"Missy Woods is a honey, plowboy. How'd you rate?" prodded Chris.

"I guess us country boys just get lucky once in a while."

"Patrick, if us being here is going to put a crimp in your evening, we'll leave if you want," offered Haley.

"Oh, we will, will we ... ooowww!" screamed Chris under his breath, the victim of a high heel driven into his foot.

"No, that won't be necessary. I just wanted to come by to say hi." Patrick got up and started back to his group. After two steps, Patrick turned back to the couple. "Oh, by the way, Chris, you and Joey don't have to avoid me at workout anymore. You were right. I'm a big boy, and I'm pretty much over the Abram's Falls stunt. I'll get even—er, uh ... I mean ... over it."

Patrick turned and headed back to his table to enjoy the food and his friends, leaving two very stunned people staring at each other in bewilderment.

"That's weird," said Haley.

"What, the fact that Patrick doesn't want to kill us anymore?"

"No. He doesn't get over things like that easily. Maybe this girl has gotten to him," surmised Haley.

After a moment's thought, Chris's face lit up. "No, I think it goes a little bit further than her. And I've got a pretty good idea what it is."

As the evening came to a close, it was time to say good night. Mackee stayed with Jeanie at the car as Patrick escorted Missy to the front door. Mackee, sitting on the hood of his car with his arms on Jeanie's shoulders, watched the two approach the front porch. "I wonder if he had a good time."

"Oh, I'm sure he did. I know Missy did. She's been looking forward to going out with Patrick since before he knew she existed."

"No kidding? Patrick's been trying to get me to set up a date with her since summer! I hope they weren't disappointed."

"I had a great time tonight," said Patrick.

"Even though you ran into your ex at the restaurant?"

"Even though. You know, you really are a neat girl," Patrick said. "Would you mind if maybe I called you tomorrow."

"No," she responded.

"No? You mean I can't call you?"

"No. No, I mean no, I don't mind if you call me. I'd like that."

"Great, I'll call you tomorrow."

"Great."

The two looked at each other, wondering which was going to make the move toward the obligatory good-night kiss. They moved closer to each other, maneuvering their heads so as not to bump noses. When both were within centimeters of each other, Missy closed her eyes and Patrick reached forward with a kiss that was intended to be just a light exchange. But once joined, their kiss became more involved, and they came together in a firm embrace. But, before they could forget where they were, the porch light ignited like a searchlight, quickly breaking them from their entanglement.

"Ehem!" Patrick exclaimed as they composed themselves. "Well then, I guess I'll talk to you tomorrow."

"Tomorrow, then. Patrick, I had a wonderful time," she said as she opened the door. "I'll talk to you then. Bye."

"Good-bye."

Patrick headed back to Mackee's car. After a couple of steps, he lifted his head to find Mackee and Jeanie in their own embrace. Patrick turned his head and began to whistle and clear his throat to announce his presence without startling them.

"Oh, I see Mrs. Woods pulled the porch light gag on you, dude," said Mackee. "Now you know why I never take Jeanie to the front door."

"Oh well, it's gettin' late. I better get inside," said Jeanie.

"All right, sweetie. I'll see ya tomorrow."

"Okay, Mack. Bye, Patrick." Jeanie gave Patrick a peck on the cheek as she walked by. "And take care of this guy," she said noticing the Cheshire Cat grin on Patrick's face. "He looks like he just won the lottery!"

"Bye, Jeanie," said Patrick, still dazed.

Jeanie jogged to the house as the boys climbed into the restored antique.

Mackee looked at Patrick as he turned to back out of the driveway. "Dude, she's right. You do look like the cat that ate the canary! What'd Missy say to you?"

"Oh, nothin' much," answered Patrick, still in his daze. "This has just been one of the best days I've had in quite some time."

"See, it pays to let yourself go sometimes."

"Yeah, I guess you're right."

The rest of the trip was quite quiet as, for the first time in a long time, Patrick's mind was on something other than gymnastics.

TWELVE

▼

"COME ON GOODMAN, this is no time to be missing routines!" yelled Coach Lowery. "That's your third blown set in a row! You better get your head out of the clouds and back into your work."

"Give him a break, Coach!" barked Mackee. "He's had a very busy weekend!"

"Stow it, Mackee. Your workout hasn't been exactly stellar. Both of you guys get back to work."

"Yes, sir," came the unison response from both gymnasts.

"Hey, Coach, where's Chris?" asked Joey.

"He said he had to take his mother to a doctor's appointment," answered Coach Lowery, not taking his eyes off of training. "He said he'd get here as quick as he could. Dallas! How many times do you plan to miss that release today?" he barked rhetorically as Dallas slammed into the eight-inch skill cushion.

Of course, Coach Lowery had reason to be upset. At a time when his gymnasts should be hitting mid-season stride, the best ones were having trouble hitting routines. This weekend would be a good test of the team's ability. The Wolverine Invitational in Ann Arbor, Michigan, always drew the best gymnasts from the eastern United States. This meet had always served as a good barometer for the teams hoping to qualify for the NTIs. Coach Lowery needed for every guy to be hitting on all eight cylinders.

As frustration mounted with each miss, Dallas could see it building more in Patrick than in the others and decided to break up the tension. He discretely motioned to AJ and whispered into his ear. AJ then approached Patrick.

"Goodman, what's that look in your eye?" asked AJ, "I've seen that look before ... oh my gosh!"

"What are you talking about, AJ?" inquired Patrick, not volunteering anything.

"Ty, come here and look at this!" said AJ, motioning to his teammate. Ty came over to the chalk bucket where they had all gathered. Ty cupped Patrick's face in hands.

"Oh my gosh. You're right, AJ," mocked Ty, turning Patrick's head as if to get a better look into his eyes. "Yep, there's definitely something here. Dallas, you better take a look at this."

"Wow, Pat, this could be serious!" said Dallas as he took his turn fussing over their team captain.

"Gentlemen," Dallas beckoned to the team, "conference."

The team, with the exception of Patrick, huddled together, looking like a football team calling a play. Patrick stood apart from the group, wondering for how long these clowns would continue their charade. Then a chorus sounded, "Ready, break!" The guys clapped their hands simultaneously and approached Patrick. Dallas, AJ, and Ty faced Patrick, with their hands behind their backs, the remainder making a circle around him.

"Well, Mr. Goodman," spoke AJ, "Drs. Dallas, Street, and myself have arrived at a diagnosis." Patrick noticed the remainder of the circle slowly closing in on him.

"How right you are, Dr. Doujmovich," said Dallas. "The medical term for your condition is *infantitus canine affectionosis.*"

"Or, in layman's terms," added Ty, "puppy love."

Then, the remainder of the team grabbed Patrick, pinning his arms behind his back.

"You know, Mr. Goodman," said Ty, in a pseudo serious tone, "it's a good thing we caught this in time, before a real infection set in." Dallas and AJ had disappeared for a moment, but returned, flanking Ty.

"And, you're very lucky that we have procured the only known cure for this dreaded disease," added Dallas. AJ produced from behind his back the spray bottle that the gymnasts use to apply water to their grips to make the chalk stick. He began spraying a fine mist on Patrick's face. This, in and of itself, is not a dreadful experience, especially after training hard. It was refreshing. But Patrick knew what would follow the water, and it was at this point that he really began to struggle. It was too late. From behind his back, Dallas produced a block of gymnastics chalk and began rubbing it on Patrick's drenched face.

"Why ... you ... guys ... ," exclaimed Patrick. "When I ... get ... out of ... this ... "

"Now, now, don't try to talk, Mr. Goodman. We'll be done applying this topical vaccine in just a minute."

Once Patrick had spent his energy, the boys let him go. Even Coach Lowery had to laugh at the sight of the team captain covered with chalk and looking like a street mime. The entire team erupted in laughter.

"Very funny, you guys," said Patrick.

"All right, Goodman," said Coach between chuckles, "go wash your face and get back out here. The rest of you juvenile delinquents get back to work."

Before Patrick could open the locker room door, it burst open with Chris emerging from within. "Nice look, plowboy. Normally you'd have to pay top dollar for that look on Rodeo Drive." Patrick took the jab in stride as he made his way to the locker room and Chris joined the group.

As the laughter subsided, it was replaced with the sounds of bars squeaking from the pressure of swinging gymnasts and the grunts and groans of the team putting every bit of energy into its workout. Patrick emerged from the locker room to the sight of even Chris and Dallas smiling and encouraging each other. The thought came to his mind that this may turn out to be a team of destiny after all.

"Holy smoke, Patrick," said Joey, "you should take a chalk bath more often!" Patrick had just hit his seventh routine in a row to the delight of his coach and teammates. It was as if the chalk bath was the break in the tension that everyone, including Coach Lowery, needed to get back on track. Suddenly, everyone was clicking exactly the way that would be needed to win the upcoming meet. The workout quickly came to an end, and it was time to condition.

"Hey, guys," said Chris, "I've got an idea. Instead of doing regular conditioning, let's do something a little different."

"I don't like the idea of replacing conditioning, McClure," said Coach Lowery.

"No, I think you'll like this, Coach," answered Chris. "If it doesn't work, fine, we do regular conditioning."

"Anything to break up the monotony of conditioning," said Joey.

"Okay, McClure," said Coach, "we're all ears."

"Okay, we've got seven guys here and six competitive events. We put a guy on each event and one on the conditioning event of his choice. At your signal, we do our routine on the event we're on and the seventh man does his conditioning as long as a routine is going on. After we're done, we rotate to the next event in Olympic order—floor, pommels, rings, vault, p-bars, high bar. After pipe, rotate to conditioning, and conditioning rotates to floor exercise, and so on. If you hit your routine, you continue to rotate. If you miss, you are out and must do regular conditioning. When it's down to three guys, we drop the conditioning part of the circuit. Just like Pioneer Circle; we go to the last man to hit."

Each team member looked at each other, no one quite sure if it was a good idea.

"I like it," said Patrick. "What better way to concentrate on hitting routines than to compete head–to-head when we're tired from the rest of the workout."

"Yeah," said Joey, "it's like gymnastic musical chairs."

"Wait a minute," said Dallas. "I think it's pretty much a foregone conclusion that Slash is gonna win this contest. He hasn't missed a routine since he moved here."

"Yeah, but we've all had days when we could hit just as good as McClure," added AJ.

"And you gotta admit, Dallas, it makes for an excellent challenge," said Patrick.

"I think it'll take a great combination of concentration and stamina," concluded Mackee.

"Then, it's settled. We do it," said Chris.

"Okay, let's try it," said Coach.

"Okay, I'm game," conceded Dallas. "But I start on p-bars!" he said, sprinting to his favorite event. Suddenly, everyone scrambled to their choice of starting event, hoping to get dibs on their favorite. Mackee to rings, AJ to pommel horse, Ty to the vault table. Patrick yelled, "I got floor!" which stopped Joey in his tracks for the same event. All that was left was high bar and conditioning. Joey looked at the bar, his weakest event, and there stood Chris.

"Hey, squirt, I'll start on conditioning if you want pipe," said Chris.

Joey thought for a minute. It occurred to him that if he started on conditioning, he wouldn't hit high bar until seventh rotation. The game would most likely be over by then.

"No thanks, dude. I'll do dips first." Joey went over to the extra set of parallel bars for conditioning.

"Is everyone in place?" asked Coach. "Ready, go!"

Everyone began doing his routine. Ty, having to do only one vault, finished first with a stuck layout Tsukahara.

"One stuck!" shouted Ty.

Dallas had a big step in one of his handstands, but saved the routine and dismounted with an effortless double backflip.

"Two stuck!" yelled the blond senior.

"Make that three!" called Mackee as he nailed his ring routine with a full-twisting double back dismount.

"Four stuck!" called AJ, still in the handstand as he pirouetted from one end of the pommel horse to the other, finishing with a light landing on.the four-inch thick landing surface.

"Bringing … home … number … five!" yelled Chris as he wound three whip giants to a stuck full-twisting double layout.

"Bring it home, Patrick!" shouted the balance of the team as Patrick was in the corner, just prior to his last pass on floor. Patrick took a big breath and sprinted across the diagonal of the forty-by-forty-foot square to a round off, back handspring, tucked double back, Stuck.

"Six!" shouted Patrick. Everyone looked over to the parallel bars, where Joey was stuck in mid-dip.

"Come on, Joey, you can do it!"

"Hang in there, dude!"

"Come on, get tough, Joey!" came the cheers as Joey strained to push the last dip upward.

"S-s-s-seven!" yelled Joey as he collapsed after locking out the last dip.

"Very good, gentlemen," came the congratulations from Coach Lowery. "Thirty seconds, then be ready for second event."

While everyone else got water, Joey lay on the mat and sucked air. I'm gonna die, he thought.

"All right, fellas, time's up. Second event!" shouted Coach

Joey slowly rose out of the pool of sweat he had created to take his place for his floor routine. Patrick moved to pommel horse, AJ switched to rings, Mackee checked his mark on the vault runway, and Ty set the parallel bars for his narrow shoulders. Dallas adjusted his grips for high bar, and Chris readied himself on the floor in push-up position for his conditioning exercise of choice.

"I really like this idea, Slash," said Dallas.

"I'm glad I could oblige, Dallas."

"I think this may be the longest high bar routine in history," plotted Dallas while looking at the high bar.

"Ready, go!"

Mackee took a big step on a front handspring, front flip vault, but stayed on his feet.

"One stuck!"he said, sighing a breath of relief.

"Two stuck," said Ty as he came to rest on the parallel bars dismount mat.

"Here comes number three!" said Joey, as he sprinted to his round off, back handspring, full twist dismount on floor.

"Make it four, fer shore," mocked AJ on his rings dismount.

"Make it five, and I'm still alive!" rhymed Patrick as he sailed to his handstand dismount on pommel horse.

Everyone turned their attention to the back of the gym, where Chris continued to do push-ups and Dallas was adding giants and pirouettes to his high bar routine to push Chris to the limit.

"That's not fair, Dallas!" shouted Joey. "That's not your routine."

Dallas yelled to the group while still doing giants. "Nobody said … which routines we … had to do. Besides … McClure never does the same … routine twice, anyway."

"Yeah, but … " said Patrick.

"Leave him alone!" came the voice from the sweat-drenched face of the Californian. "I'm gonna beat this bastard, anyway. Don't worry."

Everyone gathered around the pair, some shouting encouragement to Chris, others trying to talk Dallas into dismounting. Chris continued to push harder and harder while Dallas just laughed and continued to swing around the bar.

Finally, Dallas's plan worked. Chris pushed and strained as much as he could, stuck in mid-push-up. No matter how much his teammates shouted to rally him, Chris could go no longer and dropped in a heap on the floor.

"You can come down now, dipstick. Your plan worked," said Joey.

"Yippee!" shouted Dallas as he wound up for his double back flyaway. Dallas hadn't counted on being fatigued and dizzy after his exaggerated routine and overshot his dismount, rotating past his feet and landing on his back on the mat.

"Ha, ha. Serves you right, Dallas," said Patrick.

"You guys should thank me. At least one of you can win now," said Dallas as he clutched his back from the jolt.

"Did you ever stop to think that maybe winning was not the only goal here, brainless?" said AJ.

The rest of the team went for another drink of water before the next round. Dallas and Chris just lay on the gym floor.

"Pretty good, Dallas," said Chris, staggering to his feet and still out of breath. "It takes an awful lot … to sacrifice one's self to … screw a teammate. … Good job. .. Think I'll go … do some … sit-ups," Chris walked away, leaving Dallas on the mat by himself in a pool of sweat staring at the ceiling, watching everything spin.

Once the excitement was over, it was time to get back to the game at hand. One good thing did come out of Dallas's stunt. Everyone had a chance to catch his breath before the third round. Joey set the pommels in close on the horse. Patrick, having put on ring grips during the fracas, was ready to mount rings. AJ was standing at the ready at vault, Mackee was ready for parallel bars, and Ty was the last to get ready for his event, high bar.

"Here we go again, fellas," said Coach Lowery.

Ty became the next casualty, missing the regrasp on his release move on high bar. Everyone else had stuck their routines. Without a sound, the survivors rotated. On the coach's command, the athletes began the next round. Then, the next. Then, the next. Even though high bar was Joey's weakest event, he had very little trouble staying on, knowing that all it took was concentration. Although the scheduled ending time had come and gone, Dallas was the only one to leave, having finished his conditioning and not in the mood to watch the remainder of the game he had tried to sabotage. Those still in the game, Patrick, Joey, AJ, and Mackee, refused to fall to the other. Once the last man worked past the conditioning rotation, that rotation was dropped, and only the six competitive events remained. Chris and Ty had long finished their conditioning but had remained to cheer and encourage the others.

If any of them had begun to look fatigued, it was Joey. As the gymnasts rotated, Joey did so doubled over with exhaustion, trying to regain his breath before each routine.

They'll surely fall next event, they each thought.

On the tenth round, Joey found himself back on pommel horse. He could see Patrick out of the corner of his eye on rings. He looks haggard, Joey thought. AJ was on the vault runway sucking up wind. Mackee just stood, staring at the parallel bars.

"Go!" said Coach Lowery, growing tired of the game itself but very intrigued by the intestinal fortitude being demonstrated by his charges.

AJ misstepped his landing on his vault and quickly found himself on his bottom and out of the game. Mackee, although very tired, was showing a high level of energy in his parallel bars routine. Patrick, who decided to not hold his strength parts on rings any longer than necessary, continued to look strong. Joey had gotten into trouble early in his pommel horse routine. He had hit his leg on the side of the horse but continued to swing. It took several circles to get back up to speed, which took more energy than he thought he had. However, he had just enough energy in reserve to get him to his dismount. Mackee, however, was not as fortunate. After a strong routine, Mackee pulled in too tight on his double back dismount and found himself upended on the dismount mat, frustrated and exhausted. And, although Patrick took several steps and nearly tripped over the chalk bucket, he managed to stay on his feet.

"Well, I'll be a monkey's uncle," said Coach Lowery. " If someone had told me that you two would be left after everyone else, I wouldn't have believed them."

"You shouldn't be so surprised, Coach," said Joey. "Patrick is a very good gymnast!" This comment brought a smile to all of the tired faces.

"You guys get a drink. Catch your breath before we go again," said Coach.

The two met at the water fountain, both tired and out of breath. Patrick looked at Joey. There was something in his eye he hadn't seen much of in himself or in his teammates. It was a fire, a hunger, the edge that he and the rest of the Pioneers had at one time but now seemed to be replaced with complacency.

"You look good out there, squirt," said Patrick. "You know I'm not gonna lay down for you."

"I'd cut your heart out if you did," returned Joey, with a fire in his voice to match the look in his eye.

Chris met Joey on his way to the rings. "Come on, Joey, throttle this joker."

"Look, Chris," returned Joey, not taking his eyes off of rings while he walked, "don't bug me right now. I'm a little busy."

The team was uniformly cheering for both gymnasts, but everyone wanted Joey to win. Not being blessed with great strength, Joey's rings routine was fairly basic and over quickly. Patrick kept up the pace on vault with a well-done layout Tsukahara full twist.

The rounds continued, cheers getting louder as more routines were successfully completed. By the fourteenth round, both gymnasts were moving on sheer willpower alone, the lactic acid building in their muscles, fatigue becoming a serious factor. Joey looked at the event that he dreaded most, high bar. Patrick prepared to do his strongest event, floor exercise. Joey was into the third skill of his routine when he heard the groans of his teammates and the sound of them rushing to high bar. The unthinkable had happened. On his first pass, Patrick touched out both hands on his double back, ending his routine.

"Come on, Joey!" yelled Chris. "All you gotta do is land a dismount, and you've won."

Joey put on a burst of energy and finished his routine with a strong double tuck dismount ... stuck. A roar came from the team as Joey earned his first victory, of any kind, since becoming a Pioneer. Before he could appreciate the cheers of his teammates, Joey staggered over to the mat where Patrick lay. "You okay, dude?"

"Yeah, I'm fine. I just stung my ankles a little. I'll be okay."

"Just tell me one thing, Patrick," asked Joey. "You didn't dump on that routine, did you?"

"No way, Joey. That was a hundred and ten percent, honest. I just ran out of gas."

"You sure?"

"Yep."

"Thanks, Patrick," Joey made it to the locker room before collapsing on the floor.

"Good job, plowboy," said Chris, helping Patrick to his feet. "You did a man's job." Chris looked to the locker room, making sure that Joey was well out of earshot. "Do you think he suspects?"

"No chance. He's on cloud nine," answered Patrick. The two high-fived as the rest of the team accompanied them to the locker room, laughing, cheering, and giving Joey all of the celebration that goes with winning a major contest, including being thrown into the shower with his clothes on.

Coach Lowery just stood out in the middle of the gym, dumbfounded. Where his barking could not produce what he wanted, a simple game had brought more results than he could have imagined.

THIRTEEN

▼

THESE LONG BUS rides rate about the same as midterms, thought Patrick. The trip to Ann Arbor was the longest trip they would make by bus. Nothing quite compares with seven gymnasts, two managers, and a cranky coach confined to a bus for thirteen hours. Compounding matters was the fact that it had been raining since they hit the Kentucky–Tennessee border. By all rights, somebody should be dead before we get to Ohio, Patrick thought. But, this time, the group looked eerily different to Patrick, who sat in the backseat of the bus. Instead, the occupants looked as though they were enjoying each other's company. Dallas and Chris were actually talking to each other and sharing jokes, and Mackee and Joey played paper wad basketball with Ty and AJ three seats away.

This is how it should be, thought Patrick, not seven individuals, but a team. It really was not a surprise that the team was happy. Workouts had been going quite well. Everybody was aproaching midseason form, hitting routines and building stamina and confidence. Everyone felt sure that they could win the Wolverine Invitational. Not even the rain could dampen the spirits of these friends and teammates.

"Hey, Coach!" called Joey. "When do we stop for lunch? I'm hungry."

"You're always hungry, Johnson," returned Coach Lowery. "We'll stop in Cincinnati. I want to get at least halfway before we stop."

"Why Cincinnati? Isn't Dayton closer to halfway?" Chris said to Dallas.

"Yeah, but back when coach was competing, his team stopped to have lunch at Fountain Square before going to the Wolverine. Next day, he won the meet. I guess it's superstition. He thinks we might get some sort of religious experience, like he did, and go out and beat everyone just because we ate fast food in the open air with a bunch of pigeons and street urchins."

Joey's stomach told him that they were close to the Cincinnati city limits. The bus negotiated traffic to get off the interstate and carry its charges to the coach's appointed destination, Cincinnati's Fountain Square. The weather was unseasonably mild for mid-December—not quite short-sleeve weather, but a jacket was not necessary, and the wind was light. The Pioneers were not the only ones enjoying the weather. Many downtown workers were out and about during their lunch hour.

"So, this is to be the source of our inner strength, eh?" said Chris as he stepped off of the bus.

"Okay, you clowns," said Coach. "Fountain Square is just like a big, open air mall. Restaurants and shops are all over the place. Just get what you want, and bring it back here," he said as he pointed to a pavilion to his right.

For the most part, the gymnasts stuck to traditional fast-food choices. Mackee, Patrick, and Ty went for the "two all-beef patties" thing. AJ and Dallas opted for the "it takes two hands to handle it" thing. Coach and Chris headed for the border. Joey was the only exception to the typical fare, choosing Chinese. Once everyone had his meal, the group gathered under the public pavilion.

"I didn't think you were superstitious, Coach," said Chris.

"What's that supposed to mean, McClure?" answered Coach.

"According to Dallas, this is almost a ritual, coming to Fountain Square before the Wolverine. The guys seem to think that you find some luck here."

"They may have a point, McClure," conceded Coach. "We've always done well at the Wolverine, and we've always stopped here. I guess an argument could be made for the coincidence."

"What made you think that stopping here was the reason," said Joey, "and not some other factor like, dare I say, preparation?"

"Very funny, Johnson," returned Coach, pausing for the chuckles to subside. "Actually, superstition has very little to do with why I stop here every year. When I think of Fountain Square, I don't really think about winning and losing. Instead, I get a sense of peace."

The team just looked at each other as Coach Lowery began to drift into another world.

"When I was your age," Coach continued, "I felt many of the same things you guys feel now. Bruised and battered from hard training, drained mentally from school, worried about everything from whether or not I could hit my sets in competition to whether my grades would be good enough to get me into a good school, to whether or not I would have a date for Friday night. It seemed as though the Wolverine came at a time when my life was at the height of physical, mental, and emotional stress. No time could pass without me worrying about one thing or another.

"When my coach parked the bus at the square, I felt the same way about it that you guys feel. But then, something happened. Somewhere among the height of the buildings, the songs of the birds, the sound of the midday traffic, and the serenity of the Cincinnati skyline, something hit me. Everything that I had been so caught up in—gymnastics, school, girls, growing up—seemed so small and insignificant. I knew that shortly, everything that dominated my thoughts would pass. Some how, the knowledge of knowing that the things around me—the buildings, the fountain, the sidewalks—were all there before me and would remain long after I was gone gave me an eerie sense of how truly small I was compared to the rest of the world and how short this time was in comparison to the rest of my life.

"It was at that moment that I realized that dread, in and of itself, is the single biggest waste of mental energy. If I hadn't done enough preparation for what I was about to do, be it a routine or a math test, no amount of worry would make me more prepared. And if I was prepared, there was no need to dread the outcome. Life is just too short to be spent on wasted energy."

"So," said Chris, "do you figure we'll find this inner peace by coming here?"

"Actually, no," returned Coach. "You'll have to find your own place. Nothing I do or say can convince you of your own worth. That must come from within you in your own place, at your own moment. I come to this place mainly for my own mental healing. Each time I come back here, I remember that feeling, and it reminds me that since the last time I was here, I've let the same sort of thoughts get to me that I used to. I guess being here helps put my mind into the right perspective again."

"Kinda like your own, personal confessional, eh, Coach?" remarked AJ.

"In a way, AJ, I guess you could call it that," Coach agreed. "I guess someday, each person finds their own Fountain Square. Only then will you know how you will deal with your own mortality."

"Some of us sooner than others," said Chris.

Crisler Arena, home of the University of Michigan Wolverines, was an impressive sight for the best midseason invitational east of the Mississippi. Gymnasts competing in the Wolverine for the first time could be easily intimidated by the vastness of the venue and the quality of the competition.

Although they had been on the road the entire day, the weary Pioneers wanted to go to the arena to see the layout before checking into the hotel. Each jaw dropped as they entered the competition floor.

"I think I just realized my own mortality!" said Dallas, resting his chin on Patrick's shoulder from behind.

"I see a rebirth," returned the team captain.

"Here's my spot, right where I left it!" said Joey, jumping up on the first place position of the awards podium.

"Cute, Johnson," said Coach. "Let's get to the hotel, guys. We've got a workout set for tomorrow."

Upon arrival at the hotel, very little was said as room assignments were made, the guys opting to get into bed as soon as possible, each wanting to put the long day on the road behind him.

The arena looked very different the next day. Instead of a stoic example of athletic architecture, the arena was a alive with movement as nearly every competing gym was in the facility with the same idea as the Pioneers: get as accustomed to the equipment as possible, create an edge for themselves, and to size up the competition. There were no less than twenty gymnasts in line on each event, each trying to outdo the other for skills and equipment time.

"Boy, the mind games these guys play on each other is just amazing," said Patrick.

"You'd think these guys had never seen gymnastics equipment before," said Dallas.

With a booming voice, Chris gained the attention of everyone in the gym.

"Okay, you guys may as well go home unless you came here to lose, 'cause the Pioneers are here!" In unison, each of the Pioneers walked quickly in different directions, leaving Chris standing alone to offer himself as an easy target for the acidic stares of the other gymnasts.

"Oh, give it a rest, fellas," said Chris to the gymnasts who had stopped what they were doing to send an icy glare at Chris. "You guys take yourselves way too serious," he said. The other gymnasts returned to their struggle for equipment time.

"Great, Slash, you're gonna get us all killed before we even get on the equipment," said Dallas.

Joey had found a spot on the gym floor where the team could store jackets and extra clothing, and the Pioneers stripped down to their workout attire while the majority of the other gymnasts sized up the brash gentlemen from east Tennessee.

"That new kid ain't just a little bit cocky, is he, Jim?" came a voice over the left shoulder of the Pioneer coach. He turned to see Norm Early, a college classmate and coach for Wildcat Gymnastics in Lexington, Kentucky.

"Wha … ? Hey, Norm! How's it goin'? Oh, Chris? Yeah, he sure is a pistol."

"Well, he sure looked good in Atlanta. Where'd he come from? He sure looks familiar."

"Chris came to us this summer from California."

"California? Oh yeah! I remember him from nationals last year. Didn't he take second to Danny Diego from Austin?"

"Yeah, he's the one."

"Man, you got a weapon on your hands."

"If I can control him," returned Coach Lowery.

"If anyone can, you can. Well, I gotta get back to my guys, Jim. Good luck this weekend."

"Thanks, Norm. Good luck yourself." Coach Lowery turned to see his charges starting warm-up on floor. Then, just for a moment, the thought crossed his mind of just how good his team really was.

"This could be a very interesting weekend, indeed," Chris said to Patrick, who was stretching out Chris's shoulders.

"How so?" asked Patrick.

"About half of these guys were in Atlanta. Chances are they've improved quite a bit since then."

"Yeah, so have we. So what?"

"It's gonna be very interesting to see who's on and who's out."

"I didn't think you worried about stuff like that, Chris," joined Joey.

"Oh, I'm not thinkin' about me, squirt. I was talking about—"

"Hey, McClure!" came a voice from a stocky redhead crossing the floor exercise carpet.

"Marty, Marty Reynolds, what do you know, dude?"

Marty Reynolds, the Lake Erie team captain, dressed in street clothes with his gym bag over one shoulder, had come to talk to his old pal and nemesis.

"We just finished workout when I saw you guys come in. You know you dusted most of us in Atlanta. How dare you show your face in my backyard," said the Michigander jokingly.

"Yeah, but it's just not the same as makin' ya look bad in front of the hometown crowd. So, what's new with you, Marty?" asked Chris.

"I think I'm gonna throw a new dismount off pipe."

"Let me guess. You're gonna try four flips, right?"

"Close, but no cigar, dude. I've been working a triple-twisting double layout. I do it in about half my routines. I warmed it up today. You must've missed it. If it feels good, I'll do it tomorrow. How about you? You gonna show us anything new?"

"As a matter of fact, yes," said Chris, obviously fabricating his story as he went on, "I've been working real hard on a new opener on floor." The remainder of the Pioneers looked at each other, wondering what skill Chris could possibly be talking about. "I think I'm going to put in a full and a half-twisting, two-and-three." Chris's teammates looked at him in disbelief, knowing that no gymnast in the world had ever tried this most impossible, and possibly lethal, head-first entry skill, much less had the skill ready for the second pass of a floor routine.

"No way, dude," said Marty. "You've always had balls, but I never thought you were that stupid."

"Stupid! You calling me stupid and a liar, you little dwarf? Patrick, you tell him," Chris turned to the surprised captain, catching him completely off guard. "Tell this pea brain that I've been training this trick."

Patrick tripped over his words. "Uh … sure, uh … Marty. If Chris says that he's been working it, uh, he certainly has."

Joey jumped in. "Yeah, he's calling it a woofus!"

"Woofus? What kind of name is that? Is it named after his dog or something?" asked Marty sarcastically.

"No, dude," Dallas decided to join the fun. "That's the sound he made after the first one he did knocked the wind out of him!"

Marty looked at the faces of the Pioneer teammates, not sure whom or what to believe. "You guys are full of crap, right? McClure, you haven't really been working that trick, have you?"

"If I'm lyin', I'm dyin', my friend."

"I think you'll be dyin' if you're not lyin'. Oh well, it's your funeral, pal. I thought I was crazy. Happy hunting, dude."

"Thanks, my friend. Have a good meet, but not too good, okay?"

"Sure thing. See ya later, McClure. We're headed for a pizza." The Lake Erie team leader walked back to his teammates, who were already heading out the door.

"You know what this means, you guys," said Chris as soon as Marty was out of earshot.

"Yeah," said Patrick, "you've got to come up with some excuse for 'pulling' this trick from your routine."

"Wrong, plowboy," Chris returned very seriously. "I've got to figure out how to do a full-in, Arabian one-and-three by tomorrow." All of the Pioneers stopped and looked at each other in disbelief as Chris made his way to the corner of the floor exercise mat to start warming up his tumbling.

"Patrick," said Joey, "you gotta talk him out of this! He's gonna kill himself!"

"Now what makes you think that I have any power whatsoever in preventing that clown from doing anything?"

"You're the captain, Captain," said Mackee. "Do some captaining!"

"I guess you guys aren't gonna let me out of this, are you?" said the dejected team leader.

"No!" came the chorus.

Patrick retraced Chris's steps to the corner of the floor exercise carpet, trying to think of the words that would coax his teammate out of risking his neck, literally.

"How tough could this really be?" asked Chris before Patrick could get out the first word.

"Chris, I … uh … really think you should—"

"After all, I've done a Thomas before, a one-and-a-half twisting, one-and-three, and it's just another flip. That can't be all that tough."

"Chris, I think you … uh … need to give this … uh … a little more … uh … thought." Patrick tried to find the right words, but nothing seemed to work.

"Wish me luck, plowboy!"

"Chris, don't, really!"

Chris panted a couple of times and checked to see that no one was coming from another corner. Then, he was off and running. Patrick's hands went over his eyes, not wanting to see what was certain to be the end of his friend and teammate, but at the last moment, his curiosity got the best of him as he peeked through his interlaced fingers.

"Go, Chris, go!" came the shout from Joey.

"Jam, baby, jam!" shouted Mackee.

"Get up, Slash!" even Dallas had gotten into the act.

The entire gym had stopped to see what the commotion was about, not knowing what was in store.

Chris turned over a blazingly fast round off, back handspring and punched into the air. Full twist in the first flip, half twist in the second! Chris quickly spotted the floor rushing up to meet his outstretched hands.

"Whhooofff!!" came the gasp of escaping air as Chris bounced across the spring floor on his back. His momentum carried him off of the floor exercise carpet and onto the hardwood floor. He stood up to the cheers of everyone as he made his way back to the corner where he started, passing a frozen Patrick, his fingers still laced across his staring eyes and his mouth hanging open in disbelief.

"Cool," came the response from the Californian, pretending not to be affected. "I think it goes in tomorrow." Patrick calmly excused himself to the restroom, where he coughed his breakfast into the first available toilet.

Later that evening, the hotel where the Pioneers were staying was filled with gymnasts from all over the eastern United States. Each gymnast was trying in his own way to relax, to let the body rest up for next day's competition, and to find a way not to get caught up in the mind games that often take place in a gymnast's head. The tricks the mind can play can cause havoc with a gymnast's confidence. All it takes is a bad workout or just one bad turn to cause an otherwise solid, confident athlete to doubt his ability to perform.

Some watch gymnastics video to keep their minds centered on the task at hand. Some do conditioning to make the body tired so sleep comes fast and easy, without the burden of contemplating a failed performance. Some try just to escape through video games, movies, or books. Some just pace and worry.

On this eve, Patrick's pacing took him to Chris's room. Patrick knocked on the door and was let in by Chris. Chris, who was sharing a room with Ty and AJ, had been reading from the room service menu while Ty and AJ were playing the video games that Ty had brought from home.

"Man, this selection sucks!" said the Californian. "And what looks edible costs more than my monthly on my bike! Hey, plowboy, you wanna go in on a pizza?"

"Sure. What delivers?"

"I'll check," Chris called the front desk to get the number of the nearest pizzeria. He was given the number of a resturaunt with a thirty-minute delivery guarantee. He was quickly connected with the pizzeria. "What do you like on your pie, plowboy?"

"Anything but fish."

"Cool. Send me two supremes and four diet sodas," Chris said into the phone. "Okay, $24.75. I'm setting my watch now. I'll meet the delivery guy in the lobby. Thanks." Chris hung up the phone and grabbed his jacket.

Patrick looked at Ty and AJ, then back at Chris. "Aren't you gonna order something for these guys?"

Chris looked at AJ and Ty, mesmerized by the video game. "Hey, you guys want some pizza?"

No answer. Chris and Patrick looked at each other.

"Hey, guys, you want some pizza or what?" asked Patrick.

Chris and Patrick were surprised to see the two glued to the video screen, oblivious to everything else.

"Yo, Fred and Barney, me and Patrick are gonna pick up some loose women we saw on the corner. You want us to bring a few girls back here for you guys?" said Chris.

"Thanks, no," said Ty. "We're not hungry."

Chris and Patrick looked at each other again and laughed as they walked out the door.

It didn't take long for Chris to start the conversation. "You look pensive, my friend. What is on your mind?"

"What makes you think something is on my mind?"

"It was *you* who came to *my* room. I don't think you were looking for a food buddy, and you sure weren't interested in the videobots in there, so I figured you want to talk. What's up?"

"Okay, you got me. Ever since this afternoon, I've been very puzzled. Did you know there was a risk in doing the woofus, or did you know you could do it, or do you just not like your body very much?"

"Hmmm … that's a hard one. On the one hand, I do respect my body. That's why I don't put much junk in it. On the other hand, I did realize that there was a risk involved. So, I may be crazy, but I'm not stupid. I think I knew inside of me that I could make the trick."

A silence overcame the two as Patrick tried to process what Chris had just told him. It all made sense, but something just didn't fit.

"That's all fine and good, but how can you put yourself in that position?" asked Patrick.

"What do you mean?"

"What do I mean? Do you have any idea how close you were to buying the farm out there today? And all just for silly pride. You didn't have to prove anything to anybody. We all knew you were just stringing Marty along, and I'm sure Marty didn't take you seriously."

"So?"

"So, why the risk?" Patrick prodded.

"Okay, let me get this straight. You think that I put myself at what you believe is unacceptable risk just to do something that seems to be impossible, with very little regard for my own safety or the questionable or risky outcome, right?"

"Exactly!"

"My friend, that's what gymnastics is all about. Every skill that you, I, and everyone else does in that arena is considered risky, and someone had to have the balls to do it the first time. Sure, many of them learned their skills in a belt or over a safety pit, but there eventually had to be that moment when that skill that no one had ever done before had to be done without the safety of a spotting belt or a pit. At that moment, each one of those pioneers of gymnastics had to realize that they had to take responsibility for their talent and put their bodies on the line. Most gymnasts, excellent gymnasts, go through their entire careers just learning what others had done before them. These guys are all excellent for doing what they love, but they will pass like sand in an hourglass compared to those whose names will live on forever for risking everything they had to do what no one else had done!"

"Is that what you're after? Fame?" asked Patrick.

"No. Hell no! You're missing my point. Columbus didn't set out for the new world to be famous. Lewis and Clark weren't out for headlines when they pushed through the Northwest Passage. And, Armstrong didn't land on the moon for the fame. They did what they did because someone had to do it. Eventually, someone would've put aside their fear of the unknown to discover that the earth was round. Someone eventually would've braved the fear of the darkness of space to get to the moon. And, yes, someday, someone would've gotten the balls to do a full-in, Arabian two-and-three. Just as you think that I was crazy to try what I did, I bet critics of the explorers, the settlers, and the astronauts felt the same. I'm not trying to compare myself with these great people, but the way I see it, I do have a common quality with the Columbuses, the Armstrongs, the Kurt Thomases and the Tsukaharas. I just happened to feel, at that moment, that the desire to try outweighed the risk of failure. Besides, in the final analysis, we will not be judged for what we can do, but what we are willing to do. Lots of others could have done what they did, but they were the ones who were willing to ignore the odds and the negative opinions to try."

Although Chris's answer explained his reasons, Patrick still was puzzled. It became obvious to Patrick that Chris's threshold for risk was much, much higher than his, or any humans for that matter.

"Then tell me this," Patrick continued, "have you ever found a risk that was, in your mind, too great?"

"No, not yet," Chris answered in an eerie calm, "but I know it's out there. I don't know it's name, but I'll know its face when I see it."

"What does that mean?"

"Someday, plowboy, someday. Look, the pizza's here. What time is it?"

"Nine thirty-six."

"Darn it, twenty-seven minutes. No free pizza tonight. I'll get the pizza. You get the tip."

"Deal."

Every palm was sweaty. The tension was visible on each gymnast's face as Chris saluted the head judge and stepped up onto the corner of the floor exercise carpet. With a deep sigh, Chris hopped into his run for his first tumbling pass. Those who had witnessed the previous day's workout pictured in their heads the amazing skill that the "crazy Californian," as the gymnasts were now referring to Chris, threw only a day before. Those who weren't there had heard about it. Everybody stopped what they were doing. Even judges motioned for other gymnasts, ready to compete, to stand by while they witnessed the most amazing skill they had ever heard attempted. The paramedic crew, present at all major gymnastics competitions, noticed the attention and rose with anticipation. Though most competitions were spent taping ankles and nursing sprains, they knew that the time had come to be on their toes.

The steps taken by Chris were the fastest he could muster. His teammates, with strained faces of concern, shouldered the burden of the potential consequences just as much as he. As he did his preparation step for the round off, Chris gasped for one more breath, one that could very well be his last, and held it as he put as much energy as possible into the turnover phase of the round off. Coach Lowery stood at the edge of the ring tower, his head in his hands, not wanting to see what could be the end of not only the best gymnast he's ever coached, but also a human life for which he was responsible.

Chris turned his back handspring over as fast as he could, trying to create as much speed as possible to turn into vertical height and rotation. When the time came to push off the floor, Chris felt the strain on both of his Achilles tendons. Everyone counted in silence the number of revolutions and twists Chris's body went through, hoping he had enough rotation to keep safe.

As he opened from his tucked position to receive the floor with outstretched arms, he could sense that he had opened too early. Those who could guess the inevitable outcome either turned their heads or continued to watch with morbid curiosity.

Chris's arms were not strong enough to protect him from his mistake. They crumbled from the force of his fall, forcing the brunt of the fall onto his head and neck.

Before his body could come to rest on the carpet, the Pioneers were already running to his aid, twenty steps ahead of the paramedic crew.

"Chris!" cried Patrick, his vision obstructed from the tears that had welled up in his eyes. The Pioneers arrived at Chris's side as his crushed body finally came to a stop from his savage fall. Chris was lying motionless on his back.

Patrick was first to reach his friend's side. "Don't touch him!" he screamed, knowing never to touch a person with a severe neck injury. "Chris, can you hear me?"

Two eyes opened, and two dilated pupils tried in vain to focus in the direction of the concerned voice. "Plowboy, is that you?"

"Yeah, pal. I'm right here. Don't try to move."

"I don't … think I could … even … if I … wanted to." The paramedics arrived and moved the teammates back so they could get to the fallen gymnast. All except for Patrick obliged.

"I guess I should've … stayed in my tuck … a little longer … eh, plowboy?" Chris' words became more labored.

"Yeah, I guess you'll have to work on it when we get back to the gym." Patrick was beginning to realize that Chris may never go back to the gym again. "You … you just hang in there, pal."

"I'm hangin', plowboy … I'm … hangin' … . Remember … you've … got to … be … crazy … unh … " Chris lost his fight for consciousness.

"I've lost a pulse," said one of the paramedics. "Everybody, get back!"

"Noooo!" screamed Patrick as Mackee and AJ pulled him from his friend.

"Start CPR!" said the other paramedic.

As the paramedics worked feverishly to bring life back into the body of the fallen Pioneer, Coach Lowery, eyes red from tears, approached the group of grieving teammates. "You know, Goodman, this didn't have to happen." The rest of the team had released Patrick and had taken a place beside their coach.

"Yeah, Goodman," said Dallas, "this was your fault!"

Then, all of the teammates, with their coach, stood over a cowering Patrick, index fingers extended accusingly in his face.

"It's your fault! It's your fault! It's your fault!"

"Nooooooo!" Patrick sat up suddenly to find himself soaked with sweat, short of breath, and his pulse racing. He looked at the clock on the night table of his hotel room. 3:32 AM. "Oh, crap! It was just a dream." Unable to sleep, Patrick lay in his bed staring at the ceiling. "I'm gonna be worthless tomorrow."

Patrick was, understandably but uncharacteristically, late for breakfast. As he arrived at the table, he noticed the absence of Chris, who was often late for breakfast, and Coach Lowery, who was usually the first to get coffee. "Where's Coach?" he asked.

"He's off talking to Chris," said Joey, his attention buried in the back of a cereal box.

"Yeah," said Mackee. "The first time McClure is on time for breakfast, and Coach drags him away before he can get in the first bite."

"Hey, did any of you guys have any weird dreams last night?" asked Ty. All of the Pioneers answered in the positive, except for Dallas, his head still buried in his arms, sound asleep.

"Yeah," said Joey, finally pulling his attention from what his saved box tops could buy. "I had one of those fallin' off a cliff, helpless kind of dreams."

"My dream really messed me up," said Ty. "I was doing gymnastics. I was at the NTIs, and everybody was watching. I kept falling off of everything, and there was nothing I could do."

"I think I know why we had those crazy dreams, guys," said Patrick. Before he could expound upon his theory, Coach Lowery returned to the table with Chris.

"Fellas, I think Mr. McClure has something he wants to tell you all."

Chris, his head hung low, stepped in front of the coach. "I'm sorry if I embarrassed anyone with that stupid stunt I pulled yesterday. I was stupid for trying that skill. I could've killed myself. Needless to say, I won't be competing the woofus today."

The rest of the team looked at each other. Each breathed an uneasy sigh of relief.

"That's okay, Chris," said Ty. "You don't have to do a woofus to embarrass us. We can manage that on our own." The laughter was just the needed touch to release the tension.

"Come on, you guys," said Coach. "We've got a meet to win. Somebody wake up Dallas."

As the team started to file out of the hotel restaurant, Patrick seized the opportunity to confront Chris about his conversation with Coach.

"So, did you guys have an interesting conversation?"

"You could say that," said Chris.

"So, are you gonna do the woofus or not?"

"I said I wasn't doin' it. I'm not doin' it."

"Why not?"

"Coach said I'd be off the team if I throw it."

"Yeah, he's said that before, and that didn't stop you then. What made this threat more believable than the others?"

"Let's just say that I didn't sleep so good last night."

"You, too, eh?" asked Patrick.

"You have trouble sleeping, too?"

"We all did, except for Dallas."

"That figures."

The quick van ride was somehow different. Each gymnast withdrew into his own world, with Dallas still asleep, his head against the window. Patrick noticed that Chris was unusually distant, staring out the window at nothing in particular. Coach was busy working on the training program for the team for the next few weeks, looking beyond this competition to the next meet. That was just how Coach was, always looking ahead.

Upon arrival to Crisler Arena, the gymnasts filed out of the van and headed toward the front doors. Patrick conveniently fell behind the group to talk to his coach. Patrick waited until all of his teammates were out of listening range before speaking.

"Because I am ultimately responsible for the health of each one of you, Patrick." Coach Lowery answered before Patrick could get out the question. "You see, Patrick, at your age, you feel invincible, like nothing can hurt you. Well, regardless of what you think, I have to look out for the well being of you boys. Now, how responsible would I be if I had to call Chris's mother to tell her that she'd lost her only son because I did nothing to stop him from self-destructing?"

"Don't get me wrong, Coach," said Patrick. "I just wonder if by limiting what a gymnast is allowed to do, you don't curb his ability to be creative. I mean, we both know that Chris is capable of skills that we've never even seen before. Why be so critical when you may not know the limit of his talent?"

"You know, Patrick, I'm surprised to hear that coming from you. You know how we get things done. You work out the bugs in the gym, where it's safe and you can control most of the variables that make a skill dangerous. Then, only when it's ready, do you put it in a routine. A major competition is no place to experiment with a new, potentially dangerous skill."

"I know, but we're talking about Chris. He's different from the rest of us. For him, the first time may be all he needs to get ready."

"This may be so, Patrick, but I have to make a judgment call, and for this instance, I think I'm making the right call."

"I don't mean to disagree with you. I just hope that by telling Chris he can't do something, he doesn't lose his confidence."

"Patrick, if we were talking about anybody besides Chris, I'd be worried. But if there's anybody who doesn't have a confidence problem, it's Chris."

"If you think so, Coach," conceded Patrick.

"I hope so, Pat."

Patrick opened the doors for the man who represented the past, present, and future of Pioneer Gymnastics.

A competition arena has three faces. The first face, the day before anyone comes in, is quiet, stoic, almost cathedral-like. The second is the workout day, when the complexion of the facility takes on the persona of a playground with all of the bullies sizing each other up, either during the workout or sitting in the stands before or after their own training. The day of the competition, when warm-up begins, it takes on its third face, one of a circus, with each gymnast trying to show that he's not affected by the presence of other gymnasts trying to get his attention. He's trying to somehow find a psychological advantage to one up the competition in final preparation for battle. All the while, the entering patrons, with popcorn and sodas in hand, feast on the show as they pick out their favorite athlete to keep an eye on.

The fact that the Wolverine was perhaps the biggest invitational of the season only served to magnify the intensity between the gymnasts, the coaches, and those who relish in watching them.

Although warm-up was going quite well, Patrick could not help but notice that Chris was preparing differently from past competitions. Whereas in most meets, Chris was notorious for taunting other favored gymnasts with his loud voice and gymnastics prowess to back up the talk, this competition revealed a very different side of the Californian wonder. He was very serious and single-minded. His warm-up was methodic and not flashy. He didn't appear to be creating new routines, as he normally would. Rather, he did the more familiar routine, set after set, warming up with full routines rather than combinations. It was as though he wanted to make sure that his routines were solid, not allowing for the slightest of error.

"Hey, Patrick," called Marty Reynolds. "What's with McClure? He doesn't seem to be his verbal self today. Is he worried?"

"Highly doubtful, Marty," Patrick bluffed. "He's just getting over a little stomach virus he picked up last night."

"Sure he didn't get his bell rung from that woofus he threw yesterday?" taunted the defending national champion on high bar.

"Doubtful. Last night, we were laughing about the look on your face when he did it. We'll see who's bell is rung when it's all over." Patrick didn't know what he was saying. He was just trying to find the words that would take the heat off of Chris, who had enough to worry about.

Chris's unusual behavior, Patrick's feeling the effect of having little sleep, and his knowing that the others didn't sleep well, either, all led Patrick to think that this may not be that great a meet for the Pioneers, except maybe for Dallas.

The public address announcer blared to the gymnasts that warm-up had concluded. That all of the Pioneers survived warm-up without injury was cause for a minor celebration. The athletes made their way to a area designated for the march-in. It also was the final opportunity for a gymnast to communicate to another before the competition. Marty made a point to get in one last dig.

"Hey, McClure, I noticed you didn't warm up your woofus. You get scared?" At that point, every Pioneer but Chris rose to his feet to take apart the loudmouthed Michigander.

"Sit down, you guys," said Chris, still seated and visibly unaffected. "I figure I don't need it to kick your ass, Marty."

"Oh really? You think so?"

"Yeah, I do. In fact, I'll bet you fifty bucks you don't even medal today."

"Fifty bucks—are you serious, McClure?"

"Fifty bucks. On top of that, I bet you another ten this little guy beats you on vault," said Chris, motioning to a shocked Joey.

"You're on, McClure."

"No doubt, Marty."

The meet coordinator poked his head in the room. "Okay, you guys, get ready for march-in." The gymnasts shuffled to their feet. Joey eased up to Chris's left side. Under his breath, he asked, "How am I supposed to beat him on vault? I'm the worst vaulter on the team!"

"Don't worry, squirt. You'll beat him."

"With what?"

"Layout Tsukahara."

"Layout Tsukahara? Chris, I have a hard enough time getting to my feet when I'm piked. How am I gonna do a layout?" Joey's panic was about to set in.

"Easy, kid," said Ty. "You just run like hell."

"Yeah," added Mackee, "and pray a whole lot."

"You're serious. You really want me to try this, don't you?"

"Listen, Joey," consoled Chris, "your piked Tsukahara is awesome. All you have to do is arch fast off the table. Some of the pikes you do in the gym should be layed out. You'll do fine."

"Do you think so, Patrick?"

Patrick was in a quandary. He wanted to agree with his teammates, but he had just had this same conversation with Coach.

"Sure, Joey. You just have to believe you can," said Patrick, his tone less confident than his words. After all, he thought, the worst he could do is land short and blow out his ankles and end his career.

After much thought, Joey came to a conclusion. "All right, I'll do it." Joey punched the palm of his left hand in determination as the team made its way to the opening ceremonies.

The arena became even more like a circus. The lights had gone down, with only flood spotlights to see by. The stands were filled with more than ten thousand spectators hungry for the level of gymnastics that only comes to town so often. The promoters had done a great job bringing in the people. More than three hundred in the crowd were orphans and underprivileged children from the Ann Arbor area. Many tickets were given away by radio promotion. This meet would not lose money. The tradition of the Wolverine Invitational, with loud, supportive, feverish fans and the best gymnastics the country has to offer, had become almost as popular as the annual University of Michigan–Ohio State University football game. In fact, the scope of the competition could rattle the unprepared gymnast. The noise, deafening at times, made it hard to concentrate.

"Ladies and gentlemen," screamed the announcer, "presenting some of the greatest gymnasts in the United States! Welcome to the seventeenth annual Wolverine Gymnastics Invitational!"

The rest of the proceedings were a blur to Joey, his attention centered on his responsibility to the team, and to Chris. He was confused. If he backed out of the vault, not only would Coach Lowery not be mad, but support him in the decision to save the vault for another day. And, besides Chris would understand. Joey knew nothing special was expected of him. Wait, he thought, maybe that's why I haven't done anything special before. To back down would nullify every reason why I'm still on this team. Success, after all, is not a destination, Coach Lowery had said, it's the journey. Once the proceedings had concluded, the gymnasts reported to their first event. For the Pioneers, it was vault. Joey knew he was the first one up, the pacesetter, Coach called it. The sacrificial lamb, Joey thought. Judges don't have the guts to give a high score early, especially to the first competitor. A high score early leaves less room for higher scores to better vaults that may come along later in the competition.

Having chalked his hands, Joey walked to his mark on the vault runway. He was met by Mackee and Chris.

"Remember, squirt, fly!" said Mackee.

"Stick, Joey. You can do it. It's your time to shine," said Chris confidently.

"Thanks, guys," said Joey, who was not so sure. It's easy for them to be confident, he thought. It's not their butt on the line!

Joey almost missed the salute from the head judge, signally that it was time to go. He let out a big sigh and returned the salute. He took one more moment to visualize the vault and gestured the actions his body would go through to do the vault correctly. One more sigh and he was off. After his first step, Joey knew that he had passed the point of no return. He knew that the momentum that the team would need to win this competition rested squarely upon his shoulders and this vault. As he got closer, the board and the table got bigger. Joey felt no problems, so he accelerated to his approach. He made sure that he didn't jump too high in his approach to the board, which would minimize his flight afterward. Joey pushed the board as hard as he ever had, muscles tensing to try to get every ounce of repulsion out of the coil springboard. Upon reaching the table, Joey extended his arms to receive it, planting his first hand about midway down the table, and jamming his second hand, with a locked arm, into the far end of the table to maximize the blocking action to create height and rotation. He exploded from the table faster than he had ever before, faster than he thought possible for him. Now came the hard part—the wait. If he tried to flip too early, he'd be too low and land short. The trick to doing a layout Tsukahara is being patient, waiting for your body to turn upright and using the full effect of the pushoff, before trying to rotate the backward flip with the chest arching and hips opening, then using the abdominal muscles to pull the legs over the top.

Then he saw it. The floor seemed further away than usual. Joey picked a spot on the mat where he thought his feet would land and targeted his landing. His feet planted into the soft four-inch mat on top of the twenty centimeter landing mat, and, for a moment, he was motionless. Not only did he stick, but he could not move for seconds if he wanted to.

Then the explosion of noise. Not only from the crowd and his teammates, but from inside himself. A voice was screaming for his success so loud that it could not be contained.

"Yeeeee-haaaaw!" Joey screamed, fists clenched as he turned to salute the judges. Joey ran back to the seating area, skipping, dancing, and fist-pumping along the way.

"I'm proud of you, Johnson," said Chris. "But, you really shouldn't make a habit of screaming at the judges!"

For the first time, Joey realized his role as the pacesetter and not the sacrificial lamb. All that remained was to see the score flashed.

9.25

"Joey, that's fantastic!" said Coach. "I'm proud of you!" Joey finally felt a sense of worth and belonging to the team.

Joey's vault was the spark that ignited the team. Chris was his usual self, surpassing all the other gymnasts with difficulty above and beyond anyone, each routine punctuated with his casual smile and wink to his teammates. His style bedazzled judge, gymnast, and spectator alike. Although Chris had grown accustommed to standing at the top of the awards stand, for the first time, this season, he had at least one teammate with him on each event, including four out of six positions, when the all-around awards were handed out.

Patrick was inspired, performing his best gymnastics ever. Routines that were questionable weeks before looked solid and polished. Although Patrick had to settle for a tie for first place on pommel horse with Chris, to him, it was the same as winning.

Joey's other routines, lacking the difficulty of the McClures and the Reynoldses, but inspired nonetheless, gave him the sense of pride he had lacked since joining the team two years earlier.

While the Pioneers looked like a team of immortals, Marty looked human. With falls on pommel horse and high bar, including landing on his knees on his new dismount, and one fall on parallel bars, Marty was kept off of the awards platform for every event except rings, where he had to accept a fourth-place medal behind three Pioneers: Mackee, Chris, and Patrick. The big step Marty took on his vault caused him to not only not place, but also finish three-tenths of a point behind Joey.

When the final results came in, it was a landslide for the Pioneers. The team won by three full points over the second-place team. The top two places for each event were Pioneers, including a silver medal for the newest vault sensation, Joey Johnson.

Coach Lowery looked at his charges on the awards stand. Even Chris and Dallas were hugging each other. These guys could do it, he thought. For the first time he saw not seven individuals, but, at last, a team.

FOURTEEN

▼

"WHERE'S THE INTENSITY, Dallas?" Coach Lowery screamed at the Pioneers' parallel bars specialist, having missed his fourth routine in a row. "You can't rest on your laurels. I know you guys had a pretty good meet up in Michigan, but that victory won't get you through the rest of the season, much less get you ready for our meet a week from Friday."

Coach was right. Intensity was off, not just with Dallas, but for everybody. Coach Lowery even had a hard time convincing himself that they needed more work. After all, this little group of country boys and one Californian did just throttle some of the best gymnasts in the country. All he had to do was think about years past when his teams were confident, perhaps overconfident, going into the NTIs. Then, convincing himself was easy.

"Dallas, I won't have you be the cause of us not qualifying to NTIs!"

"Why are you always yelling at me, Coach? Goodman hasn't hit a set in the last twenty minutes, either!" answered Dallas.

"Neither has anybody else," added Patrick.

Naturally, it was going to be hard to keep them motivated to train for their home invitational. The Pioneer was always small by invitational standards, typically around a hundred competitors from nearby cities: Nashville, Chattanooga, Atlanta, maybe some from Kentucky and North Carolina. It definitely lacked the intensity of the bigger competitions. What it did do, however, was set the stage for the end of the season. The Pioneer was a small enough meet to help the guys compete without the pressure of a big meet right before state championships, the regional qualifier, and, ultimately, the National Team Invitational. Although the Wolverine did a great job of building confidence, the success that came with it was going to make it difficult to keep them motivated, Coach thought. Everyone except Joey, of course. Joey had become a gymnast possessed. While everyone else had dropped his level of training to soak in the rewards of winning the Wolverine, Joey used the results to fuel his. While the other guys were laughing and cutting up, Joey was doing extra conditioning, extra combinations, and sneaking extra turns on the apparatus while whoever's turn it actually was was caught up in conversation with the others.

As Coach Lowery debated whether to push them harder or kick them all out of the gym, Mackee uncharacteristically fell from a handstand on rings, tucked his head, and landed flat on his back, laughing at a comment that AJ had made. Coach's decision was made.

"All right, you guys, get out of here. You're not helping yourselves by training stupid. Take the day off. Come in tomorrow with your heads screwed on straight and ready to train hard."

The team looked at each other and then at the back of Coach Lowery, who was heading for his office, laughing.

"Hey, Slash, why don't you buy me a burger?" insisted Dallas.

"You're the one with all the cash, Dallas. Why don't you treat us all?" returned Chris as they headed for the locker room.

"Man, I wouldn't spend a plugged nickel on you losers."

"Well, I guess it'll have to be dutch treat," returned Chris.

"You know, just like your last date, Dallas!" quipped Mackee.

As everyone was almost through the locker room door, Chris noticed that Joey was still out at parallel bars.

"Come on, Joey, we're goin' to Burger Max!" called Chris.

"You guys go on. I've still got a bit more to do."

Chris knew that meant Joey wouldn't be joining them. He called into the locker room, "Hey, you guys go on without me. I'll catch up to you later."

Without a word, Chris went over to the pommel horse and started swinging circles for endurance. Just then, Ty leaned out of the locker room door. "Hey, Chris, what do you want us to order … " He looked to see Joey and Chris hard at work. He looked back into the locker room and then walked back into the gym, strapped on his grips, and started working on his rings swing.

One by one, each Pioneer looked into the gym to see what was holding up the other, discovering the rest of the team training basics and conditioning, then finding themselves joining in.

"Come on, you guys, the burgers are gonna get cold!" Dallas said, walking out of the locker room and seeing what his teammates had seen before him. "Aw, you guys, we just got a reprieve from all of this." Dallas watched as his teammates worked with no signs of letting up. "Okay, you guys, let's go," he said. When no one budged, Dallas relented and joined the team.

Coach Lowery walked out of his office and was on his way out when he noticed that the gym lights were still on. When he looked in, he couldn't believe his eyes. The same guys who couldn't concentrate for five minutes an hour ago were now training harder than ever, with nothing but their own expectations to push them.

The mall had announced closing for the evening more than twenty minutes earlier. Chris barely got in, as security had already started locking doors.

"Thanks, Benny," Chris said to one of the guards he had come to know since dating Haley.

"No problem, Mr. McClure. Better tread lightly, though. Your lady expected you over an hour ago."

"Oooh, not good," winced Chris. "Did she look very upset?"

"Let's just say I'm glad I don't have to answer to her."

"Thanks for the heads up, pal. Got any ideas?"

"Yeah, chocolates, flowers, and a helluva good story."

"Well, I'm oh for three. I guess I'll have to throw myself on the mercy of her heart."

"Good luck. But, let me get a look at your butt. I don't think there'll be much left of it after Haley gets finished."

"Ah, thanks just the same, Benny. You have a good night."

"You too, Mr. McClure," and Benny locked the remaining door and went on his way.

Chris hid himself behind the planter outside Pizza Roma to see Haley before she could see him. Haley was doing her normal cleanup routine and talking to herself. Paying more attention to what she was thinking than what she was doing, Haley dropped a salt shaker that she was refilling. In her rage, she kicked the shaker across the restaurant floor.

"Damn it!" she screamed.

Chris could contain his laughter no longer. His sudden outburst gave his hiding position away. With catlike reflexes, Haley turned and, without focusing on her target, hurled the box of salt at the plant, hitting Chris in the forehead, causing the container to explode, knocking him to the ground and covering him with salt.

"Hi, honey. Nice to see you, too!" Chris said sarcastically as he gathered his senses and rubbed his head. By the time Chris's eyes could sharply focus, Haley had arrived at his side, pushing a broom and dustpan in his face.

"You're here. You might as well do some work," announced Haley as she returned to the task of filling condiments. "You know you were supposed to be here an hour ago. We've missed the movie."

"Look, I'll make it up to you. We'll go get something to eat."

"I work in a restaurant, doofus. I've been eating all day. I don't want to go eat."

"Well, I'm starved. What have you got?"

"You know the menu as well as I do. Whatever you want, you have to make it yourself."

"Right," answered Chris as he dumped salt remnants from his dustpan into a nearby trash can and shook his head violently from side to side to release the salt from his wavy blonde hair. He then made his way back to the grill.

"So, why are you so late?" asked Haley, focusing on her work and not looking at Chris.

"Well, actually, Coach let us go about two hours early."

"And that made you an hour late?"

"Not exactly. See, when Coach kicked us out, everybody left the gym except for Joey. He either didn't hear or didn't want to hear or didn't care if he heard. He just kept working. One by one, each of us kept coming back into the gym and started training."

"So, why did you guys get kicked out of the gym?"

"Nobody was in the mood to train. Just cut up. That is until we saw Joey goin' off after we all started to leave."

"So when did you guys finish?"

"About half an hour ago." Chris put several slices of different meats on the grill. "It's amazing what he has done for this team. Here's a guy that, on any given day, won't count for team score. His routines are not strong enough, and he knows it. But he gets in there every day and busts his ass to try to put himself in a position just in case we need his score. A lot of guys would've given up by now or jumped to another team where his score would count."

"But see, that's the way Joey's always been," said Haley, adding pepper and salt to Chris's sandwich meat. "Always wanting to be the best, even in a hopeless cause."

"But his approach to training is different than anyone else's. It goes way beyond just wanting to be better."

"How so?"

"Joey doesn't consider workout as work. To him, it's another opportunity to do the best at whatever he's doing. For instance, if Coach gives us an assignment, say fifteen double backs, Dallas and some of the others might try to talk Coach down to, say, ten. Joey would just keep doing them. He'd do, like, twenty. And if Coach asks him how many he's done, he'd lie and say ten so Coach would have to watch him do at least five more. That way, he's got at least twenty-five tries to do the best double back he's ever done."

"Then why isn't he as good as the rest of you guys?"

"He will be, someday. His strength and talent just haven't caught up to his desire yet. With the others, it's just the other way around," Chris surmised as he took a bite of his sandwich.

"Well, it's too late to get anything accomplished. What do you want to do?"

"It's after ten," said Chris, looking at his watch. "We both have to be up for class tomorrow. We better make it an early evening. I need to drop by the drugstore on the way home."

"Finish your sandwich so we can close up here," Haley instructed him. She turned off the lights as Chris choked down the last bite of his sandwich. "Chris, how good do you think Joey can be, really?"

"I think that Joey will be the team captain someday. He's already becoming the leader."

"But how good a gymnast?"

"Very good. His strength is improving every day, and his difficulty is coming around. I think Joey could be one of the best. I only hope I'm around to see it."

"Don't talk that way." Haley turned the key on the grating that covered the entrance of the restaurant. Chris held the door to the outside open for her to pass. They kissed and parted ways, each thinking about what it was like to be Joey's age and how far they had come since then, and how far they each had yet to go.

The gym has a funny, surreal look to it while the lights are warming up, Patrick thought. It was still early, ten minutes before workout was scheduled to start. Patrick, Dallas, Joey, and Ty were stretching on the mat, and the others had yet to show. It was a foregone conclusion that Chris would be his customary twenty minutes late.

"I can't believe it!" yelled a voice from within Coach Lowery's office.

"Oh no, I bet we're gonna get our butts kicked today," said Dallas, who was used to getting the brunt of Coach's wrath.

"Relax, Dallas," said Patrick. "I don't think that yell was from anger as much as amazement." Patrick had noticed that Coach Lowery was emerging from his office with several sheets of paper in his hands.

"Patrick!" Coach Lowery called to his team captain as he approached. "What teams do we usually get for the Pioneer Invitational?"

"Well, not many, Coach. Mostly, just the smaller clubs around here. Firestorm came up from Atlanta, and Pyramid Gymnastics came from Memphis, but that was it. Why?"

"That's all about to change, Patty, me boy," Coach Lowery said in his worst Irish accent. "I hold in my hands entry forms from just about every big team in the country! Lake Erie, Texas Star, Empire State—they're all coming!" he said, shaking the entry forms in his clenched fist. "This will be the biggest Pioneer Invitational ever."

"Don't suppose it's 'cause we run such a good meet?" asked Joey.

"I don't think so," replied Coach Lowery.

"I guess everyone is gunnin' for us," said Dallas.

"Yeah, everyone wants one more shot to knock us down a peg before NTIs," concluded Patrick.

"Sure," added Ty, "but in our own gym?"

"Where better?" asked Patrick. "If anyone can beat us in our own house, what better way to set us up when we meet them at nationals?"

"We just better make sure it doesn't happen," a voice came from the locker room door as Chris walked in, on time for the first time in two months.

"Yeah," added Mackee, also entering. "It sounds like a good idea, but they're gonna have to go through us first."

"Well, since we're all in agreement here," added Coach Lowery, "I suggest we get to work. Let's start on 'pig'. Everybody hit five routines on each event."

The gymnasts gathered their bags and made their way to pommel horse, their first event.

"Hey, Slash," called Dallas. "I bet I hit my five before you do."

"Dude, that's not even a fair bet. You know I'll hit faster than you"

"Okay," added Dallas, "I'll double with Ty, and I bet we hit our ten before you and anyone else hit your five each."

"You're on. What's the bet?"

"Who's your partner?"

"What's the bet?"

"Steak dinner."

"Cool. I'll take Joey."

"Are you serious?" asked Dallas, breaking into uncontrolled laughter.

"Dead serious. Joey and I will finish our ten sets before you and Ty. The stakes are steaks, so to speak."

"Wait a minute," interrupted Patrick. "Can anybody get in on this?"

"What do you say, Dallas? Let Patrick combine with AJ and Mackee for ten routines?" asked Chris.

"Ten? Why not fifteen?" replied Dallas.

"We are obviously the weakest pommel horsemen on the team," added Mackee.

"Okay, your team has to hit ten sets between the three of you," concluded Dallas. "The teams that lose combine to buy steak dinner for us ... I mean the winners."

"Everybody got it?" asked Chris. With a nod, all were in agreement, and the contest was on.

Each gymnast took his five minutes to warm up.

"Okay, so who goes first?" Chris asked Dallas.

"Well, Patrick has the weakest team on horse. They go first."

"That's okay for pommels, but what about when we get to their strong events?" asked Joey.

"It won't matter," said Mackee. "We're gonna be so far ahead of you guys, who's goin' first will be the least of your problems."

"Right," said Chris. "How 'bout you lead it off, loudmouth?"

"My pleasure."

"Here's the rules." said Dallas, breaking Mackee's concentration. "We alternate guys. If you fall, you're done, next guy's turn. Got it?"

"Yeah, we got it. Now, can we get on with it?" asked Patrick.

Mackee chalked his hands again, spit into his palms, blew a heavy sigh, and mounted the horse. He was only five skills into his routine when trouble started. His leg brushed the horse, which threw him off balance. Before he could recover, he found himself under the horse, flat on his back.

"Okay, so this may take a little longer than I thought," concluded Mackee.

"One down," remarked Dallas. "Go ahead, Joey. Age before beauty."

Joey gave Chris a look that seemed to say, "Hope for the best." Chris's return glance was one of reassurance. Joey mounted the horse and got into early trouble. He missed a hand placement on the pommel and found himself just trying to stay on the horse. Skills that were normally easy now were made more difficult because instead of having a pommel in one hand, he now had both hands on the horse leather, swinging around the pommel.

"Come on Joey, stay with it!" shouted Patrick, the rest of the team giving him an odd stare for supporting the opposition.

Joey continued to struggle but never fell off. By the time he got to his dismount, everyone was on his feet, rooting. Well, everyone except Dallas, who was busy in the chalk bucket, more concerned about his own upcoming routine. Joey managed a labored but successful dismount.

"Way to go, squirt!" said Chris, giving his partner a hard pat on the back that nearly knocked him to the ground. Joey didn't mind, however, because he had successfully led off his team.

Although the attention continued to be on the routines that followed, Chris took the opportunity to bolster his partner.

"Do you have any idea what you just did?"

"Yeah, I just hit my first set. Got us closer to a steak dinner."

"Right, but you did more than that," Chris said. "You know where you got into trouble early in your routine?"

"Do I remember? It scared me to death. I don't know how I stayed on."

"I'll tell you how you stayed on. You did three skills that have more difficulty than the rest of your routine. You just increased the start value of your pommel horse routine by almost two full points!"

Joey looked at Chris with amazement. "That was an accident. I probably couldn't do that again if my life depended on it."

"But you did it! You proved you could make it. If you worked on it, I bet you could put that in your routine. You would have one of the most difficult routines in the country!"

"Gee, Chris, I don't know."

"What's to know? Listen, I could care less if I gotta buy part of a steak dinner for Dallas. I want you to try that combination in each of the routines you have left."

"What if I miss?"

"Who cares? It's just a stupid game. Besides, if you can increase the value of your routine, isn't it worth a steak dinner?"

"I guess you're right," Joey pondered a moment. "Okay, I'll go for it. But you gotta tell me one thing, Chris"

"Okay, what?"

"What did I do?"

Chris laughed and then proceeded to describe in detail the combination that Joey had accidentally put into his routine.

The game worked through the order, everyone hitting his routine. Then, it came back to Joey.

"Okay, Joey. Come on, you can do it. Do it just how you see it in your head," said Chris.

Joey worked the combination in his next routine, but he fell.

"Don't get down, squirt. That was real close. It'll be there. Keep working, keep your chin up."

The team continued the game, some hitting, some falling. Chris continued to encourage Joey to do the new combination, but each time he tried, he fell. Joey was beginning to get discouraged.

"That's ten!" boasted Dallas. "We pick next event, and we're going to vault! See you losers in the showers. By the way, McClure, I like my steak rare, very rare." Dallas laughed and moved on to set the vault table for Ty's best event.

"Chris, I gotta go back to my original set. Otherwise, we'll get smoked." Joey had become dejected.

"Look, Joey," said Chris, "I'm not gonna worry about this stupid game. Besides, we're not that far behind." Chris was becoming more concerned with Joey's attitude and mood than the game. It was time for a concession. "If you don't hit your next routine, go back to your old routine. If you're concerned with catching up with those guys, we'll catch up with no problem."

Patrick hit his fifth routine, bringing his team total to nine. It was now Joey's turn again, Chris having finished his five, the most a single partner could make. Joey took a breath and mounted the horse. Without thinking about the combination, Joey just turned himself to face the length of the horse and tried only to swing his legs as fast as he could and try to keep up with his hands. A smile came over his face as he made it through the new combination with almost simplistic ease. The rest of the routine moved with Swiss timing. Joey flew to his dismount, raising his clenched fists in defiance upon his landing.

"That's it, Joey!" Chris yelled at his partner. "That's seven. We just need three more sets."

Within minutes, Chris and Joey found themselves only two routines away from Patrick, Mackee, and the team's weakest pommel horseman, AJ.

"Finally!" said AJ, hitting his second routine, making ten for his team. "Let's get to vault. Dallas and Ty already have seven!"

By the time Joey hit his fifth routine, Ty and Dallas were already on their third event, high bar.

"Hey, Dallas!" shouted Chris as he and Joey headed for vault, "these are legitimate routines, right? Releases and all?"

"But, of course, my friend," Dallas responded with a chuckle and a one-event cushion.

"This is where we catch up, Joey," Chris said to his partner in a volume that only they could hear. "You just haul down the runway. As soon as you land, move fast. I'm gonna be right behind you."

It took Patrick, AJ, and Mackee just twelve vaults to stick their ten, putting them on high bar with Dallas and Ty, who had hit only three routines. Ty was having trouble catching releases.

"Here we go, squirt," said Chris.

The two proceeded to put on a vaulting exhibition. Joey would lead with his new vault, the layout Tsukahara. No sooner did he stick his landing did he sprint back to the other end of the runway, moving just in time to avoid a collision with his senior teammate, who was practically on his heels with his own vault. Joey paused at the end of the runway just long enough to check his starting point on the floor. Then, he was off again for his next vault. Chris passed Joey going the other way. Chris didn't bother to check his starting point, just making a quick U-turn without breaking stride and racing down the vault runway for his next vault.

By the time Chris and Joey had landed six of their vaults, the rest of the team had stopped to watch the amazing display of endurance and stamina.

"What are you guys doin'?" Dallas barked at the teammates that were watching in jaw-dropped awe. "Those guys are gonna catch us if you don't get goin'!" Dallas was beginning to panic.

"Those guys are incredible!" said Patrick.

By the time the next high bar routine was finished, Chris had landed the final vault of their tandem.

"Uuhhnn!" yelled Joey as he dropped to prone position in a pool of sweat on the carpet next to the high bar chalk bucket.

"Now the fun begins, eh, Dallas?" said Chris, trying hard not to show that he was nearly spent from vault.

"Maybe for you, McClure. Ty and I are still five routines ahead of you guys," answered Dallas as he mounted the bar.

"We'll see. Joey, get your grips on!" called Chris, already in his grips and chalking up his hands.

Dallas caught his release. "Ha, I'm on my way to six, Slash!" Dallas cranked his last giants and dismounted with a double back in layout position, landing effortlessly on the dismount mat.

"That's six! Come on, Ty, let's keep it going."

Mackee was the next to go. The rings specialist of the team, he did not have the most difficult high bar routine, but you couldn't tell that to him. To Mackee, his routine was as hard for him to make as any of the better guys. Then, Mackee's release move, a front flip regrasp, was short. He fell to his chest, missing his third routine in a row.

Joey was still slow to get his grips on. Chris sat next to him on the folded mat. "Okay, we don't have the luxury of a warm-up, so we'll have to do cold routines," said Chris.

"What about my release?"

"Don't worry. If you don't make it, consider that turn a warm-up. If you do make it, we've got a routine in the bag."

Mackee, in disgust, stormed off of the mat, pulling off the tape that wrapped around his grips to help keep the old, worn Velcro attached. Mackee plopped down next to Chris, mumbling incoherently. The wad of tape ended up on the floor in front of Chris.

"What's that, Mack?" asked Chris. Upon getting no response, Chris bent over to pick up the wad. Mackee, still visibly upset and tearing at the tape on the left wrist in a spastic rage, slipped, his hand coming off of the tape just as

Chris was sitting up. Mackee's right elbow collided with Chris's left temple. The force knocked Chris off of the mat.

"Oh, wow, Chris. I'm sorry. Are you okay?"

Chris, woozy from the collision, tried to regain his balance. The hit had made him dizzy and blurred his vision for a moment.

"Yeah, I'm okay. Did you ever think about joining professional wrestling, Mack?" said Chris, still shaking off the effect of the blow.

"That makes seven!" yelled Ty upon landing his double-twisting dismount.

"Chris, do you want me to go first?" asked Joey, who could see that Chris was still trying to gain his composure.

"No, I'm fine, kid. You rest a little more. I'll get us going."

Chris got chalk, looked at the high bar, and wondered when his vision would return.

"Hey, plowboy," Chris called, "which bar do I grab?"

"How many do you see?"

"Three."

"Go for the one in the middle."

"Thanks."

No one could tell if Chris was serious or putting on. Then again, they never could.

The first sign that Chris was okay would come with his first combination. Once he got through a series of difficult one-arm giants and pirouettes, everyone breathed easier knowing that he was in fact back to normal.

Chris cranked his giants faster, readying for his release move, the full-and-a-half twisting Geinger. Just prior to his release, Chris's vision went blurry again. He knew he had to do his release; Joey was counting on him. His release came later than usual. Everybody knew that meant trouble, even for Chris. They all stood frozen, except for Coach Lowery, who jumped in under the bar to catch Chris as best he could. Chris knew the release was late, and lost in midair, he extended his arms blindly, hoping to somehow find the bar. Instead, his body collided with the bar, his upper arms and the bridge of his nose taking the brunt of the impact. The hit caused his body to lash backward and rotate. Coach Lowery made the spot of his life, grabbing the 165-pound senior around the midsection, suspending him just inches above the floor before his body took the force of a fall onto his neck.

All of the Pioneers gathered around. Chris, his nose obviously broken and his arms badly bruised, fought to maintain consciousness.

"I'm fine, I'm fine. Let me get up and finish." Chris tried to get to his feet but was restrained by his coach.

"I don't think so, Chris. You're done for the day. If you're okay, you better go get that nose looked at."

It was at that moment that Chris noticed that his nose was bleeding.

"My nose! It's bleeding! It's *bleeding!*" Chris began to panic.

"Chris! It's okay. You took a shot. Joey's getting ice. Just relax," said Coach.

Chris was not about to relax. "No, you don't understand! My nose is … I have to leave!"

Before Coach Lowery could give Chris the okay to leave, he was gone. For a moment, everyone stood looking at each other. Dallas broke the silence. "Well, I guess Slash can talk a good game, but when it comes down to it, he's just as human as the rest of us."

"Shut up, Dallas," said Joey. "He just had his life pass in front of his face and his lights knocked out."

"Yeah, Dallas," added AJ, "If that had been you, you'd still be cryin'."

"Give him time to clean out his shorts," added Patrick. "He'll be right back out here, ready to kick your ass, Dallas."

"All right, you guys, break it up." ordered Coach. "Let's call it a day. You guys hit the showers. I'll see you tomorrow."

Before they could get to the locker room door, the team heard the roar of Chris's motorcycle as it hastily left the parking lot.

"Good," Joey thought, "Haley's not home yet." This meant that she was probably still at work or at the gym getting a late workout and probably hadn't heard from Chris. Joey quickly went into the study, where he knew he'd have privacy, and dialed Chris's number.

"Hello?" came the voice on the other end.

"Chris?"

"Yeah, speaking."

"Chris, it's me, Joey. You okay?"

"Oh, hey, squirt. Yeah, I'm fine. Just a bloody nose and a couple sore arms is all."

"Good. You had all of us worried."

"Why? 'Cause the mighty Chris finally missed and landed with his foot planted squarely in his mouth?"

"Hey, man, we all miss. It's just human. In fact, it was kinda refreshing to see that you belong to the same race as the rest of us. I just wanted to make sure you were okay."

"Thanks. Naw, I'm fine. I don't think anything is damaged too bad."

"You sure don't sound very convincing."

"Well, maybe my pride is bruised just a tad."

"If your ego is the only thing that takes a beating out of this, consider yourself lucky."

"I already do. Thanks for the call, Joey."

"Don't mention it, dude. By the way, you talk to Haley yet?"

"No. Should I?"

"Well, if I know her, you better talk to her before she hears about it from somebody else. The way stories go around in this town, by the time she gets wind of it, they'll have you dead and still hanging from the high bar!"

"Maybe you're right. I think she's working tonight. I'll give her a call after I get off the phone with you so she doesn't worry."

"Good idea. Keep your chin up. I'll see you at workout tomorrow."

"Okay. And, Joey … thanks."

"Sure thing, pal."

Chris hung up the phone and stared at it.

"You really should tell them, Chris," came the voice behind him. "They have a right to know."

"No. Not yet, Haley. I'll tell them when the time is right."

"What if that time never comes?"

"You let me worry about that."

FIFTEEN

▼

It was not unusual for Chris to be missing at the beginning of a workout. In fact, yesterday was the first time he had ever been on time. But today, everyone was looking for him to show up. The fall that Chris had taken was not unlike any fall that anyone else on the team had endured a hundred times. But for Chris, it was noticeably different. He never missed. So, aside from being painful, the crash was also visably traumatic for him. No one could start workout until they knew that everything was back to business as usual. Tension was an understatement.

"All right, you guys," said Coach, trying to break the nervous gridlock that possessed the team. "We've come to expect McClure's tardiness. Let's not procrastinate at his expense."

"I talked to him last night," said Joey. "He sounded down, but he said he would be here."

"If you ask me, I bet he's too scared to show his face after the shot he took yesterday," said Dallas.

"Well, nobody's askin' you, Dallas," answered Mackee.

"Yeah," added Patrick, "I seem to recall a blond sophomore a couple years ago who took a whole week off after facing a double back off p-bars."

"I missed a leg on my tuck."

"Yeah," joined AJ, "and if my memory serves me right, you bawled your eyes out. Seems to me you've got no room to talk."

"But at least I didn't bail out on the team right before the biggest meet of the season." Dallas, growing tired of the attack he had started, was now nose-to-nose with AJ.

"Nobody said Chris is bailing out on the team. He's just his customary late is all," said Joey, trying to squeeze himself between the two.

"All right, you guys, break it up," came Coach Lowery's commanding voice. "It doesn't matter whether McClure graces us with his presence or not today. We have a meet to get ready for, and it is not getting done while you guys sit around acting macho. Now get to work!"

All agreed that regardless whether Chris was absent or just very late, there was a job to be done, one that each had to do on his own. But in the back of each of their minds, they wondered if the team would ever be the same.

Workout was nearly finished. Those who hadn't started their conditioning were finishing their assignment of routines.

"Champions are not a flash in the pan, Dallas," said Coach, who was pushing the senior, who had fallen behind to finish his routines. "If you are not willing to invest the time and energy now, how can you expect to have what it takes when the time comes?"

"I don't know, Coach," answered Dallas in a cocky tone. "Why don't you ask Johnson? He works his brains out, and still, he's number seven on the team."

"But he's climbing right over you, Dallas," said Mackee.

"Not in this lifetime, Mack."

"Don't be so sure, Mr. Dallas," quipped Patrick. "Don't let him get to you, Joey."

"I never have," answered Joey, who, although acting unaffected, doubled the pace of his sit-ups.

Dallas finished his routines and started over toward the others, who were midway through their conditioning. Dallas looked at the clock, noticing that there were only ten minutes remaining in the workout. "Well, I guess Slash is a no-show, eh, fellas?"

"Put a sock in it, Dallas," said Patrick.

"You gonna help me, Goodman?"

"If he doesn't, I will," came a voice from the locker room door.

"Christopher!" said Dallas, surprised to see Chris, who sported two black eyes, the result of his nose injury. His sullen appearance gave Dallas the feeling that Chris was in no mood to retaliate his verbal attacks.

"We've been worried sick about you, pal," he said sarcastically. "How you feelin' after that thumpin' you took yesterday?"

"Just strong enough to kick your a—"

"McClure!" shouted Coach. "Where have you been? We have a meet to prepare for!"

"That's why I came by, Coach. I didn't want to disturb workout, but I wanted to see everybody before you all left." Everybody gathered around Chris.

"I didn't want to leave you guys hangin', so I figured I better come in and tell you guys in person."

"Tell us what?" asked Joey.

"I'm quitting gymnastics."

"You're *what*!" demanded Coach.

"I just can't do it anymore," admitted Chris.

"Come over here, Chris," Coach said, leading him away from the others for a little privacy. "I realize that you've been through a helluva thing. It hurts to take a shot like that, especially for someone like you, who's not accustommed to falling, much less taking a buster like you took."

"Coach, I really do appreciate what you're trying to do, but believe me, it goes much deeper than just a fall off of an event. I just can't explain it to you now."

"I know, Chris. You think that the weight of the world is on your shoulders, and you just want to get away. I understand."

"No, Coach, I don't think you do. I just don't think I can do it anymore."

"Look, Chris. Don't make any decisions right now. I realize what happened yesterday was quite devastating. I imagine for someone like you, never having missed a skill like that, when you do take your first fall, well, you must think that the world is falling in on you. You may not believe it, but that's what each of us feel each time we expect to be on and find ourselves on our butts beneath the equipment. But, you can't end your career over a fall.

"Everybody thinks that this meet is the most important of the season. Even though it is our only home meet of the season, it's the results from state championships that get us into the NTIs. Go ahead and take some time off. We'll get by this weekend; don't worry about us. You just get away and do some thinking. There will always be a spot for you on this team. I think if you just give it some time, you'll see, you'll be okay. It happens to all of us. But to the rest of us, it happens a lot more often. You just have to learn how to live with disappointment. Remember, the mark of a true champion is not how talented you are, but rather your ability to overcome adversity. I think you'll come back stronger."

"I hope you're right, Coach," conceded Chris, knowing that there was no need in debating the issue.

"Me too, son. Me too."

Coach Lowery led Chris back to the rest of the team.

"Fellas, Chris is gonna take a little time off. As you can probably guess, Chris is still a little shook from the shot he took the other day. He'll be back before you know it."

Coach's words brought very little consolation to the other Pioneers. Although Coach's delivery sounded like Chris was just taking some time to think, everybody felt that Chris's words spoke the real truth. He may never be back.

"You guys train hard and kick some tail." Chris's words of encouragement seemed somewhat shallow as he made his way toward the exit. All the team could do was watch him leave. Joey stood in obvious shock, eyes glazed over in blind stare.

"Bullcrap, Chris!" said Patrick, running to catch Chris before he made the door. "While the rest of us have to come back each day after taking as many busters as we can tolerate, you fall one time and you think that's it? It's time to hang up the grips? Something's going on here, McClure. We've sweat blood together. You can't just walk out on us, not now. You owe us, man."

Chris just stared at the floor. Patrick glared at Chris, waiting for a response, any response. The old Chris would've retaliated with fists flying and wisecracks coming out both sides of his mouth, but this time, nothing. Joey stood in disbelief with the other Pioneers. Coach just ran his hands through his hair, scratching his scalp.

Patrick realized that his challenges would not be met. "Alright. Go ahead and quit, Chris. We don't need you, anyway. We were great before you got here. We'll do fine when you're gone!" Patrick the locker room door open, nearly ripping it off the hinges.

The rest of the Pioneers, save Joey, slowly made their way to the locker room, talking to themselves in disbelief. Joey just stood and stared at Chris, eyes watering. Coach Lowery walked up to Chris and put his arm around him.

Chris and Coach Lowery shook hands as Chris left for the parking lot. Just as Chris turned to leave, he looked back to see Joey, still standing in the same position he was in when Chris came in, his eyes filled with tears, his lip trembling.

"Joey, call me later, okay?" Chris said, unable to get Joey's attention. Joey just continued to stare into space, unable to react to what he had just heard.

Though each Pioneer realized that he could get through a workout without Chris, few doubted how the season would end if Chris were not a part of the team.

Joey could not say what he wanted to say to Chris on the telephone. The telephone is reserved for polite conversation or business. For real conversation, there is no substite for face-to-face.

Joey didn't know exactly what he was going to say to Chris. He figured that it would come to him before he got to Chris's house, but as he steered his bicycle into the McClure driveway after school, he realized that he was no closer to what he was going to say than when he started the six mile trek. Ringing the doorbell did nothing to bring his thoughts to a logical assemblence, either.

The door opened to reveal Chris's mother. "Hello, Joey. How are you?"

"Fine, Mrs. McClure. Is Chris around?"

"Who is it, Mom?" came the voice from within the house.

"It's Joey Johnson, dear."

"Don't just stand there. Let him in."

Joey entered the house to see Chris in the living room, his feet propped up in a big recliner. He was using the TV remote like a six-gun, shooting down the programs that didn't meet his approval, revealing another, similarly repugnant program.

"I tell ya, there are no good programs on TV anymore."

"Can I get you anything, Joey?" asked Mrs. McClure.

"No thanks, Mrs. M. I would like to talk to Chris alone, if I could."

"Why, sure, Joey. I'll be in the basement, finishing the laundry if you need me. Do you need anything, Chris?"

"No, thank you, Mom. I'm fine." Chris turned off the television and discarded the remote. "So, Joey, what's on your mind?"

"Okay," Joey had an angle, "so you come back and you don't do the really hard stuff. Just do really *good* stuff. "

"It won't work, Joey."

"Sure it will. You just have to take out a couple of skills, and your routines won't be as risky but will still score well."

"It won't work."

"Why not?" asked Joey, now frustrated.

"Because … it's not me. I … can't go just halfway. Sooner or later, I'd try the hard stuff again, and then where would I be?"

"You should hear yourself," barked Joey, turning from frustrated to digusted. "If somebody told me three months ago that you'd be sounding like this, I'd say they've got the wrong Chris McClure. You were the one who convinced us that the goal was worth the risk. You made us believe in ourselves when we had nothing else to believe in. You were the one trying to convince Patrick to try the bigger skills so he could be a champion. You convinced me to try harder when I had no reason to. You turned our team into a team. With you, we knew we could win. You gave us the attitude and the drive to win. You were the one who taught us how to approach a meet in such a way that we knew walking in that we would all hit our sets. You made our team a contender. Or was all that a lie?"

Chris sat in his chair with his head down. In his struggle to find the words, he could not look Joey in the eye. "No, Joey, it wasn't a lie. But it wasn't me, either. You guys had it inside yourselves to do what you've done. You didn't need me. Look at the Wolverine. You take my scores out of the team score, and you guys still win. And as far as what I've meant to the team, Dallas is probably happier now that I'm gone, and now you don't have to worry about being seventh man anymore."

"All right, I didn't want to talk about what you've meant to me, but since you brought it up, let's talk about me. You're right. Without you, I don't have to work to be the number six man on the team, but what you did in coming here was make me work three times as hard for any of my scores to count. The thing you probably didn't count on was that by making me work harder, I've become competitive with the other guys on the team. If you quit now, I have no reason to work as hard. You get to walk away, and I have to put up with everybody else telling me that I haven't earned anything, that if it hadn't been for you quitting, I'd still be the seventh man on the team. Well, I'm not gonna let you screw me over like that just because you've found out that you're not perfect, and that, just like the rest of us, the results of your efforts are not predictable, automatic, or guaranteed. You're just gonna have to go on with life like the rest of us, unsure. And, if that means me being the seventh man on a championship team, so be it. If I had to choose between being the sixth man without effort or have to struggle to break onto the team, I prefer the challenge. Anything else is cheap."

Chris let down the ottoman on the recliner, rose, and walked to the window, avoiding eye contact with the gymnast that meant the most to him. "I appreciate your concern for me, Joey, really I do. But nothing you can say will make me come back. My problems are just too big right now."

"So that's the way it's gonna be, Chris? Well, I don't buy it. No problem should have kept you out of the gym if you really wanted to come back."

"If only you knew, Joey," said Chris. staring out the window.

"Well, maybe someday, you'll share what's really bothering you. Until then, you can count on me to bother you, continuously." With nothing more to say, Joey excused himself and left the house of his best friend.

Chris watched as Joey mounted his bicycle and rode away.

"Were you listening?" Chris said, still looking out the window.

"Yes," came the voice of his mother, entering the room. "I think Haley's right. You've got to tell them the truth. They have a right to know."

"I think you're right." Chris nodded his lowered head. "I'll tell them when the time is right. I hope they understand."

"If they're your friends, they will, son."

"I hope you're right."

SIXTEEN

▼

"Welcome to Pioneer Gymnastics and the Pioneer Gymnastics Invitational"

The computer-generated sign hung over the gym entrance. Joey looked at the sign and tried to imagine what it would be like to be on the awards stand and hold the first-place trophy high over his head with the rest of his teammates, including Chris. After all, it was with Chris that the team enjoyed so much success this season, and, in Joey's mind, the only way the Pioneers could hope to take such a lofty position again. Of course, the others thought there was a chance, but Joey knew better. Joey entered the gym and reported to the locker room to try his best to prepare for the competition, only hours away.

"Joey, I'm glad you're here," said Dallas upon entering the locker room. "I need to talk to you."

"Look, Dallas. I got nothing to say to you. Ever since Chris first came here, you've been trying to get rid of him. Well, now he's gone, and I hold you partially responsible. I wish it had been you that got wrapped around that pipe and not him."

"Listen, I know you don't like me very much, and Chris and I didn't get along, but I had nothing to do with Chris getting hurt, and I certainly had nothing to do with him quitting the team. I know we need him as much as you do, but we just have to go on."

"Yeah, but there's a big difference between me going on and you going on."

"And what's that, squirt?"

"I'm hoping Chris will come back and make us champions. You don't want him to come back and could care less if it costs us a national championship or a great friend."

"Hey, I know things were never peachy with Chris, but that doesn't blind me from the fact that we are really gonna need him if we're gonna win, and without him our chances are pretty slim. Either way, we have to train and prepare ourselves for competition. We can't waste time hoping he's gonna come back and save us."

"I guess it's just easy for some of us to go on as if this were the desired outcome." Joey punctuated his dig by moving himself to another part of the locker room, as far away as possible from Dallas.

Mackee, Ty, and AJ entered the locker room together just as Joey had positioned himself away from Dallas and threw his gym bag to the floor to further accent his anger.

"Ooh," said Mackee, "do either of you guys sense what I'm sensing?"

"Um, could it be ... tension, Mack?" returned AJ sarcastically.

"Give the man a cigar. He got it on the first try," poked Ty.

"Better to give him a knife," quipped Mackee. "I think we'll need it to cut through all this bad karma these two are putting out. Hey, fellas, lighten up a little."

"But, Mack, he—" Joey began.

"Forget about it, little guy," interupted Mackee. "It's past. Let's get on with the business at hand."

"Hey, guys. What's up?" Patrick greeted his teammates upon his entrance.

"You don't want to know, Pat," said Ty.

"Well, I can probably guess, and I bet it has something to do with one Chris McClure."

"Who else?" confirmed Mackee.

Patrick decided that it was time to step forward and try to lead his teammates. "Look, fellas, I'm as worked up about losing Chris as the rest of you, but we gotta look at the big picture. When we stomped those guys at the Wolverine, Chris had a lot to do with us doin' a great job, but he was not the only Pioneer looking good out there. You take away his performance, and you still have a darn good showing by the rest of us. In fact, you take his scores completely out, and we still win by a pretty convincing margin."

"Yeah, but his contribution is much more than the score. He pushed us. He motivated us," added Joey.

"Oh, I don't deny that we were inspired, but Chris can't be the *only* source of inspiration and motivation. Use your knowledge of what you were capable of in the last meet to move you to do better. Use the knowledge that even though we all looked good in Michigan, none of us have hit our peak yet, and our only limitations are the ones we place on ourselves. Look, I know we're all coming into this meet with a slightly different perspective than what we had before Chris got hurt, but that shouldn't stop us from havin' some fun and showin' these guys that they can't just walk into our backyard and take our trophies away."

All eyes were on Patrick. "I say we go out and be cocky as hell, do our best routines, and show these guys what it's like to come up against Pioneers on our turf."

"Yeah," added Dallas, trying his best to help motivate the troops, "we don't need that waste. We never did."

"That does it, Dallas!" screamed Joey, who had heard all he wanted to hear against his pal. Joey lurched forward, his hands outstretched toward Dallas's throat. As a reflex, Patrick and Ty grabbed Joey before he could reach his mark. Mackee and AJ then had to restrain Dallas, who was not about to be intimidated.

"What the hell is goin' on here?" screamed Coach Lowery, entering the locker room to the sight of his charges trying to dismember one another. Upon the boom of his voice, the Pioneers broke their hold on the combatants, and the hotheads became cool.

"Dallas started it, Coach!" said Joey.

"I don't care who started it, Johnson, I'm finising it, right here. We've got enough to worry about out in that gym without the team trying to tear each other apart! Now, you guys kiss and make up, and let's get out th—" Coach Lowery's words suddenly fell off as the attention of the athletes shifted to the dark figure that filled the entrance to the locker room.

"Chris!" screamed Joey. "You're back! I knew you couldn't stay away! Hurry and get changed. Warm-ups start in five min—"

"I'm not here to compete, Joey," said Chris in an apologetic tone. "I felt that I owed you guys an explanation for leaving the way I did."

"You sure picked a heckuva time to share this with us, Slash," said Dallas coldly.

"Well, if it's worth anything, I didn't want you guys thinking I intentionally meant to let you down."

"I don't think you intentionally meant to try to cram that high bar up your nose either, Chris," said Patrick.

"No, I didn't. But, it's a little deeper than that. I thought I was dying," confessed Chris.

"You punch my lights out like that," added Mackee, "I'd think I'm dyin', too!"

"No, really, Mack. I thought I was starting to die. For real," said Chris with a tone of finality in his voice. "You know I told you guys that my dad left me and my mom when I was a kid? Well, that was kind of a half truth." Chris sighed, then continued.

"My dad died when I was very young. He died from a brain aneurysm. He had a rare disease called Berry's Aneurysm. It's a genetic defect. You have a weak blood vessel in your brain. The cruel thing about it is that it doesn't affect, in any way, your growth and development. To everyone else, you look, act, and grow just like normal. The difference is that at some point in your life, regardless of health, diet, temperament, or age, the aneurysm grows, eventually pops, and you just drop dead."

The Pioneers and their coach stood in dumb silence. Then Patrick spoke. "Chris, do you—"

"Yeah, I've inherited it."

"How long have you known?" added Joey.

"Since I was about eight. I had a pretty nasty bike wreck, and it knocked me out. Being a nurse, my mom had all kinds of tests run on me. That's when they found it."

"So," asked Joey cautiously, "how long do you have?"

"I have no clue. Could be today, tomorrow, next week, or next year, or even ten years. I have no way of knowing. I just know that since I was eight years old, I've been looking for warning signs."

"And then Tuesday ... " added Patrick.

"The blurred vision, the bloody nose, the hyperventilation, all symptoms that the vessel had broken. Sometimes it takes days, even weeks. Sometimes you have about five minutes before you check out. And, those are the lucky ones. With others, the aneurysm doesn't blow right away. With some, it just swells and presses on your brain as it grows. Then, it starts with blurred vision, and you lose coordination, and then you can't control your muscles at all. Eventually, you lose speech and eye movement, then you become a vegetable." The team looked at him in disbelief.

"And if that's not enough ... " Chris paused to choke back his emotion, "then, the last thing you actually do feel is excruciating pain. Pain you can do nothing about because nothing works. You can't even cry."

"Chris," said Patrick, "we had no idea."

"Of course you didn't."

"But, Chris," surmised Mackee, "you're still here. Obviously, it wasn't time, was it?"

"No, Mack, I don't think so. Your elbow into the side of my head probably had something to do with my blurred vision."

"And, I bet that bar crashing into your face had a little to do with the nosebleed and disorientation," added AJ.

"Do you think maybe a degree of panic could cause hyperventilation?" asked Ty.

The look on Chris's face changed from fear and depression to calm. Tension had given way to relief. Smiles had replaced shock.

"So, I guess you'll be back soon?" asked Joey. The room fell silent once again.

Chris's face became sullen and his eyes dropped to the floor, avoiding contact with his teammates. "No, not now," he said.

"Why not?" demanded Joey. "You know you're okay, at least as okay as you were. Why not come back?"

"Well, first of all, I still have some tests the doctors want to put me through, and, besides, I'm still a little shook. I don't know when I'll come back, if ever."

The room fell silent a third time as the Pioneers realized yet again that they would have to pursue their quest without their strongest gymnast.

"Look, you guys," said Coach Lowery, "I know how much we would like to have Chris out there with us, and I bet Chris would like to be out there just as much. However, we do have a job to do, and it won't get done from in this locker room, so let's get to it!"

"Coach," asked Joey, "can Chris stay on the floor with us instead of sitting in the stands?"

"Naw," said Chris, "it's not right. I'm not a competitor."

"But," added Coach Lowery, "you are a Pioneer. If anyone has earned the right to be with the team, you have. I'd be hurt if you didn't."

"All right, you guys," said Patrick, "Pioneer Circle." The gymnasts, including Chris, stood in a circle. At once, all shouted "Pioneers!" And, all did a standing backflip to a stuck landing. Then, arm in arm, the Pioneers emerged from the locker room.

Nothing had prepared them for what they saw. The gym that they trained in on a daily basis was usually occupied by no more than thirty or so gymnasts at a time. For the first time in Pioneer history, every available space in the gym was taken by either gymnasts or spectators. The Pioneers stopped in their tracks.

"I don't guess all these people are here to see me, are they, Coach?" said Joey in a sarcastic tone.

"Somehow, I don't think so, Johnson," answered Dallas.

"All right, you guys," said Coach Lowery, "let's not get rattled. This is your gym, this is your equipment. You guys train here day after day. All you have to do is what you do every workout, just hit one set on each event, and we walk away with the team trophy. Now, let's get a good warm-up. We start competition on high bar."

But, this was not like the day after day. It was unreal to have so many people in their home away from home. And, the caliber of gymnasts there made it difficult to concentrate on the job at hand without stopping to look at the incredible gymnastics going on around them. Patrick caught Joey staring at the other gymnasts.

"Hey, Joey," said Patrick to the gawking youngster, standing with his mouth hanging open, "you tryin' to catch flies or what?"

"Oh, sorry, Patrick," said Joey, regaining his composure. "It' just weird seeing those skills by so many guys on our equipment."

"Yeah, it's kind of amazing what can be done when you put your mind to it. But, remember, it's okay to look around at the stuff goin' on, but don't get caught looking, or the intimidation show put on by your opponent has worked. And besides, if you miss your turn in warm-up because you're watching someone else, Coach will have your butt!" Joey was not the only gymnast taking in the sights. Many of the other gymnasts were finding it hard to maintain their concentration while some of the best gymnastics in the country was going on.

Chris had assumed the role of assistant coach. In addition to helping Coach Lowery keep the gymnasts focused, Chris had also become the designated guidance counselor.

Some say warm-ups is the best time to watch. Although the warm-up doesn't contain the pressure of hit or miss that competition has, a spectator can see gymnasts not only make skills that may be missed in competition, but also attempt them several times as they try to fine-tune the skill or a combination for the meet. Then, the spectator shares in the suspense, knowing what skill comes next and whether the gymnast will feel confident, because they hit it several times, or nervous, because they were less than perfect in the warm-up.

Warm-ups on floor went fairly well for the Pioneers. All of the boys were solid. Pommel horse was another story. While Mackee and AJ found it as difficult as usual to stay on, Joey was having trouble with his new combination. His frustration led him to revert to his original routine.

"What are you doing?" asked Chris.

"I'm warming up a routine I can hit!" said Joey.

"But you have a beautiful routine. Why change it now?"

"I'll score better if I hit my old routine instead of falling with the new routine."

"But you'll hit!" exclaimed Chris with confidence. "You just have to believe you can."

"But I tried! You saw what happened. I can't hit it. I only hit it half the time."

"But you will. And the confidence that you'll get from doing it in competition will fuel you for the rest of the season, and you'll really be able to help the team with the higher scores."

"That's if I hit."

"You'll hit." Joey realized that there was no point in trying to argue with Chris.

"Hey, Pat, check out pipe," called Mackee. Patrick glanced at high bar to see Marty Reynolds do his a combination of three consecutive releases, a double back over the bar to legs together reverse Hecht, to a straddled reverse Hecht, without breaking form or pace on his giants.

"Nice. Very nice," concluded Patrick.

"Now, that's what I call crazy," said AJ.

"Crazy is an interesting word, AJ." said Chris. "You have to be crazy to try it, but you have to be great to compete it." Chris threw a glance to Patrick, who knew that he, not Marty, was the subject of Chris's comment.

At the conclusion of the rotation, Chris also assumed the role of gofer, picking up whatever the other gymnasts had left behind.

"Hey, Slash," called Dallas, nearly empty-handed, "get my bag for me, will ya, pal?"

"Get it yourself. I'm not your slave!" came the defiant response.

"Just whose slave are you then?" came a voice from behind Chris. He turned quickly, prepared to fire off a sharp response until he realized the comment's origin. Standing in front of him were Marty Reynolds and Danny Diego.

"Danny, Marty, what are you guys doin'?"

"I think anybody in the joint could see what we're doin'," replied Danny. "The big Q is, what are you doin'?"

"Yeah, dude," added Marty, "what are you doin' in civilian clothes?"

Chris thought for a moment. He hadn't figured out how to tell the guys that he had been competing with and against for so long that his competitive career was over. After careful consideration, he decided to tell them everything.

"Well, you guys, I don't know exactly how to tell you this, but … I'm … quitting—"

"He's quit putting those stupid anchovies on his pizza!" Patrick cut him off before he could reveal the truth. "Gave him such a stomach bug, he had to scratch for today."

"Yeah, we're hatin' it," added Mackee. "You feelin' any better, pal?" Mackee turned Chris around as if to give him an examination.

"Well, I … uh … oof!" Chris had received Mackee's fist squarely in the stomach, out of sight of the others.

"See," said Mackee, "it still has him doubled over. Come on, Chris, you better sit down." Mackee led Chris to the next warm-up event.

"You sure he's okay?" asked Danny.

"Sure," said Patrick, "it's not like he's gonna die or anything."

The visitors looked at each other in curious disbelief. Satisfied, they headed back to their respective teams to continue their warm-up.

"That was close, Chris," said Mackee.

"Close to what? I was just going to tell them the same thing I had already told you guys."

"Look, we've got enough problems competing without you," added Patrick, rejoining the team. "We don't need them knowing that you've quit to give anyone an even greater psychological advantage."

"Besides," added Joey, "once quit isn't necessarily forever quit." The team was in silent agreement with Joey's wishful comment.

The remaining events warmed up predictably, with each gymnast looking true to form for his level of training. Mackee's strength on rings drew loud cheers from the crowd that was present for the pre-meet festivities. Ty looked sharp on vault, with each turn going higher and higher, as if fueled by the crowd's cheers of approval. Joey looked even more confident on vault than he did in Michigan. The crowd's cheering was new to Joey. The team began to notice.

"Hey, Pat, check out Joey," said Ty. "Every time he vaults, the crowd cheers a little louder."

"And the louder they cheer, the faster he runs and the higher he vaults."

"And then the louder they cheer. I think he's addicted," concluded Ty.

By the time the Pioneers got to parallel bars for their warm-up, what at first seemed like a sureal experience had turned into just another competition, except for Joey, for whom it was a coming-out party. Each turn for Joey had become another opportunity to please those who were watching. Dallas, who had become somewhat silenced from the intensity of the event, had become vocal again, challenging anyone on the team to match his level of expertise on his favorite event. It quickly became a contest between Dallas, the strongest p-bar worker on the team, and Joey, who had a new fan club. Each turn was followed by a one-up by the other, Dallas's turns fueled by his ego, Joey's by the shouts of his supporters in the stands.

"Fellas, this looks great," said Coach, "but I hope you intend to save some of this savvy for the competition," which meant for them to quit horsing around and focus on the meet.

The warm-up on the last event was crucial. Since it was also the first competitive event, the warm-up would set the tone for the start of competition. If the warm-up was good, not only would the gymnast gain confidence for the first event, but also a good warm-up on the last event could set the pace for the rest of the day.

Chris looked at Patrick, who himself was looking pensive going into the crucial warm-up.

"What's the matter, plowboy?"

"What do you think?"

"I think you've got a heck of a sweet routine that you're gonna hit. Your warm-up is awesome!" returned Chris, trying to bolster his pal.

"Yeah, sweet set, with no teeth. How am I supposed to compete with the likes of Marty Reynolds when he has such a beefy set and I've got nothing in mine."

"But he has to hit, dude. And you can only do what you can do."

"Still, I don't want to have to count on every gymnast who has more guts than me to miss their sets so my puny routine will be competitive." Patrick had become dejected.

"Listen, Miss Optimism, you pull your 'pity me' attitude out of the dirt and realize some facts. First, you have a meet to finish. No amount of moping is gonna change that. So, whether you have a competitive set or not, you *do* have to compete it. Second, if you're so steamed about the content of your exercise, change it. When this meet is over, get your butt up on the pipe and do something positive to beef up your routine instead of whining about it when you get into competition."

"Gentlemen, timed warm-ups have concluded. Please prepare for march-in," came the voice on the loud speaker.

The march-in proceedings were simple in comparison to the past few meets. Looking around at the other competitors, Patrick wondered why such great gymnasts would bother to come to such a reletively small competition. Could the Pioneers be that good? he thought. Perhaps they were there to gun for Chris. No, the whole team had to be the reason for the turnout. When the biggest prize is the team title, you don't gun for one gymnast. The plan is simple. Beat the favored team at home and squelch their momentum right before postseason competition. No, it *was* the team, not just one gymnast, that they all had come to challenge.

During the national anthem, Patrick glanced over to where the team would sit during its first event to see Coach Lowery standing to the left of Chris, both with their hands over their hearts. Chris was even singing. Although

Patrick couldn't hear his voice, he could see his lips moving. Patrick thought to himself that while it was unusual to see the Californian in anything other than tattered gym clothes or leather, it was most unusual to see him in a tie. A leather tie, but a tie all the same. There was one more unusual thing about Chris that Patrick was the sole witness to: tears were welling in his eyes.

"Gentlemen, report to your first event, and good luck."

As the boys reported to the judges, Coach Lowery was checking mats and Chris had assumed the role of cheerleader.

"All right, Joey," Chris cheered, "you're our starter. We need a good set to start us off. Remember to stretch all of your giants, especially in your blind changes, and don't forget to compress deep for your jam-in so the jam-out tops off in a handstand. Get a good tap before the dismount, and spot your landing early. We really need a stick!"

As he chalked up, Joey tried to absorb everything that Chris had said. Mackee, who followed Joey on high bar, was also getting chalk.

"Kid, rough translation: 'Do your best.'" Mackee gave Joey the simplified, *Reader's Digest Condensed* version of Chris's overzealous encouragement.

Joey stood under the bar, with his coach at his side, while waiting for the judges signal to begin.

"Start us off good, Joey," said Coach Lowery as he lifted his youngest athlete to the bar.

"I'll try, Coach." Joey blew a breath while adjusting his grip. As though he had started a tape player in his head, Joey could hear Chris's words while he was swinging. "Stretch your giants … ." The giants came with ease. "Especially in your blind change … " The blind change half turn, which could at times be tricky to Joey, came easy with the stretch he gave, according to the instruction in his head. "Compress deep for the jam-in … ." At the top of his swing, Joey pulled his legs to his face into a deep pike and pushed his feet down between his arms to create the compression at the bottom of the swing that pitched him back on top of the bar, dislocating his shoulders and extending his body to open his jam-out right to the handstand, right where Chris said it would be! The remainder of the routine was easy: a couple of giants and a dismount. "Get a good tap before the dismount … ." Joey cranked the giant prior to the dismount. The swing that followed put his dismount five feet higher than usual, but Joey expected it somehow and kept his composure, making his tucked, full-twisting double back easier than it had ever been. "Spot your landing early so you can stick … ." Joey's technique allowed him to spot the landing mat throughout the second flip. He was still above the bar. With catlike ease, Joey extended his legs to slow his rotation as well as to nail his target. Joey drove his feet into the twenty-centimeter mat like a dart, standing straight upon landing for a perfect dismount.

As though sticking his landing had released the spectators' and his teammates' cheers from bondage, the gym exploded. The Pioneers jumped to their feet and grabbed their smallest teammate, who had done his job well with a stuck set. As they high-fived and back-patted the leadoff man, Joey looked into the stands to see Haley with his parents and Chris's mother, all giving him the thumbs-up and okay symbols, Haley had fingers from both hands in her mouth to blow a wolf whistle that could be heard above all the other cheering going on in the cracker box gym he called home.

"Come on, Mack. Keep us going, bud!" Joey could barely catch enough breath to shout encouragement to the next man up.

Chris was now giving Mackee his instructions. "Okay, Mack, make sure on your—"

"I know, I know. Just pray I catch my release. I can handle the rest," said a nervous Mackee.

"You got it, pal. Kick some butt."

"Eight-six-five—not bad, little guy," said Chris, who was the last to congratulate Joey after giving Mackee his last-minute support.

"Eight-six-five! That's my best High Bar score, ever! I couldn't have done it without you, Chris."

"What, are you kidding? That was all you up there. Don't give me credit."

"Yeah, but you were talkin' me through it. I could hear you."

"Not during the routine. I was too jazzed to say anything. Nobody said anything during your set. You've discovered the secret."

"What secret?" Joey asked.

"When you don't have to think about what you're doing, and all you have to do is react to the voice in your head, gymnastics becomes simple. It won't be long for you now, buddy." Chris's attention was diverted back to Mackee, who was putting the finishing touches on a hit routine. "Come on Mack, Bring it home!"

Before Joey could contemplate what Chris had said to him, it was forgotten as he got wrapped up in the competition. Mackee landed his dismount with a small step but a fine routine. Once again, the team and the partisan hometown crowd erupted with cheers.

The next two routines, AJ and Ty, each missed their release moves, bringing scores down into the lower eights. Then, it was up to Dallas to get the team back on track. "Come on, Dallas, we're still in this!" shouted Mackee.

"No worries, Mack," said Dallas confidently.

Dallas had had plenty of practice hitting his high bar routine with all the extra sets Coach had given him for causing so much conflict during workouts. Now, all would see if it paid off. The first indicator would come early in his routine. Like most high bar routines, the harder skills, especially releases, come early, while the gymnast is fresh. Dallas's routine had two releases in a row: a reverse Hecht directly into a Geinger. Dallas cranked two fast giants and executed his releases effortlessly to the cheers of the crowd and his teammates. The remainder of the routine was fairly easy by comparison. By doing his hardest elements first, all Dallas had to do was fulfill the rest of his routine requirements and dismount with a relatively simple double back in layout position. Dallas landed lightly with a small step for a score of 9.1. Loud cheers from the crowd and congratulations from his coach and teammates followed his exercise. As Dallas waved to the crowd, acknowledging their cheers, the cheers grew. Chris extended his hand to congratulate Dallas on a fine set. Dallas accepted his hand and pulled Chris close enough to deliver a message. "It's gonna be hard to walk away from this, ain't it, Slash?"

"We obviously do things for different reasons, Dallas," countered Chris.

"Perhaps not as different as you might think, my boy."

The final routine was left to the most solid Pioneer, Patrick. The public address announcer made sure that the crowd was aware of that fact.

"Now up on high bar for the Pioneers, the senior captain and defending Tennessee state all-around champion, Patrick Gooodmaan!"

The cheers became deafening before Patrick saluted the judges.

"Come on, plowboy!" shouted Chris. "Get crazy up there!" Patrick knew exactly what Chris's comment meant, but with two missed high bar routines behind him and no score to drop, Patrick knew that his set had to be good. This was no time to risk trying a new skill if they hoped to win their own meet.

Patrick had an idea. He had done the Tkatchev before with his legs together, which was worth more than straddled. Patrick started his routine the same as he always had, a stem rise clear hip circle to blind turn, but from there, the routine took on a new personality. After cranking several giants, Patrick launched his modified Tkatchev. Although he caught the release, to the cheers, delight, and certain surprise of his fans, coach, and teammates, the effort left him with no momentum to continue his routine smoothly, and he was forced to do several easy elements and elements of no value just to get his routine back on track. This, he knew, would cost him a few tenths. To try to make up for the error, Patrick added the same release combination that Dallas had used, the straddled Tkatchev to immediate Geinger. That combination went flawlessly, but the effort left him with little energy to do his normal dismount, a full-twisting double layout. Instead, Patrick opted to end with an easier, tucked full-twisting double back, the same as Joey's.

When he landed, the cheers went up again, but he knew they would change to jeers when the score came up. Chris was the first one to reach Patrick after his landing.

"Great job, plowboy. You almost looked crazy up there."

"Yeah, I hope it's crazy enough."

When the score was flashed, Patrick was not surprised.

"Eight-nine-five. Not bad. Not good, but not bad, either," Chris said, putting his arm around his captain's shoulders.

"Well, Pat," said Coach, "it was a good effort. You almost pulled it off. If you hadn't had all the extra stuff after your first release, you probably would've gone 9.4 or better." Coach's words came as little consolation.

"But the effort was worth it, plowboy," added Chris. "You increased the value of your routine by two-tenths. You just need to add your other dismount, and you're up to a 9.6!"

"Yeah, but it needs to be worth a 9.8 to compete with the big dogs," Patrick confessed.

"At least you're willing to make a change."

Both agreed that it was a start, but silently, both knew how much still had to be accomplished.

"At the end of one rotation," the announcer blared, "in third place with a score of 48.85, from Austin, Texas, Texas Star Gymnastics. In second place, with a score of 51.5, Lake Erie Gymnastics. And, your leaders after the first event, with a score of 51.95, the host team, your Pioneers!"

"All right, fellas," Coach Lowery delivered a synopsis of the first rotation, "we escaped the first rotation without too much damage. Although we are leading, I don't expect it to hold up if we continue to do routines like we just learned them. We were lucky that Lake Erie started on pommel horse. We had to count two falls, they had to count three, and I don't know how long that three-point lead will last over Texas. They got their weakest event out of the way. Now they go from Rings to Vault, where their scores should rise quite a bit. Our job is clear: we have to go to floor and hit six sets. Let's go."

As the gymnasts rotated to their next event, Chris could see the doubt in Patrick's face.

"Hey, pal, forget about the last event. You learned a lot there, but it's time to go hit a floor set. You ready?"

"Yeah, yeah, I'm ready," came the less than enthusiastic response.

"Well, you better be. We need some stuck landings here."

"Right."

The next rotation went by without too much trouble. Although the Pioneers could count six hit routines, a pretty nasty fall by a Texas Star gymnast on Vault brought the festive mood back to serious as each competitor was reminded of how a lapse in concentration could have disasterous consequences. After several minutes, the Texas vaulter was carried away on a stretcher. Patrick, Chris, and Joey, who had already hit his routine, looked at each other.

"I guess no amount of preparation can prevent an accident, eh, Chris?" said Joey.

"Nor prepare you for it mentally," added Patrick.

"Point taken, you guys," conceded Chris.

The highlight of Floor was Patrick's routine. Every pass stuck, and strength and balance parts were done with control and command. Patrick was beginning to show why he deserved to be ranked with the best in the country. The 9.55 that Patrick received gave him the shot in the arm that he was looking for.

"Good job, plowboy," said Chris. "Now, let's have some fun on pig."

As the gymnasts rotated to their next event, the meet announcer gave the updated team standings.

"Ladies and gentlemen, after two events, in third place, with a 102.75, from Atlanta, Firestorm Gymnastics. In second place with a 104.3, Lake Erie Gymnastics, and still leading after two events, with a 104.55, your Pioneeers!"

"Okay, gentlemen, Lake Erie is just two-and-a-half-tenths away from us, and we're on our toughest event, Pommel Horse. I don't want you guys to worry about scores or leads, or trying to save the day. I just want you to concentrate on hitting your set, that's all. If you hit your sets, everything else will take care of itself."

"That's easy for him to say," Mackee told Patrick. "If we hit three out of six routines, it'll be a miracle."

"Then I suggest we go out and produce a miracle," concluded Patrick.

Mackee led off the rotation. Before he had a chance to settle into his routine, he found himself standing at the edge of the mat wondering how he fell off. Two falls and a struggled dismount later, Mackee found himself digusted and angry for not being able to help his team.

"Don't sweat it, Mack," said Chris, in his best encouraging tone. "Keep your head. We're really gonna need you on Rings." Chris could tell that his words did little to console his teammate.

Joey was next.

"Joey, don't try anything silly," said Coach. "Just try to keep the set moving, and try to stay clean, and maybe we can get a hit set."

Joey cast a glance at Chris, who was pointing to his own temples, gesturing for Joey to think. Joey looked at the horse, visualizing his routine. As soon as he saw his imaginary self land the dismount, he looked to the judges for the signal to start. Once the head judge gave him the customary salute, Joey heaved a heavy sigh and approached the horse. No sooner had he jumped into the first few circles, the voice had come back into his head. "Just stretch your circles … " Joey went into his first combination of complex hand placements. With each placement, the voice came back again. "Stretch … stretch … *stretch* … " Joey decided that his routine felt good enough to go for the new combination. He reached down to the leather, and, easier than ever, the complex combination of travels and spindles happened without a hitch. He flew through the single legwork and back into circles and to the dismount. Joey planted his feet into the vinyl-covered surface for his third stuck dismount in a row.

Joey's landing started another chorus of cheers from the crowd and high fives from his teammates. Joey's routine was enough to even bring Mackee out of his doldrums.

"Great set, Joey!" said Coach Lowery, hugging his youngest charge. "You have really come around!"

All the Pioneers waited for the score to be flashed—9.05.

Joey jumped and screamed at the sight of his first Pommel Horse score above a nine. Joey's new fan club jumped as well. With one look into Chris's eyes, Joey immediately became aware of the words that Chris had given him earlier. There was a secret, and he was on the edge of discovering it.

By the time Patrick was ready to start his routine, AJ and Ty had to count three falls between them, in addition to Mackee's three falls. Dallas had managed to stay on, but only by the slimmest of margins. Patrick knew that each time he went up, he would make the difference between the Pioneers staying ahead of the pack and becoming another team looking to see where the leaders were.

Patrick was not a stranger to this position, so it was no suprise that he could handle the pressure of having to hit a set. He was determined not to disappoint this time, either. From the mount, it was evident that Patrick had a mission—to win. Patrick's routine came at the end of the rotation. The other events had finished, and all eyes were on him. The feeling that everyone was watching was not a feeling that he was comfortable with, but he was learning to like it. Patrick mounted the horse with confidence. His opening sequence carried him from one end to the other and back again without using the pommels. This brought a cheer from the partisan crowd. Once Patrick did get on the pommels, it was a blur of difficult hand placements on a single pommel. With each hand placement, the crowd noise grew. Patrick split his legs and began doing Thomas flairs, hopping from the middle to the end, spindling his body, turning his trunk opposite to his circle direction, and hopping back to the center, all to an even greater cheer. Then, seemingly without effort, Patrick was in a handstand, pirouetting on the pommels, and, without breaking rhythm, dropped back into flairs. And then, turning backward, he rose back to the handstand on one end of the horse and pirouetted from end to end before closing his legs in a perfect handstand and dropping to the dismount mat for a stuck landing! The cheers, which had become deafening, were from not only the crowd and Patrick's teammates, but also the other gymnasts. The score reflected the appreciation of the judges as well—9.65.

"Wow, Patrick! That was awesome!" was the universal cry of the Pioneers as they grabbed their team captain. Patrick not only felt the satisfaction of hitting his routine, but also he knew that his success was just what the team needed to stay in the meet. The meet announcer blared the event update.

"The standings after three events: In third place, with a score of 155.75, your Pioneers! In second place, with a score of 156.2, Texas Star Gymnastics, and your new leaders, with a score of 158.3, Lake Erie Gymnastics!"

Just as the announcer gave the current standings, Coach Lowery gave his update to the team, not only assessing the last event, but also telling the Pioneers what to do and expect for the next event.

"Not bad, boys. Not especially great, but we didn't shoot ourselves in the foot, either. I think the rest of you guys ought to thank Johnson and Goodman for keeping us in this thing. Those were stellar routines, you two. Now, we go to Rings. Mackee, I need the set of your life up there. Patrick, be sure to hold your strength parts. The rest of you guys, be sure you swing tight and concentrate on your focal points on giant swings. Texas hit five out of six on P-bars, and Lake Erie just lit up the end of the vault table. They both go to strong events, so we can't hope to gain here. Let's just try not to lose ground. Firestorm and three other teams are right on our heels. No mistakes."

That's easy for him to say, Ty thought. He didn't have to do the routines. Ty, being the weakest on Rings, would go first. From the start, Ty had problems. The object of a rings routine is to keep the rings as still as possible while the body swings both ways in and out of handstands and with motionless strength moves held at least two seconds each. From the first handstand, Ty began to develop swing in the ring cables. The more he tried to correct his swing, the more he swung, until Coach Lowery stepped in to stop his swing, an automatic five-tenths of a point deduction. From that point, the only thing on Ty's mind was getting through his routine without getting killed. He managed to labor through the remainder of his routine and finish with a tucked double back dismount that under-rotated, causing him to touch both hands on the mat. Ty walked off in disgust. This was not turning out to be a good meet for him.

"Ty, don't fall apart, son," said Coach. "I need you on vault." Ty couldn't hear his coach. He had already walked away, peeling off his grips and throwing them at his gym bag. His teammates knew that this was no time to offer consolation. Ty was left to brood on his own.

Joey had grown up a lot that day, but the thought in his head was whether he had grown up enough to maintain his concentration on his most difficult event, Rings.

"Okay, Joey," said Chris, while Joey was chalking up, "just remember to look up into the ring tower as long as you can on your back giants, the floor on your front giants. On your strength parts, just try to breathe. And on your dismount, do just what you did on high bar, tap big and late, spot your landing, and bury your feet into the mat."

Joey listened intently, processing the information and storing it for later use. Once Joey had a full supply of chalk, he stepped onto the mat under the rings. "You're in a groove, Johnson," said his coach, while awaiting the judges signal. "Just keep moving."

The judges gave the signal to begin, and Joey returned the salute, breathing another heavy sigh. Coach Lowery lifted his gymnast to allow him to adjust his grip before lowering him to arrive in a still hang. Coach Lowery stepped back to his spotting position and crossed his fingers. Joey pulled up to invert his body and begin his routine. His first skill swung backward and upward to a straddle planche, his body horizontal, facing the floor, arm's length above the rings. "Breathe, Joey, breathe … " the voice had begun to speak. "Close your legs and press … " Normally, Joey would remain straddled while pushing up to his first handstand, but the voice instructed him to close his legs first, not only making the press more difficult, but also raising the value of the strength hold and the press. Coach Lowery's jaw dropped just a little. He glanced over to Chris, who shrugged his shoulders and shook his head to acknowledge the same level of astonishment and disbelief.

Joey continued to listen to the voice in his head. "Look into the tower, keep your arms straight, push!" Joey's giant swing was immaculate, arriving in the handstand in a hollow position with no swing errors. "Focus on the floor, hollow your chest … " the voice said as Joey swung the other direction with the same results, a handstand without error. Joey swung forward again to a double forward roll to another back uprise, legs together, planche. No extra swing. Joey lowered to a support and took a breath before dropping into his iron cross. Although he held it only two seconds, it was one second longer than he normally held it in practice. Joey rolled back to start his dismount sequence. "Tap late, pull hard, focus up, tap late, pull hard, focus up, tap hard, pull!" said the voice. Joey pulled the rings as hard as he could before releasing for his dismount. He spotted the landing early and adjusted his body to prepare for contact with the floor. Once again, Joey's stuck landing triggered an explosion of cheers from the crowd, most of which had, over the past three events, become members of the newly formed Joey Johnson fan club.

No sooner had Joey landed and saluted the judges did his teammates grab him once again. The score of 9.15 was his highest ever on Rings, by almost a full point. Joey's teammates and coach were begining to realize that this was no fluke. Joey was in a zone.

All the team needs to do is follow his example, and they could really challenge for NTIs, Coach thought.

AJ, who was not having a spectacular meet, rose to the occasion with an 8.95. Dallas followed with a 9.1. Suddenly, Coach Lowery felt that the fears of this event could be laid to rest with two of the finest ring swingers in the country up next. Patrick mounted with a very strong strength combination consisting of three different crosses. Each time he came to rest in a cross, the cheers became louder. With each increase in volume from the crowd, Patrick responded with even more command of his routine. As Patrick set up for his dismount, he could hear the cheers and shouts of encouragement from his team. Patrick tapped his dismount high above the rings. He made sure to throw the rings far away to the side. He knew he would be high, and the last thing he wanyed was to do a high dismount only to collide with the rings on the way down. There was enough difficulty in the body of the routine that Patrick could dismount with an easy full-twisting tucked double back. Upon his landing, the cheers were every bit as loud as they were for Joey, and the accolades from his temmates were just as jubilant.

"Way to go, plowboy!!" came the shout from Chris. "Nine-four-five—that's great!"

"Thanks a lot, pal," said Mackee. "Did you think to leave any cheers for me?" Mackee slapped hands with his fellow ringman.

"Oh, I left plenty up there, Mack," returned Patrick. "Just get after it!"

"Roger."

If Patrick's routine was the main course, Mackee's was the dessert. His routine started with a butterfly cross. Without so much as a tight lip, he continued to press upward while rotating forward until he was in a flat Maltese cross. After a three-second hold, he pressed and rotated his body until he arrived at an inverted cross. Once having held this position for another three seconds, he finished his press into a rock-solid handstand to deafening cheers. The remainder of the routine consisted of two giant swings to handstand, one forward, one backward, to another motionless handstand. Before the audience could catch its collective breath, Mackee lowered straight down to an inverted hang, lowered down to a back lever, and bounced back upto another cross, L cross, cross pullout to support, press handstand combination. The dismount seemed like an afterthought, but his double back in layout position to stuck landing brought the entire house to its feet. As if the crowd couldn't get louder, when the 9.75 was flashed, the team thought the roof would come off of the gym.

"I couldn't let you show me up on my event, Pat," said Mackee.

"How could I, brother? That was awesome!" said Patrick.

"And somewhat familiar," said Chris, joining the party.

"Yeah, I wondered if you would notice," said Mackee.

"You opened with the same strength combination I did the first day at the gym," said Chris.

"I hope you don't mind."

"Mind? Heck, I'm honored!"

"Guys, check out pipe!" cried Joey.

The boys turned their heads just in time to see Danny Diego anchoring high bar for Texas Star. Danny started his set with a difficult release combination: one-arm giant, one-arm Tkatchev, legs together Tkatchev, straddle Tkatchev, Geinger.

"How does one get enough swing for that combination?" asked Joey.

"Genetics and exremely quick muscle twitch, I guess," answered Chris.

Danny's set finished with a double-twisting double layout. The cheers were again deafening as the fans realized that they were experiencing the greatest exhibition of gymnastics talent they had ever seen.

"I guess 'wow' would be an understatement, eh, Pat?" said Mackee.

Patrick was speechless.

"Well, Texas just went six for six," said AJ.

"And, Lake Erie only had to count one fall on P-bars," said Ty.

"Well, there's nothing we can do about the other teams," said Coach Lowery. "All we can do is continue to rock sets and let the other teams worry about themselves."

The meet announcer made that point all too clear: "Gentlemen, rotate to your fifth event. ... The standings after four events: In third place, with a score of 210.1, your Pioneers. In second place, with a score of 211.7, from Austin, Texas, Texas Star Gymnastics, and your leaders after four events, with a score of 212.2, Lake Erie Gymnastics!"

SEVENTEEN

▼

"THREE LOUSY TENTHS!" said Patrick. "Not even a fall. A fall is a five-tenths of a point deduction. Just a straight leg here, one less step on a landing there, and history is rewritten." Patrick lay with his head in Missy's lap as his eyes and mind searched the clear blue sky for the magic that would change the outcome of the Pioneer Invitational.

"Let it rest for a while, Patrick," said Missy. "You guys did a great job. Sometimes, no matter what you do, your best is just good enough for second."

"That's easy for you to say," said Patrick, rising to his feet and assuming an adversarial posture. "You weren't out there. We could've won. One more stuck landing, one less mental error. Shoot, if we had had Chris—"

"Would you listen to yourself? What good is second-guessing what you could've done? For every mistake that you could take back, there's another the other teams would have back, and you still wind up three-tenths down to the winner. It has been three days since that stupid meet, and it's all you ever think about or talk about."

"I'm sorry, Miss, I've just been bugged lately about the direction the team is going."

"I think you need to wake up and realize that no matter how much this means to you, there are things you just can't control. Some care as much as you. Some, like Dallas, don't care half as much. The point is no matter how much it means to you, you can't do anything about anybody else. That must be left up to the individual. You know deep in your heart everybody tried as hard as they could. Some things just aren't in the cards. You guys did great, and it was just one meet. You guys still have the rest of the season ahead of you."

"I guess you're right, but—"

"No buts! This is the third time we've been out this week, and I don't think that you've said more than three words to me that didn't have something to do with gymnastics. You're out with *me*! When you're with me, you owe it to me to relate to me. I love to watch you do gymnastics, Pat, but I like to leave it in the gym, where it belongs.

"The way I see it, you have two choices. You can come back down here and relax and talk to me about things I care about, or you can take me home and talk to yourself about your team, for which you feel so personally responsible."

"You're right," conceded Patrick, returning to his previous position to ponder the clear blue sky. "It's really stupid to try to think of how things could've been different when there's really nothing to do about the past."

"That's my boy. You just relax, and let Missy rub those worry wrinkles out of your head." Missy began gently rubbing at the forehead of the Pioneer captain. It took nearly thirty seconds for Patrick to finally relax and let his mind go elsewhere.

Soon, the warmth of the sun, the sound of the gentle breeze, and the touch of a loving hand put Patrick in a temporary state of relaxation. Just when Missy thought that she had soothed the savage beast in Patrick, she could feel his brow begin to tense again.

"I just can't belive that these guys don't want this as much as I do," said Patrick, his eyes still closed.

"That's it, Goodman," raged Missy, pushing Patrick's head from her lap. "Take me home!"

"Missy … I'm sorry—"

"Too late, Patrick. If you can't take your mind off that stupid gym, you don't want me. You should date a chalk bucket. I've got much better things to do than be a sounding board for your childish suppositions. 'What if this, what if that?' I don't care, Patrick!" Missy wrapped her white sweater over her shoulders, walked over to Patrick's car, and positioned herself in the passenger's seat. "I'm not asking you to choose between gymnastics and me, Patrick, I just want equal time. And I guess I'm not going to get it, so just take me home."

Patrick stood dumbfounded. Once realizing that he had no argument, Patrick took his position in the driver's seat, started the car, and proceeded, in silence, to take Missy home. His thoughts were leaning not toward a resolution with his girlfriend, but rather the true cause of his dismay, his own shortcomings as a gymnast.

Amazing! Chris thought. Videotape has an uncanny knack for making mistakes that were not perceivable during competition stand out when viewed in the comfort of one's home. Chris had spent the past three days in his basement looking at video of his past competitions, meets with Danny Diego and Marty Reynolds. He had come to accept his early retirement. What a fabulous death it would've been. Not the worthless wasting away that comes with disease, rather something spectacular, like attempting a skill that few had ever dreamed of, let alone tried. Being able to say that you met life and death head-on in every moment, willing to accept either. That would be right, the way it should be, not what it had become: lying around the house, afraid to accept what might come in the next minute.

Chris's thoughts were interrupted by the doorbell.

"Hey, pal!" came Joey's voice as he descended the basement steps. "Whatcha doin'?"

"Hey, Joe. Just watchin' some video. Gymnastics."

"Cool! Who you watchin'?"

"Just some old meets when I lived in California."

"Hey! Isn't that Danny Diego?"

"Yeah, this was two years ago. California State Invitational."

"Gosh!" gasped Joey, "he was crazy then, too."

"Yeah, we all were. It was kind of an unorganized fraternity. Your pledgeship amounted to doing something that would make other gymnasts say, 'That boy is crazy!' We were the best at giving coaches gray hair!" Both laughed.

Joey watched the tape, occasionally looking at Chris, watching his body language as he tried to imitate and manipulate releases, strength parts, and dismounts as if his gyrations could alter the video.

"So, Chris," Joey took a big gulp, "do you miss it?"

"Sure, kid. There are very few things I ever wanted to do. Gymnastics was the one thing I could do, and do well, and get real satisfaction from."

"Then, why stop now?"

"Man, we've been down this road before. At any time, it could hit me. Then, that would be it, lights out, end of story."

"True, but that could happen to anybody. You don't have to be carrying a genetic defect to wrap yourself around a high bar. Just one moment of seriously bad luck—the rest of us have to deal with that uncertainty, too."

"Yeah, you aren't carrying this thing in your head. It kinda makes you appreciate your time left."

"By wasting hour upon hour reliving the days when your perspective was more favorable?" said Joey, pointing to the television.

"Listen, twerp, I've spent my life running from the inevitable. I think I deserve a little time to embrace what time I may have left."

"And how much time is that, Chris? An hour? A day? A month? A year or more? Just how much of that time can you afford to waste reflecting back instead of creating new memories? I believe that we all have eternity to look back on what we did with our short time on this rock. I think the time we have here is short, no matter how long it is. It's up to you whether you spend your time living or dying."

"Don't you think that you're being a little too serious? You just want me to come back and help the team."

"My, aren't we just a little full of ourselves? Actually, I could give a rat's ass whether you come back to the team or not. We'll manage fine. It's not about that. I do, however, care about the mental health of my best friend, the only person who had an ounce of confidence in me. Whether you spend another second in that gym doesn't matter to me. What does matter is that you realize that, regardless of how much time you have left, I think you should spend it enjoying what life has to offer, not feeling sorry for yourself because fate dealt you a lousy hand."

"How dare you come into my house and talk to me like that. I think I want you to leave, Joey."

Joey turned to climb the steps. Two steps up, he turned to deliver his final thought to his friend. "No, Chris. How dare you. How dare you come into my life and make me believe that anything is attainable. How dare you make me believe that if I were willing to try, I could succeed. How dare you give all of us the feeling that the risk of failing is always an acceptable cost for trying, that beating fear is always more gratifying than giving in, even more gratifying than the victory that succeeding eventually leads to. I guess that was all just fine and good for as long as you believed it. Well, I just hope you get better, pal, 'cause gymnastics aside, you're still the greatest guy I've ever known. See ya later." Joey turned and climbed the steps of the basement and slammed the door, which shook Chris from his blank stare. He threw the remote control into the couch.

"Crap." Chris sat and cried.

Although he had spent most of his life in the confines of the Pioneer gym, there was still an eerie strangeness to the warming up of the metal halide lamps lighting the dark of the empty training floor.

"Okay, Goodman," said Coach Lowery upon entering the dimly lit facility, "what is so important that you drag me out of sound sleep at near midnight? You do have classes tomorrow, don't you?"

"Yeah, but the choice was easy—be sleepless at home or be sleepless here. At least here, I can be productive in my insomnia." Patrick grinned as he covered his wrists with tape, wristbands, and his high bar grips.

"So, what kind of productivity are we talking about tonight, Pat?"

"Oh, I don't know, I was thinkin' about a little 'Def' productivity? Sound interesting?"

"I see. Got a few demons to beat tonight, eh?"

"Yeah, I guess," Patrick pondered for a moment while making his final preparations before starting his swinging. "Have you ever been so consumed with something that everything else is just, well, kind of a blur?"

"You mean like you and this silly notion that you have to become more than you are to be what you think you ought to be? Sure, everybody does. It is the nature of the beast to project an image of what we want to be, only to find that we all fall far short of our expectations. It's very unsettling."

"What did you do when you were in my shoes?"

"Well, back when I was an up-and-coming gymnast, I got an idea stuck in my head that I had to be first at something. Noticing at the time that no one did more than two double backs in a floor routine, I got the idea that I should become the first gymnast to compete three different double backs in one routine. Just as you have become obsessed with adding a full twist to an already fine Geinger, I measured myself against my ability to pull off the hardest floor routine being done at the time. It haunted me day and night. At night, I could see myself executing a perfect full-twisting double back, double back in pike position, and dismounting with an effortless double back tucked. During the day, I would find myself daydreaming about the cheers that would arise upon my landing. In class, I would forgo whatever assignment we had to list the perfect conditioning regimen to get me fit enough for such a taxing routine. Yes, I would say I was somewhat obsessed."

"So, what happened?"

"First meet of the season, and I was ready to spring this new routine on the fans and competitors alike. I anchored the team, so my routine came last. I found it hard to hold back the snicker I felt, seeing the other routines go before me, none with two double backs, let alone three."

"So, did you hit, or what?"

"I would say that I hit. Good, solid landing on my first pass, the full-in. Only one step on each of the other two passes. It was actually pretty good for the first time out."

"And, did everyone react the way you thought they would?"

"Well, there was a lot of cheering, as I recall, but nobody hoisted me upon their shoulders like I thought they would."

"And did you win floor?"

"Oddly enough, no. I took third, behind my teammate, who did only one double back, a two-and-a-half twist, and a clean front tumbling pass, and a guy from the other team who only did one double back, a triple-twisting layout, and a very clean combination of whip back, whip back full-twist, immediate double-twisting layout for a dismount."

"Oooh, sorry."

"Don't be. I learned two very valuable lessons that day."

"What, that audiences are fickle and judges have no sense of what is harder?"

"No, smart guy. In that brief moment, I realized that, first, if you devote enough time and energy, any goal is attainable. And second, and probably more important, quality will always beat content. No matter how hard you make something, if the quality of what you're doing doesn't keep pace, the difficulty won't matter."

"So are you saying that this little quest of mine is, perhaps, silly and fruitless?"

"Not at all, Pat. Just remember what you're in it for. You seem to think that the only way to bring your gymnastics to another level is to add these difficult skills to your repertoire. Just remember, if it can't be done well, these new skills will bring your gymnastics to another level, but it may be a lower level than where you are now."

"Right." Patrick listened to every word of his mentor, but Coach Lowery could tell that he only heard half. Patrick hopped up on the high bar to start work on this elusive skill.

"Faster … faster … faster!" is all that Chris could think. The whine of his motorcycle engine and the pounding beat of the heavy metal music pushed him to go faster—120, 125, 130 miles per hour. The broken lines on the two-lane road had become a blur. His bleach-blonde hair whipped against his helmetless head. The blackness of night made it easier to concentrate on the images illuminated by his headlight. Chris wondered just how big a splat he would make if something went wrong as he crouched lower in his seat to minimize drag while he opened up the engine on his Kawasaki.

None of it made sense. He had lived his life fearlessly, knowing that at any moment, for no reason and without warning, his life could be snuffed out as though it had never happened. And there was nothing he could do about it. No amount of success or measure of risk made any sense. When it's all over, that's it, it's over. All along, he had though that with each death-defying stunt, he had cheated the grim reaper, when, in fact, he hadn't cheated anyone but himself. What was the point in trying?

Perhaps if he were back in California, where the back roads were long and straight for miles, he could come up with an answer. The roads in east Tennessee were too hilly and winding to just let the bike do its thing and let him think. But for now, he would have to slow down as he approached a tricky intersection. The two-lane road he was on crossed a four-lane main artery connecting Knoxville with the interstate. Commuters seldom obeyed the traffic light on the larger road. To them, a yellow light meant speed up, not slow down, and a change from yellow to red would mean that four more cars might still go through.

As luck would have it, as Chris closed in on the intersection, the light was with him, and the opposing traffic was stopped at the light, uncharacteristically obliging for late-night. Chris began to open the throttle to take advantage of the unusual display of driver etiquette.

Before Chris got to the light he noticed something wrong. A transfer truck coming from the other direction was making a left turn, crossing directly in front of Chris. Without enough distance to stop, and cars everywhere, Chris could see that his options were limited, each ending with a large splat. Perhaps this is how it should end, with a fiery crash, he thought. But, just as the thought of ending it all had become comfortable, his mind went to images of Patrick, of his mother, of Joey, and of Haley. In an instant, Chris aimed his bike for the rearwheels of thesemi. His only chance was to lay his bike down and slide underneath the trailer of the turning rig. Chris shifted his weight to the right, pushing the rear wheel to the left. As the motorcycle went into a controlled slide, Chris tucked his legs up into the leg guards to try and protect them from the friction of the road. Sparks and smoke arose from the disintegration of his bike frame against the road. He could feel the fabric of his Levi's and his leather jacket shredding away against the pavement. Chris watched as the enormous frame of the trailer passed over his head. Then, when the star-filled sky emerged on the other side, Chris knew that he had cleared the trailer. All he had to do now was hang on to his bike until everything came to a halt, hopefully before he ran out of clothing.

Then, another problem. While still sliding, Chris noticed that the road banked to the left, leading him on a head-on course with a curb and the parking lot of a shopping center.

Before Chris could react, the wheels made contact with the curb, standing the bike up and throwing Chris into the air and toward the parking lot.

With catlike reflexes, Chris reached down for the ground, doing a round off to turn him around, and started turning back handsprings as fast as he could to try to control his speed. The asphalt pavement stung his wrists and ankles. Glancing to his left, Chris could see his motorcycle tumbling just as fast as he. His chest burned as he tried to keep pace, burning more energy than his breathing could restore. Fifteen, twenty, twenty-five back handsprings before Chris reached a point where he felt he could control and slow his momentum. He did one last back handspring and reached back with his feet, creating a long, low block angle with his body, which changed his direction from horizontal to vertical. Chris pushed his body skyward, watching as best as he could the ground beneath him. Once he felt the apex of his flight, Chris pulled his head back slightly and tucked his knees to do a nearly perfect backflip. Although he had to take a few steps to regain control upon landing, Chris soon found himself at a standstill some ten feet from the shopping center wall. Chris examined his right side for damage. Not too bad, he thought. Nothing that some neosporin, gauze, and some new clothes couldn't fix.

Chris walked back to the scrambled heap that was once his motorcycle. All traffic had stopped, as many motorists had gotten out of their cars, initially to help what was certain to be a major accident but whose roles had been reduced to slack-jawed onlookers.

He started gathering the parts of his bike. The engine still running, Chris turned the radio off, then the engine. What an instant ago was the roar of a motorcycle engine, the pounding of rock music, and subsequently the crashing of metal on cement was now eerie silence.

"Hey!" Chris shouted, waking the dumbfounded crowd from its disbelieving trance. "I don't think my bike is goin' anywhere, so could someone give me a lift?"

EIGHTEEN

▼

"COACH, HAVE YOU seen Patrick?" asked Mackee as he poked his head into Coach Lowery's office.

"Sure haven't, Mack. What's the matter, you guys not able to start warm-up without him?"

"Very funny, Coach. It's just that I've trained with this guy for almost ten years, and over that whole time, I don't think I've ever known Pat to be late for a workout."

"Perhaps Missy kept him out late last night. It was Friday, you know," answered Coach.

"Doubtful. He and Missy broke up on Wednesday."

"Hmm … funny, he didn't mention it to me. I guess the coach is always the last to know. At any rate, I'm sure he'll be in soon or have a good reason for not being here."

"Man, I wish you were this laid back when I miss workout!"

"I would, Mack, if I thought it wouldn't become a habit."

"Who, me?" replied Mackee in mock innocence.

Before the Kennedy senior could pull his head out of Coach Lowery's office door, Patrick, looking out of sorts, pushed the door the rest of the way open.

"Sorry I'm late, Coach. It won't happen again," he said while tucking his T-shirt into his shorts

"Looking a little disheveled, there, pal," quipped Mackee.

"Goodman looks a little panicked, boys," said Dallas from the floor exercise mat where the rest of the team was stretching out.

"I knew he couldn't keep it up," alluded Joey.

"Keep what up?" asked Dallas. "Has Captain America found a new girlfriend that he can't keep pace with?"

"Oh, nothing … nothing. Just forget I said anything," replied Joey, realizing that he had let the cat out of the bag.

"Too late, Johnson. Spill it," prodded Dallas without mercy.

"Okay, but you guys gotta promise not to let Patrick know that you know. Heck, he doesn't even know that I know."

"Know what, Johnson?" added AJ as the rest of the team began to converge upon the freshman. Dallas grabbed Joey's shirt in both hands and pulled him closer to increase the intimidation factor.

"Yeah, what's he doin', Joey?" Ty jumped in.

"Well?" insisted Dallas, his grip tightening.

"Patrick has been training alone at night. Sometimes way after midnight."

The three stood in disbelief, frozen at the anticlimax of Joey's revelation.

"That's it?" said Ty, nonplussed by the lack of payoff they had anticipated.

"Yeah," confessed Joey, thinking that his information would pardon him from the pounding that he felt was sure to take place. "He's been comin' in after workout for the past three nights, staying sometimes past three in the morning."

While Ty and AJ suddenly became disinterested with Joey's less than shocking news, Dallas's curiosity heightened.

"Has Coach been here with him?" asked Dallas, whose two-fisted grip on Joey's shirt was the only thing keeping him from dropping to the floor .

"You bet. You know Patrick won't break the rules and sneak in, so he asked Coach, and Coach has been here, too."

"Hmm … looks as though I need to have a talk with my bud. Johnson, don't tell Patrick what you've told me."

"What, are you kiddin'? He'd kill me if he knew I knew! Um … Dallas?"

"What kid?"

"Could you let me go now?"

"Sure, kid." Dallas dropped Joey to his back.

"Unnooofff!"

"What are you clowns doin'?" demanded Coach Lowery.

"Nothin', Coach," Dallas covered. "Just having a little fun with Johnson."

"At whose expense, I wonder?" Coach asked rhetorically.

Just then, the sound of loud rock music began to blare from the overhead speakers. Instinctively, the group wheeled around toward the direction of the black metal stereo rack, they saw the source of the commotion. There, in tattered denim shorts and his best faded tank top, stood a familiar guest at the controls.

"Gentlemen, it's time to rock!" Chris was back.

NINETEEN

▼

As IF HE had never left, Chris was right back on his game—joking, bashing, and being cocky, just like before. But this time, he was more focused, more intense. Chris became obsessed during training, taking twice as many turns as the other guys, instead of his previous one turn to their three. Instead of paying attention to only himself, he began to help his teammates, lifting them to the rings and high bar, moving mats in and out.

Chris had become driven. Although he was still a jovial, happy-go-lucky gymnast, he was now one with a fixed vision. He could still joke, but he kept it short, never enough to divert him away from his quest, his focus squarely fixed upon his training and that of the team.

Soon, everyone had become infected, taking almost twice as many turns as normal, each one barely able to catch his breath before his next turn, except for Chris. He set the pace. No one dared slow down, not because of the coach's drive or Chris's noble effort, but rather the thought of Chris's tounge-lashing for any slackers and the knowledge that the other teammates would kill the guy that didn't keep up.

Even Dallas, who tried several times to draw Chris into the usual verbal confrontation, to no avail, picked up his intensity. Dallas realized that he was becoming more tired from taunting a nonreactive Chris than from training. Before long, Dallas was sucking wind so hard from just trying to keep up that talking at all became difficult, sometimes impossible.

Coach Lowery could do nothing but watch. The turns were coming faster than his ability to correct or praise, not that they needed either. Once the guys got used to the pace, knowing when to breathe to get the best of each turn, their pace increased.

With the increase in workload came an increase in efficiency. Hit routines came in bunches. After two workouts, the hit–miss ratio on made routines was five-to-one. By the fifth workout, that ratio had grown to ten-to-one. With each hit routine came the pressure to hit another. The relief of hitting a routine gave each gymnast the fire to encourage the next to hit his.

"Come on, AJ!" shouted Joey.

"You're almost there, A!" added Ty.

"Bring it home, dude!" Dallas encouraged AJ to finish his Parallel Bars routine. "This one makes seventeen! We're goin' for steaks!"

Encourage as they did, no amount of cheering could keep AJ from missing a pirouette on top of the bars. He landed on the mat two skills away from hitting a routine that would have kept the streak alive. AJ crumbled to a heap on the mat.

"Come on, Coach," pleaded Joey, "we hit sixteen. That should be good enough for something."

"Nope, you guys set the mark. Twenty hit sets in a row for steaks or nothing."

"But we got over 75 percent there. That's gotta be worth somethin'," added Mackee.

"That's 80 percent, to be exact, Mack. However, that's not the point," said Patrick. "Coach offered us pizza for fifteen. But noooo, Dallas had to negotiate for steak dinner or nothing."

"It's all Doujmovich's fault," said Dallas. "If he had hit his silly little routine, Slash, Goodman, and I would've cleaned up easily, and I could be savoring the smell of sautéed mushrooms and onions for my eighteen-ounce sirloin, instead of inhaling the toxic fumes of your collective body odor!"

"Don't blame AJ, Dallas," added Chris. "I think he has a better hit–miss rate than you."

"Big deal. At least I can hit under pressure," boasted Dallas.

"Oh you think so?" barked Chris. "What do you say we make things interesting."

"Oh, how so?"

"You willing to put a steak dinner on the line?"

"If I was ready earlier, I'm just as ready now."

"It's not the same. That was not a bet earlier. Nobody lost. Coach just offered if we hit. We wouldn't have to come up with the goods if we missed. This is us," Chris said. "I'll take AJ and whoever you want and go up against you and whoever you want. We win, you buy. You win, I buy."

"You mean you guys buy."

"No, I mean you and me. Nobody else puts up a buck. Just you and me. That's what makes it interesting."

"Okay, you're on. You get AJ, Ty, and Mackee. I'll take Patrick and Joey."

A look of terror overcame Joey. On one hand, he wouldn't be teamed with Chris, for whom he would gladly hit as many routines as neccesary to win. Instead, he would be competing *against* Chris and *for* the one person who had caused all of the turmoil in the first place. On the other hand, Dallas did choose him for his team. That was a compliment. A backhanded one, considering he probably wouldn't have picked him for anything else, but a compliment just the same.

"What makes you think that Joey and I would want to hit sets for you, Dallas?" asked Patrick.

"Simple, you two could care less about this game. You are gonna try your best every turn because you both think that your success in competition depends upon consistency in your training. Hitting enough routines to feel confident about how you'll compete is important to you. I don't think either one of you thinks you can afford to miss routines, accidentally or otherwise."

"He's got a point there, Pat," said Mackee.

"Yeah, but a big hat should just about cover it," joked Ty.

"Very funny, Ty," returned Dallas. "So, Slash, what are the rules?"

"Simple, each hit set is worth ten points. If you have a major break, like a major loss of form or extra swings, you lose a point each time. If you fall, you lose five points."

"Five points!" barked Ty. "That's awful steep, don't you think?"

"Not at all," answered Chris. "This is a contest about hitting routines. I think hitting should be placed well above junk sets."

"Fine," agreed Dallas. "Now, since you guys have one more than us, you'll have to drop a score."

"Drop low score?" asked Ty.

"No way, dude. You guys drop your high score," answered Dallas. "Okay, so who judges, Slash? I certainly don't want you judging my routines."

"Well, Coach? If you would be so kind."

"My pleasure, boys. This will be the first thing I've had to do since you guys started setting such a frantic pace."

"Cool. Well, I set the rules. Dallas, you pick the event."

"Fair enough. Let's see how you guys do on AJ's favorite, parallel bars."

"One warm-up turn each?" asked AJ

"Sure," answered Dallas, "you're gonna need it."

The gymnasts each took a warm-up turn. Dallas, Patrick, and Joey warmed up with full routines. Chris's team did the same, except for Chris, who only did swings.

"I'll go first," ordered Dallas.

"Why not go last? That way, you'll have a scapegoat if one of us misses first," said Patrick.

"Yeah, since we're talking about hitting under pressure, you should be last, where the heat is," added Joey.

"Fine. I'll go last. Johnson, you go first."

"But, they have more guys. Shouldn't they go first?"

"Okay," said Chris, "we'll start off."

"You mean I'll start off," said AJ. "This whole thing started with me, so let me put this thing to rest. I'll hit first!"

With a look of determination, AJ mounted the bars with a vengeance. Each skill topped off at a handstand and each swing was effortless as he glided past his previous trouble spot, the pirouette. AJ ended with a double back, easily six full inches above his normal height, and landed without a movement.

AJ blew out a breath of both relief and satisfaction. He walked back to his team with a small deviation toward the captain of the other team.

"Pressure *this*, Dallas," taunted AJ as he was greeted with high fives for both his routine and his retort.

Joey was next. He looked to Chris for advice, but all he got was a look of support and a thumbs-up. Joey looked at the bars, trying to find motivation. Then, a thought hit him that gave him instant resolve. Without another moment's hesitation, Joey mounted the bars and executed a flawless routine, punctuated with a stuck landing on his dismount.

Joey looked over to Chris to get the same look as before, including a more deliberate thumbs-up.

"Good job, kid," said Dallas.

"Shut up, Dallas. I'm not doin' it for you," returned Joey.

"What got into you up there?" asked Patrick.

"Easy, just before I mounted, I tried to imagine what the greatest pressure to hit could be."

"So what did you think of? State? NTIs?"

"Nope. The greatest pressure a gymnast has."

"And that is?"

"Hitting when you just don't care."

Then, it was Mackee's turn. Being a Rings specialist, his sets were neither difficult nor consistent. Proving true to form, Mackee missed three skills in his routine but didn't fall off, which, by Mackee standards, was a pretty good routine.

"That's seven points, Mack," shouted Coach Lowery. "Good job."

"Okay, Patrick, your turn," said Dallas.

Patrick returned a glare to Dallas as if to say, "Like I care."

Patrick, known for his consistency, hit his routine in a business-as-usual manner. Upon landing, Patrick walked casually over to Joey first for a high five, then turned his attention to Ty, who had just finished chalking up for his routine.

"Come on, Ty!" shouted Patrick, ignoring Dallas's outstretched hand.

"Let's go, Ty. Hit one!" added Joey, joining in the encouragement given by all of the Pioneers except Dallas.

Ty's routine ended with a successful dismount, save for a small hop. "Nine points, Ty," said Coach. "Dallas, you're up."

"Like a walk in the park," answered Dallas in a tone both confident and arrogant.

"Wait a second, Coach!" Chris broke in. "Since my routine only counts if I miss, how about if I go before Dallas?"

"Yeah," added AJ, "if it's pressure Dallas wants, shouldn't he be very last?"

"You have a point. Dallas, do you have a problem with that?" asked Coach Lowery.

"Why should I? This is my event," which in a way was true. Dallas had been the highest scorer and most consistent on that event.

Chris chalked his hands and stared at the bars while visualizing what routine he would do. After a minute of contemplation, Chris positioned himself at the end of the bars.

"What's he doin'?" Joey whispered to Patrick, pointing to the fact that Chris's routine usually started from the side of the bars, not the end where he was now standing.

"I'm not sure," answered Patrick, "but I think Chris is gonna rub some crow in Dallas's face."

Chris jumped from the springboard to mount on the end of the bars. After the first three skills, it became obvious what Chris was doing.

"Hey! He's doing Dallas's routine!" said Ty.

"Yeah," added Mackee, "and maybe just a touch better." Mackee's remark drew a cutting glare from Dallas.

"Come on, Chris! Bring it home!" shouted Joey. Soon, everyone was cheering Chris as he got close to the end of Dallas's routine. Everyone except Dallas.

Then, Chris surprised everyone. Instead of dismounting where Dallas normally did, Chris turned his body ninety degrees and swung down on one rail, kipped back up on top of the bar, turned back to balance on both bars, and began adding skills.

"Oh my gosh!" shouted AJ. "Now, he's doing his own set!"

Chris, barely breaking a sweat, performed his own routine as if he hadn't started with a full routine. He punctuated his turn with a double back dismount in the piked position, his feet sinking into the four-inch landing mat. The cheers from his teammates, which had begun with his imitation of Dallas's routine and grew to a roar upon his landing, came from both his ability and his in-your-face manner that put Dallas in his place. Chris's actions spoke volumes over any remark he could've made. If there were any question of Chris' ability to come back, it was answered in that moment.

While the rest of the team congratulated Chris for his style and audacity, Dallas quietly chalked his hands, waiting for the cheers to subside.

"Nice, Slash, very nice. You did my set almost as well as I do. Almost. Regardless, that whole stunt was for nothing. It didn't count for your score, and since we're up by four points, I'm due to be suckin' down some steakage. That is if I can manage to stay on my favorite event," Dallas's tone turned to sarcasm.

Patrick and Joey looked at each other as if to say they would have gladly missed their routines if it would have quieted the cocksure, blond senior.

Poised, Dallas approached the end of the bars. He closed his eyes for a moment to visualize the routine that he had trained, completed, and competed hundreds of times in his Pioneer career. With a smirk on his face and a wink toward Chris, he mounted. Dallas's routine was all too familiar to the rest of the team. It had rarely changed over his year-and-a-half history with the Pioneers. It was also rare for him to miss.

Dallas moved effortlessly to the last skill in the routine, setting up his double back dismount. A chuckle could be heard coming from Dallas. He swung through the support phase and up off of the bars. Then, the unthinkable happened. One of Dallas's hands missed its assigned leg. Before he could regrasp his knee, he found himself on the dismount mat, face down. Dallas lay motionless, more from embarrassment and shame than pain.

The rest of the team was in shock as Chris knelt down to Dallas. "You okay, pal?" he asked quietly with genuine concern. Dallas answered with a numb, "Uh-huh."

"Good," said Chris, "I don't want your steak. That crash was more than worth it." Chris patted Dallas on the back. Dallas remained still on the mat, his face pressed into the vinyl surface.

AJ knelt down in the same position that Chris had taken. "I'm not so forgiving, Dallas. I like lots of mushrooms and my steak well-done!"

"Right," said Dallas, taking inventory of his body parts. The team all shared high fives and headed to the locker room. Coach Lowery just shook his head, ran his fingers through his quickly graying hair, and walked over to help Dallas up.

TWENTY

▼

"Chris, come in," Haley spoke into the small microphone connected to her headset. "Chris, do you read me?" Still only silence. "Chris, this is no longer funny. You talk to me, or you'll be eating Mickey D's for supper."

"You really know how to ruin a moment of serenity, Haley," came the familiar voice over the voice-activated communicator.

"Cute, honey, real cute. I think I already have a reason to be somewhat paranoid when it comes to you. I don't think I can deal with your little mind games on top. By the way, where are you?"

"Comin' in over your right shoulder."

Haley turned to her right just in time to see the familiar red, white, and blue markings of her hang glider as it emerged from behind a bluff several hundred yards away, with Chris at the controls.

"It's getting late, Chris. We need to start heading back."

"Just a few more minutes, babe. I found this excellent thermal back over the ridge."

"No! We need to start heading back. You've been up there for two hours! I would like to get back into town before it gets dark. There will be plenty of time to hit that thermal the next time." Haley bit her lip. The words had come out of her mouth before she had the chance to think about what she had said. To her, and everyone else, there was plenty of time. With Chris, nobody knew.

There was an eerie, prolonged silence. Obviously, he had heard her offhand comment.

"Okay, I'm coming in."

"Chris, I'm sorry for the comment about—"

"Don't give it another thought. You're right, There's plenty of time to explore that thermal."

Although Chris had become an accomplished flier in a relatively short period of time, Haley thought, he still needs a little more work on his landing technique. Chris floated into the open glen effortlessly. He tilted the front of the glider up to act as a break. The maneuver worked, as the kite came to a complete stop, only eight feet above the ground. The glider dropped the remaining distance, straight down, leaving Chris awkwardly trying to get his feet under him to avoid planting his face into the grassy surface.

Haley jogged the twenty or so feet to help him get out of his harness and disassemble the glider.

"You're getting pretty good at this, McClure. You are a quick learner."

"I do have an excellent teacher. I think I need to work on my landings a little more."

"That's why you wear a helmet, dear."

The two finished packing the nylon wing and the fiberglass and graphite skeleton into the back of Haley's car. Before long, the two were driving out of the park located deep in the Smoky Mountains. There was a noticeable silence. Haley spent most of the ride just looking at Chris. Chris continued to watch the road, enjoying the weight of her stare.

"You know, Chris, if Coach Lowery ever found out that you were hang gliding so close to state championships, he'd have both our heads."

"Well, what Coach doesn't know won't hurt him."

"Yeah, but what hurts you would kill him!" Haley winced again, realizing she had used the K word. "Sorry, Chris."

"Sorry for what?" he inquired.

"You know, 'hurt you, kill him'—"

Chris slammed on the brakes, controlling his steering to avoid flipping the small Suzuki and bringing it to a dusty halt.

"Look, I'm getting pretty tired of everybody walking on eggshells when they talk to me! I'm no different than before, when nobody knew what was wrong with me! I'm a tough guy. I can deal with it. But, if there's one thing that I won't deal with, it's my friends acting like if they say one wrong word, I'm gonna go slit my wrists or jump up on a tower with an M-16! Just forget about it. Sure, I could kick tomorrow, but I could also go twenty years from now. In either case, I don't think I can stand another minute of you and the rest of the team treating me like I'm on my deathbed! I neither want nor need your pity. Is that clear?"

"Listen, Mr. McClure," returned Haley in a volume and intesity to match Chris's, "I'll make you a deal. You stop acting like you have a death wish, and I and everyone else will stop acting like we might be the trigger that sends you over the edge!"

"Fine!" returned Chris.

"Fine!" repeated Haley. The two glared at each other, neither knowing what the next word should be. Then, at the same time, they broke into laughter and lunged to hold the other as best as they could, fighting the restriction of their seat belts.

"I just don't want to think about life without you, Chris," Haley whispered into his ear as she began to sob.

"Then don't," Chris returned, consoling his love and containing his own tears.

TWENTY-ONE

▼

"SOMEBODY WAKE UP Dallas!" Coach Lowery shouted.

Mackee moved from his seat on the bus to the seat occupied by Dallas. Mackee made sure he had everyone's attention before he went into his act. He carefully lifted Dallas's right arm, placed it around his shoulder, and nuzzled up to Dallas's chest. Dallas instinctively reacted by pulling Mackee closer. A noticable smile came over Dallas's face. Likewise, everyone, including Coach Lowery, was trying to contain his laughter at the gag.

"Oh, Dallas," Mackee wooed in his best southern belle falsetto, "I think you are just the dreamiest!" The smile on Dallas's face became more pronounced. It was becoming more difficult for everyone else to hold in what everyone knew was sure to be an explosion of laughter. The more that Dallas bought into the fantasy, the further Mackee took the act.

"Oh, Dallas, it's getting late. My daddy says I have to be home before eleven."

"No … baby, no … let's just stay here … a little … longer," Dallas uttered in almost a mumble, pulling his "date" even closer. The giggles were beginning to escape from the rest of the team.

Realizing that Dallas was fully immersed in the gag, Mackee decided to take the fantasy to another level. "Oh, Dally, you feel so good!" Mackee began to rub Dallas's chest, much to the delight of the subconscious senior. Dallas began to return the caress of his partner. "Oh, baby … you feel … good, too!"

The caresses turned to petting. Mackee leaned up to Dallas's ear. "Did you bring … protection?" Their faces beet red, the rest of the team contained their laughter as best they could to allow the charade to come to a conclusion. Patrick had to cover Joey's mouth, who was beginning to lose control.

"Protection? We don't need … protection. … Baby … I'll be careful—" Mackee then stood up and smacked Dallas across the face. "You irresponsible bastard!" Mackee said in his own gruff voice.

The laughter could be stifled no longer. The bus exploded, including the bus driver, who was finding it hard to keep the vehicle in the middle of his lane on the long stretch of interstate between Nashville and Memphis.

The sharp pain in his cheek and the loud howl of the team only added to Dallas's disorientation as he tried to regain consciousness. "What's up with you guys?" he asked, still very confused.

Coach Lowery controlled his laughter just long enough to ask everyone else to settle down. "Okay, guys," he said, trying to maintain a straight face, "we're about a hundred miles from Memphis, and I know this is a boring drive, but I want to make sure everyone knows what we're trying to accomplish this weekend."

"Win states, right, Coach?" chirped Joey.

"Right, Johnson, but that's not all. This is not just state championships. It's your national championship qualifier. Every state in the country is having its state championship this weekend. How each club does at states will determine placement for competition session at NTI's … assuming we get that far."

"Why wouldn't we get that far?" asked a surprised Patrick, who, having been to two NTI's, thought he knew all there was to know about the season's most important competition.

"There are only six automatic bids this year. In the past, each of the six national regions sent its six best teams based on their state championships scores. This year, only the top team from each region has a lock on getting in."

"So even winnin' states doesn't guarantee anything," said Mackee.

"That's right, Mack," answered Coach Lowery. "It's possible that we could win state and miss NTI's."

"That sucks," remarked Dallas, still rubbing his bruised cheek and regaining an exceptable level of awareness.

"And, the fun doesn't stop there. NTI's is a grueling two-day competition. Saturday's competition starts with thirty-six teams: the top finisher from each of the six national regions and the next thirty teams in rank order from state championships, regardless of region. They are seeded based on their score from states. Those teams compete over three sessions. The lowest twelve seeds compete in the first session, where we all know the scores are tight. The middle twelve compete the afternoon session. And, the top six regional finishers, plus the top six rank order teams compete in the much-desired late session.

"The top six teams after Saturday's competition will go head-to-head in the late session on Sunday night. The final session will be televised live nationwide, in prime time. It'll be a madhouse. And, it all starts here, at state championships. Not only do we need to win, but also how we score determines a lot of what happens to us down the road."

"No problem, Coach," said Mackee. "I think we are more than ready."

"I couldn't agree more, Mack," returned Coach, "which is why I felt that now would be a good time to let you guys in on the NTI format. You guys have trained well, are relaxed yet focused, and loose but with a sense of purpose."

"So, from here on out, it's a battle of attrition," added Ty.

"That's right, Ty," said Coach. "The team that can remain coolheaded and tend to the job at hand will emerge victorious."

"I guess that means no improvisations on routines, eh, Coach?" asked Dallas, referring to Chris's knack for inventing new routines at a moment's notice.

"Not if you can't hit your set, Dallas," answered Coach Lowery. "What we need for the next four weeks is consistency."

"What about high scores?" asked Chris.

"High scores will come with hit sets. This late in the season, I don't think that the two- or three-tenths of a point you might gain by putting something new in your routine is worth the risk of losing a half point for falling."

Although everyone was in silent agreement, all looked at Chris, who, although known for adding and changing his routine in a heartbeat, had yet to fall when doing so. Chris noticed that all eyes were upon him.

"What?" exclaimed the Californian. "Hey, listen, you guys have nothing to worry about. My sights are set on winning! And that means doin' exactly what Coach says, so … relax!" Chris turned his head to look out the bus window as if something more interesting lay in the Tennessee landscape. The team then looked at each other, not knowing whether to believe Chris's words or his history.

"I hate it when he says relax," Mackee whispered to Patrick

"That's enough, guys. From now until we get to the arena, I want you focused squarely upon your routines. When we get in, I want a quick, efficient warm-up, and everybody hits three sets on each event. Got it?" The team answered with a mumbled chorus of agreement and nods, except for Chris, who was already focused, either on his routines or counting telephone poles.

The team looked in silence at each other, searching their teammates' eyes for the look that matched their own resolve to finish the job that they had all started together. Upon the conclusion of Coach Lowery's speech, Dallas pulled his CD player out of his gym bag, put the headphones over his ears, and disappeared into his own world as the rest of the team sharpened its focus on the goal it had trained for all season, the National Team Invitational.

"Wow!" exclaimed AJ upon entering the Pyramid Arena, the site for the state championships. Joey could say nothing and just stood, mouth open, his eyes as big as saucers.

"Relax, fellas," said Coach Lowery, pushing Joey's chin up to close his mouth. "Sure this place is enormous … "

"And gorgeous … " added Mackee.

"And decked out … " added Ty.

"And *huge*!" concluded Joey.

"It's all of those things, guys. But, if you go over and take a look at the equipment, it's no different from anything you've trained and competed on all season long," concluded Coach. "Don't think of this as anything more than just another meet."

"With a hundred-foot ceiling," said Mackee.

"And, like, twenty thousand seats!" added Patrick.

"And *huge*!" repeated Joey.

"Can we get to work, Coach?" asked an annoyed Dallas, removing his headphones and totally removed from the others' conversation. "I don't know about you guys, but I've got a meet tomorrow. I'd like to get into bed sometime tonight."

"Dallas has a point, fellas," said Coach Lowery. "Let's get to work."

"Welcome to Memphis and the state gymnastics championships!" said a local team mom as she greeted each gymnast and handed each a goody bag on his way to the locker room. The parents club had gone out of its way to make each gymnast feel special, with decorations galore and plenty of free Elvis memorabilia and other souvenirs. The Memphis Chamber of Commerce had donated other gifts, and the Pyramid and Mud Island, both local attractions, added to the booty, along with the the host club, Pyramid Gymnastics, that had donated the grip bags that were being handed out to the gymnasts.

"Look, Chris," said Joey upon entering the gym and receiving his gift, "now you don't have to use a brown paper bag for your grips and stuff."

"I happen to like using a paper bag for my stuff," he returned.

"Not a bad setup, not bad at all," said Mackee, upon receiving his bag.

"All right, you guys," said Coach, "let's get to work. I'd like to check in sometime today. The lockers are right over there." Coach pointed to a doorway with a banner over it that read:

"THROUGH THESE DOORS GO CHAMPIONS"

"They must've known I was coming!" said Dallas upon reading the banner.

"They had no idea you were coming, Dallas," said AJ. "Had they known you were coming, it would've read, 'Through these doors go champions ... and David Dallas.'"

"Very funny, pizza face."

The guys made their way to the locker room to change clothes for workout. Joey, still in awe of the size of the gym, had stopped in the doorway. Moving too slowly for Dallas, Joey was brushed aside by the arrogant senior.

"Out of the way, Johnson. Some of us would like to get going."

"Oops, sorry, Dallas," said Mackee sarcastically, returning his shove. "I didn't see you standing there." Mackee winked at Joey. Dallas gave a thought to confronting Mackee but thought better of the obvious mismatch and continued into the locker room..

"Hey, Mack, what's up with Dallas?" asked Joey as Mackee helped him to his feet. "He's not his usual butt-headed self. It's, like, intensified! It's like he has no desire to be here at all."

"Don't let his attitude fool ya, kid. He loves this town. He's just a little nervous about this meet."

"Why? He hasn't cared about any competition all season long. Why start getting nervous now?"

"It's not the competition, Joey," added Patrick, joining the conversation. "Dallas is from Memphis. He's got a lot of old friends here. He's nervous about competition only to the extent that he doesn't want to look bad in front of his homeboys."

"Come on, guys," said Mackee, putting an arm around each teammate, guiding them through the locker room door. "Let's not keep our adoring coach waiting."

By the time the three made their way to the door, they were met by a sullen Chris, already dressed for workout, headed toward the competition floor.

"Are we in a hurry, Christopher?" asked Mackee as Chris brushed by.

"Nope, just doin' what Coach says," answered Chris without turning his attention away from his intended course. Joey, realizing that Chris was right, hustled ahead of Mackee and Patrick to get dressed and catch up to Chris.

While the rest of the Pioneers were slowly emerging from the locker room, Joey and Chris stretched on the floor exercise carpet. Chris, Joey noticed, had turned inside himself, methodically and quietly stretching and warming up. Joey looked around to find that, unlike most of the competitions the Pioneers had been to, the gym was surprisingly empty, with the exception of volunteers making last-minute preparations.

"Gosh, Chris," asked Joey, "where is everybody? You'd think for state championships, everyone would want to get in and spend as much time on the competition equipment as possible."

"I don't know, Joe. Maybe we're just early," Chris replied, not looking around.

"Don't you see?" said Dallas, approaching the royal blue plush carpet. "It's a foregone conclusion. The rest of the state is conceding the championship to us."

"Yeah right, Dallas," added Mackee. "Now if we can just get the rest of the region to do the same, we can avoid the inconvenience of having to compete!"

"Heck, while you're at it, Dallas, why don't you just inform the rest of the country that we accept the national title without contest!" joked Ty.

"What are you guys jabbering about?" asked Coach Lowery, joining the group.

"Well, sir," barked AJ, snapping to attention and saluting his coach, "Dallas has proclaimed us national champions without so much as token resistence from the opposition, and we are awaiting the terms of surrender from the rest of the gymnastics teams of the United States, sir!" AJ's right hand was still at a salute, his eyes fixed on a distant wall.

"At ease, Doujmovich," returned Coach Lowery, barely able to hold back a smile. "That's all fine and good, Dallas, but isn't it customary to at least throw a couple of routines and get some scores before the other side lays down and dies?"

"They're blowin' everything out of proportion, Coach. All I said was that no one else is bothering with being here for the workout because they know we're gonna slaughter 'em. So, what's the use?"

"Or, it could be that we're an hour early for the open workout, Dallas," returned Coach Lowery. "I just talked to Guy VanCleeve, the coach of Pyramid Gymnastics, and it appears that we forgot to take into account that we crossed over a time zone coming here. We gained an hour coming to this end of the state. Workout isn't supposed to start for another forty-five minutes."

"So, are we supposed to sit on our hands 'til then, Coach?" asked Mackee.

"No, we can go ahead and get started, but I just want to remind you guys that, even though we may be heavily favored this weekend, Dallas, we still have to hit routines to win. If the guys from Volunteer, Lookout, Music City, or Pyramid come out and hit routines, not only will our cockiness cost us our ranking in the region and, ultimately, the nation, but also we could lose the state title and end up watching NTIs on television. So, get focused!"

As the boys dispersed to get ready for their first event, Joey noticed that Chris had gone off on his own, warming up his swing on high bar instead of starting with floor with the rest of the team. Taking a cue from Chris, Joey walked over to the pommel horse to start his own work. Soon, each Pioneer picked up on the cues of the others and, before long, each of the Pioneers was on a different event: Mackee on rings, Dallas on Parallel Bars, Ty and AJ on Vault, and Patrick on Floor Exercise. Being the only ones on their events, it was no time before each gymnast was up to routine form.

The first team to enter the arena for open workout was Music City, from Nashville.

"Why'd you guys stopp?" barked the Music City head coach. "Let's get into the gym and get—" His words were clipped when he saw why his charges had stopped at the end of the entrance tunnel. Each piece of equipment was occupied by a Pioneer, each a likely state champion on the apparatus that they occupied, doing full routines easily above the grade of any other routines that would be done that weekend. The coach was also in appreciative stare.

"Ken Billings! Hey, pal, how ya doin'?" said Coach Lowery as he extended his right hand to the coach of Music City Gymnastics.

"Great, Jim! How are you?" returned the Nashville coach after being shaken from his daze. "You want to just let me know when we should come back and get *our* workout in?"

"Oh, that. We goofed up on the time change, and the guys just took advantage of the early start. Just jump in anywhere."

Soon, the other teams began filing into the gym, and in no time, the gym was full of athletes. Coach Lowery sat in the front row of seats looking over the meet information packet. His concentration was interrupted by the sound of cheering. When he looked up to locate the source, he noticed it was coming from everywhere there was a Pioneer gymnast. With each release, each complex combination, each stuck landing, the appreciation of fellow gymnasts was shown to each Pioneer, who was proving to easily be head and shoulders above the rest of the state. The other gymnasts knew this and were just glad that this team represented their state. For the first time, Coach Lowery realized that the rest of the state identified, appreciated, and were a part of this machine, and everyone was along for the ride.

"Okay, fellas," said Coach Lowery as the bus pulled into the hotel parking lot, "usual room assignments. AJ and Ty, you're in room 237, Joey and Chris in 239, Patrick, Dallas, and Mackee, you're in room 241."

"Hey, Coach," asked Dallas, "can I swap out with Slash? I want to bunk with someone who doesn't snore."

"Who snores?" asked Mackee, knowing full well that he was the culprit.

"Face it, Mack," said Patrick, "I have witnessed plaster falling off of the ceiling from your sonic vibrations."

"Johnson, you got a problem with this?" asked Coach.

"Shoot, it's just sleepin'," answered Joey, trying not to show his displeasure.

"Chris?"

"It don't matter to me, Coach. Once I'm out, it'll take much more than Mackee's snoring to wake me," Chris concluded.

"Okay, then. It's settled. Chris, you're in with Mack and Goodman. Dallas, you're in 239 with Johnson. You guys get into bed. You've got a very big day ahead tommorow. You'll need the rest. Lights-out in thirty miniutes."

The gymnasts grabbed their gear, collected room keys from Coach Lowery, and made their way to their rooms.

"I wonder why Dallas *really* wanted to room with Joey?" asked Mackee of his roommates as they climbed the flight of steps to their second-story hotel rooms.

"Could it be that you really do snore so loudly as to disturb a normal person's slumber?" asked Patrick rhetorically.

"Either that or Dallas is up to no good," said Chris suspiciously as they entered their room.

"Man, Dallas, did you see the eyes on us during workout?" asked an astonished Joey, throwing his bags into a chair and falling on the bed, gazing at the ceiling. "They were mesmerized! I'm surprised nobody asked us for our autographs!"

"Yeah, whatever," said an unconcerned Dallas, throwing his bag into a corner and heading for the phone.

"Who you callin', Dallas? Pizza this late? You heard Coach. We've got lights-out in fifteen minutes!"

"Shut up, squirt. I don't have to tell you ... oh ... Hello? Benny? ... Yeah, Dallas ... Naw, we just got in. We had a long workout ... I know it's quarter to eleven ... Yeah, come get me. We're in room ... Joey, what room is this?"

Joey was too stuned to answer.

"Never mind. Listen, Benny. There's a Kwikmart next to the hotel. How soon can you be there? ... Fifteen minutes? Excellent, I'll see you then ... cool. Later, dude."

As soon as Dallas hung up the phone, the interrogation began.

"Dallas, where do you think you're goin'? We've only got the biggest meet of the season tommorow, and you're gonna break curfew?"

"Don't worry about it, kid. This is my hometown. I rarely get to get out and hang with my boys. I'm not gonna pass up the opportunity because of some meet. Don't worry. I'll be back before you know it. Just don't say anything to anyone. I'm counting on you to keep quiet."

"You know that if Coach finds out, you'll be scratched from the meet!"

"That's right! So, it's probably a good idea if Coach doesn't find out! You get me, kid?" threatenened Dallas.

"That's why you wanted to room with me. You knew the others would rat on you."

"You're not as dumb as you look, Johnson. Look, I'll be back in a couple hours. You keep your mouth shut, and everybody wins. You blab, and the team will be short six scores … mine!" Dallas looked out the door to see if anyone was in the hallway, grabed his leather jacket, and then, as he pulled the door closed, he motioned his index finger to his mouth, looking at Joey, signaling him to keep quiet, which was no problem since Joey was standing still, dumbfounded and mute.

No sooner had the door closed, Joey heard a knock on the door. Joey's eyes lit up. "Dallas! You've had a change of—" Joey opened the door to reveal Chris instead of Dallas.

"Hey, where is Dallas headed?"

"Did you see him?"

"Yeah, but he didn't see me. I was getting some ice when he slithered by. Where is he goin'?"

"Chris, I tried to stop him! I told him he was gonna get into trouble! It's the biggest meet of the season!" replied Joey, hysterical and incoherent.

"Joey, slow down. One thing at a time. Now, where is he going?"

"He was meeting some friends at the Kwikmart in about ten minutes! From there, he didn't say. Do you think we need to tell Coach?"

"Naw, not yet. No sense creating more trouble than there is."

"Chris, where's that ice?" came a voice from behind Chris.

"Pat, come here," said Chris in a whisper just loud enough for Patrick to hear.

"What's up, fellas?" asked Patrick.

"Looks like I was right. Dallas bailed out. Seems he's got some nocturnal activities planned."

"Hey, guys, what's holdin' up that ice?" came Mackee's voice from the room next door. Patrick grabbed Mackee by the scruff of the neck, and all three filed into Joey's room, closing the door behind them.

"It appears Dallas has decided to go out to play tonight," said Chris.

"I didn't think my snoring was as bad as he said," said Mackee.

"No, your snoring *is* that bad, Mack, but that's beside the point," said Patrick. "What are we gonna do about Dallas?"

"I say we let him go. It's his butt if he gets caught," said Mackee.

"Yeah, but Joey gets into trouble for not saying anything," replied Patrick.

"How long ago did he leave, Joey?" asked Chris.

"About ten minutes ago. He's meeting somebody named Benny in about five minutes at the Kwikmart next door."

Suddenly, there was a knock at the door. Each looked at the other. Chris motioned for Mackee to head to the bathroom to turn on the shower.

"Who is it?" asked Chris.

"It's Coach Lowery, McClure. Open the door!"

Mackee returned from the bathroom, the shower going full blast.

"What's up, Coach?" asked Chris, only cracking the door.

"That should be my line. I thought you were sleeping in the other room with Mackee and Patrick."

"Oh, I am, but, uh, Joey called me over. He said his stomach was hurting."

"Let me take a look," said Coach, pushing the door open to reveal a roomful of Pioneers.

"It would appear we are treating by committee," said Coach. "Where's Dallas?"

"In the shower!" came the mixed chorus.

Sure that something was up, but not quite sure what, Coach Lowery dismissed the strange actions of the boys. "So, Joey, your stomach's hurting?"

Although Joey felt anxiety from Dallas's escapade, he realized that he wasn't exactly doubled over with pain, so he turned his face to a grimace.

"It's a little better now, Coach."

"I think it's just a case of butterflies, with the meet tomorrow and all," said Mackee.

"Perhaps," concluded Coach Lowery. "Well, you guys get into bed. You're about five minutes away from lights-out as it is."

"You got it," reassured Chris, subtly ushering Coach Lowery out the door and closing it behind him.

"That was way too close," said Patrick with a sigh of relief.

"Well, now what?" asked Joey.

"I bet if we hustle," said Chris, "we can catch him before his pals get there and drag him back."

"I don't think it's worth it, Chris," said Patrick. "I agree with Mack. I say we let him rot. No sense in all of us getting into trouble just because Dallas has a death wish. Sorry, Chris."

"Don't be. I don't know about you guys, but I'm goin' after Dallas," said Chris.

"I'm goin' with you!" exclaimed Joey, grabbing his jacket.

"No, you stay here, Joe. We need somebody here in case he calls."

"You know as well as I do that he's not gonna call here. Besides, I'm the one that dragged you guys into this."

"I'm going, too," said Mackee.

"Not me," said Patrick. "I'm stayin' here and getting some sleep. I'm not risking my butt because Dallas is stupid."

"As if you're gonna get any sleep now?" said Chris. "Wouldn't you much rather be with us than lying in your bed staring at the ceiling, wondering what's goin' on? Come on, it'll be an adventure!"

"An adventure?! I don't think my heart can stand another adventure. No, thanks. I'll just stay here."

"You know, Pat," said Mackee, "you're words say no, no, no, but your eyes say yes, yes, yes. Come on. What could happen?"

"Mack, it's Memphis, it's midnight. What do you think might happen?"

"That's okay, fellas," said Chris in a slightly sarcastic tone, "Plowboy doesn't want to hang with us. That's his deal. You guys ready to fly?"

"Wait a minute," said Patrick, reconsidering. "You guys will need me to keep you out of trouble."

"If anyone knows how to avoid trouble, it's you, Pat," said Mackee.

"Somehow, I know I'm going to regret this," said Patrick.

"Well, let's go. Time is a-wastin'," said Chris.

As the four exited the hotel, checking that no one has seen them, Mackee whispered the *Mission Impossible* theme.

"Dat dat *dat dat*, dat dat, *dat* dat."

"Mack, stow it, will ya?" asked Chris.

"I feel like a ninja," said Mackee, running across the parking lot in a stealth manner.

"Well, if we run into any bad guys, you be sure to use whatever brand of ninja martial arts you know," said Patrick, catching up.

The four walked into the Kwikmart, looking around in hopes of spying their teammate, but to no avail. Chris approached the clerk behind the counter while the others checked down the rows of the market.

"Excuse me, sir. Did you happen to see a young fella in here about ten minutes ago? Blond hair, leather jacket?"

The cashier, looking at Chris's imposing figure, was relieved to know that this was not a holdup. "Why, yes, a young man fitting that description was just in here moments ago. You only just missed him."

"Did he by any chance say where he was going?" asked Joey.

"Not to me," said the cashier.

"Did he meet anyone in here?" inquired Patrick.

"Wait, yes! He did meet someone in here. A couple of fellows came in. One with long brown hair. The other with black curly hair."

"Did either answer to the name Benny?" asked Joey.

"Yes, I believe that the one with long hair answered to that name."

"And, you're sure they didn't say where they were goin'?" asked Chris once again.

"Now that you mention it, they did say something about going down to the college district. There are many clubs there where the college students go."

"How far away is that from here?" asked Joey.

"About fifteen or twenty minutes from here."

"Great, are we supposed to walk?" asked Mackee.

"Sir, is there a bus that goes there from here?" asked Patrick.

"Yes, it should be along in about ten minutes."

"Cool!" said Chris. "We'll just hang out 'til the bus comes."

"Oh, yes! I remember, they were driving a new black Mustang. I do remember that!"

"Thanks a lot. You've been a big help. How much for these chips?"

"That'll be a dollar twenty-nine."

The boys left the market, each with a snack and a drink. They each had a seat on the bench at the side of the road to wait for the Memphis Public Transit System bus.

"Okay," said Joey, "let's assume we find Dallas. What are we gonna do?"

"Well, first, we'll appeal to his sense of decency and team commitment," said Chris.

"Then, we'll rationally discuss the pros and cons of breaking curfew," said Patrick.

"Then, we club him on the head and drag his sorry carcass back to the hotel!" said Mackee.

"Fine," said Joey, "it sounds like a plan."

"Hey, there's the bus!" said Mackee.

"Right on schedule. I hope the rest of this evening goes like clockwork," said Chris.

"College district!" shouted the bus driver as he opened the door. The boys quickly filed off of the bus.

"Wow! Look at the people!" exclaimed Joey, looking out over a sea of bodies.

"Must be some special occasion," added Mackee.

"Or, maybe this is what a typical Friday night is like in Memphis," surmised Patrick.

"Looks like your typical Friday night in your typical college town to me," said Chris.

"Oh, you've witnessed such celebration before, Christopher?" probed Mackee.

"Yeah, on television."

"Next question," asked Joey. "How do we go about finding Dallas?"

"Well, what do we know?" asked Chris.

"Black Mustang," said Joey.

"Black curly hair, long, straight brown hair and Dallas," said Mackee.

"All in leather," added Patrick.

"The Mustang was leather?" asked Joey.

"Very funny, Joe," quipped Patrick. "I suggest we move very fast. There's only so many places Dallas can get into."

"I dunno, Pat. After all, this is his hometown," said Mackee.

"Yeah, but he's been in Knoxville for quite a while. He may not have as many connections as you might think," said Patrick.

"But, he did have his two pals with him. That may be all the connection he needs," concluded Chris.

The boys set off. Walking quickly through the human ocean, the boys tried to peer into club after club. With each step, they each tried to find the familiar face or, even, the right combination of descriptives that might lead them to Dallas. Two hours went by with no luck.

"Man, I don't see any sign of Dallas," said Mackee.

"He could be back at the hotel by now, for all we know," said Patrick.

"I'm getting hungry," said Joey.

"You're always hungry," said Patrick.

"Well, it's not just him, Pat. I could go for a pizza myself," said Mackee. "Hey, Chris, can we postpone this manhunt for a little bodily nourishment?"

"Sure, fellas, there's a pizza stand over there," he said, pointing over the crowd and across the street. The group pushed their way through the crowd to the far side of the street to the curbside pizzeria, where they each got a couple slices of pizza and a soda.

"Hey, guys! I found a table!" exclaimed Joey. The boys sat down to enjoy their pizza.

"Just think, guys," said Mackee, looking at the crowd of late-night partyers. "Next year, this will be us, man. Except for you, Joey. You've got three more years, sucker."

"Actually, Mack," said Patrick, "I kinda picture myself buried in the books and busy in the gym when I get to college next year. What am I talkin' about? I mean *if* I get to college next year."

"You mean you still have not applied to a college?" asked Chris.

"Patrick thinks he may have to stay behind and help his folks," said Mackee.

"Man, the best way you can help your folks is to go to college and get an education," demanded Chris.

"Well, it takes money to go to college. Money that I, and my folks, haven't got, and I don't exactly see colleges jumping up to offer me scholarships," said Patrick, defending himself.

"The first step is to apply. Maybe, you're not hearing from schools because you've shown little or no interest in going to college," said Chris.

"That's easy for you to say, Chris. With your talent, you could pick your own ride!" exclaimed Patrick.

"Maybe with your brain, plowboy. I don't think I'm cut out for higher learning," said Chris, looking into the crowd. "I guess we all have our own reasons."

"Or excuses," added Joey, punctuating his statement with a straw slurp at the bottom of his soda cup. Silence followed as the group gazed different directions.

"Where the heck is Dallas, anyway?" asked Joey.

From a distance, a familiar pair of eyes spied the quartet in their seats.

"Benny, look!" said Dallas, pointing out his teammates to his pal. "Those are guys on my team!"

"Wow, man, are they, like, breakin' curfew, too?" asked the alcohol-affected friend.

"Yeah, but I bet they're not out to party, pal. I bet they're out tryin' to track me down. I've got to think of something."

"Why not send 'em a hooker?"

"Naw, that's way too obvious. Besides, McClure's probably the only one who would know what to do with one. No, I've got a better idea. C'mon," and the two slipped into the darkness.

"All right, Chris," asked Mackee, "how much longer are we gonna continue this wild goose chase?"

"Yeah, I'm pretty beat, myself," said Patrick.

"You guys go ahead and go back. I'm gonna look for at least another half hour."

"I'll hang with you, Chris," said Joey. "But, I've got to get some sleep tonight, or I'll be worthless tomorrow."

"You've got my word. Thirty minutes, no more."

"Okay, I'm in for a half hour, but no more!" said Patrick. The four got up to leave. Just as the group stepped out into the street, Mackee collided with someone.

"Hey, watch where you're goin', you Mack truck—" said the stranger before he came to realize whom he had hit. "Hey! Aren't you guys Pioneers?"

"Should we know you?" asked Chris.

"Hey, wait. Don't you compete for Pyramid Gymnastics, here in town?" asked Mackee.

"Yeah! Billy, Billy Yates. I saw you guys work out today. You guys were awesome! Hey, what are you guys doin' out here? Shouldn't you guys be resting up for tomorrow?"

"I guess the same could be asked of you, Billy," said Chris.

"Yeah, except that we don't have a prayer of winning, and our coach doesn't really care what we do outside the gym."

"Oh, well, whatever," said Patrick. "Actually, we're out trying to find our—"

"A good time!" interrupted Chris. "We're trying to find a good time, and quite frankly, we don't know this town so well. So, where do the rest of the guys go for laughs?"

"No problem, guys. There's a club right up the street, to the left. It's called Pandora's."

"As in the box?" asked Joey.

"Right. It's a no-alcohol joint, so there's no problem getting in. It's a dance club. All the cool chicks go there, so naturally, that's where the team guys hang out."

"Great! Thanks, Billy!" said Chris as they started to make their way up the street. "We'll catch you tomorrow!" The boys continued their quest.

"There it is!" exclaimed Joey upon sighting the neon cursive letters on the side of a brick wall.

"Chris, do you see what I see?" said Mackee, pointing to a black Mustang parked in the adjacent alley.

"Got it, Mack."

The foursome approached the entrance of the second-story dance club where they were met by a bouncer. "IDs, please," came his request. The guys pulled their wallets from their pockets and showed their driver's licenses.

"Sorry, fellas," said the bouncer, "you hafta be eighteen to get in here."

"We were told that anyone could get in here!" said a perplexed Joey.

"Yeah, anyone over eighteen."

"But there's no alcohol. Why keep us out if there's no alcohol?" said Patrick.

"What do you mean there's no alcohol? Of course there's alcohol! That's why under eighteen you can't get in."

"But we were told that there's no alcohol," pleaded Joey.

"By who?" asked the bouncer.

"That's not important," said Chris. "Obviously, they were wrong. Look, we have reason to believe that a friend of ours, a minor I might add, is inside, and we've come to get him out."

"Look, fellas, I'd like to help you out, but if I let you guys in, even just to look for your 'friend,' I could lose my job!"

"Then, how do you suggest we find him?" asked Mackee.

"Do you have a picture of him?"

The boys looked at each other.

"Gee, I left all of my pictures of Dallas in my other wallet!" said Mackee sarcastically.

"Well, what's he look like? I'll call in for someone to look for him."

After giving a general discription, the bouncer called into the club on his cell phone. A few minutes went by before a return call was made. The four hung on each word of his half of the conversation.

"Sorry, fellas. Nobody fitting that description is in the club tonight. Sorry I couldn't help you."

"Wait," said Joey, "he had some friends with him. One with long brown—"

"Forget it, Joey," said Chris, leading him away. "He's not here."

"But, Chris, he's gotta be here! The car!"

"I said forget it, Joe! We'll have to look somewhere else!" joined Mackee, picking Joey up by the elbows with Chris, carrying him away from the door. Once out of the bouncer's sight, they let him down.

"I'm with you, Joey," said Chris. "I think he's in there."

"Then, let's go back. They have to let us in!"

"They won't, squirt. That's why we left," said Mackee.

"I don't get it," said a confused Joey.

"Look, the car is still here, which means Dallas is still here," said Patrick, "which means we have to find a way in there."

"Do you think they have a fire escape in back?" asked Mackee.

"Do you think they could be in business without one?" returned Chris. The boys scurried around back to find the fire escape, a telescoping ladder that extended down with the weight of the escapee.

"There it is, Mack," said Chris.

"How do you suppose we reach the bottom of the ladder?" said Patrick. "It must be an easy twelve feet up there."

"Holy crud, you guys," said Chris. "We're gymnasts, for cryin' out loud. This is a no-brainer. We just build a pyramid! I'll be on the bottom with Patrick. Mackee, you're in the middle, and Joey, you make like a monkey!"

"Wait a second, fellas," exclaimed Joey, "no mats, no spotters, heck, no chalk! I don't like this."

"Joey, you want to get up there to see if Dallas is there, don't you?" asked Patrick.

"Yes, just as much as you. So, why don't *you* climb up?"

"'Cause you're the smallest," said Mackee.

"Look, you guys want to get this done, or should we just stand here and cause a scene until everyone in Memphis knows we're here? Joey, stop whining. Just do it," ordered Chris.

Joey mumbled beneath his breath while the others built their part of the pyramid. Once ready, Joey took a deep breath and scurried up the human tower as if it were a solid willow tree. Joey grabbed the bottom of the ladder, pulling it down on top of the group, scattering the older guys, causing each to fall to the ground. Once regaining their bearings, each looked up to see Joey hanging from the end of the ladder, his feet still three feet above the ground.

"You guys just gonna lie there, or are you gonna help me get this thing down? I think it's a little stuck," said Joey, looking down on his friends. Chris held Joey's legs as Patrick jumped to join Joey on the end of the ladder, forcing it free and extending it down where each could access it. The boys climbed the fire escape to the landing on the second floor.

"Try the window, Mack," said Chris.

"Won't budge. Must be locked from the inside," said an exhausted Mackee.

"That's a violation of fire code!" said Joey.

"We'll be sure to report them to the fire marshal when this is all over, Joey," said Patrick.

"We'll have to go up," said Chris. "We may have to go up on the roof and come down the stairway."

With each floor, the boys met a locked window until they found themselves on the roof.

"Wow. Memphis looks cool from up here!" said Joey, looking over the expansive cityscape.

"Great, Joe. You admire the view. We're gonna go get Dallas," said Patrick.

"Hey, I found the door to the stairwell!" said Mackee.

"Great! Let's go!" said Patrick.

"Not so fast, Pat. The door's locked," said Chris.

"What now?" asked Joey.

"Well, we could wait for someone to come out onto the roof," suggested Mackee.

"Now, who is going to come up here and open that door?" asked Patrick.

Just then, the door opened. A couple that had met in the club was coming up to the roof for some privacy.

"Excuse us. We didn't know the roof would be occupied!" said the surprised young man.

"Oh, don't mind us," said Mackee, catching the door, "we were just passing through."

"Have fun!" added Joey.

"Watch out. This door locks," said Patrick.

"Yeah, I know," said the young man, realizing he had just cooked his own goose.

"You know?" asked his date. "Who *else* have you been up here with?"

"We'll just leave you two alone," said Chris, ducking inside the doorway.

The boys made their way down the stairwell to the second floor. Mackee stopped to look around the corner as the others caught up.

"What's our situation, Mack?" asked Chris.

"Well, I got good news, and I got bad news."

"What's the bad news?" asked Patrick.

"There's a bouncer at the door."

"What's the good news?" asked Joey.

"There's *a* bouncer at the door."

"So, what we need is a diversion," said Chris.

"I'll do it," said Joey. "When he takes me away, you guys sneek in."

"You sure you want to do this, Joey?" asked Patrick.

"No, but it has to be someone."

Joey collected himself and walked around the corner, walking right in front of the bouncer.

"Hey, kid. Where do you think you're going?"

"I'm tryin' to find the bathroom, man. Where's the little boys' room?"

"It's right up ... hey, wait a minute. Let's see some ID, kid."

"ID? Why? I know who I am. Isn't that enough?" Joey prodded the bouncer.

"Okay, kid. Out you go." The bouncer took Joey by the upper arm and led him down the stairs toward the front door. The others saw their opportunity and made their way into the club. As they passed the entrance, they could hear Joey argue with both bouncers while they tried to blame each other for letting him in.

"That Joey," exclaimed Mackee, "what a character."

The club was dark, except for the flashing strobe lights, colored lights coming from the dance floor, and the neon drink advertisements over the bar. The place was packed.

"How are we gonna find Dallas in this?" asked Patrick.

"Process of elimination," answered Mackee. "Whatever doesn't look like Dallas, we eliminate."

"Very funny, Mack," said Patrick. "I hope none of these guys eliminate us."

"I suggest we spread out," said Chris. "We'll find him quicker." The boys set out in different directions looking for Dallas. Mackee squeezed his way toward the bar, looking at each of the faces he could make out in the neon glow. Patrick headed around the other side, by the table seating, trying not to be intrusive as he looked into each group. Chris headed straight across the dance floor.

"Hey, man! Watch where you're goin'!" came the voice from the stranger in front of Mackee.

"Sorry, man. This place is so crowded! How does anyone control their own movement? Everything O.K.?" Mackee asked of the man obviously fifteen years his senior, a foot taller, and at least a hundred pounds heavier.

"Yeah, you bumping into me just nearly caused me to wear this beer instead of drink it!"

"Again, dude, I'm sorry. Let me buy you another one," insisted Mackee.

"Naw, I'm fine, but you look like you could use one. Let me. What are you drinking?"

"No, nothing for me. I'm in training," said Mackee proudly.

"Training? For what?"

"Gymnastics. Our state championships start tomorrow."

"Aren't you out a little late for an athlete whose got competition this weekend?"

"Well, actually me and some buds are trying to find one of our teammates who's AWOL."

"Hey, I got an idea," said the stranger. "Can you do a standing backflip?"

"Of course."

"Great. Hold still." The stranger turned to the man next to him. Mackee couldn't hear what was being said. Moments later, the stranger turned back around.

"Hey, kid," said the stranger, as if he had never spoke to Mackee before. "I'll give you five bucks if you can do a standing backflip."

"Right here?" asked Mackee, questioning the cramped quarters.

"Sure, man. Go for it!" said the other stranger, much smaller than Mackee but still much older.

Mackee cleared a spot around where he stood, and before the space could be filled with other patrons, Mackee quickly swung his arms, jumped off the floor and executed a flawless back tuck, sticking his landing. A cheer came up from those around him as his flip put him squarely at the center of attention.

"That was great, kid. All right, Jake, pay up!" the smaller of the two pulled out his wallet and gave the other a ten-dollar bill.

"Here ya go, kid," the stranger handed Mackee a five-dollar bill. "Now, you've paid for my beer and yours, too!" He leaned in to whisper to Mackee, "Don't worry about Jake. He's drunk. He'll think he spent the money on beer. By the way, good luck this weekend."

"Thanks," said a confused, but five dollars richer, Mackee as he continued his search across the bar.

Not exactly my kind of music, thought Chris, but the babes out here are awesome. Chris maneuvered his way across the dance floor, looking at the faces of dancers. Although he was primarily trying to find Dallas, he certainly was not going to waste an opportunity to check out the feminine fare that the dance floor had to offer. Chris saw three very attractive girls dancing together. Either they can't find decent dance partners, he thought, or they are content just being with each other. Once Chris got close enough to inquire, the answer became self-evident as the three encircled him, and he became part of their little party. Chris didn't mind a bit. His dance moves were not shabby, and these fine-looking young ladies seemed to be enjoying themselves, so all was well, Chris surmised.

Just as he was getting into the dance party, Chris looked up to see just what he had been looking for. Blond hair, leather jacket. It was Dallas.

"Excuse me, ladies," Chris told his dance partners as he left the trio to walk up behind his wayward teammate and the source of everyone's turmoil that night. Chris approached from behind, tapping Dallas on the shoulder.

"You know, if I had known any better," Chris said as he turned him around, "I'd swear … you … didn't have a beard when you left this evening." Much to Chris's surprise, he had grabbed the wrong person. "Look, pal, I'm sorry. I thought you were someone else!" The shock of fingering the wrong person had completely put Chris out of the party mood. He said thank you to the trio he had shared a dance with and somberly made his way back across the dance floor.

There's got to be a hundred tables here, Patrick thought. So many faces, each one looking like someone he knew or should know. Being polite, Patrick tried not to stare. The darkness of the club, mixed with the flashes of different colored lights from the dance floor, made it a difficult task. Patrick stopped to scan over a few tables at a time.

"Hey, handsome," came the voice of a beautiful blonde seated in front of where Patrick had stopped to look over the crowd, "did you lose something?"

"Actually, I'm looking for someone," said Patrick, trying very hard not to be distracted from the task at hand.

"Well, I'm someone," she said invitingly.

"No, you don't understand. I'm looking for a guy."

"Oh, I see. You're *tha*t way," she said coldly.

"No, I'm not!" said Patrick, realizing what he had just said. "I'm looking for a friend of mine." Patrick sat down beside the blonde. "He's busted curfew."

"Curfew? For what?"

"He and I are gymnasts. Our state championships are this weekend. My buddies and I are trying to collect him before our coach notices that we're gone."

"It seems you've all broken curfew."

"You're right. We probably should be getting back. We're not having much luck."

"What does your friend look like?"

"About five nine, blond hair, blue eyes, muscular build, leather jacket, and jeans."

"Sounds like David Dallas to me."

"You know Dallas?" said a surprised Patrick.

"Yeah. I hadn't seen him for a couple of years, but I ran into him out on the strip earlier tonight. I thought he moved to Nashville or Knoxville, wherever his folks are from."

"Knoxville. Yeah, Dallas's folks own most of it."

"My dad works in the University of Tennessee system. He goes to Knoxville once in a while. I didn't know David was a gymnast."

"I'm sure it's something he's kept from his friends here in Memphis. Have you seen him here tonight?"

"Nope, not at all. The guys that he hangs out with wouldn't be caught dead in here. They're more the headbanger type."

"Headbangers, eh? This is obviously a side of Dallas that he has never revealed to any of his teammates." Patrick scanned the room once more in vain.

"I've always wondered, Patrick, how do judges come up with their score?" Patrick decided his search could wait for five minutes as he tried to describe gymnastics scoring.

"Okay, each routine on each event has a difficulty requirement, special requirements of that event, and then there's bonus. Each skill has a value. Easy skills, like back handsprings, are worth one tenth and are called As. Bs are two tenths and so on up to F. You total the number of As, Bs and so on to get your difficulty requirement. Then you have five special requirements, exclusive to that event that are worth five tenths each. Then you have the possibility of bonus by doing extremely hard elements or connecting hard elements. Add all that up and you have what's called a start value. Then the judges use their pencils like hachets and start deducting for all the mistakes you make; a tenth for a flexed foot, a tenth for stepping out of bounds, five-tenths if you fall off."

"Sounds complicated. How do judges keep up?" she asked.

"Well the judges are well trained to know what to look for, and only judges with a ton of experience can judge at high levels. That way we all know that it's as fair as it can be and the right guy gets the right score."

"So, where do you rate?"

"About the middle, I guess." Patrick decided to change the subject and resumed his scan of the room for Dallas.

"Well, I guess this search was a dead end," said Patrick, disheartened.

"I hope it hasn't been a total loss. Uh, what's your name again?"

"Oh, I'm sorry, Patrick. My name's Patrick Goodman and, no, this night hasn't been a total loss. Um, uh, I … don't—"

"Nicole. I'm Nicole."

"Let's try this again. Hi, my name is Patrick Goodman. So very nice to meet you."

"Hi, I'm Nicole Ashley. Very nice to meet you."

"Now that we've been properly introduced, would you like to come watch the competition tomorrow?"

"Sure. Where is it?"

"At the Pyramid. Competition starts about one thirty. One thirty! Holy cow! I had better get going." Patrick got up from the table.

"Great. So I'll see you tomorrow?" said Nicole.

"Sure. It's a date," said Patrick excitedly. Patrick turned to leave, then turned back quickly. "Do you know a guy named Billy Yates?"

"Yeah, he's a good friend of Dallas'. I saw them together on the strip earlier."

"It figures. Thanks again. Very nice to meet you, Nicole." Patrick turned and hurried away to meet his pals.

The three rejoined on the other side of the room.

"Any luck?" asked Chris.

"Yeah," said Mackee, "I made five bucks! But no Dallas."

"Actually, I got quite lucky," said Chris. "I got three offers to dance, and one girl offered to drive me home. But, same here, no Dallas."

"Well, I met a very interesting girl who knows Dallas and says there's no way he would've been here, anyway."

"I smell a rat," said Chris.

"And that guy we saw on the street?" said Patrick.

"Billy Yates?" asked Mackee.

"Right. Nicole says he and Dallas are big-time pals. She saw them together earlier tonight."

"Nicole, eh?" proded Chris

"There they are!" came the voice from the other side of the club, more specifically from the bouncer from the front door who was pointing his chubby index finger at them. "I told you that kid was with three other guys!" Before long, the trio was led out the front door, rather roughly.

"I take it that you guys didn't find him?" said Joey, leaning on a lamppost.

"How'd you guess?" asked Patrick sarcastically as the three picked themselves up off of the pavement and dusted themselves off.

"Hey, you guys, look!" said Patrick, pointing to the alley to reveal the squealing tires of the Mustang and the roar of the engine as it pulled away. The sound of laughter could be heard over the exhaust.

"Gentlemen, I believe we have been had," said Chris. "We had better get back to the hotel in one big hurry."

"What time is it?" asked Joey.

"Half past three," said Patrick, looking at his watch.

"Omigosh!" exclaimed Joey.

"No time to wait for a bus. We better catch a cab," said Mackee.

"Four o'clock! We're gonna get killed!" said Joey under his breath as the four sneaked back into the hotel.

"Only if you panic loud enough and wake up Coach," said Mackee.

"Look, fellas," said Chris, "get into bed fast. Get as much sleep as you can. We don't have to be at the gym until noon."

"Yeah, but Coach wants us at breakfast at nine," said Patrick. "That's only five hours away."

"Then, I suggest we all get into bed right away," advised Chris.

Joey slipped into his room as quietly as he could, trying to move around the dark room with as little noise as possible.

"Why don't you turn on a light, Joey?" came the voice from the other side of the room.

"Dallas!" Joey exclaimed with surprise. "I was just out getting a—"

"Give it up, squirt. I had you and your buddies made right from the start. Did you guys really think you could find me in my own town?"

"Dallas, it is state meet. You couldn't blame us for trying."

"If you guys wanted a night out, you should've told me. We could've had a blast instead of playing cat and mouse."

"That wasn't the idea, actually, Dallas. Anyway, I'm tired, and I don't want to talk about it. We better get some sleep. We've got a huge day tomorrow."

"Right. It should be quite interesting."

Joey quickly got out of his clothes and into bed. Dallas is right, he thought, tomorrow will be quite interesting.

"This is a switch!" exclaimed Coach Lowery, looking over the breakfast table. "Usually, Dallas is the one with his head buried in his arms. Johnson! McClure! Goodman! Mackee! Wake up, you guys!"

"Coach, are you getting ready to address the team, or can I go get seconds?" said an unusually perky Dallas.

"Not yet, Dallas. I don't think that anything I say will register with some of your teammates. You go ahead."

Dallas went back to the breakfast bar.

"All right, you guys. What's up? Patrick, why are you guys so dead?" asked Coach Lowery.

"Uh,... ... it was Mackee!" Patrick thought fast. "His snoring kept me up all night!"

"Me, too, Coach," Chris chimed in.

"What about you, Mack? Sounds to me like you're the only one who got any sleep. Why are you so dead?"

"Gosh, Coach, these two must've woke me up twenty times last night, telling me to roll over!" Mackee covered.

"How else were we gonna stop him from snoring?" asked Chris.

"Okay, that makes sense. Mackee, you might ought to think about seeing a doctor about that snoring. I think they can do something for that now."

"Yes, sir," replied Mackee.

"Johnson!" barked Coach Lowery, jostling a semiconscious Joey. "What's your excuse? Mackee's snoring keep you awake in another room?" Coach asked sarcastically.

"Uh … no, Coach. Just nerves, I guess. Didn't sleep much at all last night," said a quick-thinking, barely awake Joey.

"Well, whatever the reason for the loss of sleep, fellas, you only have your biggest meet of the season this afternoon. It would be nice if you guys were awake for it!"

"I guess some people are just not morning people," chirped Dallas upon returning to the table.

"Shut up, Dallas!" said the entire group in unison.

"All right, guys," said Coach Lowery, as he stood up on the bus, "no fooling around. We get inside, we get to work, and we get the job done. Although our goal is the NTI's, we can't afford to overlook this competition. We all know what it means. Now let's mean business."

The boys stepped off the bus, each alone with his thoughts: Chris and Mackee wishing for more sleep, Joey hoping he could count for team score, Ty and AJ focused on routines, Patrick hoping he didn't let down his coach, and Dallas wondering how long he could fight exhaustion to keep up his front.

"Man, am I beat," Joey said as he walked alongside Chris.

"Just do the best you can, Joe. No one can ask for more than that," answered Chris.

"So, do you think it was worth the bother, Pat?" asked Dallas.

"No. You're right, Dallas," answered Patrick, "my idea was to stay at the hotel and rat you out. I would've been much happier. It would serve you well to stay as far away from me as possible." Dallas slowed his pace to be the last to enter the building.

As they entered the gym, Joey noticed that there were many more spectators in the stands than usual. Usually, not many people were in the stands during warm-ups, opting to wait until just before the opening ceremonies to take their seats.

"Chris, why are their so many folks here now?" asked Joey.

"I don't know, Joe. Maybe they're here to see me."

"Maybe they're here to see me!" said Joey defiantly.

"Maybe so, Joe. Maybe so."

"Chris!" came the familiar feminine voice from the balcony rail.

"Haley! Hi, babe. Glad you could make it."

"Hi, sis."

"Hey, Joey. Are you takin' care of my baby?"

"Oh, yeah," said Joey sarcastically. "I even tucked him into bed last night."

"Hey, sis, got any idea why so many folks are here already?"

"Are you kidding? You guys are the hottest ticket in Memphis! Aside from the publicity that Pyramid Gymnastics did to get folks in here, everyone in the state is here to see the Pioneers. There's people from all over here that have heard about how great the team is this year, and those who won't be going to NTI's figure they can come here and see the national champions!"

"Seems we've got some livin' up to do," said Chris.

"Chris, it's more than that. There are college scouts here."

"Don't tell Patrick," said Joey. "He's nervous enough as it is."

"Hey, Pat," called Mackee, as he caught up to Patrick, "isn't that the chick you talked to last night at that dance club?"

Patrick turned his head to scour the crowd in the general direction of Mackee's gaze. There, among the other spectators that had arrived early, Patrick picked out the shapely frame and long blonde hair of Nicole. Sitting patiently in a flower print dress, Nicole's eyes met Patrick's, and she waved, barely raising her closed hand so as not to draw too much attention. Patrick stopped in his tracks, acknowledging her wave with one of his own, only a little larger—using his entire arm and waving high over his head.

"Wow, I didn't think she'd come," said Patrick. "I hope I don't screw up too much."

"Don't worry, pal," said Mackee, turning and pushing him toward the dressing room, "we'll probably all goof up so much, she'll never notice."

The Pioneers got dressed in relative silence. The first ones ready waited for the others to get prepared so they could enter the gym together. Upon emerging from the dressing room, they were not quite prepared for the welcome they received. Haley had coordinated many of the hometown supporters. A large banner, emblazoned with the letters "PIONEERS!" was held up by Haley and five others as the screaming began. By the time open stretch had finished and it was time for the gymnasts to begin warm-up on their first event, the seats were already half full of the twenty thousand capacity seats.

"This should be interesting," said Chris.

"If nothing else," said Patrick.

The Pioneers, being top seed in the state, would start warm-up on Pommel Horse so that their final warm-up event would be their first competition event, Floor Exercise, and follow Olympic order: Floor, Pommel Horse, Rings, Vault, Parallel Bars, and finish on High Bar.

"This could be better," said Mackee, watching as none of the Pioneers could stay on the horse during warm-ups.

"I hope this is not a sign of things to come," said Coach Lowery.

"Now, Coach," said Chris, lying flat on his back following a fall off of the horse, "you know we always compete better than we warm up."

"It would have to be much better," said a disappointed Coach Lowery.

Warm-up on rings was not much better. Strength parts were not held for an adequate amount of time, handstands were not held, and basic form was suspect. Coach Lowery rubbed his chin. Vault was the same as Rings. Landings were short or over-rotated. A scary moment occurred when Ty got lost in a full-twisting Tsukahara and landed on his side. Although there was a soft mat under him, he was still visibly shaken.

"That doesn't make sense," Joey whispered to Chris. "He and AJ had a full night's sleep."

"Who knows, Joe? They may have stayed up all night playing video games."

"Either that or *fumble-itis* is contagious," said Mackee.

Coach Lowery rubbed his temples.

The crowd had settled down by the time the Pioneers got to parallel bars. Again, the team looked shaky. Skills that should end in handstand were either short or needed several steps to save, or just plain missed, landing gymnasts on the floor, or in some cases, on the rails. Coach Lowery sat in the seating provided for the judges with his head in his hands.

High bar, although not as sharp as it could be, did show some signs of resurgence. Patrick connected his release moves without a problem but had trouble landing his dismount. Chris was his usual dynamic self, swinging big release moves and cranking giants that, should he peel off the bar at that speed, would catapult him across the gym. The fatigue was starting to set in for Dallas, as he couldn't connect anything. Coach Lowery was back on his feet. "Okay, guys, let's have a good warm-up on floor so we have a little momentum going into the meet."

The warm-up on floor was much better than the other events. Although there weren't many great landings, at least they were all landing on their feet. Coach Lowery wiped sweat from his brow.

Warm-up time concluded, the athletes moved to the dressing room to get ready for march in.Normally during this time, when the gym is quiet and clear, coaches go through their game plans to make sure they have done everything they can to help their charges succeed. Coach Lowery usually used this time to think of any last-minute corrections. However, today, given the way his team warmed up, he used this time to pray that no one got hurt.

As the Pioneers lined up for the opening ceremonies, Dallas's lack of sleep was starting to catch up to him.

"Hey, Pat," Mackee whispered to Patrick while motioning him to look at Dallas, "looks like Dallas could use a nap."

"Dallas! You catchin' flies, or what?" proded Patrick, catching Dallas in mid-yawn.

"Speak for yourself, Goodman," returned Dallas, knowing that Patrick and the others had as little sleep as he.

"Ladies and gentlemen," called the meet announcer, "welcome to the Pyramid, and the National Team Invitational qualifier and the Tennessee Men's Gymnastics Championships!"

The beginning of the opening ceremonies brought the now full Pyramid to its feet. With the introduction of each team, the hometown boosters of each club cheered their athletes. As the Pioneers entered the gym, the capacity crowd raised the volume to a fever pitch. Once the teams entered the gym, the introductions began. With each team introduced, the crowd once again screamed wildly. Upon the introduction of the Pioneers, the entire crowd cheered madly, letting the team know that the entire state was behind their quest to bring a national team title to Tennessee.

In the madness of the cheers, Chris leaned to Patrick's ear.

"Looks like we've got our work cut out for us. I hope we're up to it."

"We'll have to be," answered Patrick, determined.

As the singing of the national anthem came to a close, Patrick was filled with a sense of pride and concern. Knowing that this was the start of his final quest to a championship as a Pioneer and that his team may not be quite up to the task today bought an uneasy feeling to the pit of his stomach.

"Gentlemen," shouted the announcer, "report to your first competitive event."

"Let's rock and roll, guys," said Chris as the gymnasts collected their gym bags and headed for their first event.

"Okay, Mackee," said Coach Lowery, "you're first up on floor. Let's start off with a good routine to set the pace."

Mackee looked at Patrick and Chris, and both gestured encouragingly. Mackee then looked at Dallas, who did not return eye contact. Instead, Dallas was in a world of his own. Mackee made his way to the corner of the floor exercise carpet, saluted the head judge, and stepped up onto the spring, foam, and carpeted surface. With a cleansing breath, Mackee ran for his first tumbling pass, a round off, back handspring, double back tucked. Everyone on the sidelines, especially those who had been with Mackee the night before, held their breath, knowing that this first skill could set the tone of the entire competition.

One flip, two flips, Mackee searched for his landing, coming to rest on his feet with a near-perfect landing. Everyone in the stands burst into cheers, the Pioneers raised their fists and yelled. Mackee breathed a sigh of relief, knowing that although he was safe on his feet, he still had three more passes to complete and five more routines before he would be done for the day, and a lot could happen between now and then.

With the balance of his floor routine finished, Mackee knew all that remained was the dismount, a layout with two twists. Mackee gulped a quick breath of air before sprinting across the blue diagonal. He whipped his round off, back handspring and jumped up in the air and began to twist. One twist, two twists, Mackee opened his arms to stop the twisting and prepare for his landing, but something was wrong. Instead of seeing the royal blue carpet, all Mackee could see was lights. He had undertwisted, and before he could recover, Mackee felt the thud of landing flat on his back.

The cheers turned to gasps as the crowd rose to its feet to see if the fallen Pioneer was okay. After regaining his breath, Mackee slowly rose to his feet, saluted the judges, and slowly walked off of the carpet, his left hand rubbing his lower back.

"Are you okay, Mack?" asked Coach Lowery, meeting Mackee at the carpet's edge.

"Yeah, I'm fine, Coach. Just wounded my pride. I sure picked a fine time to land a dismount to my butt."

"Not to worry, Mack," encouraged Coach Lowery. "Your teammates and your other five events will pick up the slack."

"I hope you're right, Coach."

"Hey, Mack, look on the bright side," cut Dallas, "at least you stuck your landing. Ha, ha, ha."

"I got somethin' for you to stick, Dallas." Mackee had to be restrained by Chris and Patrick.

"Come on, pal," said Patrick, "he's not worth the bother. There are better ways to spend your energy."

"Yeah, but few more enjoyable." Mackee's teammates agreed.

Joey stepped to his ready position to start his routine. His fatigue was evident on his first pass. Joey's double twist ended well short of a perfect landing, causing Joey to put his hands down, and automatic three-tenths of a point deduction. His second pass was not much better, landing a full-twisting front layout first on his heels and then on his bottom after several steps trying to catch himself. Once on his seat, Joey realized that he could not finish his routine the way he had practiced. So he decided to improvise, doing easier skills designed to keep him on his feet through the finish.

Joey walked off of the floor, obviously dejected.

"Don't worry, Joe," said Coach Lowery encouragingly, "you've got five more events to go."

"That doesn't exactly cheer me up, Coach."

"Well, put it behind you, Joey."

"You know, it could've been worse, Johnson," said Dallas.

"How's that, Dallas?"

"It could've been *me*! Ha, ha, ha!"

Joey did not need restraint, knowing that he would be no match against Dallas.

"Don't worry, Joey," encouraged Chris, "Dallas is just as spent as we are. This should be interesting."

Dallas smirked as he made his way to the edge of the floor exercise carpet to begin his routine. Dallas saluted and stepped into the corner. Knowing that he was every bit as tired as the others, Dallas was determined not to be weak on his tumbling. He sprinted across the diagonal of the floor for his first tumbling run, turning over his round off, back handspring as fast as he could. Dallas punched his feet into the spring floor as hard as he could to achieve enough height for his tucked double back. Upon landing, Dallas realized that he had over-rotated, landing on his heels, then rolling out of bounds, taking a judges' table with him.

While the spectators had reason, once again, to gasp, the Pioneers had found amusement in Dallas's folly.

He regained his control, standing in the corner where he should have landed a correctly executed double back. Dallas sprinted toward the opposite corner to do his second pass, a front handspring, front layout, front layout full twist, front tuck. At least that was what he was supposed to do, but his pass ended early, with him on his bottom after completely mistiming his second flip. Dallas turned over to a push-up position as the arena went silent, except for the snickers that came from those who knew Dallas. Dallas tried in vain to execute his press handstand. After his second attempt failed, Dallas resorted to jumping to the handstand position, which was not held for the required amount of time to receive any credit for the skill. Dallas stepped down from his handstand. It was at this moment that everyone could see the combination of blush in his embarrassed face and the rage in his frustrated eyes. Determined, Dallas sprinted across the floor for his final pass, a layout full and a half twist to immediate punch front flip piked. Once again, Dallas mistimed his punch and found himself squarely on his seat. In a state of rage, Dallas stormed off of the floor and toward his seat.

The consolation applause from the crowd brought Dallas no comfort. He knew he would have to face the teammates that he had harassed earlier.

"You know, Dallas, you were right," said Joey as Dallas stormed by, "I could've been you!"

"Yeah, cheer up, Dallas," added Mackee, "at least you stuck your dismount!"

The Pioneers had a good laugh as Dallas tromped off to the locker room, Coach Lowery close behind him.

"Dallas, you're supposed to acknowledge the head judge when you finish, no matter how you finish!" As he got to the curtain covering the tunnel leading to the locker room, Coach Lowery turned back to address the rest of the team. "Ty, you're next, then AJ. You guys keep your heads. I'll be right back!" Coach Lowery and Dallas disappeared behind the curtain.

"Well, Ty, you heard the man," directed Patrick. "Get out there, and hit a set. Someone has to."

Coach Lowery emerged from the locker room in time to see AJ land his last pass, a layout with a full twist.

"Well, how are we doing?" asked Coach Lowery.

"I guess consistent would be a good word," said Chris, as the score for AJ came up a 7.65.

"Consistent?" questioned Coach Lowery.

"Yeah, they both fell twice," said Patrick.

"Is Dallas okay?" asked Chris.

"That depends on your definition of okay. Physically, he's fine. Emotionally, he's a wreck."

"Is he gonna be able to finish the meet?" asked Joey.

"He has finished. I've scratched him from the rest of the meet." The eyes of the entire team suddenly opened wide, and their jaws dropped.

"Coach, we need Dallas!" demanded Chris, to the shock of the rest of the team.

"Need him? I figured you guys would be glad to get rid of him."

"Oh, no, Coach," said Chris. "Sure, he's a jerk—"

"Lord knows he practices every day!" added Mackee.

"But, Dallas is still important to the team," said Patrick.

"He may be overbearing," said Ty.

"And obnoxious," said Joey.

"And rude," said AJ

"And a royal pain in the ass," said Chris.

"But, he's our our overbearing, obnoxious, rude pain in the ass!" said Mackee.

"And he is an important part of the team." added Patrick.

"And, we need his scores!" added Joey.

"All right then. I didn't know you guys were so fond of him."

"Let's not get carried away, Coach!" exclaimed Patrick, "We just need him for the meet."

"He may not win Miss Congeniality," concluded Chris, "but he is a fine gymnast, and I think I speak for everyone when I say that we may not like him at all, but we sure do need him."

"I'll go back and get him. Patrick, I think the judges are waiting for you."

Coach Lowery disappeared behind the curtain again, and Patrick made his way to the floor exercise carpet. Determined not to make any more mistakes, Patrick took out a couple of his bigger skills that he thought might give him trouble and substituted easier skills with the same value. Although his routine was less dynamic than he had planned, Patrick hit his routine with minimal errors for a 9.25.

"Way to go, plowboy," said Chris, "but I think we'll need to be a little more agressive the rest of the way out."

"I hit! That's more than anyone else so far."

"Right, but if our scores don't start coming up fast, we may be watching NTIs on TV!"

"Well, it's your turn. Why don't you show me the way?"

"My pleasure."

Chris grabbed a piece of chalk on his way to the corner of the floor exercise carpet. His head bowed as he went through his routine in his head.

"Is he reviewing or composing?" asked Mackee.

"I can never be sure," answered Patrick.

Chris raised his head and his right arm and saluted the head judge.

"Look at the smile," said Joey. "He's composing!"

Chris stood in the corner, staring at the opposite end. Raising his arms forward, upward and then sideways, Chris took in a breath and released. Then, he darted across the floor. Round off, back handspring, then Chris punched the floor and arched his back to do a double back in layout position with a full twist on the second flip, and upon landing, punched a front flip in pike position. The crowd came to life, letting out a loud cheer for the stuck landing.

For his second pass, Chris executed another double back in layout position. The cheer from the crowd became louder with the second landing. For his strength part, Chris rolled backward to a handstand and lowered to a horizontal planche. After a three-second hold, Chris straddled his legs and swung his body into two Thomas flairs that ended in another straddled planche. He then put his legs together, held the position for another three seconds, and pressed back into a handstand.

Chris stepped down into the corner to the cheers of the crowd. He then turned to face the side of the carpet and jogged two steps into a punch layout front, layout front half-twist, to back layout full-and-a-half twist, stuck. Chris then slowly reached down to the floor beside him and gradually raised his body sideward until he arived in a one-arm handstand. After a two-second hold, Chris placed his other hand on the floor and forward rolled to a stand in the corner. Chris prepared for his dismount. He grabbed a breath and started across the floor. Round off, back handspring, half-twisting double front, punch front half.

The crowd erupted.

Chris returned to the seating area, making sure to tap Patrick's chin up to close his gaping mouth.

"That's what I consider being aggressive," said Chris.

"And creative!" added Joey.

"Not to mention risky, McClure," said Coach Lowery, having returned from the locker room.

"But effective!" returned Chris upon the flashing of his 9.85 score.

"Where's Dallas?" asked Patrick.

"Well, he's not in the arena. When I went back to the locker room, he had already left. The security guard said he saw him leave in a black Mustang."

The four who had trailed Dallas the night before looked at each other.

"Coach," said Chris, "we have a confession to make."

"We saw Dallas get in that Mustang last night," added Mackee.

"After lights-out? Well, that explains the lousy floor set."

"There's more, Coach," said Joey.

"Yeah," said Patrick, "we wanted to get Dallas back last night, and we kinda snuck out and followed him."

"Say no more, boys. I'll be angry later. Right now, we have a meet to finish. Where are we?"

"Well, Chris and I hit our sets for 9.25 and 9.85."

"And, we had to count six falls on our first event," said Joey.

"And, we have five events to go with only one score to drop on each event," added Mackee.

"And, our best p-bars man has left the building," concluded Chris.

"Looks to me like we have a long meet ahead of us, boys."

A collective "Yes, Coach" came from the team.

"Let's just hope the worst is behind us, boys. Just do the best you can, and let's see what happens." Coach Lowery ran his fingers through his hair and heaved a sigh.

The gymnasts moved from event to event, catching, passing, and slowly distancing themselves from the rest of the teams, but still well behind the standard that would be set by the other teams in the country.

"Well, Coach, how does it look?" asked Patrick.

"I guess it depends on your point of view. We are making up for lost ground, but we're still not out of the woods."

"What do you mean?"

"Floor really put us in a hole. If we hit the rest of our sets, we're okay, but if we have to count two or more falls on our last three events, like we did on Pommel Horse and Rings, we will be about half a point below the minimum score that qualified to NTI's last year."

"Yeah, but a lot of those teams from last year graduated seniors."

"But, a lot of other teams have improved, too. Either way, we need to hit to stay in the running."

Patrick looked around and noticed that there were still several teams still competing, allowing plenty of time for a team meeting before going to Vault.

"Guys, gather around," ordered the team captain.

The team turned their attention to Patrick.

"Look, we've come a long way to get to this point. Sure, Dallas is lost for today, and floor sucked, but we've done okay on pommels and rings. We still have three events left, three *good* events. We've not locked NTI's yet, and it's gonna take a pretty decent meet the rest of the way out to get there. I know it's not easy, but we are gonna have to put the bad routines, the lazy form, the falls, and the fatigue behind us. We each have three sets left, and I challenge each of you to go out and do nothing less than your best routines the rest of the way out."

The Pioneers looked at each other, silently accepting the challenge set by Patrick. The team moved in calculated unison from Rings to Vault, reserving any comment until the first Pioneer came up.

"AJ, we need awesome vaults," said Coach Lowery. "Stay clean, and fight for that landing."

Without changing expression, AJ focused on the board and the vault table, visualizing his vault and his landing. Although he knew that he was the leadoff vaulter because his was the weakest vault, he was determined to make his vault count. AJ saluted the judge without taking his eyes off of his target, then sprinted toward the board. The closer he got, the louder his teammates became.

AJ hit the board and drove his feet upward, blocking the table with his hands and launching his body skyward in a front handspring. At the peak of the flight, he closed his body into a tight pike while rotating forward. Once inverted, AJ turned his head and his hips while opening his pike to a layout position, to create a half twist. He spotted his final target, the landing mat, and just like a hundred times before in the gym and a thousand times in his dreams, AJ's feet hit the landing mat, and he brought his body to a stop, under control and stuck. AJ held his landing position an extra second to make sure he was not going to move more before slowly standing up and raising his arms in victorious jubilation. The crowd again rose to its feet and increased the decibel count of its ovation.

Although the crowd could easily be whipped into a frenzy, AJ and the rest of the team knew that this was just one hit set out of eighteen that was needed to accomplish its goal. Upon returning to the Pioneer seating area, AJ gave a high five to Ty, the next Pioneer in line, then to each of the other teammates, none of whom had changed their facial expressions from that of concentration and determination.

"Come on, Ty!" came the chant from AJ as he sat down to catch a breath.

Ty, like AJ before him, focused on his goal as he saluted the head judge. Ty's vault, a layout Tsukahara full-twist, required much more speed than AJ's. Ty pounded the vault runway and gained speed as he approached the spring board. Ty hit the board solid and quarter turned his body for a cartwheel approach to his vault. He drove his far arm into the end of the table to achieve maximum block off of his right hand. As if by reflex, Ty lifted his chest hard in reaction to his block. Ty stood straight as an arrow, his feet three full feet above the top of the table. Once Ty's rotating body blocked his view of the horse, he turned his head to the left and agressively wrapped both arms to the left side of his body to execute the twist. At the completion of the twist, his eyes searched for the blue vinyl landing mat. Ty snapped his feet into the twelve inches of foam and fabric. Again, like his teammate before him, Ty came to a motionless, stuck landing, freezing for a moment to emphasize the accuracy of his attempt. And, again, the spectators rose to their feet.

With each hit vault, the intensity of the cheers grew. The Pioneer team had become one unit of singular purpose, not getting overly excited with each landing, but determined in its resolve to see its quest reach the only logical conclusion—winning the state team title and qualifying for the National Team Invitational.

The Pioneers finished step one of their immediate goal with Chris sticking his full-twisting Tsukahara, making six hit vaults out of six.

"Four down, two events to go, Coach," said Patrick. "How are we doing?"

"Not bad. Those were some special vaults, some of the best this season. We picked up about a point and a half over our season average."

"I don't suppose we've made up for any of our weaker events?"

"Maybe for Rings or Pommels, but there's no way to make up for Floor. Six falls is a lot to count."

"Well, there's still two events left. They'll be good ones."

"They'll have to be," Coach concluded. "The last routine has finished. Let's rotate to P-bars." The gymnasts, still silent, picked up their gear and headed for their fifth event. They concentrated on their immediate goal, hitting twelve more routines.

Mackee, AJ, and Ty started the team off well with three hit Parallel Bars routines, but none scored over 8.6.

"I sure wish Dallas was here," lamented Joey. "We sure could use his score."

"Well, unfortunately we are going to have to forge ahead without him," concluded Chris, "and you're up. Let's keep the ball rolling, Joey."

Joey put together a flawless routine, scoring the first nine on the event for the Pioneers with a 9.05. Although Joey wanted to join the rest of the audience in cheering his performace, one look at his teammates brought him back into focus. Easy, Joe, he thought, you still have one set left.

Joey walked back to the seating area, graciously accepting the high fives of his teammates and grabbing a cup of water from the athlete hospitality area before returning to his seat. Chris sat down beside him.

"That was a great set, Joey. You're showing great restraint. If I were you, I'd be jumping out of my shorts."

Joey chuckled, trying to hold in the laughter. "Let's go, Pat!" he yelled to the team captain, about to mount the bars.

Patrick, too, exhibited a great routine, finishing with a very high double back dismount with a small hop on the landing. Once again the crowd was on its feet, cheering the excellence that the Pioneers were providing for the second half of the competition.

"Way to go, Pat!" came the monotone cheers of his teammates, accompanied by claps, high fives, and pats on the back. The cheers from the crowd became even louder at the flashing of his 9.3 score.

Chris followed with an innovative routine that included four double flips, two forward and two backward, and a high double back piked dismount to a stuck landing. Once again, the crowd exploded in response to some of the best gymnastics they had ever seen. Chris waved politely to the appreciative crowd but quickly returned to a deadpan face upon returning to his teammates.

"Great set, Chris!" cheered Coach Lowery over the deafening noise. As Chris rejoined the rest of the Pioneers, Coach rallied his troops. "All right, guys, we've got one event to go. Six hit sets, and we are goin' to LA! Just do what you do."

The Pioneers looked in each other's eyes, each knowing his job, each checking the other for the same level of commitment they each had in themselves.

The gymnasts gathered their gear and headed for their final event, High Bar.

"This is fun," Joey said to Chris as the two made their way across the gym, "all the hoopla, the crowd, the great gymnastics."

"Of course, you do have one event left, and all of that could go away if you miss," answered Chris, his eyes still focused forward toward his goal and his last event. Joey's expression changed from cheerful to respectful and concerned.

"Oh, yeah, I know," he muttered. "Just tryin' to enjoy a little bit of the moment."

"There will be time for that later, *if* we hit."

The Pioneers arrived at their last event to the cheers of the partisan crowd.

"Mackee, you're first," said Coach Lowery, "then AJ, Ty, Joey, Patrick. Chris, you're our anchor."

Chris and Patrick looked at each other. Chris could detect a hint of despair.

"Beg your pardon, Coach," pleaded Chris. "I really think Patrick should anchor the team on last event."

"You know that the order is set to put the best routine up last. It's worked all year. Any reason why we should change it now?"

"Only that this is Patrick's last state championship. It only makes sense that the last routine for us shoud be his."

"Fine," replied Coach. "Patrick, you follow Chris. McClure, you follow Johnson." Chris could see Patrick's face change from melancholy to mellow.

Mackee began chalking his grips. Joey noticed that Mackee's face seemed twisted, somewhat confused. When Joey got within earshot of Mackee's mumbling, Mackee lifted his head to look at the approaching teammate.

"Tell me something, anything," said Mackee, in a panic.

"What's up, Mack? Are you nervous?"

"No ... yes ... no, I mean—"

"Easy, guy. Relax."

"You ever notice that the more someone tells you relax, the harder it is to relax?" Mackee chuckled nervously.

"Hey, I'm as tight as you, pal," Joey confided, "but, you've got to loosen up!"

"How?"

"Pretend the judges are in their underwear."

"I've tried that. I didn't feel more relaxed, just overdressed!"

"Okay, how about this? What are you thinking about now?"

"Missing this set, missing my release and landing on my face. That's about it."

"Do you always think about crashing before you do a routine?"

"Pretty much every time I swing pipe."

"Why?"

"'Cause that's pretty much how they end up."

"What do you think about just before you go up on Rings?"

"I just picture a perfect set."

"So, try visualizing a perfect High Bar set."

"I've tried. I fall off on mental routines, too."

"I've got an idea!" Joey exclaimed. "Try picturing a better gymnast, like Chris, doing your routine. Hitting it. Then, when your gymnast lands, he becomes you."

"Sounds good. Think it'll work?"

"I don't know, but at least maybe you won't picture yourself falling off anymore."

"I hope you're right, Joey."

"No sweat, man. Just go out there and have fun."

"My idea of fun would be watching you guys swing for me."

"Don't worry, Mack. Just do the best you can."

"You ever notice the more people tell you not to worry—"

"Mack, just do your job."

"Right."

Joey turned and walked back to the seating area. Mackee finished chalking his grips to find he had put almost three times as much chalk on his hands than normal. He began to scrape the access back into the chalk bucket.

"What's up with Mackee?" asked Chris upon Joey's return to the team.

"He's just real nervous."

"So, what did you tell him?"

"Well, he kept seeing himself crash when he went through his mental routines, so I told him to try thinking of someone else doing his routine. It seemed to settle him a little."

"Good job. Do you think it'll work?"

"It does for me."

Chris pondered for a moment and then turned his head to watch Mackee's routine.

Although brief and not very difficult, Mackee managed to keep his routine moving and got to his dismount, with no major mistakes, and landed a fairly big double back tucked dismount with only one step. Mackee raised his arms in jubilation for having hit his routine. He didn't bother to look at the 8.85 score, his highest for the season on that event. Hitting the routine was satisfaction enough.

"Way to go, Mack," "Good job, Mackee!" came the congratulations from his teammates. Mackee grabbed some water and sat down next to Joey.

"I guess it worked, eh?" said Joey.

"Yeah, I guess it did."

"So, tell me, how did it look, having Chris do your routine?"

"Oh, I didn't use Chris."

"Who did you use?"

"Well, I figured that Chris could do my routine way too easily. There's no way I could look that good. So I picked someone who couldn't make it look quite as easy but who could surely hit the set."

"Who? Patrick? Dallas?"

"Nope. You. Thanks, buddy." Mackee put his fists up for Joey to tap with his own. Joey was flattered and confused at the same time. He then stood up to see AJ's routine over the gymnasts standing in his line of sight.

AJ's routine, while not more dynamic than Mackee's, swung with comfortable ease, accenting his body line. AJ finished his routine with a piked double back with a hop on the landing.

"All right, guys," shouted Coach Lowery, "that's two. Four to go! Come on Ty, let's hit!"

Ty also performed one of his better routines, moving cleanly from skill to skill, with only minor form deductions. Ty landed his dismount without trouble and jogged back to his team. The 8.9 awarded to his routine was worth every tenth, Coach Lowery thought.

With three routines left, it came down to Joey.

Joey couldn't help but think about the results if he were to miss.

"Now, what are you thinking about, mister?" asked Mackee, mocking Joey's approach to him earlier.

"Just how much easier it is to relax when the pressure comes off."

"What do you mean?"

"Well, I know that the guys that follow me are more than likely to hit. And, you guys have already hit, so my routine may not even count. It makes it kinda hard to concentrate."

"What do you mean your routine won't count? I've seen your routine, and if you hit, you'll outscore any of the three of us."

"Maybe."

"Maybe? You know I'm right! Do your job. Hit this set. Quit bein' a wuss."

"Okay, Mackee."

Mackee smacked Joey on the back and made his way to a better vantage point to watch the remaining sets. He turned around to get in one more jab.

"Hey, Joey. When you do your mental routine, don't picture me doing your set for you!" A smile came over Joey's face.

Joey chalked his hands and joined his coach under the bar. Joey closed his eyes and began going through his routine in his head, making subtle movements with his body, trying to recreate his body positions, tightening ever slightly the muscles he would be using during his routine. Once finished, Joey opened his eyes and saluted the head judge.

Although he was a little nervous before getting on the bar, once his hands made contact with the steel rod, he immediately became relaxed, his concentration transfixed on the bar.

Joey began to swing, moving into position for his release, a straddled Tkatchev. Joey, for a moment, wanted to second-guess his timing, but at the last moment, he relaxed and let his body do what it had been trained to do: rely on his reflex and repetition rather than emotional thought. Joey tapped his final giant swing before the release. Joey threw the bar back over his head and shot skyward as he watched the metal halide-lit darkness of the top of the Pyramid. He could feel his body rotating forward and, instinctively, turned his gaze to the eight-foot-long rod suspended four feet below him. Joey opened his grapple-like hands to regain the bar once again, swinging into giants without breaking stride.

Funny, Joey thought while swinging through the easier part of his routine, they're called releases, but it's the recatching that makes it what it is!

Joey continued to swing his routine, turning on top of the bar and jamming his legs through his arms for the circle that would throw him into his inverted giant position. Upon the jam-out, Joey could feel that he was at least twenty degrees beyond the handstand position.

Darn it, Joey thought, I missed that handstand. I need to tap this inverted giant hard if I'm going to make it back over the top. Tap he did, and the result found Joey in a stretched, inverted handstand! Joey pushed through the handstand, trying to get it to swing through to the other side. If he couldn't, his body would come off the wrong way, and he would have to drop from the bar. Slowly but surely, Joey's body dropped on the correct side of the bar. On the way back to the top, Joey hopped from his inverted grip, rotating his wrists inward, to arrive in an undergrip once again.

Joey immediately half-turned on top of the bar and set up for his double back layout dismount. Once again, Joey had to rely on his reflexes to know how much swing would be enough and when to release for his dismount.

Ping! Joey heard the bar reverberate in reaction to his torque and release. He spotted the landing mat in plenty of time to know how much body shape change would be necessary to complete the second flip and land on his feet. Joey's eyes closed in on his target, and he sank his feet into the landing mat for a stuck landing. Joey stood tall, proud to have hit his routine, and the crowd fueled his pride with cheers capable of shaking the rafters.

"Way to go, Joe!" came the chant from the crowd centralized around the location of Joey's parents. Joey scanned the crowd until his eyes locked in on a slender, middle-aged man with his right arm and fisted hand extended, thumb pointing skyward. Joey returned the thumbs-up to his father.

Joey jogged back to the cheers and congratulations of his teammates.

"Well, I guess that leaves it up to you and me, plowboy."

"Yep. Oh, by the way, thanks for switching spots with me. That wasn't necess—"

"Yes, it was," interrupted Chris. "This is your final state championships. It only makes sense that you, as the team captain, should anchor the last event."

"Well, thanks, anyway."

"No thanks needed, pal. You've earned it. But, you realize the opportunity before us, don't you?"

"Oh, no. Why do I get the feeling that we're not going to be conservative and hit routines, like we're supposed to?"

"Hang on a second," Chris left Patrick just long enough to ask Coach Lowery a question, then returned to the chalk stand where he had left Patrick.

"Okay, here's the deal," Chris plotted. "Coach says if one of our routines hits, since the other four have already hit, we'll lock the NTIs. So, this is a chance for you to get a little crazy up there."

"Are you kidding? You think I want to risk looking like an idiot in what could be my final meet of the season?"

"Look, plowboy. Those people aren't going to remember if you hit or miss today. They just want to see great gymnastics, and here's your chance to give it to them."

"Assuming I'd be willing to go along with this silly idea, which I'm not, what would you suggest I do?"

"Well, how's your full-twisting Geinger coming along?"

"The Def? It's not. I've yet to touch the bar, much less catch it, much less catch it well enough to do it in combination, much less put it in a routine, much less be ready to throw it in the biggest meet of my life!"

"Okay, so much for that," Chris scratched his head. "I know. You know the release combination you already do, right?"

"Yeah, straddled Tkatchev to Geinger. So what? Wait, let me guess. You think I should add another Tkatchev before the combination, right?"

"Why not? You did it earlier this season and it was great!"

"Yeah, but I don't think that it's—"

"Don't *think*. Just do. This is your last chance to be crazy before NTI's!"

"You mean *if* we get there. What if we both miss?"

"Okay, you want some assurance. Tell you what, if I miss my set, you are a free agent. Free to do your conservative routine and hit. But if I hit, and there's no pressure, you do the new combo, okay?"

"Okay," answered Patrick after much thought. "But hit your routine, anyway, okay?"

"But, of course," boasted the Californian matter-of-factly as he made his way to the bar.

"What was that all about?" asked Coach Lowery.

"Nothin', Coach. Just me and Pat making a deal that we each hit our routines," Chris fibbed.

Chris saluted the head judge and jumped up to the bar. "Circus time," Mackee had called it. From the moment Chris grabbed the bar until he was on the ground again, it was evident that he was made to swing High Bar. With most routines, a gymnast's anxiety comes from wondering if he will hit. With Chris, there was no doubt that he would. It seemed that all that was missing was the popcorn. Although his teammates had grown accustommed to Chris's high-flying antics, it was still fun to watch, not just Chris's command and ease of execution, but the reactions of those new to his show. It resembled very much the atmosphere of a circus crowd watching a show on the flying trapeze. From beginning to end, Chris's routine was filled with one risky release after another, mind-boggling combinations, and for the climax, a tremendous triple-back dismount that stuck.

Chris milked the crowd for all of the applause it would offer as he walked back to his team, arms raised victoriously.

"And that's the way we do that, plowboy!" Chris shouted over the ovations. "Now, it's your turn." Patrick's expression of appreciation quickly changed to one of concern.

"Don't worry about it, pal," Chris said. "This is a walk in the park."

Patrick approached the chalk stand and began chalking his grips, not quite sure how much chalk would be enough to get him through whatever it was he was about to do. Patrick closed his eyes and pictured his routine. He opened his eyes and walked over to the high bar next to his coach.

"Relax, Pat. This one's in the bag. Just be clean, and bring it home healthy," said Coach Lowery.

The other events having finished, all attention was on Patrick as he saluted the head judge. He jumped to the bar and began his start-up swings. After a few skills, Patrick set up for his release sequence.

"Watch this, you guys," Chris said to his teammates. "This should be good."

Chris had no idea just how correct he was. Instead of just doing his Tkatchev with his legs together, Patrick surprised everyone, including Chris, by launching his body much higher than normal to do a layout Tkatchev into a sky-high Geinger! Upon the catch, everyone, including Chris and the rest of the Pioneers, jumped to their feet with shouts of appreciation, surprise, and joy.

Patrick was not finished. After fulfilling his in-bar and dorsal grip requirements, Patrick set up for another release combination, piked Tkatchev, straddle Tkatchev, right back into back giants without breaking form or rhythm. Then, Patrick set up for his dismount, a booming double layout with a full twist to a stuck landing. The cheers were deafening. Coach Lowery was the first to get to Patrick, trapping him in a bear hug.

"You know, you should let me know when you're gonna change your routine!" Patrick could barely hear his coach over the shrill cheers of the crowd.

"Sorry, Coach," was all that was offered in apology from the senior who had just capped his final state championship with a six-for-six day. Soon, the mob of teammates and supporters engulfed the two.

The awards ceremony had become anticlimactic with the domination of the Pioneers. All that remained was the awarding of the team trophy.

"And the winners, the best team in Tennessee," barked the public address announcer, "and Tennessee's representatives to this year's National Team Invitational, your Pioneeeeers!"

Chris leaned into Patrick and whispered, "Man, I wish Dallas was here."

"He is, dude, he is." Patrick fixed his gaze toward the only near-empty seats about twenty rows up. Chris followed his eyes to the outline of the figure in the stands with the unmistakable blond hair of their teammate. Both took a side of the team trophy and hoisted it overhead, pointing in the direction of the teammate in the stands.

The awards ceremony concluded, the crowd dispersed, and Patrick sought out his coach.

"So, how'd we do?"

"Well, I'm sure we're in the meet, but my guess is we're not in the top twelve," concluded Coach Lowery.

"I guess that's not good?" asked Patrick.

"If we're in the bottom third, it puts a lot of pressure on us the first day."

"When will you know something?"

"You go on with your friends, Pat. I'll make some calls and see what I can find out. I'll catch up to you guys at the hotel later. I've also got to try to find Dallas."

"I've got that one figured out for you. Chris and I just saw him up in the bleachers during awards." Coach Lowery turned to look in the direction that Patrick was pointing to see the familiar frame of David Dallas, still sitting in his seat, his head in his hands. "Thanks, Pat. You guys go on and have fun. I'll catch up to you later."

"Thanks, Coach." Patrick turned to rejoin his friends "Be sure to tell Dallas he's more than welcome to join us for the celebration."

"You bet. … Oh, Patrick!" shouted Coach before Patrick got too far away.

"Yeah, Coach?" Patrick turned back.

"Good job today. Bravo!"

"Thanks, Coach." Patrick continued his trot to rejoin his friends.

"What's the word, Pat?" asked Chris upon Patrick's return.

"Not much. Coach hasn't heard from the other states yet, so we don't know where we stand."

"I don't mean that. I'm talking about Dallas."

"Oh. I pointed him out to Coach. He wants to talk to him. Besides, I don't think he's gonna be quite in the celebratory mood that we are."

"I guess you're right. Well, let's get movin'. Somewhere, there's a pizza with my name on it." And, the Pioneers left the building with their friends, families, and teammates in tow.

"Rough day, eh, Dallas?" said Coach Lowery upon joining the Memphis native in the stands.

"Rough ain't the word for it. I had literally dozens of people here to see me compete, and I ended up looking like a horse's ass in front of them."

"Your emotional outburst was understandable, Dallas, but you, like everyone else, must learn to exercise restraint when overcome by emotion, good or bad."

"That's easy for you to say. You didn't take out a judge, a score flasher, and a volunteer in one pass!"

"That's true, but those things can happen. And when they do, you have to learn how to block that out and stay focused on the job left to do."

"You saw me out there. There was nothing I could do right. Everything just got worse."

"For one event, maybe. We sure could've used you on P-bars and pipe."

"I probably would've blown those sets, too."

"Perhaps, but now, we'll never know. You didn't give yourself the chance to come back."

"You were the one who kicked me out of the meet, Coach."

"Yes, and I may have been wrong. Given the same set of circumstances, I'd have done the same thing again, but when I went back to bring you back out, you were gone."

"I was steamed. I had to get away and think. The last place I wanted to be was here. I made a fool of myself, and I knew the others would never have let me live it down. Sorry, Coach."

"That's all behind us now. Why did you come back?"

"Mixed emotions, I guess. On the one hand, I knew that some of the guys were out of gas, and I thought the best way to cheer me up would be watching them fall on their faces."

"Patrick and the others filled me in on your activities last night. It's a wonder any of you had the strength to stand up. And on the other hand?"

"On the other hand, this is my team. If I hadn't come back to watch, it would've torn me apart not knowing how they did."

"We finished okay, and we're in the NTI's. I don't think any irreversible damage has been done. Why don't you rejoin your friends. I think they were going for pizza."

"I don't think they want me around, Coach. I rode them all pretty hard during the meet."

"Forget about it, Dallas. I'm sure they have. They were the ones who talked me into getting you back into the meet. Every team has a personality that can be, shall we say, volatile. Ours just happens to be named David Dallas. I think the rest understand, and even appreciate, having you on the team, despite your faults. Now go catch up to the team. I've got phone calls to make."

"Thanks, Coach." Dallas left his coach sitting in the bleachers. As he left, Coach Lowery noticed that there was a bounce to Dallas's step.

"Patrick, you were wonderful!" came the accolades from Nicole after seeing her first gymnastics meet in person.

"Oh, it wasn't that good."

"Shut up, and take the compliment, stupid." chided Chris.

"Okay, thanks."

"Really, Patrick," added Haley, "it was great to see you cut loose a little bit."

"Really?"

"Really. It was very refreshing to see you go for something new and risky."

"Yeah," added Chris, "crazy looks good on you! You should try it more often."

"What does he mean, Patrick?" asked Nicole.

"Nothing, really. Chris just seems to think that my style of gymnastics is a little tame."

"It sure looked exciting to me!" concluded Nicole.

"It certainly was," added Haley. "It's just that Patrick is not known for exciting. Controlled is the more appropriate word. I think I like this Patrick Goodman."

"Let's not get too carried away, sports fans," said Mackee. "The guy hit one wild set in his life. I don't think it's time for eveyone to get down on their knees and pay homage. After all, if his head swells too much, he won't fit through the door!"

"What do you mean *if?*" said Haley. "Look at this guy's face. He's already on cloud nine."

Just then, the door to the pizzeria swung open and in walked the familiar frame.

"Coach!" exclaimed Patrick. "What are you doin' here? Where's Dallas?"

"One thing at a time, Pat. I'm here because I'm hungry. You know I can't eat during a meet. The way you guys do gymnastics, my stomach tumbles as much as you do."

"Where's Dallas?" repeated Chris.

"I thought he was here with you guys. He left the arena about twenty minutes after you left. He said he was coming here."

"Are you sure?" asked Patrick. "What kind of mood was he in when he left?"

"Happy, I guess. He got some things off of his chest. I figured since he had resolved some of his problems, he would be here to cut up with you guys."

"Well, we have seen neither hide nor blond hair of him here, Coach," said Chris.

"Perhaps he went to a different restaurant by mistake," added Haley.

"Doubtful. This is his hometown. If last night proved anything, it's that he sure knows his way around," answered Patrick.

"I'm sure he'll turn up sooner or later," surmised Coach Lowery.

"So, Coach, how'd we end up?" asked Joey, joining the conversation, the other Pioneers gathering around.

"Oh, yeah. I nearly forgot about that. I'm afraid the news is not great."

"Don't tell me we didn't qualify." Patrick's stomach turned sour.

"Oh, no, we're in." Patrick and the others breathed a heavy sigh of relief.

"Then what's so bad?" asked Mackee.

"We qualified twenty-fifth. That puts us in the bottom third."

"Which means we start out first session," concluded Patrick.

"That's not so bad, is it?" asked Joey.

"It's just that it's an incredibly tough uphill climb," answered Coach Lowery.

"Everyone knows it's nearly impossible to get good scores in the first session," said Mackee.

"They save 'em for the late session," added AJ.

"Hey, let's not get too upset," said Chris. "We're in there. We just have to hit so hard that they have nothing to deduct."

"Yeah," added Patrick, "if we hit our sets, we should make it to finals."

"It's not that easy, Pat," said Coach Lowery. "We not only need to finish on top in the first session, but also we have to be better than eighteen other teams to get into the final round. We definitely have a long row to hoe."

The Pioneers looked at each other, none knowing what to say. Expressions changed from relaxed to concerned.

"Looks like we have work to do," surmised Patrick.

"Why is everyone looking like their best dog just died?" yelled Joey. "We're in! We are in!"

"And we are in it to win it!" cheered Mackee.

"Pioneers!" cried Joey, and all of the gymnasts, including Coach Lowery, did a standing back tuck in the middle of the restaurant.

"Where's Dallas?" yelled Coach Lowery as the team slowly filed onto the bus that would carry them across the state to their hometown.

"I dunno, Coach," came the response from Joey, Dallas's roommate. "He didn't show up at all last night."

"He must've stayed with a friend in town," surmised Mackee.

"Good thinking, Mack. Anyone have an idea *where* he would've stayed?"

"For what it's worth, I bet if you find the black Mustang, you find Dallas," concluded Chris.

"Great. Now I have to comb the entire city of Memphis to find a black Must—"

"There he is!" shouted Joey. The black Mustang pulled to within twenty feet of the bus, and the slender gymnast emerged with a gym bag and backpack.

"Thank you for joining us, Mr. Dallas," Coach Lowery said sarcastically. "I guess it would've been too much of a bother to let someone know what your plans were last night."

"Sorry, Coach. After we get back to Knoxville, you won't have to worry about me anymore."

"Now, what is that supposed to mean?"

"It's not supposed to mean anything. What it does mean is that I'm quitting the team. In fact, I'll be moving back here to Memphis." The team and Coach Lowery were dumbfounded.

"Why? Why move back here? Do your parents know about—"

"Don't worry about my parents, Coach. I'll be eighteen in two weeks. There's nothing they can do about it. In fact, they'll probably be glad to get rid of me."

"Dallas, can't we talk this over?"

"Talk all you want. Talk until we get back to Knoxville. It won't make a difference. I've already made up my mind."

"Well, I guess it would be senseless to try to talk you out of it." The other Pioneers looked on in amazement. "Just get on the bus, and we'll get going."

Dallas climbed on the bus and took a seat away from everyone else. He put on his sunglasses and headphones and stared out the window, waiting for the bus to finally be on its way.

"Aren't you gonna say anything?" Joey whispered to Chris.

"What's there to say? I think Dallas is a big boy and can make up his own mind," Chris said unsympathetically.

"What happened to all that talk back at the meet, about needing Dallas and all?"

"Oh, I feel that we do need Dallas, but that's beside the point. We need Dallas to want to be here. He's not much good to us if if doesn't want the same things we want. We want a nationl team title, and Dallas wants to move to Memphis. That's pretty different goals, if you ask me."

"But how do you know that that's what he *really* wants?"

"Didn't he just say that before getting on the bus? I think I heard him very distinctly say he was quitting gymnastics and moving to Memphis. If I missed something, tell me."

"If you'll pull your head out of your butt for a minute, you might come to the conclusion that he might be reaching out. Maybe he said he was quitting the team just to get us to say that we need him."

"Seems like he'd be going a long way to get some attention."

"I don't think it's about attention so much as a sense of belonging," Joey concluded.

"What makes you think that Dallas would listen to anyone?"

"For one thing, he didn't have to ride back on the bus. His buddy in the Mustang could've easily taken him home to Knoxville instead of riding in this uncomfortable, cold bus."

"Maybe his buddy couldn't go to Knoxville."

"Give me a break. He only stayed out all night with him the other night. I don't think he'd be the type to wait for his mother's consent before taking a cross-country trek for a buddy."

"Okay. Let's assume you're right. Why me? I'm the one he hates most. I doubt that he would want to talk to me."

"But, it has to be you. You two have been at each other's throats since you came to Knoxville. It makes sense that you two have the most to work out."

"Why do I get the idea that you have absolutely no idea what you're talking about?"

"I don't know. All I know is that if you don't talk to Dallas, we're gonna lose him, and there's no way we can win NTI's."

"I think that you're exaggerating a bit, but if it will make you happy, I'll talk to him."

"Thanks, dude." Joey punched Chris's shoulder and hopped forward several seats to sit with the rest of the team, who had opted to play cards instead of deal with Dallas. Chris could see Joey talking to Patrick and the others. Although he couldn't hear what they were saying, Joey's gestures and the movement of everyone else's eyes told Chris that Joey had decided to share the situation with everyone else. His thoughts were confirmed when Patrick's right arm came up from his cards to extend a thumbs-up in his direction.

Chris took a deep breath and stood up. He slicked his hair back, turned around, and walked back to sit down next to Dallas.

The card game was put on hold as everyone turned their heads, as discretely as possible, to observe the conversation between the two most volatile elements on the team. At first, there was no change in Dallas's outward gaze. They could see Chris talking but no response from Dallas. After several minutes, Chris reached over to remove Dallas's sunglasses only to find that he was sound asleep. The group chuckled, which drew Chris's attention. The others turned back quickly to resume their game, each pretending not to have been spying.

Chris replaced Dallas's glasses and headed to the front of the bus.

"He's a little tired right now," said Chris. "I'll talk to him later."

A bump in the road caused Joey's head to bounce off of the window he was leaning on, waking him from a nap. He looked out the window to see familiar buildings. He then looked at his watch.

Crap. We're only to Nashville, he thought. Before going back to sleep, Joey looked around the bus to see where everyone else was. In his fog, Joey could see that everyone, including Coach Lowery, was also getting some deserved rest. Everyone, that is, except Chris and Dallas, who were in the back of the bus talking. Just before dozing off, Joey noticed that the two were laughing about something. Highly unusual for those two, he thought. Then, blackness.

"All right, ladies!" yelled Coach Lowery. "Wake up. We're home." Many of the Pioneers were still asleep when the bus pulled into the parking lot, but Coach's all too familiar yell brought everyone back to consciousness.

Dallas was the first one off the bus.

"Bye, Coach!" shouted Dallas as he quickly jumped off of the bus and headed for his car. "See you Monday!"

A baffled Coach Lowery stumbled over what to say.

"We don't work out Monday. You guys get the day off!"

Dallas unlocked the driver's side door of the Jeep Cherokee he had left parked at the gym for the weekend.

"Okay, Coach," he said before jumping behind the wheel. "I'll see you Tuesday, then. Later!" Dallas quickly started his car and was out of the parking lot before his first teammate descended the steps of the bus.

"What did you say to Dallas, McClure?"

"Not much, Coach. Just this, that, and the other thing. Nothin' big."

"Whatever it was, it was enough. I haven't seen him this happy since—"

"Since I've been here, I know," said Chris guessing the end of Coach Lowery's sentence.

"What did you say to him, Chris?" asked Joey as he and the others filed off of the bus.

"Nothin' none of you haven't heard before. Just made him think about life, liberty, and the pursuit of gymnastics."

"So is he quitting or not?" asked Mackee.

"I don't know, Mack. He has a lot to think about, though."

"Well, gentlemen," Coach Lowery broke in, "this and other mysteries will have to wait until Tuesday. You guys have Monday off. Rest. That's an order."

"Yes, Coach," came the chorus as the team went their separate ways.

TWENTY-TWO

▼

"PATRICK!" CAME THE shrill voice of Patrick's mother.

"Yeah, Mom?" came the response from his upstairs bedroom.

"Are you still on the phone?"

"I'll be off in a minute."

"That's what you said a half hour ago. I hope you know that this long-distance bill is coming out of your allowance."

Allowance? Patrick thought, remembering that he hadn't received an allowance since he was a kid.

"Bill me. I'll be off in a minute."

"Don't forget, you also have school tomorrow, Mr. Hero."

"It's under control, Mom. Now, if you please, this call is costing me money." Patrick turned his attention back to his telephone receiver. "Sorry about that, Nicole. Where were we?"

"Nowhere in particular. Do you have workout tomorrow?"

"Naw. Coach Lowery gave us the day off. He ordered us to get some rest."

"So what are you gonna do with your spare time?"

"Probably go to the gym, do some conditioning, maybe play with some new stuff."

"I thought your coach ordered you to relax?"

"He did. This is how I relax. Instead of doing what Coach wants me to do, I do what I want to do!"

"What's the difference?"

"I don't know. I guess if he tells me to to do it, I feel like it's something that I have to do. If I come up with the same thing, it's kinda my idea, so I put more energy into it. I guess it's kinda like cleaning your room. If your mom says your room's a mess and you should clean it up, you're less likely to put the energy into it than you would if you had come up with the idea yourself."

"If you say so. Hey, I noticed that Dallas left the gym after crashing on the first event. Did he get hurt?"

"Dallas? Oh, he's fine. It kinda messed him up doing it in front of the hometown crowd."

"Is he okay?"

"Physically, he's fine. Mentally? You can never tell with Dallas. He walks around with this enormous chip on his shoulder, just waiting for someone to start a fight with him. He's really not such a bad guy once you get to know him. He's just a little set in his ways."

"Did he quit after the meet?"

"Well, we thought he had. He didn't come back to the hotel that night and only showed up just before the bus was ready to leave. He was spouting how he was quitting, but by the time we got back, he sounded like he was ready to get back into the gym."

"What changed his mind?"

"I'm not sure. He did talk to Chris for a long time, though."

"I thought he hated Chris."

"He does, I mean, he did, I mean, I'm not sure. Ever since Chris walked into the gym back in August, until the meet last weekend, Dallas and Chris have been like oil and water. I thought it looked kinda weird for the two of them to be buddy-buddy in the back of the bus on the way back."

"Maybe they've buried the hatchet."

"Perhaps. Whatever treaty they've agreed upon, I'll bet it'll only last so long."

"I think maybe you don't give your friends enough credit."

"Maybe you're right. Just human nature to be skeptical, I guess. So, do you think I'll get a chance to see you anytime soon?"

"What are your plans next weekend?"

"Next weekend?"

"Sure. My dad does a lot of work with the university there. When he told me that he had some meetings in Knoxville next week, I talked him into turning it into a long weekend and letting me tag along. I hope you don't mind."

"Mind? Are you nuts? This is great! I'll see if Dallas is up to getting his boat out. It'll be a blast! When will you be here?"

"Dad has meetings on Monday, so we probably won't leave until after school on Friday. I guess we'll get in sometime late Friday night."

"Call me as soon as you get into town!"

"I will."

"Patrick! Off the phone, *now!*" cried Mrs. Goodman.

"Right, Mom. I gotta go. I'll call you tomorrow night."

"No, you called tonight. I'll call tomorrow. Fair enough?"

"Fair enough. 'Til tomorrow then?"

"Dream about me."

"I already have. Bye."

"Bye."

Patrick hung up the phone and lay back on his bed, staring at the ceiling.

"Patrick," his mother began to ask "when do we get to meet … " until she noticed that her question would not be answered, as her son had fallen asleep, fully clothed, with a big smile on his face.

Although it was a day off, it was not unusual for gymnasts to show up at the gym. Coach Lowery was always there, doing some kind of work or just looking at gymnastics videos, analyzing the mechanics of a new skill or one his gymnasts may be having trouble with.

"Hey, Coach," called Patrick, sticking his head into the office.

"Patrick! What are you doing here? I thought I told you guys to relax."

"You did, but I'm so jazzed after last weekend, I thought I'd just play around a bit, you know, do some conditioning, work off some of this extra energy. Do you mind?"

"Evidently not."

"What does that mean?" Patrick asked.

"You'll see. Go ahead, Pat."

Patrick tossed his gym bag over his shoulder and walked into the gym. His question was immediately answered. In the gym swinging high bar was Dallas, watched closely by Chris, Joey, and the rest of the team.

"It's about time you got here, plowboy!" shouted Chris across the gym, "We were beginning to think you were gonna take Coach's order about taking the day off seriously!"

"Why didn't anyone call me?" asked Patrick.

"No one called anyone," said Dallas upon dismounting the bar. "Everyone just showed up. You're the last one to get here."

"Hurry and warm up, Patrick!" shouted Joey. "We've got a cool game to play."

I hate games, Patrick thought.

Patrick quickly, but thoroughly, warmed up, doing plenty of stretching while watching his teammates play on high bar.

"Okay, what's the game?" asked Patrick, putting on his grips.

Dallas explained, "Each guy has a skill to do. It has to be something that you've never made before."

"Do we have to start on pipe?" asked Patrick.

"It's my game," said Dallas. "We start where I say. Anyway, we don't leave the event until everyone makes his skill. The first guy to make his skill chooses the next skill and the next event."

"Cool enough. I guess I'll try—"

"Oh no, Pat. You don't pick your skill. The team picks it."

"That doesn't seem fair. You could pick a skill that's impossible for me to do to make it easy for you to win."

"Doubtful," added Mackee. "To move to the next skill, everyone has to make his skill, so it wouldn't benefit anyone to give you a skill that you couldn't do."

"What's your skill, Mack?" asked Patrick.

"I have to twist my double back dismount," replied Mackee, scaling the platform beside the high bar, "and I don't mind telling you that I'm just a little bit freaked."

"What could you possibly have to do, Chris?"

"Oh, they've picked a beauty for me. I have to do a full-twisting double back over the bar."

"That doesn't sound all that difficult."

"Yeah, but he has to recatch the bar!" added Joey.

"What about you, Joe?"

"Oh, mine's easy. I have to do a Tkatchev to Geinger combination with my legs together on the Tkatchev."

"That's a good combination. I guess you guys have already picked a skill out for me, huh?" asked Patrick, knowing the ultimate conclusion.

"Full-twisting Geinger!" came the chorus.

"Figures."

The Pioneers each took their turns, some getting close to making their skill, some just getting close to calamity. Dallas, who had the task of doing a double-twisting double back layout dismount onto the soft, inground 32-inch landing cushion, continued to land on his side, not able to complete the twist or the flip. Chris, who could not quite figure out the timing of his release to bring him back to the bar, had the easiest skill to try in terms of crashing. If he missed the bar he would just land on his feet as if it were a dismount. Joey's problem came from a lack of confidence.

"Come on, Joey!" shouted Chris. "Put those feet together!"

"But, what if I hit my heels on the bar?"

"My guess is that it'll hurt, but you can't make the combination without trying!" surmised Dallas.

Joey cranked his giant hard to try to launch his body high enough that his feet would clear the top of the bar.

"Yeeoowwwcch!" Joey screamed as his heels cracked the bar. He grabbed his heels as his body dropped in a clump onto the landing mat. His teammates winced at the sight of Joey's pain.

"You okay, Joey?" asked Patrick.

"Yeah. No blood, just a lot of pain."

Patrick scaled the platform once he had been assured that Joey's pain would only be temporary.

"Got any advice, Chris?" asked Patrick, arriving in a hang on the bar.

"Swing very high," said Chris sarcastically.

"Twist very fast," added Mackee.

"And look out for that darned bar!" added Joey, rolling off the landing mat, a heel in each hand.

Patrick began swinging giants faster and faster until he came to the point of no return. Patrick released the bar and watched as his body climbed higher and higher. He reached the peak of his flight and looked down on the bar.

"Twist!" screamed Patrick's teammates. Patrick, unsure of where his twisting would end up, bailed out, half turning to land on his back on the mat.

"You wuss!" yelled Dallas. "You were there. All you had to do was twist! The bar was right there!"

"I think this game is stupid!" Patrick returned as he picked himself up from the landing mat, "If you guys want to kill yourselves, that's fine with me. I don't need this aggravation."

"Get out of my way, you guys!" shouted Joey, limping back up to the bar. "I'll show you aggravating!" Joey jumped onto the bar and began swinging. Patrick, who had begun removing his grips, turned to watch the freshman. Joey sped his giants and launched his body back into the air much in the same way that had cracked his heels moments earlier. This time, however, his feet cleared the bar. His body continued to rotate and, before long, the bar was in sight. Joey's eager hands extended to grab the metal pipe. Try as he did to continue his swing into his second release, the Geinger, the pressure on the bar was too great. His hands peeled, and he pinged off of the bar and flipped wildly into the loose foam pit.

"Yeeaaah-hoooo!" Joey screamed while flipping uncontrollably and disappearing into the foam abyss.

"Way to go, Joey!" came the cheers from the team.

Joey climbed out of the pit to confront Patrick.

"You see, Pat? All you have to do is put your fear aside just long enough for your body to do its job!" said Joey.

"Yeah, well, what do you do if that fear is too big?"

"I guess then you have to have just a micromillimeter more desire than fear. You know how scared I was, especially after smacking my heels on that bar. It just has to matter more to be up there than it does to be down here. I don't know how long it would've taken me to catch that skill, but you made me so darned mad, I just had to show you that all this fear you hide behind is bogus." Joey was now looking Patrick eye–to-eye as best as he could, being eight inches shorter. "As long as I can remenber, I've looked up to you guys for being able to do what I never thought I could ever do. What I learned by watching you guys is that anyone can overcome anything if they want it bad enough. I'm no different than you, or any of these guys. I have fear, lots. Difference is, I guess, that I'm learning to face my fear head-on. So, don't you dare take your grips off unless you've given up, unless you're ready to admit defeat, that you don't want it bad enough, that you really believe that this small, insignificant skill is bigger than you are!"

"Are you quite through?" Patrick asked, feigning courage.

"Are *you*?" answered a disgusted Joey.

Patrick looked at his teammates, all of whom had stopped what they were doing to watch the confrontation.

"I'll try, okay?" said Patrick sheepishly.

"Of course you will," said Joey, putting his arm around his pal and escorting him back to the chalk dish. "You'll try, and you'll fail, and you'll try again 'til you get it. That's what you have shown me." The rest of the team went back to work. Trying, failing, and trying again.

"Now that you two have kissed and made up," teased Dallas, "can we talk you two into getting back to the game?"

"I guess I get to pick next skill?" Joey inquired.

"No way, squirt," demanded Dallas. "You caught the Tkatchev, but you never got to the Geinger."

"Fine, I bust my heels on the pipe, jump up and catch the darn thing, risk life and limb yelling at a guy that can squash me like a bug, and you're gonna say my turn doesn't count?" Joey puffed his chest.

"A rule's a rule, Joey," said Chris.

"Okay." Joey's chest deflated as he sheepishly returned to chalking his grips for his next turn. The team resumed its game, each trying harder to accomplish his new skill first.

"I'll show you how it's done, fellas," boasted Mackee as he cranked his giants prior to his attempt at his dismount.

"Uummpphhh!!" he cried, his voice muffled as his face planted into the nylon mesh cover of the landing cushion.

"You know, you shouldn't talk with your mouth full, Mack," said Dallas.

"How's that mat taste, Mack?" teased Joey.

Mackee faked not being able to pull his face out of the mat, pretending to be stuck. Then, he made a popping sound, as if he had freed himself from the mat that had swallowed his head.

"Not too bad. Needs ketchup, though," Mackee joked.

It was now Chris's turn again. He did several giants, adjusting his swing for just the right tap. He released the bar and flung his body skyward.

"Grab it, Chris!" cheered Ty.

Chris opened from his twist only to find the bar was slightly out of reach, but instead of bailing out, he extended his right arm as much as he could to try to grasp the bar.

"He's got it!" yelled Joey.

Before the words could completely leave Joey's lips, Chris's one-handed grip caused him to turn over to his back. And, with the torque being too great to control with one hand, he peeled off of the bar, and Chris front flipped twice before landing in the loose foam pit.

"Cool!" shouted Chris, emerging from the foam. "I think it's goin' in!"

"No catch, Slash," exclaimed Dallas. "You didn't control the finish."

"What do you mean I didn't control the finish? That was a near-perfect double front dismount out of a one-arm catch!"

"Yeah, but you didn't call it," cried Joey.

"If you do it again and put a one arm giant in before the dismount, you can count it," said Mackee.

"Picky, picky, picky," said Chris, climbing out of the foam pit.

"Okay, AJ," called Dallas, "it's your turn."

"Can we change my skill?" pleaded AJ.

"What's wrong with doing a Tkatchev?" asked Joey.

"It's not the flip that bothers me. It's the thought of impaling myself on the bar!"

"Just cast it way up and over the bar on the first turn," said Patrick.

"That's easy for you to say. What's to say that if I throw the bar harder, I don't throw the bar harder right into my lower back?"

"I'll take care of you, AJ," said Dallas in a very uncharacteristic act of benevolence. "I'll push this mat in between you and the bar when you let go."

"How do I catch the bar with the mat in the way?"

"One thing at a time, AJ. A minute ago, you weren't even planning on letting go," said Chris.

"Don't worry, A. Once you're over the bar, and out of harm's way, I'll yank the mat back out. If you think you can catch the bar, go for it!"

"Okay, Dallas, but if I get killed, I'll never talk to you again."

"Fine, I'm looking forward to the peace and quiet."

AJ jumped up on the bar and started swinging.

"Next swing, Dallas," said AJ at the top of his second giant.

"Gotcha!"

AJ arched his back, then kicked his legs to create the counter-rotation needed to flip his body forward from his backward swing.

"Now!" yelled the team at the point when AJ needed to release. AJ let go on cue and flew over the bar. As promised, Dallas slid the foam mat between AJ and the bar.

"Aaiieee!" screamed AJ at the thought of impending peril. His body sailed over the bar but didn't counter-rotate like it should have. In fact, there was no rotation at all. AJ's body continued to fly over the bar in a straddled sit-up position, his back parallel to the floor. His body collided with the landing mat, opening him to flat on his back.

"Well, how'd I do?" asked AJ.

"You let go," encouraged Joey.

"And, you went over the bar," added Mackee.

"And, you're in one piece," concluded Dallas.

"And ready to try again!" said Patrick.

"Right after I clean out my shorts!" said an exasperated AJ.

"Okay, plowboy, it's your turn," said Chris.

"Right," agreed Patrick reluctantly. He continued to chalk his grips for an inordinate amount of time.

"Sometime before we all graduate, Goodman," prodded Dallas.

"All right, all right." Patrick blew the excess chalk out of his grip and slowly ascended the platform, receiving pats on the back and words of encouragement, as well as condolence.

"Speak well of me at my funeral, Chris," Patrick said.

"I forget, Pat, do you prefer red or yellow roses?" asked Dallas.

"Red, please. And tell my mom I love her."

"Just go!" yelled the team.

Chris jumped up on the platform next to Patrick.

"Okay, Pat, let's think this through. You need to put the Geinger on top of the bar, just like usual. At the peak of flight, just pull your arms into a twist. Now, you're gonna lose sight of the bar, but that's okay. It's gonna be right where you left it. Be patient. *Feel* the turn. Open to the bar, and be ready to catch. Any questions?"

"There's one part I'm not sure of."

"What part is that?"

"The part right after, 'Okay, Pat, let's think this through.'"

"Very funny, plowboy." Chris descended from the tower. "And good luck. We're all counting on you," he said mockingly.

Patrick could feel his heart pound as he reached the point of confrontation.

"The longer you wait, the harder it gets," said Dallas.

Patrick puffed one more breath and casted off of the bar. He increased the speed of his giant swing, preparing for the kick that would put him in the perfect position to try the skill. As his body moved around the bar, Patrick could not hear the cheers of his teammates. All he could hear was his own breath and his heart pounding in his chest. Patrick opened his hips just before the bottom of the swing to set up the kick and release. All of the cheers had stopped as the team captain reached the point of no return. All that was left to do was wait. Patrick released the bar the way he had hundreds of times for a Geinger. His body flew above the bar, his eyes never losing contact. At the peak of the flight, Patrick noticed that everything seemed to be going just a bit slow. For some reason, he relaxed and held his breath as he pulled his arms in and turned his head to go where he had never gone with this skill before. It seemed like an eternity in the twist. Patrick waited, and waited. Then, he opened. There's the bar! he thought. But something was wrong. Instead of the bar being in front of him, the bar is still beneath him! Patrick quickly moved his hands from extended in front of him to directly below him just in time to brace himself for the impending collision with the bar. But, it wasn't enough to keep the bar from knocking the wind from his chest.

Patrick folded in half over the bar. He then dropped backward to a hang, his face flushed and wincing. He then released the bar and dropped to the mat as he gasped for air and tried to endure the impact to his ribs.

"Patrick! Are you okay?" called Chris as the team stood over the fallen captain.

"I don't think I broke anything," Patrick said between gulps of air. "Does this mean … that I … get to pick the next skill?" Patrick broke the tension, and the team shared a good laugh as Chris and Dallas helped Patrick to his feet.

TWENTY-THREE

▼

"Pioneers!" the teammates shouted in unison as they all jumped into simultaneous back tucks.

"Pioneers!" they repeated the cheer and jumped again.

"Pioneers!" Again, they flipped. Patrick over-rotated to his back.

"Darn it, fellas," he said, rolling over to his feet and, in one motion, jumping up to a full gait to the locker room door. "Sorry to flip and run, but I gotta go." Within seconds, he disappeared into the locker room.

"Where is he off to in such a hurry?" asked Coach Lowery.

"Are you kidding? Nicole comes into town tonight," said Joey.

"Where've you been, Coach?" added Mackee. "That girl is all Patrick has been able to talk about all week long."

"I thought she wasn't coming in until late tonight." said Ty.

"You know Patrick," said Dallas. "He started doin' the math on how long it would take for her to get here from Memphis. Then he started supposing, 'What if she gets out of school early?' et cetera, and the next thing you know, Patrick has her getting here four hours before he originally calculated!"

"Besides," said Chris, "he's probably got some last-minute primping to do."

"Girls!" Joey lamented. "Why is it that every time a new girl comes around, perfectly normal, intelligent guys turn absolutely stupid?"

"Someday, you'll be stupid for the same reasons, Joey," Coach Lowery replied with a smile.

"I certainly hope not."

"Oh, well," added Coach, "it's been a long day. You guys finish up and get out of here."

"Sure you won't join us on the lake tomorrow for some sun and fun, Coach?" asked Dallas.

"No, but thanks for the invitation, Dallas. I'm looking forward to doing absolutely nothing this weekend. Besides, I'd probably be a wet blanket. You guys have some fun."

"We intend to, Coach," added Chris. "Pioneers!" The team did another back tuck, and the game continued.

"Has anyone called for me, Mom?" cried Patrick, bursting though the front door.

"Hi, Mom, I'm home," Patrick's mother said sarcastically. "How was your day? Fine, son. How was yours? Just fine, Mom. By the way, has anyone called for me? Why, no, son. Are you expecting a call?"

"Sorry, Mom. I'm just a little excited."

"That's all right. Nicole hasn't called. It's only seven thirty. When do you expect her to call?"

"Anytime between now and when she gets here."

"Well, it's a long way from Memphis. Perhaps they got a late start. Are you hungry? Supper's still warm."

"No thanks, Mom. I can't eat … I mean I'm not hungry, thanks."

"I know exactly what you mean. I'll put everything away. You can heat up what you want later on."

"Thanks, Mom."

Riiiiinng.

"I'll get it, Mom!" Patrick sprinted up the steps to his room to grab his phone before the third ring. "Hello?"

"Has she called yet?"

"No, Mackee, she hasn't. In fact, I thought that you were her."

"Her voice is as deep as mine? You're beginning to worry me."

"No, you bonehead. When the phone rang, I thought it was her."

"Gee, don't get so touchy."

"It's just that when you expect to hear one voice and then you hear another—"

"Yeah, I know. I just called to see if we're on for tomorrow?"

"You mean the cliffs?"

"Yeah. You guys are coming out there, right?"

"It's Dallas's boat. I've told him about meeting out there. I'm sure we are."

"Cool. AJ, Ty, and myself will … *click* … get there around two … "

"Two is cool, Mack. I've got a call on the other line. It's probably her. I'll give you a call in the morning."

"Cool. I'll talk to you tomorrow. Tell Nicole I said hello. Later, dude."

"Later." Patrick hooked his phone to catch the call waiting on the other line.

"Hello?"

"Patrick?"

"Nicole! I didn't expect to hear from you for another couple of hours. Where are you?"

"Actually, we're still about two hours out of Knoxville. I couldn't get out of school early so we didn't leave 'til late."

"So, you guys will be in about ten or so. Cool. What do you want to do?"

"Sorry to be a party pooper, but I'm bushed. If I don't get eight hours of sleep, I'll be no fun at all tomorrow. I think we're gonna go to the condo and just crash."

"I guess getting a pizza tonight is out of the question?"

"Sorry, but I'll make it up to you. After nine o'clock tomorrow morning, I'm yours for the weekend."

"That's an interesting concept."

"That's a figure of speech, sonny."

"Gotcha. By the way, where's your dad's condo?"

"Down by the lake, but I'll give you better directions when I call tomorrow morning."

"Great. I'll talk to you tomorrow then."

"Okay. I'm looking forward to it."

"Me, too."

A pause.

"Say good-bye, Patrick."

"Good-bye, Patrick," said Patrick, dazed. "I mean, good-bye, Nicole."

"Good-bye, Patrick." Patrick could hear the click of Nicole's cell phone. Patrick hung up the phone.

"Hey, Mom! You haven't put all that food away yet, have you?"

TWENTY-FOUR

▼

"COME ON, PLOWBOY, bring it home!" Chris's approving voice encouraged Patrick as he finished another perfect high bar routine. All that was left was the dismount. Patrick cranked his giants faster and faster, then he released. flipping and twisting end over end, finally spotting his landing …

"Patrick, Wake Up!" the voice of Patrick's mother, combined with her jostling, finally brought Patrick to consciousness.

"Huh?" exclaimed a disoriented, half-awake Patrick.

"There's a call for you. It's Nicole."

As if spashed by ice water, Patrick immediately realized where he was.

"Why didn't you say so?"

Patrick looked frantically about to find his phone, which was covered by one of his pillows. As if no longer in a hurry, he cleared his throat and calmed down, putting on his 'Joe Cool' look before picking up the receiver.

"Good morning, Nicole. How are you?"

"Are you coming by to get me, or what?"

"Yeah, I was planning on it. What time is it?"

"Nine thirty. I thought you were coming to get me at nine."

"I thought you were going to call me at nine."

"If I'm not mistaken, I was supposed to call at nine, and you were supposed to come get me. Did I not just wake you up?"

"Yeah, but … I mean … I was … I mean … sure. I thought I set my alarm … oh, here it is."

"What?"

"Well, I set my alarm for eight, but I forgot to arm it."

"So, are you coming to get me, or what?"

"Of course … I mean … sure. Let me jump in the shower, and I'll be there in about a half hour."

"Patrick, aren't you forgetting something?"

"Like what?"

"Do you want to know where I am?"

"Oh yeah, sure. That would make things much easier."

Nicole gave Patrick directions. Patrick reassured her that he would be there before she knew it.

Forty-five minutes later, Patrick's Mustang pulled up to the front of a very expensive condominium on the lake's edge. Before he could climb out of his car, he saw Nicole coming out the front door. He watched as her honey blonde hair swung side to side as she jogged out to meet him. She was every bit as beautiful as he had remembered. Blue-jean cutoffs and a red checked shirt tied at the midriff accented her perfect build.

"Morning, sunshine. Daddy says he wants to meet you. He kinda would like to see who I'm running off with. It makes him feel better," she said, leaning into Patrick's convertible.

Patrick could see the tall, dark figure appearing in the doorway, pipe in his mouth and the morning paper under his arm. Patrick forced a gulp down his dry throat as he climbed out of his car. The two met on the sidewalk.

"So you're the fella Nikki hasn't stopped talking about for the past week. Patrick, is it?"

"Yes, sir. Patrick Goodman."

"Nicole says you're a gymnast. A pretty good one, too."

"Daddy! You're embarrassing him."

"That's all right, Nicole. Yes sir, my teammates and I just won the state championship. We head out west for national team championships in three weeks."

"National championships? You guys must be good. I've never heard of great gymnastics coming out of Tennessee before."

"Well, we hope to change all that, sir."

"Well, good luck, son. Where are you two headed, if you don't mind me asking?"

"Not at all, sir. My teammate, David Dallas, has a boat. We're going out on the lake."

"David Dallas? Is he from Memphis?"

"I told you that, Daddy!" chided Nicole.

"Yes sir, one in the same."

"I used to work with his father. How are they doing?"

"Oh, quite well."

"Good man, Dallas. Oh well, I'm keeping you kids from your fun, and I've got work to do. Nice to meet you, Patrick."

"Nice to meet you, too, sir." Nicole's father shook Patrick's hand and turned to go back into the condo.

"Come on, let's go!" Nicole said, grabbing Patrick's arm, spinning him into an about-face, and pulling him toward his car.

"So, what exactly are we doing?" asked Nicole as Patrick's Mustang pulled out of the drive.

"Hopefully, Dallas is still waiting for us with his boat."

"Any chance he'll go off without us?"

"If I know Dallas, he's not even there yet. He likes to sleep more than anyone I know."

"When were we supposed to meet him?"

"Twenty minutes ago or so, but don't worry. We're only a couple of miles from the marina. By the way," Patrick changed the subject, "just how well did you know Dallas when he lived in Memphis?"

"Not well, really. Although we went to the same school and our dads worked together, we never really interacted. He was pretty shy back then, not very popular. We ran with different crowds."

"Him with the stuck-up rich kids, and you with the cheerleaders?"

"Actually, Dallas was the chess club–debate team crowd, and I was the one who ran with the rich snobs."

"Why am I having trouble with this picture? Dallas lives to rip at anyone who even resembles a geek, much less is one."

"I guess we all move on, some of us trying to distance ourselves from what we used to be."

"So, I guess you don't run with the rich crowd anymore?"

"Not any more. I got tired of the status quo trying to tell me who I could and couldn't like or be with. Not that I wanted to live on the wild side, but I have found that there are a lot of things that money can't buy."

"Like … "

"Like personality, character, class. Once my freinds started getting involved in drugs and alcohol, just to be cool, I figured I needed to find a different breed of friend."

"You sound bitter."

"I guess it still gets to me. The night I met you was the night after my big falling-out with my friends."

"So, I guess that makes me a rebound relationship."

"If you say so, I guess."

"You know what they say," Patrick said, quoting ficticiously, "if you're going to date someone one the rebound, who better than a gymnast?"

Both chuckled.

"Here we are," said Patrick, pulling into the drive of the marina. "See, I told you, no sign of Dallas."

Patrick parked his car in a space close to the floating ramp that led to the dock. He hopped out of his car and opened the trunk to get a cooler packed with ice and soft drinks.

"Are you sure he's even awake?" asked Nicole, pulling a picnic basket and several towels from Patrick's trunk.

"Yeah, he's on his way."

"How can you tell?"

"That's his boat tied up there. He keeps it in dry storage in there." Patrick, his hands filled with the cooler, nodded his head in the direction of a large metal building where boats are kept in dry dock. "In order for his boat to be out here, Dallas has to call ahead so they can have it ready."

Patrick's last few words were muffled by the sound of Dallas' olive green, limited edition Grand Cherokee speeding into the lot and screeching to a halt, only slightly off-angle with the other cars.

"Sorry I'm late, guys," said Dallas, hopping out of his Jeep. "I kinda overslept. How long have you guys been waiting?"

"We just got here ourselves," said Patrick.

"Hi, Dallas," said Nicole. "Do you remember me?"

"Sure. When Patrick said he met a girl named Nicole Ashley, I knew the name sounded familiar, but I couldn't place a face. Now that I see you, it's all coming back to me," said Dallas, jumping over the side of his boat to remove the protective tarp. "Didn't our dads work together?"

"Yes, they did," said Nicole, placing her load into the boat. "Dad works in the university system now. That's how I got to come out to Knoxville this weekend."

"I hate to break up this little reunion," said Patrick, placing his cooler in the boat, "but we should be getting a move on."

"Keep your pants on, pal. Just an exchange of pleasantries," said Dallas. "You get that line, and we'll be on our way."

Dallas started the boat as Patrick untied the lines that attached the boat to the dock. Nicole pulled in the bumpers as Patrick pushed the boat away from the dock and jumped in before the boat got too far away.

"Good job, mates. Now we're ready to set sail," said Dallas, pulling the throttle down to ease the twenty-foot ski boat out of the marina.

Once they had cleared the no-wake zone, Dallas opened up the motor, pitching the bow up and throwing an unsecured Patrick head first over the seat he was leaning against and pitching him upside down into the backseat, next to Nicole.

"Hi, handsome. Did you have a nice trip?"

"Beauty," exclaimed Patrick, checking to make sure that all of his vital parts were still intact. "Hey, Dallas, how 'bout warning me before you toss me out of the boat?"

"Sorry, dude. I just don't have the patience to ease out of the no-wake. It's just hard to hold this baby back."

"Fair warning is all that I ask."

"Fair enough."

Patrick thought about resuming his place next to Dallas, but the sight of Nicole pulling off her shirt to reveal her bikini top quickly changed his mind. Patrick righted himself and pulled his T-shirt off over his head, tossing it below.

"This is the life," said Nicole, lying back to take advantage of the cloudless sky, "no cares, just the sun, the breeze, and the water."

"No kidding," said Patrick, also lying back, adjusting his sunglasses.

"Hey, I think we're being followed!" exclaimed Dallas.

Patrick and Nicole rose from their semi-reclined state to look behind the boat just in time to see the multicolored Jet Ski jumping the wake.

"Who's that?" asked Nicole.

"That's Chris and Haley," replied Patrick as the watercraft headed away from the boat only to turn and set up for another jump over the wake from Dallas's boat.

"Oh my gosh, Patrick!" exclaimed Nicole. "He's headed right for the boat!" Chris and Haley ducked their heads to cut down as much drag as possible as the Jet Ski hit the wake only feet away from the end of the boat.

"He sure likes living dangerously, doesn't he?" asked Nicole.

"You've hit the nail directly on the head, my dear," said Patrick, accustomed to and unimpressed by Chris's daring-do. "That is one Christopher Todd McClure, as daring as he is foolish."

"He sure doesn't seem to hold life in very high regard." she observed.

"Noticed that, did you?" said Patrick as the Jet Ski hit the wake once again, closer still. "Don't worry. After a while, you'll get used to Chris."

"And, isn't that the girl he was with at the pizza joint in Memphis?"

"Yeah, that's Haley Johnson. Nice girl. She teaches hang gliding, so she's used to living on the edge. They're perfect for each other," said Patrick.

"Nice match," Nicole said.

"You think *that's* a nice match? She used to date the Boy Scout here," added Dallas.

"Oh, really? So, what happened?"

"Let's just call it incompatability, and leave it at that."

"Touchy, touchy. Hit a nerve?" prodded Nicole.

"No, I just find it very uncomfortable discussing former girlfriends with ... you know... "

"Current girlfriends?" asked Dallas, filling in the blanks.

"Not necessarily, just other people unfamiliar with the situation."

"Relax, Patrick," said Nicole, "I'm not threatened."

"Can we just drop the subject?" asked Patrick.

"Consider it dropped," replied Nicole, turning back to face into the breeze.

Patrick rose from his seat and made his way to Dallas' side. "Are you headed out to the cliffs?" he asked.

"Of course," answered Dallas, his eyes fixed forward.

Chris, having had his fill of wake jumping, was now running alongside the boat. Patrick sat down in the seat next to Dallas. Looking over his shoulder, he could see Chris and Haley keeping pace with them several feet away. Chris looked back at Nicole, who was enjoying the sun, then looked to Patrick and nodded his head, showing his approval in Patrick's taste. Haley also flashed a thumbs-up. Chris then hit the accelerator and pulled away from the boat. Patrick then resumed his place next to Nicole, trying to enjoy the sunshine and contain his excitement at the same time.

Within minutes, the boat arrived at the prearranged meeting point, the cliffs. As the boat slowed down, Patrick and Nicole rose from their half-conscious state. Nicole sat up in time to see Mackee swing out on a fifteen-foot rope suspended from a tall tree that extended over a sheer cliff and drop twenty-five feet to the water below.

"And you guys do this for fun?" asked Nicole.

"To be completely honest," confessed Patrick, "I've never dropped from up there. I leave the craziness to the other guys."

"It doesn't look any crazier than what I saw you do at the meet in Memphis last week."

"Yeah, but that was different," justified Patrick.

"Really? How so?"

Nicole's query left Patrick puzzled and speechless. Patrick's concentration was broken by the boat tipping slightly to the right and an explosion of water that produced Mackee pulling himself to a support on the side of the boat, spitting a stream of water across the boat.

"Sooo, it's the dish! Remember me?" said Mackee abruptly.

"Excuse me?" said Nicole, astonished at the macho display of chauvinism.

"You have to pardon Mackee," said Patrick. "He just pulled himself from the primordial ooze."

"Yeah," added Dallas, "he spent most of yesterday learning how to walk erect."

"Are you usually this charming, Mackee?" asked Nicole.

"Naw, usually I just club women and drag them by the hair to my cave."

"Somehow, that doesn't surprise me," replied Nicole. "Yes, I remember you. You were the one who tried balancing the salt, pepper, and cheese shakers on your forehead at the restaurant last weekend."

"Until they all dumped out on his head," added Patrick.

"One in the same," replied Mackee with a bow from the side of the boat.

"Patrick has done nothing but talk about you all week," said Nicole. Mackee jumped the rest of the way into the boat, shaking the water from his head and extending his hand to shake hers. "I'm sure Patrick has told you that I am his best friend."

"Actually, Patrick has talked a lot about you guys," said Nicole, wiping the water off of her arms from Mackee's shakedown and reaching to shake his hand, "but he didn't mention that you were his *best* friend. I guess it was just an oversight."

"Geronimo!" came the cry from the cliff, where a dark-haired figure had swung out some fifteen feet away from the cliff, adding another ten feet to the height of the drop, and creating the initial rotation that easily became four flips before he hit the water.

"That would be Christopher," said Mackee, turning in time to see him hit the water feet first.

"Yeah, earlier, he tried to park his Jet Ski in my galley on the way over," said Dallas.

"Sounds familiar," said Mackee. "So, you guys gonna come play with us, or are you practicing to be wallflowers?"

"Actually, I think we'll just sit here and watch you fellas look foolish," said Patrick.

"Speak for yourself, Goodman," said Dallas. Having shut down the boat and tossed anchor, he dove overboard and swam toward shore.

"I think I'm gonna join the fun, Patrick," said Nicole. "Hope you don't mind." Nicole pulled down her cutoffs, stripping down to the rest of her bathing suit, and dove overboard to join the others.

"Looks like it's just you, pal," said Mackee.

"Naw. It's not gonna be fun here by myself. I'm right behind you." Both dove into the water and swam toward land.

As Patrick and Mackee emerged from the water, Patrick could see Joey at the top of the cliff, rope in hand.

"It's about time you guys got out of the way," said Joey.

"I guess this is no big deal to you, eh, Joe?" asked Patrick, referring to the incident at Abraham's Falls.

"None at all. And just think, if you guys had invited me out here last year, you probably wouldn't have fallen for the gag we played on you." Joey took a full swing, releasing at the peak, diving head first into the water below.

"What gag?" asked Nicole, arriving at the top just seconds ahead of Patrick and Mackee.

"Chris, Haley, and Joey tricked Pat into diving off a log at Abram's Falls up in the Smokys last fall," said Mackee.

"How did that happen?"

Patrick quickly summarized the episode, exaggerating distances and reactions to suit his perspective. The rest of the team corrected where necessary and laughed at the conclusion, embarrassing Patrick.

"Why is everyone laughing?" demanded Nicole. "I certainly don't find anything funny about someone risking his neck over a joke?"

"I guess it's what we call 'location humor.'" said Haley.

"Yeah, you had to be there," said Chris.

"Well, you guys have a sick sense of humor," Nicole concluded.

"Ya think?" asked Mackee sarcastically.

Each of the Pioneers and Haley took turns swinging and dropping into the water below. As Nicole came to the front of the line, she hesitated, looking into the water.

"You okay?" asked Patrick.

"Yeah. It just looks a lot further down from here."

"You don't have to do this."

"I know … but I want to."

"Okay, just make sure you go in feet first and keep your arms up or at your sides. You don't want to smack the water with your arms. It hurts."

"I thought you hadn't done this before."

"I haven't. That doesn't mean I haven't visualized it a bunch. And, I've seen guys hit with their arms out. It's not a pretty sight."

"I'll take your word for it. Wish me luck."

Before Patrick could get the first syllable out of his mouth, it was covered by Nicole's in a passionate kiss.

"I don't care what these jokers think. I think you're the bravest one here," said Nicole just before she swung out over the water, let go with a scream, and dropped to the water, Patrick watching all the way down. He caught the rope, gave thought to just swinging out, but thought better of it and turned to give the rope to Mackee.

"You're kidding, right?" asked Mackee.

"What do you mean?"

"You know exactly what I mean, Pat. Surely you didn't climb all the way up here just to hand me that rope?"

"You know I've never done this before, Mack. I sure don't want to look like a fool now."

"Is that what you're worried about, looking like a fool? Did it not cross your mind that you might look a little more foolish just standing there handing the rope to each person that goes by? Just swing out there and drop. You know how to swim, and you know the drop isn't gonna kill you. Just go."

"But I'm—" Patrick tried to reason and stall his way out.

"No *I'm*. Just swing out and let go."

"What's the holdup up there?" asked Nicole from below.

"No holdup," answered Mackee, "Patrick's just planning his strategy!"

Patrick reluctantly took the rope into both hands, hyperventilated for a moment, then swung out over the water, much to everyone's surprise. However, contrary to everyone's expectations, instead of releasing, Patrick held on to the rope and swung back up to the landing.

"Oh, no, you don't!" exclaimed Mackee, pushing Patrick back out over the water. But a determined Patrick held the rope again, returning to the cliff. And, he received yet another push from Mackee. "Just drop!" cried Mackee. On the third try, Patrick closed his eyes, held his breath, and released.

"Yeah, Patrick!" screamed the crowd as Patrick dropped toward the lake below. Just before hitting the water, Patrick, instinctively extended his arms sideward as if to secure a landing from a high bar dismount. The cheers turned to gasps as everyone winced at the sight of Patrick's arms smacking the water's surface. Patrick's cry of pain was unheard as the lake immediately swallowed him under. A tense moment seemed to last forever as each felt their heart stop as they all waited for Patrick to resurface.

"Yeeeeooooww! That hurt!" screamed Patrick as his face broke the surface. Everyone breathed a sigh of relief as he swam back to shore to be consoled by Nicole.

"You were right, dear," said Nicole, "it wasn't a pretty sight."

"Thanks, Nic. Is it okay if I never do that again?"

"Sorry, darlin', but you're gonna have to do it right before you can stop."

Patrick looked into Nicole's hazel eyes. "Are you sure you've never coached gymnastics before?" They ascended the cliff together to try again.

With each turn, Patrick and Nicole became more courageous, swinging higher than before each release. Patrick, having learned from his first attempt, was becoming more adept to pulling his arms overhead before entering the water. On his way to the top, the line had become jammed.

"What's the holdup?" cried Patrick from the bottom of the cliff.

"Something between Mackee and Chris," said Joey. Patrick worked his way around the others to join the men at the top.

"You guys plan on goin' off today, or should we just pitch tents and camp here?" asked Patrick.

"Look who's here, Mack," said Chris. "Twenty minutes ago, this guy couldn't muster the stuff to let go of the rope, and now, he's gettin' pushy."

"It's not just me, guys. Everyone else would like a turn."

"Well, I would go if Christopher here would just take his turn."

"It's not as simple as that, plowboy. Mackee here insists that he can do more flips before hitting the water than I can."

"Need I remind you guys that we only have the most important meet of our lives a couple weeks away? I don't think either of you are gonna do us any good in a body cast or a coffin," cautioned Patrick.

"So, what's the big deal? You go, and I'll count. Then, I'll go, and Patrick can count mine. Nice and fair, right?" said Chris, ignoring Patrick's concern.

"Fine, McClure, you name the price," conceded Mackee, also paying no attention to Patrick.

"Guys, seriously, I don't think this is a good idea."

"Cool, loser does the winner's conditioning for a week," answered Chris.

"Do we count to the half flip or quarter?" asked Mackee.

"Whatever, Mack. It's your funeral."

"I don't think I want to see this." Patrick began to climb down the cliff.

"Where are you going, Goodman?" asked Chris, "You have to count my flips."

Reluctantly, Patrick climbed back up to the perch, where he could see best.

"You guys realize that I am not to be held responsible for—"

"Shut up!" the two said in unison.

Mackee took the rope in his teeth and climbed up the tree next to the one where the rope was tied. Once at a height that he thought would give him maximum upswing, he looked down at his friends.

"You do know how to count, don't you, Chris?"

"Just go, you ape!"

Mackee pushed himself off of the side of the tree trunk and began the long pendular swing, kicking his legs upward at the bottom of the swing to increase the following upswing. Near the peak of the swing, Mackee threw the rope forward to start his backward rotation. There was no need for Chris to count his flips, as everyone watched and counted out loud as a chorus.

"One, two, three, four, five ... ooooooohh!" Everyone groaned as Mackee smacked the water with his back as he over-rotated the fifth flip. Seconds of anxious waiting followed as excitement had turned to concern for Mackee.

Then the surface of the water broke with Mackee exploding from beneath, leading with a clenched fist.

"Beat that, McClure!" he shouted, showing no sign of damage.

"Sweet," said Chris, acknowledging Mackee's attempt. "You ready to count, plowboy?"

"Chris—"

"Don't say it, Pat."

"Be careful."

"You said it. Don't you know that the worst things happen when you tell someone to be careful? Just watch and count. Mackee made, what, five and a quarter?"

"Yeah, that sounds right."

"Cool. I'll be right back." Chris climb up the same tree Mackee jumped from. Once arriving at his jump-off point, Chris looked to make sure that Mackee was in position to see his turn. Chris jumped from the tree and began his swing, tapping at the bottom as Mackee did.

Chris's release point was a little lower than Mackee's, which gave Mackee the early advantage. To compensate for the low release, Chris pulled his knees apart to speed up his rotation. Like Mackee's turn before him, the others watched and counted out loud.

"One, two, three, four, five ... oooooooohh." A more subtle sound came from the mouths of everyone as Chris, upon finishing his fifth flip, kick his body open to an arch, diving hands first into the water.

"It ain't pretty," said Joey to a sullen Mackee, "but it is five and a half flips."

"I know, a quarter flip more than mine. I guess I'm gonna be one sore puppy by week's end."

"Nobody messes wit da mastah!" shouted Chris as he emerged from the water.

At the top of the cliff, Nicole rejoined Patrick, who was holding on to the rope and staring down at Chris and Mackee, who were exchanging a congratulatory handshake.

"I wish I could do that," said Patrick.

"What, flip five and a half times before hitting the water, or survive it?"

"Just be brave enough to make my body do that."

"How long have you had this problem?"

"What problem?"

"Constantly wishing that you were someone or something that you're not."

"Actually, I'm quite happy with who and what I am."

"You just think you need a few adjustments."

"Okay," confessed Patrick, "perhaps I could use a few enhancements to be the gymnast I'd like to be."

"And, you think you can find these improvements in your friend down there."

"Okay, I admit, Chris certainly has some admirable qualities, qualities that any gymnast would want."

"Perhaps, but that may not be your answer. Why do you think Chris is so good?"

"Because he's afraid of nothing and is extremely talented."

"And he duplicates who?"

"No one! He sets his own standard. He's that good!"

"Exactly. Trying to be like him won't work for you. The two of you are entirely different. You've got to find you're own niche. Find something that you do different than everyone else and capitalize on it."

"Hey, are you guys goin' up there or what?" came the voice below.

"Keep your pants on, Johnson," Patrick called down. "I'm just trying to figure out what to do!"

"How much thought goes into swinging out and dropping off a rope, Goodman?" shouted Dallas.

Patrick looked deep into Nicole's eyes. She returned a smile and cupped his chin in her hands, catching him off guard and pulling him in for a kiss.

"Go get 'em, tiger," she said, pushing Patrick's stunned face back to arm's length.

Patrick took the rope into his teeth and scaled the tree. After a deep breath, he pushed off to create his swing. At the peak of his flight, Patrick kicked his legs to turn his body over. Not enough to do more than one flip, but it was a big one. As his body turned over, Patrick opened his arms in a swan dive position. Once spotting the water, Patrick closed his arms into his chest and began twisting. The tighter he pulled in, the faster he twisted. Upon hitting the water, Patrick entered feet first having completed five twists in a single flip.

Patrick emerged from the lake water to the sound of applause and cheers from the cliff.

"Wow, Pat!" said Mackee, pulling him up from the water, "that was way cool!"

"Who would've thought that the same guy that wouldn't even do this an hour ago could do such a sweet drop!" added Joey.

"I guess I was just waiting for the right motivation," said Patrick, turning his head to see Nicole release for her turn, flailing her arms about before hitting the water below.

"Not that I'm not having a great time, Patrick," said Nicole, emerging at the water's edge, "but are there plans to do other things?"

"Well, I figured we would do a picnic later."

"Good. Any chance that later could be now? I'm kinda hungry."

"Okay, but I don't know if Dallas is ready to leave yet."

"You could ask."

Patrick scaled the cliff face to catch up to Dallas before he took his swing. After a few minutes, Patrick made his way back down the cliff.

"Well, Dallas isn't quite ready to leave, but he said we could borrow the boat."

"That's even better. That way, we'll have a chance to be alone."

"Great," agreed Patrick.

"Patrick! Nicole! Wait up," came a voice above them. The two turned to see Haley descending the cliff.

"I would hate to spoil anything, so if I'm out of line, tell me."

"Out of line for what?" asked Patrick.

"Would you mind if Chris and I tagged along? I couldn't help but overhear you talking about a picnic, and I know a perfect spot."

Patrick looked at Nicole for her approval.

"Sure, no problem," said Nicole. "It'll be fun. There's plenty of room in the boat."

"Oh, that won't be necessary. We'll catch up to you on the Jet Ski. I'm sure Chris wants to get in a few more dives. Just head north, Patrick."

Patrick agreed, and he and Nicole swam out to Dallas's boat while Haley waited for Chris to hit the water on another of his kamikaze dives.

Patrick and Nicole climbed into the boat. While Patrick pulled the keys out of his trunks, Nicole pulled up the anchor, then moved forward toward the bow to reach down into the galley below to get a towel to dry her hair.

"He is a bit on the crazy side, isn't he?" asked Nicole as Patrick started the boat and slowly steered away from the others.

"Who, Chris? What was your first clue?" he returned sarcastically.

"You know what I mean. I've seen guys that live on the edge before, but Chris seems to have taken up permanent residency."

"Well, there is a reason for that," said Patrick, pushing the throttle forward. "Chris is the not so proud owner of a genetic defect called Berry's Aneurysm. There are some weakened blood vessels in his brain, and someday, for no apparent reason, one will rupture. And, when that happens, that's all she wrote."

"Wow, I feel bad now, having judged him for a fruitcake."

"Don't. Chris brings on that kind of reaction from everyone. How do you think we felt when he first came to the gym? We all thought that he would kill himself before the end of the season."

"How does he survive, day in and day out, knowing that at any moment—"

"What choice does he have? Live in a cave until the inevitable? Feel sorry for himself? I think he handles it better than I would."

"He certainly does handle it well."

"He puts up a pretty good front. He thinks it's all a game, that by cheating death with his antics, he, somehow, wins."

"Although, ultimately—"

"He loses." As Patrick's thoughts trailed off, his concentration was broken by the sight of Chris and Haley zooming out in front of them on the Jet Ski. While Chris's eyes were locked forward, Haley turned, and with an upward swing of her arm, signaled the boat to follow them.

Moments later, the four converged on a small island jutting up from the water. Chris rode the Jet Ski up to the shore while Patrick stopped the boat a safe distance from the water's edge and dropped anchor. After dropping Haley off at the shore, along with the picnic supplies stowed beneath the seat, Chris maneuvered the Jet Ski back out to the boat to help Patrick and Nicole bring in their supplies.

"Did anyone bring cow flesh?" asked Chris, turning the Jet Ski beside the boat.

"No beef," said Patrick. "How about turkey-burgers?"

"Great. Half the flavor and none of the fat. No thanks. I'm glad I brought some *real* meat."

"What would that be? Butt steak?" joked Patrick.

"Naw, hot dogs! Three packs!"

"You know, hon," Patrick said sarcastically to Nicole as she pulled up the last cooler, "my doctor said I don't get enough preservatives and animal entrails in my diet."

"That's why I always pack an extra side o' beef jerky," added Nicole, "'cause you never know when you're gonna run out of sodium-rich animal fat."

"Very funny, you guys. I can see already that you've been hanging out with this guy way too long, girl. You guys are two of a kind. Meet you on shore." With a small cooler stowed beneath his seat and a larger one strapped on top, Chris pulled the throttle switch to carry the picnic supplies to the water's edge, leaving only one for the two to bring in. Haley met Chris at the shore to help remove the coolers.

"They make a nice couple," said Nicole, looking at the two removing the coolers from the Jet Ski.

"I guess so." Patrick tried to avoid the subject "Let's get to shore before Chris eats everything."

"He may be an animal, but I believe he is civilized to the point of at least waiting until the food is cooked, Patrick."

Nicole got into the water with Patrick and started wading in to shore on either side of the remaining cooler. Nicole noticed Patrick looking at Haley as they got closer to shore.

"Haley seems like a nice girl," said Nicole, trying to draw Patrick into a conversation.

"She's a sweetheart, all right," Patrick responded coldly.

"So, you and Haley used to date?"

"What brought that up?"

"Just curious. So?"

"So, yes, we did. So what?"

"So nothing. Don't get so defensive. I was just curious."

"Sorry. It's just a huge story I'd rather not get into."

"Believe me, there's nothing less fascinating to me than your past love life. It's your current one that I'm interested in."

"Thanks."

"No problem."

The two waded to shore and placed the cooler with the others. While Haley and Nicole prepared the food to be cooked, Patrick and Chris walked around the beach, looking for dry wood to use for a fire.

"Hey, Pat," Chris called across the twenty feet that divided them, "come here." Patrick jogged with his supply of driftwood up to the edge of a bank of trees where Chris had sat down.

"What's up? You okay?"

"Yeah. Have a seat." Patrick placed his armful of wood on top of the wood that Chris had gathered and sat down to Chris's right.

"What's up?"

Chris sat quietly, staring across the lake to the shore, dotted with expensive lakefront homes, and over the trees to the Smoky Mountains beyond.

"Have you ever noticed how beautiful that is?"

"The houses? The trees? The mountains? What?"

"All of it. Every bit of it, from the water right up to the sky. All of it."

"Sure, Chris. That's why people come out here, to take advantage of the beauty of it all."

"Huh. Funny you should put it that way, 'take advantage' of it. I think that's exactly what you do in your situation."

"What do you mean?"

Chris turned his gaze from the scenery to Patrick's eyes, "Do you think that you really appreciate this place, or do you take advantage of it?"

"Well, I'd like to think that I appreciate it. And you?"

"Let's take a test. Look at my eyes," Chris used his index and middle fingers of his right hand to emphasize Patrick's visual target.

"Okay, now what?"

"Describe the skyline behind you," instructed Chris.

"I don't know. Four or five houses with boat docks, a bunch of trees beyond them, and the Smokys on the other side."

"Close," said Chris, not moving his eyes from Patrick's, "there are six houses: two brick two-story, two cedar two-story, one cedar three-story, and one cedar three-story A-frame that's filled with glass panes. Five of them have boat docks. The one that doesn't, one of the brick houses, third from the left, has a walkway that joins with a walkway that leads from the cedar house to its left. They share that dock. There are two boats docked, and cars are missing from the drive, so I assume that the owners aren't home. The dock at the big A-frame has a few smaller life jackets hanging at the dock, so my guess is that, since the boat is gone, the owners are retired, and the jackets are for the grandchildren.

"The trees aren't quite in full bloom yet, but the view of the mountains, especially the highest peak, which is just to the left of the A-frame, is spectacular. And, there are no clouds in that part of the sky. Shall I go on?"

"Can I stop staring at you now?" asked Patrick. As Chris released Patrick's chin, he turned around to see that his description of the skyline was dead on.

"Of course." Chris resumed his gaze across the water.

"I'm sure that there is a point to all of this. I'm just not sure what it is."

"Ever since I found out that I had this disease, I've come to realize that every moment, I mean *every* moment, regardless of how trivial, is precious beyond words. You've lived here all your life, yet you've never bothered to memorize the things around you. You remember the feeling, and you have an idea of what this place looks like, but you don't really try to remember everything exactly the way it was so you'll never forget. How it looked, how it felt, how it smelled, *everything*! It may seem trivial to you, but when I remember an experience, I want to remember everything. When my life comes to an end, now or whenever, and my life passes before my eyes, it won't be the *abridged* version. I want to recall every nuance that made my life special."

"And, you've been able to memorize every experience you've ever had?"

"Of course not, you goof, just those experiences that I find extremely special and worth remembering."

"Like this moment?" Patrick asked, looking at Chris, who was still looking at the landscape.

Chris paused, then turned his head to look Patrick in the eye. "Yeah, like this moment."

"There they are!" called Haley as she and Nicole rounded the bend.

"Do you guys anticipate eating any time today?" inquired Nicole. Chris hopped to his feet and offered his hand to aid Patrick to his feet. The two picked up what wood they had gathered and started back to the picnic site, Haley walking beside Chris and Nicole beside Patrick.

"So what was that all about?" asked Nicole.

"Not much, just a little heart-to-heart."

As the four returned to the picnic site, preparations were made for lunch.

"Get away from there, plowboy. You don't know how to build a fire," said Chris, moving Patrick aside of the gathering of sticks and brush that would eventually become a campfire.

"I've heard this one, Chris. Is this the part where you set fire to your hair with a can of gasoline?"

"Very funny. Actually, promise not to tell anyone, but I was an Boy Scout when I was a kid."

"And look how you turned out!" quipped Haley.

"Hardy har har. It seems everyone is a comedian. I'm surprised you don't have anything to add, Nicole."

"I'm afraid I don't know you well enough to be rude," answered Nicole diplomatically.

"That's unusual, Nic," added Patrick, "most people feel comfortable enough to be insulting to Chris upon introduction!"

"I'll keep that in mind," returned Nicole.

"By the way, Chris," asked Patrick, "what ever happened to the rest of your Scout troop?"

"A couple are in jail, a couple have decent jobs, one is even a congressman."

"A tribute to the survival skills learned in Scouting," said Patrick sarcastically.

"All right, all right. One more jab about my pals, and I'm gonna put this fire out," Chris said about the kindling he had just set ablaze.

"You win, no more slams on the Scouts. Their reputation is still intact, thanks to you," answered Patrick, impressed by the quickly prepared fire. Chris accepted the compliment with an exaggerated bow.

Within minutes, the food was prepared and quickly consumed.

"I'm stuffed!" exclaimed Patrick, rubbing his stomach and lying back to rest his head on Nicole's lap. "How 'bout you, Nic?"

"I'm full, too. Not only are you the chief fire-starter, Chris, but also by the way you cook, I'm sure you'll make some girl very lucky one day."

"Only if the menu is limited to hamburgers, hot dogs, and anything else prepared on a barbie," Chris replied modestly.

"That's still a far cry better than what my dad can cook," added Haley. "His cooking prowess is limited to what can be stacked between two slices of bread."

"So, Chris," asked Nicole, "did you learn to cook in the Scouts, or did your dad pass down his talent—"

"Ahem!" Patrick cleared his throat to cut off Nicole's sentence, sensing that she was treading onto an uneasy topic.

"That's okay, Pat. She didn't know." Silence came over the foursome as Chris rose to his feet and began gathering the trash to place it in the plastic bag they had brought with them. "I lost my dad when I was quite young."

"Oh my gosh, Chris. I'm so sorry!" pleaded an embarrassed Nicole.

"Don't be. You had no way of knowing. Anyway, in answer to your question, I really couldn't say. My dad died when I was nine. I wasn't quite old enough to really learn much from him. As you could probably guess, I learned a lot about cooking and other stuff from my mom." Chris poured water on the fire and continued his clean up while he talked. "I do remember that my dad was great at everything. He was the captain of the polo team in college—"

"Your dad played polo?" asked Patrick, the vision of jockeys and horses dancing in his head.

"Not the polo you're thinking of. He played water polo. He was on two NCAA championship teams and played on the 1980 Olympic team. He was good, all right."

"Did he get to see you do gymnastics?" asked Nicole.

"Not really. I started gymnastics at age seven, but he was always so busy with everything else he did, he didn't get to see me do much. You know, little class competitions, stuff like that. I didn't start competing seriously until I was eleven."

"I bet if he could see you now, he'd be really proud," added Patrick.

"Yeah, whatever. Anyway, he can't see me, so there's no point dwelling on it," said Chris sullenly.

"Well, that does it for this place," said Patrick once the site was thoroughly cleaned by the group. "I guess we better get Dallas's boat back to him before he misses it."

"Hey, Pat," said Chris, "why don't we play a trick on Dallas? You ride back to the cliffs with me on the Jet Ski, and we'll tell Dallas that you ran out of gas, or some nonsense, and watch him get all worked up!"

"I thought you guys buried the hatchet." said Patrick.

"Oh, we did, but that doesn't mean I don't like to see him get worked up once in a while."

"Is Dallas still a hothead?" asked Nicole. Both Chris and Patrick stopped what they were saying and turned to look at Nicole.

"What do you mean *still?*" asked Chris.

"Well, from what I remember, when Dallas lived in Memphis, he had to transfer schools three times for getting into fights."

"Sounds like our Dallas, all right," added Patrick.

"Cool. This'll be great. Patrick, you ride with me—"

"I don't think so, Chris. After all, Dallas was nice enough to loan us his boat. As long as I've known him, that was the first unselfish gesture on his part that I can ever recall. I sure wouldn't want to mess up a good thing," said Nicole.

"I guess you're right," Chris said reluctantly.

"It sure wouldn't kill you to give the guy a little slack," added Haley.

"Tell you what," said Chris, "we'll take off on the Jet Ski, and you guys follow in the boat. If we get there first, I'll give him the 'running out of gas' routine. Even if he buys it, you guys will be right behind me, and that will be the end of the gag."

"And, if we get there first?" asked Patrick.

"Obviously, there's no gag, plowboy."

"Fine, you have your fun as long as it lasts, but y'all can't leave without helping us take this stuff back to the boat," demanded Patrick.

"What do you take me for, Patrick, a savage? Of course we'll help."

Within minutes, the supplies, Patrick, and Nicole were safely aboard Dallas's boat. Chris and Haley then left them in the rooster tail wake of the Jet Ski as they sped off to join the others at the cliffs.

Once Nicole pulled in the anchor, Patrick turned the key to start the motor. Nothing happened.

"What's wrong?" asked Nicole.

"It won't start."

"Don't tell me it's out of gas."

"Nope, we've got plenty of gas," said Patrick, checking the gauges. "It appears that the battery is dead."

After a moment of awkward silence, Nicole laughed.

"You find this funny?"

"No, not this. I'm just picturing the look on Chris's face when his joke backfires and he realizes that we really are stranded."

"And just how long do you think that will take?" asked an exasperated Patrick, still trying to start the motor with no luck.

"Oh, I don't know," said Nicole playfully as she moved up behind Patrick, "an hour or two, maybe."

"Who knows?" said Patrick. "It could be dark before they ... " Patrick's concentration was broken as two slender hands circled around his waist, up his washboard stomach, and over his huge chest, developed from years of strength training. "I guess they could be here in just minutes once they've discovered ... "

"Then again," added Nicole, turning Patrick around, "I doubt it."

Of all of the beautiful sites to be seen on the lake, the Great Smoky Mountains reflecting against the cool, tranquil water or the majestic mother eagle returning to her nest perched high in the treetops, Patrick could see nothing but the depths of Nicole's green eyes. He knew in that moment that he would remember this day very well for a very long time. *Everything*.

TWENTY-FIVE

▼

"WOULD YOU *PLEASE* hurry up, Dallas?" cried Patrick, frustrated by the amount of time Dallas was taking to prepare for his turn on the high bar.

"Keep your pants on, Goodman," replied Dallas, his hands still in the chalk bucket. "If I don't have the right amount of chalk or have the wrong consistency, I could fly off!" To some degree, this is true, thought Patrick, but in this case, it was merely a ploy to bother him.

"Fine," said Patrick as he jumped in front of Dallas, "you play in the chalk. I'm gettin' some work done!" Patrick jumped to the bar and wasted no time, cranking his giants much faster than usual for a warm-up turn. In fact, Patrick had bypassed the warm-up part and went straight into a full routine.

"Cold sets! I love it!" said Coach Lowery, approaching from his office. "What's gotten into Patrick?" Coach asked Joey, the last in line.

"A girl."

"Is it serious?" asked Coach Lowery.

"This is his first turn up," answered Mackee, "and he's in the middle of his second routine in a row without getting off the bar."

"Is he trying to get out of workout early?"

"I don't think so, Coach," answered Mackee. "His girlfriend lives in Memphis. He just came in with a blind stare and headed to the first event without saying much to anybody. He doesn't act stupid, like the last time. He looks more … uh … "

"Focused," said Chris, finishing Mackee's sentence, his eyes on the team captain putting the finishing touch on his third consecutive routine without dismounting the bar. "I've seen this look before. It's called tunnel vision. This man is on a quest. Come on, plowboy! Bring it home!"

"You think any of us are gonna get a turn in today, Goodman?" said a perturbed Dallas.

"Sure." Patrick put mustard on the last two giants before pinging a huge full-twisting double layout dismount to a labored, but stood up, landing. He then collapsed.

"Nice, Patrick," said Coach, bending over the exhausted senior. "I hope you didn't put your whole workout in that turn."

"Not … at all … Coach," Patrick gasped for breath. "Now that I have the assignment done, can I work on some new stuff?"

"Patrick, you know that the week before NTI's is no time to start messing with new skills."

"Then when? This may very well be my last competition, Coach. If it is, I sure don't intend to go out thinking that there was more I could've, should've, or would've done."

"Son, this is the time to polish what we have, to squeeze every tenth of a point out of each routine to get the best score we can. We've worked so hard to get to this point. Besides, who says this is your last meet? There's always college."

"Yeah, right. The way colleges are dropping gymnastics programs, I'll be too far down the ladder to get a full ride, and that's the only way I'll be able to get in."

"I'm sure there will be other aid … "

"I hope so. My folks can't afford it and I have been procrastinating, like, forever to apply for other aid. I guess it's a full ride or retirement."

"Don't give up hope, son."

"I'm not givin' up anything. I just want to make sure that I'm doin' my best gymnastics this weekend."

"Fine. Tell you what, Pat, as long as the others still have high bar routines to do, you can work on whatever, but as soon as the last guy is done, you rotate to the next event with the group. Got it?"

"That's all I wanted, Coach," Patrick popped up as if refueled.

"Remember, Pat, nothing new goes in without my okay, okay?" said Coach Lowery to a nodding Patrick, already in the chalk for his next turn.

Dallas, having taken his first warm-up turn, made his way next to Patrick at the chalk box. "Look, Patrick, I don't know what you're tryin' to prove, but—"

"Nothing to you, Dallas," said Patrick, glaring at Dallas, "so don't worry about me." Patrick turned his attention to the bar where Mackee was wrapping up his first attempt at routines, " Come on, Mack! Bring it home!"

Each of the Pioneers took his normal turn. Each focused on the string of correct thoughts that would signal his muscles to react precisely the same way each time to secure a hit routine, hoping that the same thought and result would be repeatable and reliable for the upcoming competition. Only the sound of the music from the speakers could be heard. Not that it was loud, but each of the Pioneers trained silently as his focus had turned inward.

Then, Patrick got up to take his turn.

Although the composition of his turn was the same as his competitive routine, that's where the similarities ended. With each skill, however simple, Patrick put in a new wrinkle. Each giant swing ended with a hop that rose six inches above the bar and was accented with both arms flairing to his sides and recatching the bar with a bounce.

The focus of the rest of the team was squarely on him.

Instead of releasing the bar near the top of his swing to do his blind change, Patrick lifted his left hand off of the bar at the end of the previous giant, doing a one-arm giant to the top of the bar, where he once again flaired his arm to the side as his body turned 180 degrees and stopped at the top of the bar in a momentary one-arm under-grip handstand. He then regrasped the bar with both hands, straddled his legs, and dropped into a endo circle to handstand that also ended with a hop and arm flair well above the bar.

Seven jaws dropped.

From the catch, Patrick pirouetted and tapped a setup giant to prepare for his Geinger. Although he was still unable to add a twist, like Chris had once suggested, Patrick changed the technique of the skill to make it his own. He put a gigantic tap behind his swing, putting his release way above the bar. He rotated through upright vertical, his body laid out, his head tucked in, and still no sign of twisting back toward the bar. His body rotated another ninety degrees, his chest pointing to the ceiling. Only then did he pull his arms across his waist to initiate twist toward the bar. Once he regained sight of the bar, Patrick extended his arms to catch the bar, his body nearly sixty degrees above the bar, almost in a handstand.

Fourteen eyes popped out of their sockets.

Since his catch point was well above the bar, Patrick decided to tap into another Geinger. Although it was not as high as the first, it still left him high enough on the catch to swing into a giant without a form break. Once arriving at the top of the bar, he stooped his feet through his arms and used the next circle swing to jam his legs out to a German Giant. His shoulders twisted, Patrick kicked his legs through another German giant before throwing the bar down, launching his body above and over the bar, like a reverse hecht. Before recatching the bar, Patrick again flaired his arms out and to his side to emphasize the flight over the bar, and caught the bar in perfect position to swing two more flawless giants before finishing with another full-twisting double layout, this time finishing the twist soon enough to flair his arms to the side before nailing a perfect landing.

Normally, such a routine would be followed with the explosion of cheers from his teammates. However, when Patrick turned to accept the applause of his team, he was instead confronted with dumbfounded silence from the unbelieving Pioneers. Even Chris, who was used to seeing excellence, was uncharacteristically speechless.

"What? You guys act as though you've never seen a routine before," said Patrick, quietly enjoying the effect.

"If what you just did was just a routine," said Chris, "then you're right, I've never seen a routine before. That was great!"

"Great? That was friggin' *awesome!*" added Mackee.

"I just want to know one thing," said Coach Lowery. "Can you do that again?"

"Every time. That was easy."

"This weekend?" asked Coach Lowery, suggesting that Patrick had his permission to put his new routine on the competition floor at the NTI's.

"*Every* time, Coach," said a newly confident Patrick, heading back to the chalk box to prepare for his next turn.

"What in the world has gotten into you?" asked Mackee.

"It's actually quite simple, Mack. I just realized that I have to quit tryin' to be like everybody else and just find what I do best and emphasize it."

Not to be outdone, Dallas mounted the bar to give his attempt at a routine. Like Patrick, Dallas put a little flash behind his easy skills and a bit more pace on his bigger elements.

"Woo-hoo, Dally!" screamed Ty, as the rest of the team joined in cheering for Dallas's attempt. "You got some relish to go with that mustard, son?"

Dallas worked through the hard part of his routine and quickly approached his dismount.

"Bring it home, Dallas!" shouted Patrick.

"Nail it, boy!" added Chris. Dallas increased the pace of his giants to prepare for his dismount, another full-twisting, layout double back. Everyone gasped as Dallas's release came later than it should have, putting his body dangerously close to the bar. Each Pioneer cringed as Dallas passed the bar, scant inches away. Dallas landed on his feet, but his momentum caused him to over-rotate to his seat. He continued his roll until he was on his feet. Dallas stood up to look at the bar, still vibrating from his release.

"Wow! I don't think I've ever seen the bar in front of me after a dismount before!" he exclaimed.

"Well, lets hope it's the last time that happens, Dallas," said Coach Lowery, looking on from behind the rest of the team. "Look, fellas, I realize that Patrick's routine was, to say the least, exciting. But, let's focus on the job we have before us." Coach Lowery motioned the boys together and positioned himself in front of them.

"Okay, in three short days, we are gonna get on a plane and fly to Los Angeles for NTIs. I don't have to tell you that this is the single biggest meet in Pioneer history. In fact, this is the biggest meet of your lives. Just getting here was a goal that you've all met. We have just one more step to go. I don't know if it has entered your heads yet, but there is a chance that we could place."

"We know, Coach," said Patrick, speaking for the team. "We also know that if each of us goes out and does our job, we can win!" Patrick's words were followed by cheers and high fives by the rest of the team.

"Okay, guys, settle down, settle down. True, there is a chance that if everyone has a good day, we could be on the top of the awards stand. However, it is going to require a great deal of intensity and focus. No more hotdogging, no more crazy attempts at skills that are not going into routines. Just maintain your focus on hitting your sets."

"Coach," asked Chris, "does Patrick's new routine stay in?"

"Well, that kind of puts me over a barrel, doesn't it? I tell you what, Pat, you do your sets the way you just did it. If you miss even one routine from here on out, you go back to conservative, got it?"

"Got it, Coach," said Patrick, reaching out to slap the hand of his buddy, Chris.

"Okay, if that's settled, let's get back to work. Three hit sets from each of you on each event." The team turned its attention back to the chalk bucket and the bar.

"Hey, I've got an idea!" shouted Joey. "Let's do our sets as though were already at the meet!"

"What a dumb idea," said Dallas.

"Naw, it's a great idea, Joe," countered Patrick. "Who's up next, Mackee?"

"Duh, ya think?" said Mackee sarcastically as he was already hanging from the bar, getting ready to do his routine.

"Get down from there, Mack. Let's do this right."

Mackee dropped from the bar and reapplied chalk to his grips.

"Okay, are you ready?" asked Patrick.

"I was ready a minute ago when I was hanging on the bar!"

"All right, wise guy, straighten up."

Mackee shook off his silliness and put on a straight face. Chris walked up next to Mackee to lift him to the bar, as Coach Lowery would do in competition.

"Okay, Mack," said Patrick, "here's the situation. We're in the final rotation of competiton in the first round, and we're counting on your routine to get us into the next round."

"Why not the final round?" asked Mackee.

"We've gotta leave some excitement for the other five events," replied Joey.

"Besides, you think we're gonna count on your routine on pipe to win the meet? Fat chance," smirked Dallas.

"Hey, it could happen," said Mackee, defending himself.

"It's gonna happen, gentlemen," Chris interjected. "Unless you guys have been sleeping and missed the news, we are gonna need every routine just to *get* to the final round. So, it's just as likely that *everybody's* routine will matter, on *every* event! So, let's get serious!"

"Okay, where was I?" said Patrick. "Oh yeah, we're in the final rotation of the first round, and let's say we already have a fall on this event, so we don't have another score to drop, so your routine will count for team score."

"Who fell?" asked Mackee.

"What does it matter who fell?" asked Patrick.

"A lot! If Ty or AJ fall, we still have four good routines to count besides mine."

"Okay, let's say it's Chris," said Patrick.

"Another fantasy. Like Chris is gonna miss a set," retorted Mackee. "If this is supposed to simulate a real meet, you better make the situation at least believable!"

"Okay," obliged Patrick. "Let's say it's me."

"Now that's believable!" said Mackee, throwing his right arm up in the air, signifying his readiness to start.

Ty, AJ, and Joey all returned his salute. Chris helped Mackee to the bar. Mackee started his routine with a powerful upswing.

"Come on, Mack!" shouted his teammates in support.

Mackee set up his release move and, uncharacteristically, caught it. "Woohoo!" shouted Joey. Mackee continued his set, hitting all of his parts, and set up for his dismount. One, two giants to gain speed for the tap swing that would give him enough rotation to do a tucked, full-twisting double back to a stuck landing.

"Yeah!" shouted the team.

"Way to go, Mack!" cheered Chris, as the team gathered around Mackee, offering high fives and pats on the back.

"Okay," said Patrick, "who's next?"

The game continued.

"Johnson!" came the shout from Coach Lowery's office.

"Hang on, Coach, I'm up next on p-bars!" answered Joey.

"Okay. After your next turn, I need to see you in my office."

"Yes, sir."

Patrick and Mackee looked at each other with looks of concern.

"Wonder what I did," Joey said to his teammates.

"Who knows, Joey?" said Mackee. "Maybe, he just wants to give you a pat on the back."

"Naw, he could've done that out here. Whatever it is, he doesn't want you jokers to know about it."

Joey took his turn. His concern for whatever it was that Coach wanted to talk about proved to be a distraction, causing him to miss two elements in his routine and over-rotate his dismount to his seat.

"I guess I have three more of these to hit when I get back." Joey picked himself up off of the floor and headed to Coach Lowery's office.

"So what do you think is up, Pat?" asked Chris.

"Well, I can only think of one thing, but I'd rather not speculate," said Patrick.

"You know exactly what's up, Goodman," said Dallas, fully aware of Patrick's thought.

Before anyone could elaborate, Joey burst out of Coach Lowery's office and made a beeline for the locker room. Soon after, Coach Lowery emerged from his office, running his hands through his hair. The team approached him.

"So, Coach," asked Patrick, "you gonna let us in on what that was all about?"

"Sure, Pat," answered Coach Lowery, grabbing a breath. "I just let Joey know that he would be the odd man out for NTI's."

"*What?*" demanded the team.

"Just like that, huh," asked Patrick, "no trial, no challenge?"

"No vote?" asked Mackee.

"Look, fellas, you guys all know we can only put six on the floor at NTIs. Someone has to sit out. It certainly can't be one of the seniors, and once you get to the rest of the team, everyone is about even, so I did the only fair thing I could think of: cut the guy with the least seniority."

"Doesn't hardly seem fair, Coach," added Chris. "Seems to me that Joey has worked harder than anyone else. You'd think he should have a better shot."

"Who would you rather I cut, Chris? You?"

"I'd gladly give up my spot. Joey's earned it."

"Yeah, right," Dallas butted in. "You're our ace in the hole, Slash. There's no way on earth you *couldn't* be on the team. Johnson is good, but he ain't you."

"Maybe there's another way to do it," said Patrick, "maybe set up a mock competition during tomorrow's practice. The top six compete."

"Good idea in theory, Pat, but what if you happen to be the one who misses?"

"Then, I stay behind."

"Yeah, I see that happenin' … *not*." added Mackee.

"It's a no-win situation," said AJ.

"Exactly my point, A," said Coach. "Believe me, fellas, this was not an easy decision, by any means."

"Coach is right, fellas," said Patrick. "Somebody had to be number seven, and, unfortunately for Joe, it was him."

"This is true, plowboy," added Chris. "But, right now, one of the most loyal and dedicated gymnasts any of us will ever know is sitting in that locker room feeling that everything he's ever worked for has been for nothing. I don't know about you guys, but I think Joey needs pals right now, not judgments."

Chris left the group and headed for the locker room.

"Chris is right," said Mackee. "Joey has definitely busted his butt to make this team. Sure, somebody has to be the odd man out, and maybe it should be Johnson, since he's the only freshman on the team, but if I were in his shoes, I'd sure feel like a waste."

"I told him that he was still very valuable to the team and that he needs to stay keen with his routines in case something happens to one of the other six."

"And, how much of that do you think he heard beyond the 'You don't get to compete in the biggest meet of your career' part?" asked Mackee.

"My guess is he sure doesn't feel very valuable," added Ty.

Chris emerged from the locker room. "He's gone. He must've just gone home."

"I'll give him a call later on," said Coach Lowery.

"I can't wait that long," said Chris, throwing his wristbands into his paper bag and hustling toward the door.

Patrick put his arm around a saddened Coach Lowery. "It's a crappy job, Coach, and I'm glad I didn't have to make the choice you had to make. But, don't worry, we'll come through this okay."

"Maybe some of us will, Pat. I sure hope I did the right thing."

"We all sounded it out, Coach," added Mackee. "You really didn't have much other choice."

The rest of the team gathered their belongings and, with heads lowered, headed for the locker room.

"I sure hope everyone is happy!" said an angered Haley, opening the door to Chris. "That poor kid is devastated!"

"Can I come in?" asked Chris, stepping inside.

"How in the world could you let this happen, Chris? I thought you told me that Joey was one of the best on the team?"

"It wasn't my call! Patrick and I tried to convince Coach to come up with another way of selecting the odd man out, but by then, Joey was already gone! I came as soon as I could to let Joey know that he still has friends."

"He's in his room. The door is locked. He won't talk to me. I don't think he thinks he has any friends."

"I'll find out." Chris stepped around Haley and made his way back to Joey's room. He could hear sobbing on the other side of the door.

"Hey, Joe, you okay?"

"Oh, just fine, Chris," said a sarcastic and hurt Joey. "How are you?"

"Not so good myself, pal. You want to let me in?"

"I don't think I would make good company. I'm not sure of anything anymore."

"Joey, I don't know if I can make this thing make any sense to you, and that's really not my job. I just want to come in and be your friend."

A long silence ended with the sound of the lock being turned and the door opening. Without revealing his face, Joey went back to his original position, tucked up in a ball in his chair, rocking back and forth, looking at the trophies, medals, and ribbons he had earned over the season, with tears streaming down his face.

Chris sat on the edge of Joey's bed, facing the distraught freshman.

"Look, Joe," said Chris, trying to make eye contact, "there's no way I'm gonna be able to make this make sense to you, so I won't even try."

"Oh, it all makes perfect sense to me, Chris. Just because I'm the youngest one on the team, I'm not going to be able to compete in the biggest meet of all our careers. It makes perfect sense. I started out this season lowest on the totem pole, and I have busted my ass day in and day out, putting up with Dallas's crap, doing the extra work, the extra conditioning, busting my butt every workout so I could break into the team score, and for what? So I can be excluded from the meet that I helped us get to? No, this all makes perfect sense!" Joey's tears increased.

"No it doesn't, Joey. Don't think I haven't seen what you do in and out of the gym to get where you are. I, more than anyone else, want to see you on the floor, Joe. But don't forget, everyone has contributed. And, anyone who had to be excluded, not just you, but anyone, would be a loss to the team and would feel exactly the way you feel now. It sucks, I know, but as tough as this may seem, you've got to find the positive in this."

"Are you so sure there *is* a positive for me in this? I don't see much to be excited about when I feel like my entire life has been a waste of time."

"*Nobody's life is a waste of time!*" Joey's words had thrown Chris into a rage, jumping to his feet and raising his hand as to stress his point like a fire-and-brimstone preacher driving home salvation. Before going off the deep end, Chris turned away and rubbed his hands across his face and through his long blonde hair, breathing a sigh, regaining his composure, and remembering why he had come to Joey's room. "Look, Joe," he said, turning to face his friend, "I want to be here for you. You can always count on me, and you deserve to feel just how you feel. But, it is not gonna help you do your job."

"What job?"

"You may not be competing, but you are still part of the team. You know this has been a team effort. We all feel lousy about this. If this is how it has to be, I guess it just has to be that way, but we still need you. You can still do what you can to help everybody else get ready."

"We have less than three days to get ready. What do you think I'm going to do that isn't already being done?"

"Push and motivate the team. Don't let anyone slack off. It would be real easy for the others to ease up now, knowing that they get to compete. Stay on top of those who would give less than their best."

"Yeah, like they'd buy it from the guy who's obviously not as good as them."

"Nobody believes that, Joey."

"I still feel it, Chris. I know this feeling well. I felt inferior when I made this team. It hasn't been so long ago that I forgot what it was like to be the least common denominator."

"And that's how you feel now?"

"How can I not?! If I didn't feel that way before, Coach Lowery's decision sure didn't leave any doubt."

"I think you're the only one who feels that way."

"Yeah, right."

"Yeah, *right*! You want to feel sorry for yourself, be my guest. Or, do you want to find the truth and prove your doubters wrong at the same time?"

"And how exactly do I do that?"

"Push yourself."

Joey looked puzzled.

"It's simple. Push yourself. You really are in an enviable position, you know."

"What do you find enviable about my misery?"

"If you're not good enough, as you say, prove yourself. Stretch the limits of what you do. Even if you don't compete, you have the advantage of no risk. You have the chance to learn something new or make what you already do better. If you don't earn your way into competing, I bet the effort will push those who may have doubts about the decision being irreversible, and I bet they pick up their intensity."

Joey sat in silence, knowing that what Chris said was right.

"And, what if something happens to one of us, and we can't compete? You have to be ready to step into someone else's shoes if they get sick or hurt."

"Yeah, who's gonna get sick or hurt before this weekend, you?"

"You never know, Joe. Sure the odds look slim, but you never know. You just have to make sure that you're ready, just in case."

"And if no one gets sick or hurt?"

"Then, you have to become the assistant coach, tracking scores during the meet, being a contributor in every way you can. You make sure you've done everything you can to help. You'll have your day."

"When? After this season, you, Patrick, Dallas, and Mackee will be gone. Who is gonna get us there next year, a new batch of freshmen? This, I think, will be my only shot. After you guys leave, we're nothing more than just another rebuilding team, marginal difficulty, limited experience, no depth. Unless four more Chris McClures move into town, I don't think there's much hope in me returning to NTI's before my career's over."

"I'm sure that's what Patrick and the other seniors thought when they were freshman. You never know what you're gonna end up with. But, if we assume that this is in fact the case, and this will be the only trip for you or any Pioneer for the next twenty years, don't you owe it to your team and yourself to make this trip count?"

"Yeah, I guess you're right."

"Of course I'm right. It would be too easy for you to toss in the towel. I seem to remember someone giving me the same speech about giving up not too long ago. Some wacky kid thought that by me giving up, it made it too easy for those who remained."

"I get the point."

"I sure hope you do. If you give up now, you would just confirm what your detractors think: you're too young, you can't handle the pressure, when the goin' gets tough—"

"I get the point."

"You can keep pressure on the rest of the team by not buckling under. Become stronger! Set the example!"

"I get the point!"

"Good! So, I'll see you at workout tomorrow?"

"Of course, you think I'm just gonna quit?"

"I would've if it hadn't been for you. I owe you my life."

"I wouldn't go that far."

"No, seriously, gymnastics is life and death to me. After I crashed on the bar that day, I was ready to pack it in, but you convinced me that there are some things more important: friends, commitment, trust, faith. I never really had a chance to thank you for that … thanks."

"No, thank you."

"Joey, you convinced me that these things are more important. Now, you have to find this to be true."

"Okay, you're right. But I don't like it." For the first time, Joey showed the beginning of a smile.

"You bet," Chris grabbed the teary-eyed freshman by the back of the neck and pulled him to his chest for a much-needed hug.

TWENTY-SIX

▼

THE FACADE OF the gym always looked so cold and univiting, Chris thought as he rode his motorcycle up to the entrance of the gym. Cold compared to the heat and energy produced within the metal walls of the building that had become home for the Californian.

As was always the case, Chris had arrived late again. Not so late as to miss any training, but late just the same. No one was in the locker room when Chris arrived. The rest must have started without him. He quickly changed into his workout clothes and hustled into the gym. The rest of the team was finishing warm-up and preparing for Floor Exercise.

Chris ran around the carpeted spring floor a few times to stir circulation into his legs, which had stiffened after the fifteen-minute motorcycle commute.

"Nice of you to join us, Mr. McClure," said Coach Lowery sarcastically.

"Can't think of any place I'd rather be, Coach." Chris then planted himself on the floor, off to the side so as to stay out of the way of the rest, who were warming up their tumbling passes. Chris sat in a straddled position for hamstring and torso flexibility exercises. He watched the others train while he stretched.

This late in the season, it didn't take long to get warmed up. Once ankles and wrists were taped and the conditioning and adrenaline kicked in, the body picked up where it left off the day before. This day was no exception. Five minutes into the event, everyone was ready to do routines, except Chris, who was still stretching.

"Do you think you might be ready to join us before we move to the next event, Christopher?" pleaded Coach Lowery.

"Sure, Coach," answered Chris nonchalantly, "just put me up late in the order."

"You're always late in the order," added Joey. "Why should today be any different?"

But it was different, Chris thought. Instead of a team of seven guys, it seemed more like six. Joey seemed to stand apart.

"Good afternoon, Mr. Johnson. How are we today?" said Chris, approaching Joey, who was headed to his corner of the floor to start his routine.

"Today we are just peachy, Mr. McClure. Ready to play my part." Chris was not quite sure which meaning Joey intended: the part of a contributor or outcast.

"Johnson, you're first!" called Coach Lowery over the top of his clipboard.

"Watch this," he said to Chris from the border of the floor. Joey thrust his arm into the air to signify his readiness to begin. Coach Lowery did not look over his clipboard. Instead, he continued to make notes.

Joey took a deep breath and started his routine. From the corner, he sprinted across the diagonal. He pushed his body as fast as it would carry him into a round off, back handspring and punched as hard as he could, driving his arms up over his head to start the rotation for his first big element, a tucked double back, which he kicked out of to a stuck landing.

Patrick, Mackee, and Ty cheered upon his landing. Joey, happy with his landing, glanced quickly over at Coach Lowery, his face still buried in the clipboard. Joey refocused and headed back across the diagonal. This time his round off, back handspring set him up for his second skill, a layout double twist to a rare stuck landing.

The other Pioneers were now on their feet cheering as Joey maneuvered into his corner elements: Thomas flairs, counter-rotating around his torso, and finishing in a pirouetting, straddled handstand that stopped and dropped into an effortless middle split. If Coach had seen any of Joey's routine, Joey wouldn't have known it, focusing instead on his routine.

"Come on, Joey!" shouted the team. "Finish strong!"

Joey pushed himself into a straight handstand with a five-second, motionless hold, then stepped down. Facing a near corner, he took only a few steps before doing a front handspring to a layout forward somersault to an immediate tuck front one-and-a-quarter flip to a push-up position. Using the momentum from the drop, Joey bounced off of his stomach and pushed himself back into another handstand and pirouetted twice and stopped on a dime in a handstand that he held for another five seconds before stepping down into the corner of the carpet, ready to finish his routine.

"Let's go, Joe!" shouted Mackee. "Bring it home!"

Joey caught a breath during his routine by lifting his left leg to a 160 degree split, his right hand pointing at the floor and his eyes following his right arm. Then he returned to his original upright position to prepare for his final pass. Joey exploded out of the corner, finishing with a round off, back handspring, one-and-a-half twisting layout to an immediate punch front. Stuck.

The team cheered and offered congratulations to the freshman, who had just hit a perfect set. Joey looked over to his coach only to find him still involved with whatever it was that he was writing on his clipboard. Joey's attitude dropped from confident to useless in the timespan of a heartbeat.

"Doujmovich, you're up!" called Coach from behind his clipboard.

Joey sulked over to the spot on the floor where Chris was finishing his stretching.

"Great set, pal!" said Chris, offering his hand for a low five. Joey dropped down next to Chris.

"I'm glad *you* noticed," said a disgruntled Joey. "I guess a positive comment from Coach would've been nice. He didn't even see my set."

"Don't kid yourself, Joe. I watched him. He saw everything. Look at things from his perspective. He had to make a tough decision. It's still tough on him. I don't think he's purposely ignoring you. He probably doesn't want to get either his or your hopes up only to be disappointed later."

"Nice try. I still think he's ignoring me."

"Just watch. He will act ambivalent toward everyone's routine until someone misses a set. Then watch him show that he's been paying attention."

"I guess you're right," Joey rose to his feet, "but I don't have time to pay attention to everybody else. I have work to do."

"Like what?"

"Like some harder tumbling. What was my last set worth?"

"I had your routine starting at a 9.6. It probably would've scored a 9.2 or 9.3."

"Right. I need some harder tumbling. Excuse me." Joey turned and headed toward Coach Lowery. Chris hopped to his feet and started warming up his tumbling on the strip adjacent to the floor ex carpet.

"Coach?" asked Joey.

"What is it, Joey?" answered Coach, not making eye contact, looking at either the floor routine that AJ was finishing or back down to his clipboard.

"Did you see my routine?"

"Of course I did. Good job."

"Thanks."

"Is that all you came over here for, Johnson, to pat yourself on the back?"

"No, sir. I just wanted to know if it's okay to work on some harder tumbling."

"This close to NTI's, I should say no, but I guess it would be okay."

"Thanks." Joey jogged off to the edge of the tumbling strip.

"Okay," said Chris upon Joey's arrival, "what great new tumbling are you hoping to create?"

"Well, let's look at the double back. What is the easiest way to improve the difficulty?"

"You can either stay tucked and add a full twist to make it a full-in or stretch your shape and make it a double layout."

"Which is easier?"

"Depends. If you can twist fast and still turn over the double back, the full-in is easier. On the other hand, if you can flip fast, the double-lay might come faster."

"Which is worth more?"

"They're the same value."

"Okay. I think I'll try the full-in. Got any suggestions on how to start?"

"Yeah. Drag one of those huge mats over here, and put it at the end of rhe strip. Space your steps so you can punch and over-rotate one flip up onto the mat. Once you can over-rotate a full up there, you're at least ready to turn the second flip over into the pit."

Joey set forth to create his training station while Chris continued his warm-up tumbling. Joey looked at the floor and saw that Ty was still in the middle of his routine, giving him plenty of time to work on the new skill before everybody got through routines and the team rotated to the next event. Joey dragged the six-foot-wide, twelve-foot-long, thirty-two-inch-tall training mat to the end of the strip at the edge of the loose foam pit. Joey then paced his steps away from the end of the mat to mark a line on the carpet as a target for his hands for the round off, about fifteen feet from the mat, to make sure his other tumbling would fit before the mat. There's nothing more embarrassing than completely missing the landing mat, he thought.

Joey's first two attempts were good enough to try to over-rotate a twist up onto the mat. His first two tries landed him squarely on his feet on the mat, still not rotated enough.

"Try reaching over the top of the flip this time," came the voice behind Joey. He turned to see Dallas, who had positioned himself at the edge of the carpet to await his first routine. "You'll rotate the flip a little faster and finish the twist a little sooner."

"Thanks, Dallas."

"Don't mention it, kid. You got some balls."

"How's that?"

"If it had been me scratched from NTI's, I probably would've wrecked the place and then quit. You got class, more than anyone else on this team."

"Except you, of course."

"Of course. Now leave me alone, you little bug. I have to concentrate on my routine." Dallas returned his focus to the floor, as he went through his routine in his head. Joey turned his attention toward getting his arms up faster.

That turn was a little better, he thought, missing his feet and dropping softly onto his back. "Cool," he said. He tried two more, both resulting in successful landings on his back.

"Good job, Joe," said Patrick, walking by Joey, still on the mat. "It's time to move that 'whale' out of the way and chuck that bad boy into the foam."

"If you say so," replied Joey, who had intended on doing just that, with or without Patrick's endorsement.

Joey moved the mat out of the way and pounded the chalk line he had made on the carpet until it was gone. Joey looked up to see that Mackee was finishing his routine, which gave him the time of only three routines, Dallas, who was in the middle of his set, Chris, and Patrick, to get somewhere with the full-in.

Joey hustled back to the end of the strip and eyed his approach to the pit. He visualized what his body would go through in the skill, identifying at what point he would finish the twist and then pull his legs around the second flip, the only part he hadn't actually done yet.

He took his normal tumbling pass run, stretched his hands to the carpet and turned over the round off, back handspring and lifted his arms up into the air, pulling his left elbow over his head first to start the twisting. His left arm was soon followed by the right, coming over the top of his head and down to his legs to pull his lower body around for the second flip. The next thing Joey knew, he was flat on his back, covered with six-by-six-inch cubes of blue pit foam.

"Woo-hoo, Joey!" shouted Chris above everyone's cheers. "That was right on the money!"

"And high, too!" added Mackee.

Joey climbed out of the pit. Everybody was there to pull him out, except Dallas, who was finishing his routine, and Coach, whose focus remained between his clipboard and the current floor routine.

"That was great, Joe!" said Patrick. "That would've stood up on the floor. It was so high."

"Cool, let's do it!" exclaimed Joey, turning and heading for the 40 x 40. Patrick grabbed him by the shoulder.

"Hold on, pal. You may need to work this a little more just to be sure—"

"Why? You said yourself it's ready for floor."

"No, I said that one would've stood up on floor. There are no guarantees that the next one doesn't end in a face-plant. I said nothing was ready."

"Great. When then?"

"Gee, I don't know, Joey. Work your way up. Throw some mats in the pit to firm your landing a little more, then raise your landing by adding mats. In no time at all, you'll be floor level and ready to be spotted out on the floor."

"I don't think I can wait that long," said an anguished Joey.

"Don't worry, Joe, you've got plenty of time. I'd love to stay and chat, but I have a routine to do. Keep pluggin', pal." Patrick retreated to the corner to start his routine. Out of the corner of his eye, he could see a figure in the corner to his left. It was Joey.

Before anyone could react, Joey had started across the floor. All they could do was hope and pray that he could get around to his feet.

From the beginning of the round off, Patrick could tell that Joey was in trouble. By not getting his feet around fast enough, the round off caused the back handspring to be too high, making his contact angle too high, forcing his body to drive backward, not upward.

"Pull in, Joey, pull in!" yelled the Pioneers. Try as he did, Joey got as small as possible in his tuck, hoping to create more rotation. He managed to clear his head in the flip, but nothing could cushion his collision with the floor.

SLAM!

Joey hit the floor on his face and knees and bounced several times before coming to rest in a clump on the floor exercise border tape. Everyone rushed to his aid, except Patrick, who had already headed to the ice machine.

"Joey, are you all right?!" asked Chris, the first to get to him.

"Uuuhhhn," replied Joey, visibly shaken but trying to get up.

"Don't try to get up, son," said Coach Lowery. "Just roll over to your back and relax. Let's make sure you got all your original parts. Are your ankles hurt?"

"I never made it that far, Coach. My ankles are fine, but my knees kill!"

"I'm not surprised, Joey. Aside from the normal bruises, I think you've created a few new colors," added Mackee.

"Not to mention the fashionable gymnastics equipment logo embedded in your forehead," added Dallas. "Sure took some guts, though."

"Guts? Maybe. Brains? Certainly not!" exclaimed an enraged Coach Lowery. "That was a stupid thing to do! You could easily have gotten killed or at least ruined the rest of your life with a catastrophic injury that could have left you paralyzed! What the hell were you thinking?"

Joey jumped to his feet, feeling no pain, only anger. "I'll tell you what I was thinking, Coach. I was thinking that the only way you were gonna notice me was for me to do something so completely stupid that maybe you'd pry your fat face out of that damn clipboard and see that I'm still a part of this team!"

Joey turned around and limped toward the locker room, snatching one of the two bags of ice from a dumbfounded Patrick and placing it firmly on his rug-burned forehead. "Thanks."

The entire team stood frozen until the slam of the locker room door brought everyone to their senses.

"I guess I better be the one to talk to Joey this time," said a cowering Coach Lowery as he headed toward the locker room and grabbed the other bag of ice from Patrick.

"Ya think?" Dallas whispered to Mackee.

"How's the head?" Coach asked as Joey applied and removed the bag of ice from his head, examining the bag for any sign of blood.

"It hurts. My knees hurt. I think I bit my lip, too."

"Do you think you need to see a doctor?"

"No way. I'm fine. Just a few bruises and carpet burns. Nothing permanent. I'm sure I'll make a full recovery."

"Joey, what would provoke you to do something so foolish this close to NTI's?"

"Close for who? I'm not competing this year, remember? I figure I've got all summer to heal up."

"Joey, you've got to stay on top of your gymnastics. What if something happens to one of the others? I may need you."

"May need, may not need, may never need. What does it matter, Coach? I bust my butt out there, day in and day out, and for what? Just to be an expendable tool, to use as a spare part if one of the more important pieces doesn't work just right. I'm afraid this logic doesn't help to boost my confidence."

"Joey, I'm sorry about this whole mess. Really I am. I wish I could put the whole team on the floor. You are very valuable to this team. You are one of the reasons we are where we are. Unfortunately, I can't put everyone on the floor. I know my team score automatically drops without you on the floor. But, you aren't the only contributor to this team. The team score drops regardless of who's left out. I don't want you to think that I think less of your gymnastics, or you as a person, because of this whole ordeal."

"It's kinda hard not to when I'm the only one in this situation," lamented Joey, fighting tears.

"Joey," pleaded Coach Lowery, sitting next to him on the pine bench, putting his arm around the shattered boy, fighting tears, "you are the future of this program. I know this is tough for you. But, believe me, this was especially tough for me, too. I have a team of seven outstanding gymnasts. It nearly killed me to have to exclude any of you. If it had been up to me, I'd compete everyone and take our best score, but it's not my call. I had to pick six. I knew I'd be having this talk with whomever the odd man out was. I'm sorry it was you, but unfortunately, my hands are tied. It has nothing to do with your ability or potential, but rather how the cards fall. You will be there again, Joe."

"Yeah, I know. I've already had this conversation. So how am I gonna get back, with Ty and a bunch of snotty-nosed freshmen?"

"You *are* a snotty-nosed freshman. These guys thought the same thing about you at the beginning of the season, but look how far you've come."

"Yeah, but I've had Chris and Patrick and Mackee, and even Dallas. Who are the next group of guys gonna look up to?" pleaded Joey, the swell of tears no longer welling in his eyes, but trickling down both cheeks.

"You, Joey." Joey turned his head and looked at his coach. "You have grown so much in a year. It's amazing to me the man you've become. Whoever does compete for me next year, they won't have far to look to find their leader. They will look to you, and you will lead them, and lead them well."

"Don't even say that stuff, Coach," said Joey, dropping his head. "I don't need you to pump up my ego."

"This is not just an attempt to cheer you up. I really do need for you to see your place in all of this. You are an asset to this entire program, not an expendable spare part. Your job now is not to feel self pity, Joe. I need for you to stay on top of your routines. Yes, it's possible that you won't see any action at this competition, but I really do need for you to be ready just in case someone else falters."

Joey felt bad that he had taken the situation so personally. After all, he thought, someone had to be excluded. At that moment, he couldn't think of anyone else that he would want to see in his situation.

"I'm sorry for behaving so poorly, Coach," said Joey, rising to his feet. "It just all seems like such a waste to get this far only to have to watch from the sidelines."

"I'm glad to see that this all means so much to you, Joey."

"This is all I am, Coach. It means the world to me."

Just then, the locker room door burst open.

"Coach, you better get out here. We just had an accident," exclaimed Mackee, grabbing one of Joey's ice bags and turning back to rejoin the team.

Coach Lowery and Joey charged out of the locker room to see the team huddled at the parallel bars.

"Quick! Get some paper towels!" called Patrick from the middle of the mob. Joey turned and rushed back into the locker room. He made a beeline for the lavatory to pull handful after handful of paper towels out of the dispenser. Several thoughts went through Joey's head. He knew someone was hurt because of the need for ice, but paper towels? He hurried as fast as he could and bolted for the door. Upon arriving at the group, Joey could see that everyone was gathered around AJ.

"Joey, quick! Hand me the towels!" shouted Coach Lowery taking the towels in one hand and removing Chris's tattered T-shirt from around AJ's left hand.

"What the heck happened?" asked Joey.

"Stupid mistake," said AJ, grimacing from the pain. "I was setting up parallel bars ... ouch ... and ... like an idiot, I didn't hold the rail. I held the post, and the darn thing slipped out of my hand, and slid down into the upright, pinching my other hand." Once Coach Lowery removed the shirt, it was evident how much damage had been done. AJ's hand was open and bleeding from the second knuckle of his index finger down to first knuckle of his thumb.

"Geez, AJ, that looks pretty bad!" said Mackee.

"It feels kinda bad, too, Mack!" answered AJ.

"I think you're definitely going to need some stitches, son," said Coach Lowery. Everyone knew what that meant.

"Well, Joey," said Ty, "I guess you'll be competing at NTI's, after all."

"This is not at all how I wanted it, Ty," said Joey.

"This is not how *anybody* wanted it, Joe, least of all me!" replied AJ, whincing, "but now it's up to you to pick up my slack!"

"I think I have the bleeding under control, AJ," said Coach Lowery, "but you need to get to a doctor and have that taken care of right away."

"I'll take him, Coach," said Patrick.

"No, you need to train, Patrick." replied Coach Lowery. "AJ, are your folks at home?"

"Yeah," answered AJ, looking at the clock on the wall, "my dad got home from work about a half hour ago. He can be here in five minutes."

"Good. Patrick, would you ... " Before Coach Lowery could get the words out of his mouth, Patrick had already started running toward the phone on the wall to call AJ's house.

"This really bites," said AJ, angrily.

"I know, son," said Coach Lowery. "I know this is little consolation, but it could've been much worse."

"I know, but believe me, Coach, it's bad enough." AJ could only stare at his hand, bandaged in gauze and paper towels, thinking of the thousands of times he had set those very same bars without so much as a close call. And now, with one microsecond's thoughtlessness, he would be missing the meet of his career.

"Your dad's on the way, AJ," said Patrick, returning from the phone.

"I really feel like such an idiot," said AJ, more embarrassed than hurt. Everyone stood motionless, not knowing what to say.

"I guess it just goes to show, folks," said Mackee, trying to break the tension, "nothin' is a sure thing."

"Great," said Patrick, "what else can happen?"

TWENTY-SEVEN

▼

"WHOOOAA!" SCREAMED JOEY as he spun several times on his back on the end of the pommel horse before flying off and landing on the mat with a thud. Joey gathered his senses and found his way to his feet, clutching his forehead to try to stop the spinning that was going on inside. "That could've been a little better."

Coach Lowery glanced at the clipboard that a stitched-up AJ was holding. "In fact, Johnson, that could've been much better. That's the fourth fall, and you're not through your first routine."

"I guess it's just not a pommel horse kind of day, Coach," said Joey, trying to make light of his errors.

"Well, it needs to become one, Mr. Johnson. What excuse are you going to use if Saturday is not a pommel horse kind of day?"

"Sorry, Coach," said Joey, dropping his head. "I'll try harder."

"Thank you, Mr. Johnson."

"That may be his problem, Coach," said Patrick in a low tone as he walked by Coach Lowery.

"What do you mean, Pat?" replied Coach Lowery, maintaining his gaze on the next routine.

"Do you think maybe Joey is trying too hard? I mean, he seems too tight, too wound up."

"Probably. Let's hope he loosens up before this weekend."

Joey was not the only Pioneer feeling the tension. It was the last workout in their gym before flying out to UCLA, the site for the National Team Invitational. Nerves were short for all of the Pioneers as they tried to hone every skill, minimize every error, and perfect every routine. It was only natural for some to feel a little more pressure as the meet drew near.

"Ouch … damn it!" screamed Joey, as once again, he made another error during his routine, this time smacking his legs into the hard wooden pommel, which not only hurt, but also stopped his legs, throwing the rest of his body over the horse into a side roll that planted the freshman on his back on the opposite side of the horse from where he started.

"Joey, lighten up!" said Chris. "You're gonna kill yourself!"

"I can't lighten up, Chris!" said a now bruised, as well as frustrated, Joey. "This is our last workout at home, and I can't hit a friggin' pig set! How exactly do you expect me to lighten up?" Joey pulled himself to his feet, walked over to the chalk dish, and pounded his fist into a block of chalk, shattering the block and causing a cloud to explode from the top of the dish.

"You can start by not wasting any more chalk, Johnson," said a monotone Coach Lowery, slowly running out of patience. "Then, you walk to the water fountain, get a drink, splash your face, and get ready for Rrings. You can come back to pommels when you're done."

Joey swallowed the anger and pain and followed Coach Lowery's direction, heading for the water fountain on the other side of the gym.

"I certainly hope he comes around soon," said Coach Lowery.

"It's not like he hasn't been through an emotional roller coaster the last couple of days, Coach," said Patrick.

"Yeah," added Mackee, "he probably feels like the weight of the world is on his shoulders."

As the others gathered their grips and headed toward Rings, Chris looked toward the water fountain to see what was holding up Joey. He had gotten his drink and splashed his face, but instead of returning to the group, he had sat down next to the fountain, his head buried in his folded arms and propped on his bent knees. Chris jogged over to him.

"You okay, Joey?" asked Chris.

"Would you be?" sobbed Joey, lifting his head to reveal his face, red from his crying. "All this time, it never mattered if I hit or missed. Now, when it counts, I mean *really* counts, I'm gonna be worthless, and I'll let everyone down, and it'll all be my fault."

"Joey, you gotta stop putting so much pressure on yourself," Chris sat down. "You've worked way too hard to fold now. Just do what you can. If you hit, you help. If you miss, big deal. We've got five more routines to back you up."

"And, what if someone else misses? Then, where will we be?"

"We'll have to cross that bridge when we get to it. Besides, you can't take responsibility for everyone's routines. You just concern yourself with your job. We'll do our jobs, and we'll let Coach Lowery worry about the big picture."

"I guess you're right."

"Of course I'm right. Now, let's get back to work before someone suspects that we have a thing goin' on." Chris hopped to his feet and helped Joey up as the two rejoined the group.

"Is he okay?" asked Patrick.

"Is anybody?" answered Chris as he strapped on his grips.

"Great job, fellas. Let's wrap it up. Come over here, and have a seat." The team had finished its conditioning, with the exception of Joey, who had to go back to Pommel Horse and make up for the routines he had missed earlier. The team gathered in the middle of the floor exercise carpet.

"None of us has any idea of how this weekend is going to go. We may be on top of the world Sunday night, or we may be watching from the stands, but one thing is for sure. When it is all said and done, we will know that we put the best Pioneer team possible on the floor, and, regardless of the outcome, each one of you will have done his very best. Not just this weekend, but this entire season. You've all grown a lot, overcome a lot, and have shown me more guts, talent, and determination than any group of guys it has ever been my honor to coach.

"So, regardless of where we see the final session of competition from this weekend, be it the bleachers or the competition floor, I want you guys to know that you have already won. Whether you walk away with hardware or not matters little. What does matter is what you guys have done, since day one, to get ready for the chance to be where you are. If this weekend finds us not at the top of the awards stand, it will not come from a lack of effort, preparation, determination, and, not least of all, courage.

"You've all stepped up and accepted the challenge before you. All that's left is finishing off the job you started. The honor comes in finishing. No matter where we finish, we will hold our heads up high because we were gallant in the attempt and courageous in our efforts. For it is the effort, not the result, that makes us champions. And to me, you are all already champions."

The team rose to its feet and in unison yelled, "Pioneers!" and did a standing back tuck.

"All right, fellas," said Coach Lowery, "you guys go home and get ready. I'll meet you at the airport in two hours. Everybody got it?"

"Got it!" replied the team. Everyone headed toward the locker room, except Joey, who went to the back of the gym.

"Where are you going, Joe?" asked Coach Lowery.

"I'm going to finish my conditioning."

"You don't need to do that. Besides, you got plenty of conditioning just trying to stay on that horse."

"It's not the same, Coach. And you said it yourself, it's what we've done all year that's gotten us here, and this is what's gotten me here."

"You're gonna be just fine, Johnson. I've got a little work to do in my office. Just let me know when you're done so I can lock up."

"Sure thing, Coach." Coach Lowery turned to retreat to his office.

"Hey, Coach?" Joey called. Coach Lowery turned around. "Thanks. Thanks for everything."

"Thank *you*, Joey."

"Mom! Have you seen my jeans?" Chris called out to his mother.

"Which ones, son? You have so many."

"You know, my favorite ones. They're bleached, holes in the knees …"

"Faded in the seat where you can almost see through them?"

"Those're the ones!"

"Chris, you've just described every pair of jeans that you own! How do I know which ones you mean?"

"You know. The ones I bought … wait a minute … never mind, I found 'em."

"Chris, I don't know what I'm going to do about—"

"Oowwww!" screamed Chris following a loud thud. Chris's mother rushed to his room to find him sitting on his bedroom floor rubbing his head.

"Are you okay?"

"I'm fine. I just slammed into the doorjamb of the closet."

"Here, let me take a look."

"No, Mom. I'm fine. Just a bump. No real damage. Go back to your life, citizen. There's nothing to see here."

"Okay, if you say so." Chris's mother went back to the task of packing her own clothes. Even though she didn't go to all of Chris's competitions, there's no way she was going to miss the biggest meet of his career.

"So, Mom," Chris called from his bedroom as he continued packing, "you and Haley gonna wait until Friday to fly out?"

"Yes, son. We'll be in late Friday night. You know nervous I get watching workouts. I can't get off work, so we'll just have to miss the training day But, don't worry. We'll be there in plenty of time to see Saturday competition."

Chris spoke under his breath, "That's not what I'm afraid of."

"Chris, I bought you a gym bag for your things."

"Mom, you know how I hate those things. Why do you think I haven't used one before now?" Chris finished packing his duffle bag and headed toward the living room.

"I know, dear, but I just couldn't bare the thought of you being on national television carrying your grips around in a paper—"

THUD!

Chris's mother turned at the sound to see her son on his bottom after slamming into the archway that separated the hallway from the living room.

"Honey, are you all right?"

"I'm fine, Mom. It's just my navigational skills that are a little off-line."

"Are you sure that's all it is?"

"I think so," replied Chris in a very unsure tone, rubbing his head once again.

"I'll take a personal day. Haley and I will see you tomorrow night."

"Mom, I don't think that's quite necessary."

"Maybe to you, but at very least, we'll get to see workout. I'll see about changing our tickets when we get to the airport. Now, not another word." Chris rose to his feet and carried his bag out to the car.

"There's Chris!" called Joey as Chris and his mother entered the doors of the airport.

"Hurry, Chris," said Coach Lowery, opening the door for his gymnast, "the plane leaves in forty-five minutes. Do you have bags to check through?"

"Naw, just this bag. I'll carry it on."

"What about your grips and stuff?" exclaimed Joey.

"All in the bag. Let's go," Chris turned back to his mother to give her a good-bye kiss, "See ya tomorrow night, Mom."

"You stay healthy, son."

"You know it," Chris said reassuringly.

"Come on, Chris," said Joey, "we're gonna miss our flight!" The three rushed to their gate. Mrs. McClure wiped a tear from her eye as she watched the trio disappear into the airport. She then walked to the ticketing agent to change her tickets for herself and Haley..

"It's about time, McClure!" said Mackee, as Chris, Joey, and Coach Lowery made their way back through the jumbo jet as the flight attendants started their preflight safety speech.

"Sorry, guys. You know how I like to make an entrance."

"Great. You're seated with Patrick, Chris."

"Thanks, Coach." Chris made his way back to the row where Patrick was seated.

"Flip ya for the aisle seat, plowboy."

"You're on," replied Patrick, stepping out into the aisle with Chris. Unlike when most people flip for something, instead of producing a coin, both did standing back tucks in the narrow aisle. Patrick landed squarely on his feet, Chris squarely on his knees.

"Uhhhnn! I guess you win," exclaimed Chris as he crawled to the center seat.

"Are you alright, Chris? I don't think I've ever seen you not get around on a back tuck."

"I think I clipped an armrest on the way up. Slowed me down. Don't worry. I'm fine." The guys settled into their seats and prepared for the flight.

During the flight, Chris excused himself to use the restroom. Upon returning, Patrick heard a commotion and turned to see Chris apologizing to another passenger that he had tripped over. Patrick stood up to allow Chris to reclaim his seat.

"Eveything okay back there?"

"Oh, yeah, that guy just had his foot out in the aisle, and I didn't see it." Patrick was puzzled. He had never seen Chris so clumsy before. Was it nerves? The thought stayed with Patrick for a while after they had settled into their seats. The silence was felt by Chris as well.

"Really, Patrick, I'm fine."

"You're sure."

"I'm sure. I'm just havin' a bad day on my feet. I am allowed one or two, you know." Chris pulled the complimentary magazine out of the pocket in front of him and opened to no particular page and buried his face in it to avoid Patrick's stare.

"I guess I'll just have to take your word for it," said Patrick, still not quite convinced.

"Thank you." Chris pulled the magazine away from his face to a normal reading distance, realizing only then that the magazine was upside down.

For most of the flight, Patrick watched Chris out of the corner of his eye, so as not to appear to be staring. Chris spent most of the flight just staring into space or looking out the window. Once the plane approached the Rocky Mountains, Chris broke the chain of silence.

"Over those peaks, and I'm home," he said.

"You don't consider Knoxville home?" asked Patrick.

"Not really," replied Chris, leaning over the empty seat next to him to get a better look out the window. "I'm sure in time, I may come to like Tennessee as much, maybe even a little more. But, let's face it, California is where I grew up. It'll always be home. As they say, you can take the boy outta the country—"

"But you can't take the country out of the boy. I guess you're right. If I were to move away from Knoxville, no matter where I went, or how long I lived there, I would still call K–town home."

"That's what scares me about you, plowboy," Chris said jokingly as he turned back to face forward in his seat. "Say, have you heard from any of the colleges you've talked to?"

"Well, it seems that the schools that I've been accepted to don't have gymnastics programs, and those that do have gymnastics teams have already assigned all of their scholarship money to other guys. What about you?"

"I haven't applied anywhere. I figure I don't want to waste someone else's money."

"What do you mean? You're one of the best gymnasts in the country. Any program would be better with you."

"Yeah, right. Do you really think a college would take me if they knew about this problem in my head? I could just see a school investing good money in me only to watch me croak on them halfway into the season."

"Or, you could be a tremendous help to a team and this disease not affect you until later in life, after you've helped your school win several national titles."

"Maybe you're right, but it still goes back to whether or not a school would take me if they knew."

"Okay, for the sake of argument, let's say that the value of what you can do for a program is worth the risk to a school, any school, where would you like to go?"

Chris turned and looked out the window once again. Patrick realized that he had struck a nerve. For years, Chris had surpressed any feelings about the future, living only in the present, to avoid the pain of unfulfillable dreams. Patrick opted to drop the subject and picked up a magazine, leaving Chris to his thoughts.

"UCLA," replied Chris still looking out the window. "My mom and dad were both UCLA graduates. I remember my folks taking me to gymnastics meets there. My folks were in school back when Mitch Gaylord, Peter Vidmar, and Tim Daggett were Bruins. In fact, I remember watching videos over and over again of the 1984 Olympics when they won the gold medal. I met Peter Vidmar when I was a kid and he even let me wear his gold medal. I think that's when I decided that I wanted to be a gymnast."

"That's incredible, Chris," said Patrick, astonished. "How come you never told us about that before?"

"No one ever asked. I'm not the kind of guy to go name-dropping. I hate that crap."

"Kind of ironic that we're gonna be competing in the same place where those guys won gold."

"Yeah," sighed Chris.

"Welcome home, Chris."

The remainder of the trip was quiet as each thought about the job they had to do. Patrick put on his headphones and listened to motivational tapes. Chris continued to look out the window, searching out familiar landmarks that told him he was home.

"Chris, what are you doing?" cried Patrick as Chris climbed over his lap to open the overhead bin that held his duffle bag, "You heard the flight attendant. You're supposed to stay seated with your seat belt fastened until the captain has brought the plane to a complete stop and has turned off the 'Fasten Seat Belt' sign. Do you want to get us in trouble?"

"They can sue me. I've spent enough time on this bird. I don't want to get caught behind some lard butt who doesn't have a hurry-up bone in his body, keeping me from getting off this plane."

It was too late. By the time Chris could rescue his bag from the overhead storage, a line had already formed in front of him that would prevent him from deplaning early.

"Oh well," said Patrick, "better luck next time."

Chris leered at Patrick. "I doubt I'll be in as big a hurry on the trip back."

"Guys!" called Coach Lowery from across the plane. "If we get separated, meet at baggage claim!"

"What if we don't have bags checked, Coach?" called Chris.

"Baggage claim. That's also where we pick up the van."

The passengers slowly filed off of the plane, each thanked by the attendants and pilots with their cheerful 'buh-byes'. The boys dragged themselves up the jetway to the concourse. As they passed security, Chris saw a familiar face on a tall imposing figure.

"Rick?" Chris called, perplexed. "What are you doing here?"

"Hello to you, too, Chris. Your mother phoned me and told me when you were coming in. Just thought I'd meet you here. Is there a problem?"

"No, none at all. I was just a little surprised to see you is all."

"I knew we would probably be meeting friends of yours when we got here," said Coach Lowery, joining the group, "but, who is this, Chris?"

"I'm sorry. The flight must have scrambled my manners. Coach Lowery, Patrick Goodman, I'd like for you to meet Dr. Rick Gardner, my physician. He's a neurologist on staff at UCLA Medical Center." Coach Lowery and Patrick shook hands with the rather imposing figure. Dr. Gardner was six feet three, with sandy blonde hair and blue eyes, and obviously older than his youthful appearance would imply.

"Jim, Jim Lowery. Nice to meet you, Dr. Gardner."

"Call me Rick, please."

"Nice to meet you, Rick," said Patrick.

"You can call me Dr. Gardner, young man," he sternly commanded. Patrick blushed. "Just kidding, son. Call me Rick."

As each of the Pioneers emerged, they were introduced to Chris's doctor.

"Is this everybody?" asked Dr. Gardner. After a quick head count, Coach Lowery confirmed that he had his full complement of athletes. The group began making its way to baggage claim.

"Chris, what is your schedule for this afternoon?" asked his doctor.

"Well, we have to check in, and we have a workout scheduled for tonight."

"Can you get away for a while?"

"Why?"

"Just to run some quick tests. Your mother said you had some problems this morning."

"No biggie. Just ran into some stuff, but I'm fine. But, let me check with Coach." Chris walked over to his coach to see what the schedule was for the remainder of the day. "Coach says that since I don't have any bags checked, I could leave now and meet them back at the hotel later."

"Great. My car is right outside. Let's go." The two separated from the group and headed for Dr. Gardner's car.

"Nice Jag," exclaimed Chris. "Is it new?"

"About a month or so. So, Chris, your mom said you had an episode this morning?"

"Cut right to the chase, eh?" exclaimed Chris as he slid down into the leather seat of the doctor's Jaguar. "It wasn't an 'episode,' Rick. I ran into the doorjamb of my closet and again into the archway going into the living room."

"Is that all?" prodded the doctor as he sped away from the passenger pick-up area of LA International Airport.

"What do you mean? Did my mom say that there was more?"

"No, but she seemed to think that it was important enough to call me. I just thought that maybe there might have been more, more that maybe your mom didn't see, that maybe you would keep from her."

"Why would I keep anything from her?"

"Obviously, to protect her. Chris, you sound just a little defensive. Are you sure—"

"What do you mean defensive? I don't appreciate everyone reading hidden meanings into my little blunders!"

"Relax, Chris. I'm not trying to accuse you of anything. I just want to make sure that you're okay."

"I'm fine. But if you must know, I did have two other little problems today."

"What?"

"Nothing big. I messed up trying to do a back tuck in the aisle of the plane, and I tripped over some guy's foot that was stuck out in the aisle on my way back from the bathroom."

"Sounds like normal mishaps to me."

"See, that's what I mean. Normal mishaps. Nothing to get worked up over."

"Except that you are not a normal person."

"Thanks, I think."

"Nevertheless, I'll run some quick tests and a CAT scan, and we'll know a lot more."

"Hey, Patrick," called Joey, leaning into the hotel room that Patrick and Chris would share, "is Chris okay?"

"Sure, Joe," replied the Pioneer captain as he flipped through channels on the television from his bed. "It's just been awhile since he's been back to California, and the doc just wants to give him the once-over to make sure everything is normal."

"As normal as normal can be for Chris."

"Exactly. At any rate, we do him and everyone else no good at all worrying. We all have a job to do, and we need to channel our energy towards this weekend."

"And just not think about what Chris might be goin' through?"

"That's right, Joey," said Patrick, turning toward the freshman as if to give a direct order. "You need to forget about Chris for a while and concentrate on what you're doing here."

"Could you?" Joey turned and went back to his room. Patrick knew that neither he nor his teammates could get Chris out of their minds.

"Good! You left me the bed by the window!" said Chris, barging into the room and tossing his duffle bag over Patrick to bounce off of his bed and come to rest on the floor on the other side.

"So, Chris, what did the doc say?"

"Same thing that I've been telling everyone else for the past two days. Nothing more than a series of klutzy moves by a less than graceful gymnastics superpower."

"Good, I'm glad your sense of modesty hasn't been affected."

"Goodman, get ready to … McClure! You're back!" said Coach Lowery. "So what did the doctor say?"

Chris doubled up two fists and thrust the thumbs of each up into the air. "Two big thumbs-up, chief. Everything checks out just fine. I'm ready to tear into it tomorrow."

"Well, we need to head over to the gym. We have a workout scheduled for an hour from now."

"Hey, Coach," asked Chris, "do we have a workout scheduled for tomorrow?"

"Of course. Tomorrow morning at ten. Why?"

"Well, I was hoping that I could skip this workout tonight. I'm pretty beat after the workout this morning, the flight out, and Rick poking every manner of probe into me. I don't think I'd be worth much tonight."

"Okay, Chris. I guess you're right. We've had a full workout already today, and tonight is just a quick touch. We'll swing back by here after workout and pick you up for supper."

"Great. Thanks, Coach."

"No problem. Pat, are you ready to go?"

"I, uh … I'm pretty beat too, Coach. Do you think it would be a problem if I stayed here with Chris? You know, keep him outta trouble and such?"

"I guess it'll be okay. Besides, I don't like to leave anyone here alone. We'll see you guys in about three hours."

"Thanks, Coach. We'll see ya later," said Patrick.

The door closed, and Chris picked up the remote control for the television and began channel surfing. Patrick watched Chris change channels in a trancelike gaze.

"Okay, so are you gonna tell me what really happened?" demanded Patrick.

"What do you mean? I told you what happened. Everything checks out just fine."

"I'm not buying it. If everything was fine, I doubt that you would be missing a workout."

"Quite the contrary, plowboy. If something was wrong, wouldn't I be trying to cover things up by trying to behave as normal? Go to the workout, joke around, try to make everyone believe that everything is fine?"

"Yes, if you thought that by going to the workout you could make people think you were fine."

"Look, Patrick, I don't have to try to convince you that me staying in this room has nothing to do with my condition and everything to do with the fact that, frankly, I'm beat. With everything that has happened today, I don't think I would be very productive out on the training floor tonight. Now, would you please just give it a rest?" Chris's voice had risen to the point where Patrick realized that Chris had had enough.

"You win, you win. I won't mention it again. Just do me a favor."

"*What?*"

Patrick pointed to the television, "Can we watch something other than the Home Shopping Channel?" Chris turned his head to see that there were still thirty-five seconds left on the great bargain on a genuine imitation cubic zirconia-studded Star Wars commemorative plate.

"You know, I have one just like that," said Chris jokingly before turning to the sports channel and settling in to get caught up on the day's action.

An eerie silence fell over the two as neither paid attention to the television.

"It's started, Pat," said Chris, still staring at the TV.

"What's started?" asked Patrick, hoping against hope that it was not what he thought it was.

"The aneurysm. It's growing."

Patrick began to panic. "Chris, you've got to do something!" Patrick jumped to his feet. "We've got to get you to a hospital or something."

"Pat, settle down," said Chris, still seated on his bed. "Anything there is to do has been done."

"Like what?"

"Just sit down, get ahold of yourself, and I'll tell you."

Patrick looked at Chris with panic-stricken eyes. Chris motioned with both hands for him to sit down, and as if controlled by Chris's gestures, Patrick sat down on the edge of his bed.

"According to the CAT scan, the weak blood vessel in my brain has grown about 2 percent over the past year."

"What does that mean?" Patrick spoke still in a panicked tone. "How long do you have?"

"Take it easy, Pat. They don't know. Since I haven't had a scan since I was here last year, it could mean that it's growing two percent a year, which means I could be thirty-five or forty before it goes."

Patrick breathed a sigh of relief.

"Or on the downside—"

"There's a downside?" asked Patrick.

"On the downside, if the growth started this morning, when I became disoriented in my closet, Rick says it might be a matter of days."

"A matter of days!?" Patrick jumped to his feet. "Chris, what are you gonna do?"

"There's nothing to do. Rick gave me some pills to thin my blood a little, to take some stress off of the blood vessel. And, hopefully, I won't have any problems this weekend."

"But, Chris! What if … "

"What if nothing, Pat. Anything that can be done has been done. You feel right now the way I felt ten years ago when I found out. What I have discovered is that no matter how much you worry about it, it doesn't help. You just have to do what I've learned to do—just know that it's there and try to get on with life trying not to think about it. The more you think about it, the more you rob yourself of productive time."

"How in the world do you do that?" said Patrick, pacing the floor.

"You know how. You do it all the time in the gym. You put the fear of crashing aside so you can train difficult, dangerous skills."

"That's easy for you to say."

"Believe me, pal, there's nothing easy about it."

"Man, you must be brave."

"I don't know. I once heard that the definition of courage is the ability to put your fear aside long enough to do your job."

Patrick stood, speechless and dumbfounded.

"Look, Pat, I didn't tell you this so you could have a panic attack. And, I certainly didn't tell you so you could heap pity on me."

"Then, why?"

"Well, first, there's the obvious. You're my best friend, and you deserve to know. Second, if Coach finds out that the aneurysm is growing, he'll do something stupid, like keep me from competing. I know my mom said that she would honor my wish to let me keep competing until I just couldn't. But, even she might buckle if it gets bad."

"Where do I come in?"

"You have to make sure that, no matter what, I get to compete as long as I can."

"Chris, this all sounds so morbid," Patrick resumed his pacing.

"It is! But who else can I count on? And when else could I ask you these things? After it's too late?"

"I guess you're right. But how am I supposed to keep your mom, our coach, or anyone else for that matter, from keeping you from competing?"

"Be creative, plowboy. You have the gift of persuasion; use it. You just make sure no one keeps me from competing. Oh, there's one more thing."

"What?" Patrick stopped and faced the Californian.

"No matter what happens, or when it happens, everyone else goes on."

"What do you mean?"

"If for some reason I can't finish this weekend, I don't want you or anyone else thinking that I would be better served by some damned fool notion that you guys should pull out of this competition."

"Chris, I can't control how I, or anyone else, is going to feel if something happens—"

"*Listen, Patrick*," Chris jumped to his feet. "I have no idea how much time I have left. Right now, I feel fine, but if things start to fall apart, not only do I not want my last thoughts to be guilt because my problem caused you guys to quit, but I don't want to be your excuse, either. The whole reason I came back after Mackee hit me in the head was to get here," Chris turned away and walked to look out the window. "I've never wanted anything more in my life. It scared me to death to think of coming back into the gym, but what scared me more was the thought of not being a part of this team and what it can do."

"I'll do what I can, but I can't promise—"

"*Promise!*" Chris turned back and planted his face just inches from Patrick's.

"Okay! I promise. No matter what happens, we'll finish the meet." The two shook hands.

"Thanks, Patrick," Chris dropped his head and sat on the edge of his bed.

"No, Chris, thank you." Patrick sat next to Chris and put his arm around the shoulder of his best friend.

TWENTY-EIGHT

▼

"So how do you feel today, Chris?" asked Coach Lowery as the team kicked off its shoes to begin morning workout.

"Reborn, Coach. I slept great, and I've never felt better in my life."

"That's great. I sure hope you guys have a good workout this morning."

"We're gonna need it," said Joey.

"What does that mean?" asked Patrick.

"That's right," said Mackee, taping his wrists, "you guys missed the show last night."

"What show?" asked Chris.

"Oh, you should've been here, Slash," said Dallas. "You'd have been right in the middle of it. Danny Diego, Marty Reynolds, and a whole bunch of guys goin' off in a big chest-pounding contest."

"First, Reynolds starts with his triple-twisting double layout off pipe," said Joey.

"Then, not to be outdone," added AJ, his hand still bandaged, "Diego jogs into a sweet double-twisting double-lay on floor!"

"Sounds cool!" said Chris. "I'm sorry I missed it."

"Oh, that's just the beginning," added Ty. "Pretty soon, everybody was into it, and the gym looked like a circus! Stuff I'd never seen before was goin' on, all at the same time! Multiple releases on high bar, wild combinations on p-bars, flips twisting and flipping so fast that you couldn't even count 'em."

"Sounds like we missed it," said Patrick. "Anyone do routines?"

"I think we were the only ones doing sets," said Joey. "Everyone else was busy trying to one-up the other guys."

"Sounds like we had the better workout," surmised Chris.

"We looked like wusses, if you ask me," added Dallas.

"And what feat of greatness would you have added if you could've jumped into the fray, Dallas?" asked Chris.

"I dunno, but anything would've been better than just watchin' everybody else have fun."

"Is that why we're here, Dallas, to have fun?" asked Patrick. "I thought we were here to win a national championship." Dallas was speechless.

"Well, gentlemen," said Chris, rising to his feet, "what do ya say we show these lightweights what championship gymnastics looks like?" The Pioneers marched out into the gym like storm troopers ready to take prisoners, Chris leading them.

If Chris's ability to do gymnastics was diminished by his disease, he covered it well. Starting on floor, Chris's tumbling was far and above what anyone had ever seen. Patrick, concerned that Chris would not be able to cover the fact that he was affected by the disease, was put at ease to see Chris's power and command of skill. Once he was assured that no one would suspect that Chris might be affected, Patrick took the cue from Chris and began opening up his gymnastics.

Even their teammates were amazed with the explosion coming from the senior captains. While others looked on with astonishment as Chris and Patrick started putting on a show, Chris was determined to show everyone that the exhibition that they saw the previous night was minor league.

"What was the big trick thrown on floor last night, Joe?" Chris asked Joey while in the corner waiting for their turn.

"Ummm ... Diego's double-twisting double layout, I think."

"Cool. Watch this." Chris took off across the diagonal and did a round off, back handspring and lauched his own version of a double-twisting double layout, only Chris finished by punching off of the floor and turning a front somersault to a stuck landing. His effort was met with a mixture of deafening cheers and dumbfounded silence.

"I wonder how that would've fared last night?" Chris asked Dallas as he walked off of the carpet.

"Pretty darn up there, Slash. I tell you what, man, I've never been a member of the McClure fan club, but if you hit like that for the next couple days, I'll write the friggin' charter for ya."

"Why, thank ya, Dally, I'll do my darnedest, just for you, dude." The two pounded doubled fists in agreement. Chris' energy became addictive. Each of the Pioneers elevated his level of gymnastics to match his. He was determined not to let any of his teammates think about anything aside from performing their best gymnastics.

From event to event they moved, leaving frozen onlookers in their wake. Before long, they had reached their last event, High Bar. As they began their warm-up swings, Joey noticed a new group of gymnasts entering the gym.

"Look, it's Lake Erie," he said.

"And there's Marty Reynolds right in front," said Ty.

"And he's coming right over here," added Mackee.

"This could be interesting," said Dallas.

Chris finished his warm-up swings by over-rotating an effortless triple back. As he got up, he found himself face-to-face with Marty Reynolds.

"Marty! I can't believe they let you out for this."

"Missed you last night, McClure," said the Mighigan native in his most intimidating voice.

"Whoa, Marty, you need to ease up on the vitamins. They make you moody."

"Heard you cracked up earlier, man. You sure you're okay to compete?"

"Marty, if it's okay for a Neanderthal like you to walk the streets, believe me, it's okay for me to nail your skanky butt."

"We'll see."

"Nice retort, Marty. You learn that on TV?"

"We'll see who's learning what, McClure. Did you happen to see who qualified first?"

"Last I heard, shorty, they don't give the title to the team that scored the highest to get here. Seems I read somewhere that you have to be the last team standing on Sunday night."

"Right. And what was that I saw in the draw? Pioneer qualified at what, twenty-fifth? Oh well, good luck. Really, I mean it." Marty could not have sounded more sarcastic.

"Luck? We aren't hoping for luck, Marty. See, we're in *my* neighborhood now. And, me and my boys here plan to carry that hardware back to the Volunteer State."

"Over my dead body."

"Certainly over someone's dead body. What say we just have a kick-butt weekend and see who's left Sunday night?" Marty's attempt to intimidate Chris had fallen short. All that was left was for Marty to accept Chris's handshake of good luck. Marty then walked away in a huff.

"Man, you should've kicked his ass, Slash," said Dallas.

"An opponent is much easier to deal with once disarmed, my friend," replied Chris.

"He sure seemed a whole lot different from when we saw him earlier this season, Chris," said Joey.

"Yeah, he does this act every year, Joe. During season, he's Mr. Friendly and buddy-buddy as long as nothing is on the line. Then, once the meets start to matter, he turns into Robo-Jerk and gets an edge on the weaker guys by intimidating them. I fell for it once a couple years ago. By the time I figured out what I had done to piss him off, he had psyched me right out of the competition."

"Well, you sure told him," said Ty.

"Don't be so sure, Ty," said Coach Lowery, joining the group. "There's still a couple days of competition to come, and Marty's no slouch. You guys done?" Everyone nodded. "Then, I suggest we get out of here. We have a long day and hopefully a long weekend ahead." The Pioneers gathered their things and headed for the locker room.

SLAM!

The closing of the hotel room door woke Patrick from his nap.

"Hey, pal. How did it go?" asked Patrick.

"It doesn't make sense. It just doesn't make sense!" said an angeredChris as he sat on his bed.

"What doesn't make sense?"

"Rick says the aneurysm has grown another 3 percent since last night!"

"How?"

"I don't know how. It just did. I feel great. I've never felt better in years, and he says I've got less than a week at this rate!"

"Holy crap, Chris! Could he be wrong?"

"That's what I'm thinking. There must've been something screwy with his measurments, or something."

"What are you gonna do?"

"I'm gonna keep doin' what I'm doin'. I'm gonna train my butt off. If I'm gonna blow this weekend, I'm gonna go big. I'm gonna do the biggest, baddest gymnastics anyone has ever seen."

"No, I mean about your head?"

"Nothing I can do. Rick is gonna give me another scan tonight. Maybe he's wrong."

"I hope so."

"Me, too."

"When are you gonna tell Coach?"

"I'm not!" said Chris defiantly.

"Don't you think he needs to know?"

"Believe me, he'll know soon enough."

A knock at the door broke the awkward silence.

Chris opened the door to reveal his mother and Haley.

"Mom! Haley! When did you guys get in?"

"About an hour ago. How are you?"

"I'm fine, Mom. Have you had a chance to talk to Rick?" Chris asked with his fingers crossed.

"No, I haven't," she replied.

"I just got here myself, Chris. Are you ready to go?" replied Dr. Gardner, approaching from down the hall and catching everyone off guard.

"Go?" asked Haley. "Go where?"

Before anyone else could provide an answer, Chris jumped in, "Rick hasn't seen me in so long, he's running all the tests he can to make up for lost time. Oh, hi, baby."

"Hi, yourself. Are you okay, Chris?" inquired Haley.

"Of course I'm okay. Why wouldn't I be okay?" Chris was giving his best effort to deflect a direct answer about his condition.

"Chris," said Rick, "you haven't told them—"

"Look, can we continue this conversation on the way? I really don't feel like discussing this—"

"Chris, are you keeping something from us?" asked Coach Lowery as he and the rest of the team filed into the hall from their rooms.

"Look," said Chris, trying to keep his thoughts straight as to who knew and who didn't, "I have to go with Rick. He's got a couple of tests for me, and when I get back from there, I'll tell everyone what's up."

"Just a minute, young man," said Chris's mother. "I did not drop a day's work and fly thousands of miles only to sit on my hands. I'm going with you."

"Me, too," said Haley.

"Us, too!" said Joey.

"I don't think that having everyone there is a good idea. Right, Rick?" said Chris, looking to his physician for some support.

"You're right, Chris," said Rick. "It won't help to have everyone there."

"Gentlemen, you have a meet to get ready for," said Coach Lowery. "We'll go get some food and meet you back here, Chris."

"Thanks, Coach. I'll fill everyone in when we get back."

The gymnasts and their coach collected themselves and headed toward the exit where the van was parked, while Chris, with one arm around Haley and the other around his mother, followed Rick in the opposite direction toward the hotel lobby, where Rick's car was parked out front.

"Regardless of what these tests say, Mom, I feel fine."

"I know, son, but what do the tests say? Rick?"

"So far, unfortunately, we have a sick boy on our hands, Hanna." Chris's mother and Haley both started to cry.

"Now stop, you two. I'm still here, and I feel fine. I'm sure at some point, there will be a reason to cry, but not now!" demanded Chris. "I have a feeling that after this test tonight, you'll see that I'm fine."

"Rick," Chris's mother began to ask in a trembling voice, "how long …
"

"I don't know, Hanna. I've only run a couple of tests. I've seen some growth, but I still don't know how fast it's growing. After tonight, I'll know more." Chris and Rick split from Haley and Mrs. McClure to go to their separate vehicles.

"I'll meet you at my office, Hanna," said Rick.

"Gotcha," she replied, and the four separated.

"Here, Chris," said Rick, tossing him the keys to his car, "you wanna drive?"

"Are you sure you can trust me behind the wheel of an automibile?"

"After watching the control you exhibit out on the gym floor, how can you not handle this simple task?"

"Can we take the long way, through the Hills?"

"Sure, whatever you want."

"Cool!" Chris grabbed the keys and jumped behind the wheel.

"Okay, Chris," came the voice over the speaker, "you know the procedure. Just lie still."

"As if I have a choice," he said as the table moved into the large cylinder that housed the MRI.

"How long does this take?" asked Haley.

"Not long, about twenty to thirty minutes. It takes a picture of the inside of Chris's head, like an X-ray, in slices from every angle. That way, we get a three-dimensional model of the inside of Chris's brain, and we can isolate the aneurysm and measure its progress. If we're lucky, it'll show little or no growth since this afternoon."

"How much growth has there been?" asked Mrs. McClure.

"A total of 5 percent growth since last year about this time."

"That's not very much, is it?" asked Haley optimistically.

"Not if the total growth was spread over the year. That would mean that he would be one of those that would lead a normal life for about the next ten or fifteen years. But, I've measured 3 percent of that growth between yesterday and this afternoon. So, you can see, this is still very unpredictable."

"So, as far as how long he has … " asked Mrs. McClure.

"No way of knowing, based on what we have now. If there's significant growth from this morning, then we know the aneurysm is becoming aggressive.

If not, it could be the result of a state of remission, or the effect of the blood thinners, or any number of things, making it even more difficult to predict."

"Isn't there something you can do, I mean with advancements in medicine? I've seen on television new operations … " Haley was slowly losing her grip.

"Haley," said Dr. Gardner, grasping her at her shoulders, "believe me, everything that can be done for Chris is being done. The best thing anyone can do is support him. As long as he is healthy, he should be happy. If there is growth, it'll only be a matter of time. He deserves the dignity of living his life the way he sees fit."

"Rick, I know this is insignifcant, but what about the competition? Can that damage him?" asked Mrs. McClure.

"He and I have already discussed it. The activity itself is not going to aggravate the aneurysm. And, according to him, he seems driven to compete this weekend, so I think it will be okay. Now, once the aneurysm grows to the point where he is incapacitated in some way, his ability to perform will be affected. But, we won't know that until it becomes visible."

A chime was heard in the holding area where the trio was talking. "That's my cue. Chris will be out in a minute." Dr. Gardner disappeared behind the door. Haley and Chris's mother fell into each other's grasp and both began to sob.

"My … my boy … " cried Mrs. McClure.

"All right, already!" said Chris, emerging from behind the door, still in his gown, "You guys are gonna have to stop this nonsense right now, or I'll ship both of you back to Tennessee. I don't know what Rick has told you guys, but until I start acting like I'm dying, I'm gonna go on like I'm gonna live, and I expect those around me to do the same. You got it?" Both nodded their head but without the same conviction.

"Good news, Chris," said Dr. Gardner, coming through the door with a chart in his hand. "No noticable growth since this afternoon."

"Wahoo!" shouted Chris as Haley and his mother both stood to embrace him.

"Now, don't get overly excited, folks. This is just one test. It could be a state of remission, but it could just be a pause in the growth. There's no way of knowing without a series of tests. I'll need you to be admited in to the hospital, and we'll need to monitor you for a week or so to be sure."

"Will it make a difference?" asked Chris.

"Will we be able to stop the growth? Probably not, but if after the tests we determine that you are in remission, you'll be able to go home and resume your normal life until something else happens."

"You mean I could actually plan on going to college?" asked Chris.

"Or plan a family?" asked Haley.

"Well, let's not get too far ahead of ourselves. We still have a lot of work to do, but yes, if you are in remission, I don't see why you couldn't make some plans."

"What about this weekend, Rick?" asked Chris.

"I would like to admit you as soon as possible, Chris, but if your heart is set on competing, I see no reason why it couldn't wait until Monday morning."

"Yes!" Chris punctuated his happiness with a fist thrust skyward.

"But right now, I suggest you get some rest. You have a big day tomorrow. I'll see you in the morning."

"Are you coming to the meet, Rick?"

"Of course! You know, I was a gymnast, too."

"Really?" said a puzzled Haley. "But you're so tall."

"Heck, yeah! I competed for Ohio State when they won NCAAs. I wasn't a major factor, but I was on the team. My growth spurt is what forced me out. So I sympathize, Chris. I wish I had one more try. I'll be there. Don't you worry."

"Thanks for everything, Rick," said Chris.

"Anytime, Chris. Good luck."

The three left Dr. Gardner's office arm in arm, leaving the doctor to study the test results of the past two days.

Upon returning to the hotel, Chris, Haley, and Mrs. McClure found the entire team in Chris and Patrick's room. The somber tone of the room was in contrast to the giddy nature of the three.

"Geez," said Chris, "what a bunch of sad sacks."

"I trust then that the tests went well?" asked Coach Lowery.

"They went great!"

"Well, while you were gone, I forced Patrick to tell us everything," said Coach Lowery.

"That's okay. You were all going to find out sooner or later." Chris could not get the smile off of his face.

"So tell us. How did it go?" asked Joey.

"If Patrick told you everything, he probably told you about the growth that my dotor had found with my aneurysm. Well, the test done tonight showed no growth. Now, that doesn't mean that I'm out of the woods, but it might mean that I could be going into remission."

"Which means?" asked Patrick.

"If I am in remission, this may not crop back up for years."

The room erupted with joy. Pillows were flung across the room as the weight of the world had come off everyone's shoulders. After a half hour of reveling, Coach Lowery brought the party to an end.

"Boys! Settle down!" shouted Coach. The team slowly ceased the horseplay. "Have a seat. Unless you guys have forgotten, we do have this matter of a competition to get through." The team settled down and had a seat where ever they could find one.

"Tomorrow begins the end of what we have worked toward for the entire season … "

"Our entire career … " added Patrick.

"Our entire lives!" added Chris.

"Amen!" sounded the chorus.

"All that I ask of you is that when the day is done, we each can look back on what we did this weekend and have no regrets. I don't want anyone to look back and say, 'I could've done better' or 'I shouldn't have held back.' I want each of you to know that when you step off of the competition floor, you will know that you did your very best, without reservation, without excuses, and with honor and dignity for what you tried to accomplish."

"Coach?"

"Yes, Chris."

"Could I talk to the team?"

"Of course." Chris got up from his seat on the floor and took his place next to Coach Lowery. Chris gathered his thoughts.

"I have only been a part of this team for less than a year. Heck, Joey has more seniority than I do. I have never been a part of a team. In this sport, I never saw a reason for a team, other than for earning a team trophy. But, I have learned a lot about what a team really is by being with you guys. Team translates into family. Just like every family, we have ups and downs, but we have them together. Just like brothers, we have fought each other and fought alongside each other. Until this year, I've only known my mom as my family. Now, I find I have brothers, brothers I would lay down my life for. I came back to you guys not because of the need to do this sport, but my need to be with my brothers. Now, we stand at a threshold. We have a chance to accomplish what, singularly, none of us could do. Now, you need to feel what I have felt all of my life, the sense of urgency.

"What would you do if this were your last chance to do gymnastics? Would you do things differently? Dallas, if you knew that tomorrow was your very last chance to do gymnastics, how different would it be? Would you try harder? Mackee, if you were told that tomorrow would be your last chance to do a Ring routine, would you hold back, or would you hold each strength part just a little bit longer to relish the moment? Patrick, if you knew that tomorrow was your last chance to throw a High Bar set, could you get crazy? Could you, for one moment, put your fears and inhibitions aside and do your very best?

"What if you knew last week that this weekend would be the last chance you would have to ever live in that light? Would you have prepared differently? Would you have trained a little harder? Conditioned a little longer?

"It will be easy for me tomorrow. How do I know? Because I have lived most of my life knowing that the next day could be my last. Just like Coach said, I've lived my life knowing that if I don't do it now, I would regret it tomorrow, because that chance will never come again.

"And if you believe, truly believe, that tomorrow is your last chance for greatness, then, and only then, will you rise above your fears, step outside your cushy comfort zone, and create your very best. That's exactly what I intend to do, for as long as I can do it. I hope you're with me."

A silence felt across the room. Tears emerged from every eye. Chris's mother walked over to hug her only son. Soon she was joined, first by Haley, then by all of the Pioneers.

"Okay, men," said Coach Lowery, wiping a tear from his eye, "it's late, and we have a big day tomorrow. You guys need to rest." The group hug dispersed, and everyone departed for their rooms, but not before giving Chris a handshake and a pat on the back. Joey, whose eyes flowed freely with tears, gave Chris a big bear hug. "I won't let you down, Chris!" he said.

"I know you won't, Joey."

"I'm proud of you, son," said Coach Lowery, after his hug.

"Thanks, Coach. Let's get 'em."

"I love you, son," said Chris's mother as she wiped a tear from her eye. "You make me very proud."

"I love you, too, Mom. I got my strength from you."

"I'll see you in the morning."

"You got it, Mom."

Haley was the last to leave the room, but not before giving Chris a big kiss and whispering in his ear.

"I love you, too, babe. Sleep well. I'll see you in the morning." Chris watched Haley disappear down the hall before closing the door.

"Man, you should be a preacher!" said Patrick as he took off the remainder of his clothes and crawled under his covers. "You have a gift. You could make millions as a motivational speaker."

"I should live so long," Chris said as he turned out the light. "Good night, Pat."

"Chris?"

"Yeah, Pat."

"I'm honored to be your friend."

"Same here, pal." The two had no trouble falling asleep.

TWENTY-NINE

▼

"How are people expected to function this early?" lamented Joey as the van pulled up to the entry to Pauly Pavilion on the UCLA campus, the sun having yet to rise above the Rockies to the east.

"Now see?" said Mackee, stumbling out of the van. "If we had done a little better at state, we could've slept in a little."

"Great. Fat lot of good that does us now."

"Exactly," Dallas chimed in. "So, let's drop it. This is where we are, and we have to make the best of it."

"That's right," added Coach Lowery as the last man exited the van, "we have a job to do, and crying over spilled milk will get you nowhere. Okay, here's how it goes. There are three rounds today. Because of our less than stellar performance at state, we find ourselves in the first session, which is not enviable, but not bad, either. We are going up against the bottom eleven teams in this session. We should fare well, but we still have to be able to crack the top twelve to get into finals and have a shot at the title. Without today, there is no tomorrow!"

"Amen," Patrick whispered to Chris.

The Pioneers marched into the arena with their game faces on.

While the gymnasts were stretching, Coach Lowery went to the coaches meeting to get the competition start list.

"Wow," said Joey, looking around the gym, "these guys don't look like the bottom of the barrel!"

"What did you expect, Joey?" said Patrick. "These guys deserve being here as much as anyone else. This is the best of the best this weekend. We can't afford to mess up at all."

"Okay, fellas, we have a pretty good draw," said Coach upon his return. "We start on Parallel Bars and rotate to High Bar, Floor, Pommel Horse, Rings, and finish up on Vault. We're doing a warm-up–compete format, so we'll warm up our first event in another gym, then come back in here to compete. Then, we'll march back out to the warm-up gym to warm up our next event, come back in here to compete, and so on."

"Cool. When do we start?" asked Patrick.

"Well, we're in the B flight, which means we sit for the first rotation."

"That's another half hour I could've spent in bed," said Joey.

"Just don't compete like you're still there," said Mackee.

"Gentlemen in squad B, you may begin your warm-up period," came the voice over the loudspeaker.

While the other Pioneers began with basic support swings to warm up, when Chris's turn came up, he began with full-out high-flying combinations, tossing his body above the rails with effortless ease.

"I guess you feel good today, eh, Chris?" said Coach Lowery.

"Never felt ... better in ... my life ... Coach!" Chris replied between landings on top of the bars in perfect, bouncing handstands. Chris concluded his first warm-up turn with an effortless double back to a stuck landing.

"Be sure to save some of that for the competition, hotshot!" said Patrick, as he mounted the bars for his warm-up turn.

"Oh, I am, plowboy. Believe me, I am."

Although only half of the teams competing that session were in the gym, they all found it hard to concentrate. Instead, they were all watching the Pioneers, who had turned the warm-up into a fullscale workout. By the time Joey mounted the bars, all eyes were on that event, and Joey looked visibly tight.

"Come on, Joey, loosen up!" shouted Mackee.

"That's easy for you to say, Mack," Joey exclaimed, obviously labored in his swing. "It's not easy to relax with all these eyes on me."

"Forget about the eyes, Joey!" shouted Chris. "Just go one skill at a time." Joey tried in vain to swing his stutz into a handstand, a skill he had done easily all season.

"Hop down, Joey!" shouted Coach Lowery. "You'll get it next time." Joey tried a layout somersault dismount with a full twist but came up short on the twist and crashed to the floor.

"You okay, Joey?" asked Chris as he helped the freshman to his feet.

"Yeah, I guess. Just my pride got hurt."

"Hey, man, don't feel like you have to win warm-ups. Just get warmed up and make it happen out there."

"I hope I can, Chris."

"Just relax, and listen to the voice in your head, Joe."

"But it seems like there's a dozen voices in there. Which one do I listen to?"

"The one that's talking gymnastics."

"Great. That helps a bunch," Joey said sarcastically.

The Pioneers wrapped up their warm-up with solid routines, except for Joey, who was still having trouble finding his rhythm. He jumped up on the bars to try to get one more warm-up turn in when the chime sounded, ending warm-up.

"That's it, Joey," said Coach Lowery. "It's time to go."

"Wait!" he exclaimed. "I'm not ready!"

"You'll have to be, son. It's time to go."

Joey dropped off of the bars, gathered his things, and caught up to the team before they marched out to the competition gym.

"You nervous, kid?" asked Ty from in front of Joey.

"A wreck," answered Joey.

"Get over it, 'cause the show is about to begin!"

The teams marched out according to event in Olympic order. The Pioneers were fifth in line. They cleared the tunnel and were astonished to see that, while they were in the warm-up gym, the seats that only had a few hundred occupants were now near capacity.

"I thought you said no one comes to the early rounds," Joey whispered to Mackee, "especially the morning session!"

"I guess they're all eager for the show."

"I suggest we give 'em one," said Dallas.

But what kind of show will it be? worried Joey.

The crowd welcomed the athletes with loud cheers each time a team was introduced...

"And, beginning on Parallel Bars, from Knoxville, Tennessee, Pioneer Gymnastics!" came the voice on the loudspeaker, followed by a loud roar from the crowd.

Ty started the competition with a solid, hit routine for an 8.85. Joey was next and still visibly nervous. Chris did his best to boost his confidence.

"Come on, Joey," said Chris, "you've worked all season to get to this moment. You just think about what you have to do. You have a great routine. Just let it flow, and you'll be fine."

"I'll be fine?"

"You'll be fine. I'll be right here when you finish."

"Okay, Chris," Joey blew out a breath and focused his attention on chalking his hands. Joey stood at the end of the rails and looked at the statuesque apparatus, chrome gleaming in the bluish metal halide light. He took another breath and turned to address the judges that were patiently waiting for him. The head judge raised a green flag, signaling the okay for him to begin. Joey signified his readiness by raising his right arm.

Joey mounted with a glide kip on the end of the bars to a solid press to a handstand. His next skill dropped from the handstand to a giant swing through the bottom, release both bars when his body returned to the height of the bars and recatch the rails in a support; only something was wrong. Joey could not feel the bar with his left hand. The next thing he knew, he was hanging on the bar by his left armpit. Joey hopped up to his support and needed an extra swing to get back into the rhythm of his routine. Although the remainder of the routine continued without much mishap, Joey found himself struggling to push his body back into the handstand on his stutz, and like the dismount he tried in the warm-up gym, Joey once again found himself having to get up off of his seat from the failed attempt.

Joey's routine did not trigger the cheers that Ty's did, nor did the flashing of his score 7.35. Joey sulked his way back toward the designated seating area for his event.

"Don't worry about it, Joe," said Chris, the first one to greet him. "You still have five more sets to go, and the rest of us will pick up your slack here." His words were encouraging, but nothing was going to keep Joey from feeling like he had let himself, his team, and most of all, Chris, down.

"Go ahead, Dallas," Joey said, waiting for the customary cheap shot that Dallas was prone to give anyone who blew a set, especially him, "tell me what a loser I am."

"You'll get 'em next time, killer," said Dallas, unusually sincere. Joey sat down and tried to focus on the next event.

Mackee followed Joey with a solid 8.95 routine. Patrick followed Mackee with a reliable performance, scoring a 9.55. Dallas was next, throwing a routine that showed why he was the leader of the Parallel Bar routines of the Pioneers, scoring a 9.75.

"Way to go, Dally!" shouted Joey over the deafening roar of the crowd.

"Top that, Slash!" boasted Dallas as he accepted high fives and chest thumps from his teammates.

Chris turned to address his teammates. "Fellas, this is my meet, my house, and my crowd. If I never compete another day in my life, I want you to remember the skills you are about to see. AJ, make sure you get this on video." Chris took high fives from his teammates and turned to attack the chalk dish as AJ got the camcorder ready.

"I don't suppose you're gonna save your best for Sunday, are you, Chris?" asked Coach Lowery.

"I think we both know the answer to that question, Coach."

"Fair enough. Anywhere in particular you want me to be?"

"As a matter of fact, yes." Chris motioned for Patrick to join them at the chalk dish. The remainder of the team looked on in bewilderment as Chris was making gestures with his arms and Coach Lowery and Patrick were shaking their heads and chuckling.

While Chris walked over to address the judges, Patrick and Coach Lowery positioned themselves, one on each upright at either end of the rails on the side where Chris stood facing them. Chris saluted the head judge and mounted the bars with a straddle position glide kip to a straddle L on one rail and continued to press to a handstand on one bar. Chris dropped down the side as if doing a giant swing on high bar. It became evident why Patrick and Coach Lowery were holding the uprights. Chris continued to swing through the bottom of the rails and just when his forearms were about to touch the far rail, he released the bar he had to grasp the opposite rail and continue his ascent to a handstand on the far rail. The crowd erupted at the sight of this unorthodox, new skill. Chris then did a series of skills that finished in perfect handstands. Then, for spice, Chris launched a back toss with a full twist to a locked-out handstand. Then, without breaking rhythm, Chris drove his swing into a full-twisting double back dismount to a stuck landing. The crowd erupted with chants of, "Ten! Ten!" When the score 9.9 was flashed, it was met with boos that were almost as deafening as the cheers.

"You just got robbed, McClure!" shouted Dallas over the maddened crowd.

"It's early," replied Chris, barely audible over the crowd noise. "I guess they felt that they had to leave some room for Reynolds!" The team laughed as they rotated to the warm-up gym for their next event, High Bar.

Upon returning to the warm-up gym, Coach Lowery needed to bring the team back to earth. "Okay, fellas, that was fun, but we still have five more routines to do today. That was a great start, but we still have to hit sets if we're gonna be here tomorrow."

High bar warm-up was easier than the first event, since the butterflies were gone. Joey's warm-up was somewhat better, although he still struggled. Once again, the Pioneer warm-up became an exhibition as full routines, with high releases and tight form, were the norm. Even Mackee's routines looked like they belonged at a national championship. When the chime sounded the end of the warm-up period, Joey was still trying to correct some directional problems with his release combination.

"Come on, Joseph." said Patrick, "it's time to cut loose." Joey hopped off of the bar with a little more bounce in his step than he had in the previous rotation. Again, the Pioneers marched into the arena to cheers, but this time, the crowd erupted with chants of, "Chris! Chris!"

"I guess you're a star now, Chris," said Patrick.

"Careful, or my head won't fit through the tunnel for the next event."

"Okay, Mackee," said Coach Lowery, "get us started here."

Mackee chalked his grips and went through a mental routine. Once ready, he took his position under the bar and saluted the head judge. Coach Lowery assisted him to a hang on the bar to start his routine. Although his lines were more favorable for Rings than for High Bar, Mackee put together a sucessful routine with a solid landing for a score of 8.75.

"Way to go, Mack!" came the cheers from the Pioneer bench. Mackee returned to the chairs and let out a huge sigh of relief just to have gotten through his routine without a fall.

Next was Ty. Although his body line was better than Mackee's, his difficulty was still not on par with the rest of the team. However, a hit routine and a stuck double back dismount earned him an 8.95. Ty's successful routine garnered cheers from the crowd and congratulations from his teammates.

"Okay, Joey," called Coach Lowery, "it's up to you." Joey jogged to the chalk dish eager to get the monkey off of his back from the first rotation. He quickly chalked his grips and presented himself to the judges. Coach Lowery boosted the youngster to the bar to begin his exercise. Push out and squeeze your legs, he told himself. The part of his routine that gave him the most trouble came early. Once he was through the tricky beginning, the remainder of the routine would be fine. Joey put his Tkatchev up extra high to make sure he could catch the bar, but instead, it resulted in his coming into the bar too close to add the second release. Joey turned his head just in time to keep from hitting his chin on the bar. The catch stopped his momentum, causing him to take an extra swing to get back on top of the bar. Joey over-rotated his dismount and had to take three steps to keep from falling. He saluted the judges and headed back for his team, disappointed once again.

"Joey, what are you mad about?" asked Mackee. "At least you didn't fall!"

"I might as well have. That routine stunk," Joey ripped the Velcro straps off of his grips as the score came up. 8.5.

"Man, I wish I could blow a set and score 8.5. I have to hit *and* smile at the judges to score higher than 8.5. Cheer up. It could've been much worse!" Mackee concluded.

"Good job, Joey," Chris added. "Someone else might've tried to connect those two releases. That would've been a huge mistake. You stayed on the bar and fought that landing. Don't worry. The hardest thing to do in this situation is relax. You're gonna be fine." Joey still found it difficult to see what the others saw. Everyone else was doing fine, but he was still making mistakes.

"Don't worry, kid," said Dallas, now on his way to the chalk dish. "You'll get into the swing of things when we really need you. Watch this. This should be comedy!" referring to his own routine. Dallas gave Joey a wink and swaggered toward the bar.

Dallas's routine was very similar to Joey's. His release combination came early and without error. Determined to make up for not getting to compete at state, Dallas showed the crowd who the number three gymnast was. Gone was the animosity with Chris. Instead, Dallas showed his teammates what he could be, a great gymnast. Dallas finished with a clean double back in layout position to a stuck landing. The cheers from the crowd and his teammates were well-deserved for the 9.25 score.

"See, Joe? Just have fun," said Dallas upon returning to the team.

"Let's go, Patrick!" shouted the team and the crowd. Patrick applied chalk to his grips and quickly scanned the crowd. It took very little time for him to find the honey blonde hair of a girl waving as she hung over the railing, nearly falling over. Yep, that's Nicole, he thought. He returned a wink.

Patrick saluted the judges and mounted the bar. He knew that scores were tight so far in the early round, so he would have to put as much flair in this routine as he had in the gym earlier in the week. Each giant swing ended with a pop that bounced the bar. Each time his hands came off the bar, he accented with his arms flairing to his sides and recatching the bar with a bounce. It felt exactly the same as it had before.

Patrick lifted his left hand off of the bar at the end of his giant, and began a series of swings, turns, and hops, all with dramatic flair, finishing in handstands. He tapped a huge setup giant to prepare for his Geinger. The tap launched his release way above the bar. He rotated through upright vertical, his body still facing away from the bar. His body rotated another ninety degrees, his chest pointing to the ceiling, his legs rotating to keep up. Only then did he pull his arms across his waist to initiate twist toward the bar. Once he regained sight of the bar, Patrick extended his arms to catch the bar, only this time, his body did what no one before him had done. Patrick found himself bouncing in a handstand!

Patrick finished his routine with more flair and dynamics, ending with a double-twisting double layout, finishing his twist soon enough to flair his arms to the side before nailing a perfect landing.

The crowd was breathless until his landing and then erupted once again, cheering even louder when the score of 9.6 was flashed.

Patrick jumped into the arms of his teammates.

"I did it! I did it! I finally broke a 9.5 on high bar! Waa-hooo!" he shouted. "Come on, Chris!" shouted Patrick. "I gotta see you pull something big to top that!"

Chris smiled and blew the excess chalk out of his grips and tilted his head backward, as if to try to think of how he could top Patrick's routine. Chris gestured his head side to side with his eyes closed as he saw combinations of skills in his head. While Chris went through this ritual, the audience had settled down and became quiet as they watched Chris go through his movements. He concluded his cranelike motions by circling his head and dropping his chin to simulate a dismount. Then, Chris opened his eyes and looked at Patrick. A smile and a wink came from the Californian, like punctuation to a statement. One more puff through his grips and he was ready.

"Where do you want me to stand, Chris?" asked Coach Lowery, who was required by the rules to be near the bar to spot in case of a fall.

"Just find a comfortable place to watch from, Coach. And look out."

"Right." Coach Lowery stood behind Chris. Chris saluted the judge and Coach Lowery put him on the bar and quickly moved to the side of the upright.

Chris began his routine with a simple straddled back uprise to a half pirouette. There, the simplicity ended. After cranking a fast giant swing, Chris paid honor to 1984 Olympic gymnast Mitch Gaylord with his two signature releases, tossing a half-twisting double front over the bar, the Gaylord I, right into a double front over the bar, the Gaylord II. Chris's routine swung from one hair-raising skill to another. After swinging a front giant with a half pirouette, Chris tapped one giant into Marty Reynolds trademark dismount, a triple-twisting double layout. One small shuffle of his feet on the landing prevented Chris from scoring a perfect score. Instead, he would have to settle for a 9.95. The crowd went berserk. The second rotation was completed. The Pioneers' confidence was building.

Although everyone was excited, the boys knew that they were only one-third of the way through only the first stage of what had to be done. The teams marched back to the warm-up gym, passing the teams that were coming out into the gym for their third rotation. As the teams came in, the Pioneers snickered as they saw heads drop and shake as they saw the electronic leader board show that after two rotations, the Pioneers had already built a three-and-a-half-point lead.

By the time warm-up began on Floor, there was little need to get loose. The first two events were enough to warm the body and get accustomed to flipping. Now, all the gymnasts had to do was be sure of takeoffs and landings. When the chime sounded to end the warm-up session, even Joey was ready to march out.

The team entered the gym to thunderous applause. Mackee was the first Pioneer up. His routine included only two difficult elements, a double back tucked and a double-twisting layout. Mackee still had thoughts of his back-smacker he did at the end of his routine at state.

"Remember, Mack," said Chris, whispering in his ear before saluting the judge, "two twists at the end, not one and a half."

"Thanks, Chris, like I need this kind of pressure." Chris patted Mackee on the back and wished him good luck. Mackee saluted the head judge and stepped into the corner. He took a deep breath and sprinted across the diagonal for a good round off, back handspring, double back. Having successfully landed his first pass, Mackee allowed himself to breathe a sigh of relief. The remainder of the routine went without a problem. Finally, Mackee found himself standing in the corner facing his dismount pass.

"Come on, Mack," he said to himself under his breath as he turned in the corner to prepare for his last pass. "You've done this pass a gajillion times." Mackee took another breath, and sprinted across the diagonal. Round off, back handspring, block! Mackee drove his body skyward and opened his arms to set for his twist. Then, he pulled his arms in to speed up the twist, and he closed his eyes and guessed. Mackee then opened his arms and his eyes and prepared for what he hoped would be a landing. By the time everything stopped moving, Mackee looked around to discover that he had stuck his landing. He was so happy, he almost forgot to salute the judges at the conclusion of his routine. Mackee screamed almost as loud as the crowd and jumped into the arms of his teammates. The score was flashed, 8.8. Mackee screamed, "I'll take it!"

"Okay, Joey, you're next," said Coach Lowery. "Are you ready?"

"Oh, yeah, Coach. I'm fine." Joey walked to the corner to begin his routine. He saluted the head judge and stepped up onto the spring floor. He stretched his arms over his head and ran across the floor. He turned over the round off, back handspring with good speed and launched his body into the air and spun his piked double back with ease to a solid landing. Finally, maybe something is gonna go right today, he thought. Joey caught a quick breath before beginning the run for his second pass, a front handspring, forward layout with a full twist. Joey realized he had over-rotated the full twist and at the last moment, added a punch-front somersault, which kept him from landing on his face but caused him to take three extra steps, his last step going outside the boundary line. Joey recovered and finished his routine with a fine double-twisting layout with one step on his landing. The extra movements cost him several tenths, and Joey was disappointed that his 8.6 was nowhere near the 9.3 that Chris had evaluated his routine at earlier that week.

"Great set, Joey!" said Chris, trying to cheer up the downtrodden freshman.

"Yeah, I especially liked the lousy press handstand," returned the dejected freshman.

"So what? So you bobbled in your handstand. You covered great on the end of your front-full with that punch front." Chris found it difficult to console Joey.

"Yeah, and made up the difference by waltzing out-of-bounds. What did I lose, four-tenths there?" Joey crossed his arms in disgust.

Coach Lowery leaned in quickly between routines. "Good job, Joey. That punch front cover was quick thinking. The couple of tenths you lost stepping out was much better than the face-plant you would've taken after over-rotating the front full. Nice job." Coach Lowery hurried back to the others.

Chris rose to his feet and turned to face Joey. "So, is this is the way you would compete if this were your last meet? It's not easy, is it? Oh, of course it's easy to give your best when your best is working for you, but it sucks when things don't go quite as planned. You know the difference in losers and winners, Joe? Winners refuse to accept setbacks as an excuse for failure. You look for every little advantage to turn a weakness into a strength. Look for the positive in every negative to create success out of failure. You've got three events left, Joey. You have to choose your own fate. You can make it happen, or you can let it happen. It's up to you," Chris turned to look toward floor. "Crap, I missed Ty's routine." Chris walked over to get a better view of the other routines.

Joey sat and thought.

Ty broke through the handshakes and high fives to sit in the chair that Chris had vacated.

"Whew! I'm glad that's over," Ty said, catching his breath.

"Sorry, man. I missed your set. How'd you do?"

"Eight-eight-five. I missed your score. It came up after I started my routine."

"Eight-six."

"Not bad. Oh, hey, wasn't that the first time you competed the double pike? Most guys would face their first try at something like that, especially after just learning it this week."

The thought had not occurred to Joey that he had competed a new skill. Suddenly, Chris's words came back to mind: " … look for every little advantage to turn a weakness into a strength … ." Joey quickly rose to his feet.

"Good job, Ty, and … uh … thanks."

Ty furrowed his brow and tried to think of what he had done to be thanked for.

Joey fought through the crowd in time to see only the end of Dallas's routine. Dallas darted across the diagonal and finished with a solid front handspring, layout front full, layout full-and-a-half, punch front tucked. Dallas sauntered off the floor with a swagger. The 9.3 posting barely drew a blink from the blonde senior.

Chris and Patrick watched as Dallas coolly moved to the seating area.

"Dallas is the only guy I know that can shrug off a 9.3," said Patrick.

"That's just on the surface. You know he's jazzed on the inside," said Chris. "Hey, you're up, pal. Go get 'em, tiger."

Patrick stepped up into the corner of the floor and saluted the judges. Like Joey, Patrick had increased the difficulty of his routine. Patrick sprinted across the diagonal to a round off, back handspring, double back layout. He monitored the balance of his routine to make sure he would have the energy for his dismount. By the end of the routine, the other end of the spring floor looked so much farther away. Patrick turned in the corner before his last pass and immediately thought of what had happened to Coach Lowery when he lost the NTI's on his dismount pass of his floor routine. The situation was similar, as Patrick's dismount, the full-in, was the same dismount as Coach's.

The Pioneer senior breathed deeply and sprinted across the diagonal. With pressure building in his lungs, he turned over his round off, back handspring and punched off of the floor as fast as he could. Arms rotating overhead, Patrick pushed his chest skyward. At the last moment, he pulled his knees in and rotated an effortless double back tucked to a stuck landing.

Patrick jogged off of the floor to the cheers of the crowd, but his teammates were still staring at the floor exercise carpet when he returned.

"What are you guys lookin' at?" he asked.

"We're all still waiting to see the full twist in that double back," teased Dallas.

"Man, I was tired. I figured an easier dismount was worth more than landing a full-in to my face."

"Yeah, but imagine the entertainment potential," replied Mackee.

After a judges' conference, Patrick's 9.55 was flashed.

"Good bet, Pat," said Dallas.

Chris had grown weary of waiting while the judges deliberated over Patrick's score, so he began bouncing on the edge of the spring floor to loosen himself up. Once the meeting concluded, Chris saluted the head judge with all of the respect due to an official of a national championship. He stepped up onto the spring floor, looked at Patrick with a wry smile. Suddenly, Patrick's mind went racing back to the nightmare he had had the night of the woofus incident.

Chris sprinted across the blue carpet and whipped through his round off, back handspring, and at that moment, Patrick's fears were realized. Chris punched off of the floor and pulled his left arm over his head to turn his body and initiate the full twist. Instead of wildly out of control, as the one earlier in the season had looked, this version looked fluid from the start. Chris spotted the floor through the entire skill. He kicked open, looked over his shoulder, his hands searching for the floor, capping the end of his full and a half twisting, two and a half flipping element that would surely bear his name after these championships. Chris made contact with the carpet, ducked his head and rolled up to his feet as though he had trained it forever. Those who were not completely stunned cheered madly. Patrick and the rest of the Pioneers felt their hearts jump up into their throats. Chris pivoted on his right foot, turning to his right to face the other way.

No one could guess what his next pass would be, so the team just sat back to enjoy. Chris sprinted out of the corner to a round off, whip back, immediate double-layout to a punch front tucked, and punched again into a statue-solid handstand. Chris straddled his legs and began alternating between swinging in flairs and popping into straddled handstand pirouettes. Chris brought the circling action to a dead stop in a rock-solid handstand. He then slowly piked his feet down to the floor to come to a stand.

The crowd was silent but on their feet as every skill took their breath away. Chris bolted out of the corner to finish with a front handspring, whip front, and finished with a double front somersault tucked with a small shuffle on the landing.

The crowd erupted as Chris threw his fists skyward. He closed his eyes, and it all came back to him. It was the same location, but a different year. It was 1984, and the Americans had just won gold. Chris opened his eyes and sought out his mother, in tears but nodding her approval. He pointed to her with both hands, then turned to jog off of the spring floor, waving to the adoring fans and choking back tears.

Chris was met by a mob of Pioneers. Patrick poked his head above the crowd to see the 9.95 score. The crowd noise became deafening until the announcer broadcast the standings:

"The standings at the halfway point: in third place, with a score of 127.5, Midwest Gymnastics. In second place, with a score of 130.45, Rocky

Mountain Elite Gymnastics. And, your leaders after three events, with a score of 140.95, Piooonneeeer Gymnastics!"

Coach Lowery pushed the guys toward their belongings so they could prepare for the next rotation. "Come on, fellas, we're only halfway through! We've got three more events to go! We're doing great, but you have to stay focused."

If Coach Lowery's efforts to settle the team had failed, the reality of the pommel horse would bring them back to earth. The sound of legs hitting leather and the sight of gymnasts spinning off the end of the horse quickly reminded the boys that their work was far from finished. Joey, who had come into the warm-up gym with a different attitude than he had the three previous times, found it particularly difficult, having fallen on three attempts at his difficult circle combination using only the leather.

"Joey," called Coach Lowery, "think maybe you should go back to your old routine?"

"*No!*" yelled Joey defiantly as he picked himself up from another fall. "So far, I've contributed zilch to this team, and I certainly don't plan on watering back. That won't help."

"But I think you'll come closer to hitting—"

"I'll hit the set, Coach. Besides, if I'm gonna crash, I'm gonna crash doin' my best gymnastics."

"You can hit this set, Joe," said Patrick, supported by the rest of the team. "You know you can hit the set. And, don't worry, we got your back."

No sooner than Patrick finished speaking, Mackee went sailing off of the horse.

"You think so?" asked Coach Lowery.

"He'll hit," said Patrick confidently.

Before Coach Lowery could give his approval, the chime sounded.

"I'll hit, Coach," Joey said, still looking into his coach's eyes. Coach Lowery nodded.

The teams were welcomed back by a full crowd that had gotten its money's worth. When the Pioneers entered the hall, a roar became a din. The teammates had their game faces on, especially Joey, who, for the first time, had blocked out everything else.

Before the first routine went up, Coach Lowery brought the team together. "Boys, I don't have to tell you that this is the toughest event, but if we can get through this, well, you know what that means. Now let's kick some pony!"

Mackee was the first up. His history with pommel horse had never been good. He jumped up to start his routine. Although the first part of his routine went by without much problem, some inadvertent brushes with the pommels caused him to lose the rhythym of his swing. But, he fought to stay on and managed to get to the dismount without actually stopping.

"Hey, at least I didn't fall off!" Mackee said as he rejoined his teammates.

"For the life of me, I don't see how, Mack. Good job," said Patrick.

The score came up, 8.15. Mackee rejoiced over his first Pommel Horse score over an eight.

"You ready to go, Ty?" asked Coach Lowery. Ty nodded.

Ty's routine went with only minor problems for a score of 8.4. Joey knew that he needed to hit not only to count in the team score, but also to keep the team score high. Without a hit set, the team would have to count two weak scores.

Joey looked to his coach, who gave him a thumbs-up. Joey saluted the head judge and approached the horse. The first few skills in his routine out of the way, Joey dropped his hands down on the leather to attempt the combination that had given him so much trouble in the warm-up gym. True to his word, Joey pushed and stretched his body while circling over the pommels from end to end. At the end of the combination, he reached for the pommel to move into the middle of the horse and felt his leg brush the horse. Instead of panic, Joey remained patient and exerted a little more energy to get back into the middle of the horse and countinue his routine.

Joey fought the temptation to rush the end of his routine and dismounted with a clean straddle swing up to a handstand pirouette. He dropped lightly to his feet, throwing his fists into the air in triumph.

Joey saluted the head judge and ran to jump on the closest teammate, which turned out to be Dallas. Before he could grab him, Dallas raised his hand, stopping the freshman in his tracks.

"Good job, squirt!" he said. "Just don't jump me. I have a routine to do!"

"Sure, Dallas. Go get 'em."

Joey watched for his score. When the 9.1 score came up, Joey couldn't jump into anyone's arms, as he was covered with Pioneers.

Dallas began his set with several turning circles on one pommel and moved to the other pommel to do the same. He worked through his single-leg skills with ease and moved to his dismount with style, scoring a 9.2. Once again, Dallas took his score in stride but found it hard to act humble once swarmed by teammates.

Patrick jumped into his routine and exhibited a very different style from Dallas. As much as Dallas'style leaned more toward a rhythmic, fluid swing, Patrick attacked the pommels with a vengeance. Patrick's muscles bulged with every hand placement, and at any moment, it appeared that he could rip the pommel off of the horse or tear the hide off of its frame. Patrick shot to a handstand, pirouetted, and planted his feet into the vinyl surface of the landing mat. After saluting the judges, Patrick wanted to howl to match the roar of the audience but instead opted for an air punch. Patrick exchanged high fives with Chris as he made his way to the chalk dish.

"Good job, plowboy. You may be a gymnast yet, you keep scoring like that!" said Chris, acknowledging Patrick's 9.75.

"Tear it up, Christopher!" Patrick demanded.

Chris took a moment to meditate and see his routine in his head once more before the point of no return. Chris lifted his head and saluted. He was ready. He started his routine on the end of the horse and began swinging circles on the leather, facing the other end. He then moved from end to end without using the pommels. Once arriving at the other end, he became a blur, circling faster and faster, twisting as he moved from end to end, back and forth. Chris gave the judges a chance to get caught up by hopping from circles on the end of the horse to a momentary handstand on the pommels, and down into the required scissor work. His final scissor swung back up to a handstand. From the handstand Chris straddled his legs and dropped into flairs that spindled and traveled from end to end. Chris concluded his routine by doing several skills on one pommel, finishing in another handstand and dropped to the landing mat to the thunderous applause of a crowd that increased as his 9.8 was posted. The Pioneers knew they were on a roll but resisted the urge to get carried away as they rotated to the warm-up gym.

"Only two left, Chris!" said Joey.

"Two left," said Chris, smiling reservedly.

The Pioneers had made it to the tunnel when the announcer's voice sounded the update.

"The standings after four events: in third place, with a score of 171.2, Midwest Gymnastics. In second place, with a score of 178.45, Rocky Mountain Elite Gymnastics. And, your leaders after four events, with a score of 187.20, Piooonneeeer Gymnastics!"

"This is our event, Mack," said Chris, as the two put on their ring grips. "Here's where you shine."

"You damn skippy!" Mackee said with a glazed-over stare.

"Let's have a contest, Mack!" said Chris.

"What kind?" Mackee replied, monotone, still looking forward, deep in thought.

"What else, Mack? A strength game." Patrick and Joey looked at each other as they put on their grips. Mackee, now interested, turned his eyes to Chris.

"Go on," he said.

"Ten points for an easy strength part, twenty for a tough one, and thirty for any part that invokes religious expression."

"So far, I like it," Mackee forced a small smile.

"Two points for every second a static strength part is held."

"And the dismount?"

"Triple back, of course."

"Pizza to the top?"

"Winner buys the pitcher."

"You're on, bub," Mackee and Chris pounded fists in agreement.

Chris used his warm-up turns to warm up each of his static strength skills, while Mackee only used one turn. Oddly, he did no strength, only a quick press to a handstand to swing one giant into an open-body double-tuck to a stuck landing.

"I'm ready," said Mackee.

The remainder of the Pioneers used the extra time to put finishing touches on their more difficult skills. There was no need for the chime to tell the team to stop. They were ready.

Once again, the Pioneers raised the decibel level upon entering the gym. The atmosphere was more that of a carnival than of a gymnastics meet. Banners were waved from rafter to rafter, and screams for favorite gymnasts shook the roof.

Mackee stayed cool and reserved, saving his strength for his routine. Ty competed first and managed an 8.5. Joey followed with a solid swinging routine for a matching 8.5.

Needs more strength, Mackee thought.

Dallas did an acceptable routine to score a 9.25. Patrick's routine was worth watching as the team captain moved well between swing and strength to score 9.45.

Mackee had tuned out the crowd noise and looked at Chris, standing between him and the rings.

"I believe it's up to you, sir." Chris swung his arm open to allow Mackee to approach the ring tower.

"No, sir, after you. I insist."

Chris bowed to his teammate, acknowledging his gesture, and walked to the chalk dish at the tower. After applying his chalk, Chris stepped under the rings to await the judge's signal and Coach Lowery's assist.

"I thought Mackee was next." asked Coach Lowery.

"I think Mackee will be the showstopper here, Coach." Coach Lowery quickly alerted the judges as to the order switch. With their approval, Chris saluted the judges and jumped to the rings. His first strength skill was the butterfly cross. Mackee had seen this combination before. His first cross was held for three seconds before he continued to press upward while rotating forward until he arrived in a Maltese cross.

"Look," said Joey, "he's doing the same combination he did the first day he was in the gym!"

After a three-second hold, and a bead of sweat beginning to show at the end of his nose, he pressed and rotated his body until he arrived at an inverted cross. Once having held this position for two seconds, he finished his press into a rock-solid handstand. lowered himself down and rolled through two more strength combinations before pressing to handstand. Chris gasped for a breath, then swung one forward giant, one backward giant, and an almost effortless triple back. Stuck.

Chris, nearly exhausted, walked over to Mackee. "That's … one easy … three hard … three … 'Oh, my Gods' … and … eight seconds held. … That's … 176 points." Chris looked over to the scoreboard for his score,. "And a … 9.85 to beat." Chris, having made his point, staggered to a chair.

Mackee chalked his hands and stood under the tower. "Hi, Coach," he said nonchalantly.

"I don't guess you're doing your normal routine, are you?"

"Sorry, Coach," appologized Mackee, "but it will look familiar."

Mackee saluted the judge and jumped to the rings. To start, Mackee did the same elements that Chris had done, butterfly cross, rotate forward to a Maltese cross, and rotate again to an inverted cross and pressed to the handstand, all with three-second holds. From there, Mackee showed why he was the spotlight dance of the party. He lowered to another inverted cross for three seconds. Then he swung forward into a giant, returning to his inverted cross. To balance the routine, he dropped the other direction and rolled over to a frozen Maltese cross! Assured that the contest was well in his hands, Mackee pressed back to his handstand and dropped into a triple back dismount. Stuck!

The crowd erupted once again as Mackee stepped off of the landing mat, and, as if to show that there was plenty of energy in reserve, dropped to the floor and pumped out a quick twenty push-ups. Upon completion, Mackee jumped to his feet and let out a roar.

"You win, Mack," Chris cheered. "I told you, you were the man!" Mackee pounded his chest at the sight of his 9.9 score.

The Pioneers, knowing that the session was in hand, for the first time acknowledged the applause of the audience with waves as they made their way back to the warm-up gym for their final event. The loudspeaker told the story.

"The standings after five events: in third place ,with a score of 212.6, Bayou Gymnastics. In second place, with a score of 222.95, Rocky Mountain Elite Gymnastics. And, your leaders with one event to go, with a score of 233.85, Piooonneeeer Gymnastics!"

The team marched back to the warm-up gym to get ready for its last event, Vault. Being the quickest event to warm up, it took very little time for the boys to get ready.

"Hey, Joey," called Chris.

"No games, Chris. There's no way I can keep up with you."

"Ah, but can you keep up with *you*?"

"Huh?"

"Do you know when you're ready to take that step?"

"What do you mean?"

"Are you ready to snap off a twist on this Tsukahara?"

"Not on your life!"

"No pressure. I saw your layout. It looks sweet. Twisting it will be easy. But, you're right. You should probably wait 'til you're back home."

"Chris, you're not being fair. I've never done it before, and it's not like I get two chances. Just one shot!"

"Okay! Okay! But, do you think you *could* do it?"

"I dunno. It feels like I could."

"Then do this. When you warm up, see if you can feel where the twist comes during the flip. You know, right as your feet come underneath you. If you don't, there's nothing more to say. But, if you do, well, you gotta make that decision on your own."

As Joey got set for his next turn, Chris reminded him to try to find the twist point in the flip. Joey shooed him away so he could concentrate on his vault. Joey sprinted down the runway and hit the board hard and fast. Pulling his lead arm over his head, Joey stretched his chest to get the most snap when his hands blocked the table. Upon contact, Joey forcefully pushed the table as hard as he could. At the end of the push, he stood up straight as an arrow, pushing his chest skyward. Now! Joey thought as his body snapped up to vertical, accelerating his rotation. Joey spotted and nailed his landing.

Hmmm? Not bad, Joey thought. He jogged back to the end of the vault runway with visions of a full twist in his Tsukahara.

"Did you feel it?" Chris asked as Joey rejoined the team at the end of the line.

"Yeah. I think so, but there's no chance on this planet that I'm gonna try to twist that today. It's too risky."

"No, you're right, Joey," Chris agreed, "but it's there if and when you need it."

"I guess." Joey had a funny feeling that Chris meant he would need it sooner than later.

While Joey pondered Chris's challenge, Coach Lowery called the team together.

"Guys, I don't have to tell you what you've done. We've got almost eleven points over the next highest team. I don't know if these scores will hold up for the rest of the day, but you guys have set an incredible mark to match. All I want you guys to do is go out and stick six vaults. I'm confident that if you can stick six, we can sleep in tomorrow!"

"Stick six!" the team shouted.

"Pioneers!" Joey shouted, and the team all did standing back tucks before lining up for the march out. The crowd had reached a fever pitch when the teams entered the arena. As the Pioneers marched around the floor to get to the vault runway, fans were hanging over the rail to touch their heroes. Each had followers, calling the Pioneers by name as they marched to their final event.

"Okay, guys," said Coach Lowery over the din of the crowd, "six vaults and we watch the rest sweat. Be safe, boys. Good luck." Coach Lowery then jogged back to the other end of the runway to set the springboard for each gymnast. Halfway between the boys and the table, he felt that the time had come when he could release the excitement that he had contained for an entire season. It was subtle, as he clenched his fist and mouthed the word, "Yes!" For regardless of how things would go from that point on, whether they made it to finals or not, everyone who was lucky enough to be there got to see in one moment the culmination of all the joy that he had felt since the first day each and every one of those boys, now men, walked into his gym. Each had made such an impact on his life like nothing else. He could not only see, but also helped create the fruit of their passion, which brought to his heart and to his own passion the realization of his own dreams.

It was too exciting an experience for anyone to sit during the competition. Rather, the Pioneers stood around the end of the runway to cheer their teammates. Being heard over the crowd would be a difficult task as the audience shared with the Pioneers the excitement of capping off the session with some of the best gymnastics ever witnessed.

"Come on, Mackee!" Patrick watched and cheered. "Get us started!"

Mackee took his position at his marker on the floor. He shook off a bit of fatigue left over from his overzealous Rings performance. He shrugged his shoulders and jumped to pump up his legs, like a prizefighter before a world title match. He closed his eyes and visualized each body position in his front handspring, double front vault, including the stuck landing. He opened his eyes to the waving of the start pennant by the head judge. Mackee raised his massive right arm to signify his readiness and stepped onto the runway at his marked point. He glanced quickly at the board and table before him, then closed his eyes and tilted his head backward for a moment. He then regained his focus on his target eighty feet away.

Mackee took his usual approach of two steps and a hop into his run. His legs pounded the one-inch-thick runway, punishing the resiliency of the foam under his feet with each pile-driven step. The springboard was spared no less as Mackee's size ten triple E feet hit the carpeted surface of the fiberglass composite board and immediately compressed the nine heavy-gauge coil springs to their maximum, only to recoil in a tenth of a second, catapulting the Pioneer skyward over the one–by–one-meter suede-covered surface, where Mackee then exploded through the table's tan top, jamming his arms downward to compress the table and recoil again. His legs flew over his head with the release of the compression and launched his body skyward. Mackee pulled his heels into the salto, stretching his abdominal muscles, then reacted to the pull by snapping his chest over and into a deep tuck, speeding up the flip. One, two flips. Mackee kicked out of his flip, and his feet attacked the vinyl-covered landing surface. Mackee's thigh muscles bulged into action to stabilize the landing to ensure that any balance error would be quickly neutralized. Mackee raised his arms triumphantly to the roar of the crowd and his team.

The crowd remained on its feet as the first score for the Pioneers was raised. The already vocal audience raised its volume another twenty decibels upon sight of the 9.6 score.

Mackee came back to the team with high fives and fist punches flying. "All right, gentlemen," said Mackee, "the table is set. You may feast when ready!"

Joey was the only Pioneer not in on the congratulations as he was next to go. He received the green signal from the judge and stepped onto the runway.

He tried to create the same feeling as he had in the warm-up gym. The run, the approach, the block, and all of the timing had to be correct if he was going to twist. In an instant, the punch off of the board, the cartwheeling action into the block off the table, and finally, the snap. In that instant Joey could feel the point where the twist would take place, but not now, he decided. Joey snapped his feet to the floor and nailed the landing, just as he had for months. Joey, happy nonetheless, ran back to his team as the 9.5 score was flashed.

"I thought you might try to twist that one," Chris said. "It was right on the money. You would've made it easily."

Joey looked at Chris with a sly smile. "I thought about it," he said through a grin.

Next was Ty, then Dallas, each with great lift and turnover, each with 9.65 scores.

Patrick took his place at the runway.

"Okay, plowboy," said Chris with a southern drawl, "y'all jest haul 'er down there as fast as yer feet'll carry ya, and if anythin' gits in yer way, well, you jest jump over'n it."

"Like, dude," Patrick replied in his surfer accent, "that is, like, a totally tubular, cosmic, like, radical concept!" Patrick then assumed his straight face. "I think I can handle this."

"Have at it, compadre."

Patrick raced down the runway with a grim focus on the end of the vault table. Like thousands of times before, Patrick instinctively combined power with reaction time as he blocked the board and the table in such a sequence that the result was an effortless layout Tsukahara with full twist to his familular stuck landing. Patrick raised his fist triumphantly as he jogged back to his team. Chris quickly met Patrick first so he would be ready when the judges signaled. "I think you can handle that," said Chris.

"Your turn, pal!"

Chris jumped back to his starting point as the head judge waved the green start flag. Chris stepped onto the runway and returned a salute. Chris bolted down the runway. If Mackee looked like a raging bull as he made his way to the table, Chris looked more like a cheetah attacking its prey. Chris hit the board, and with lightning quickness, sent his body flipping upward onto the table. He cartwheeled up off of the table then snapped his arms into his chest and wrapped two twists before nailing his landing almost twenty feet from his takeoff point. Chris paused to accent his landing as the crowd jumped to its feet and the explosion of ovation shook the rafters of the pavilion. Chris stood in triumph and saluted the crowd as the score flashed behind him. Only after what seemed like the loudest noise he had ever heard instantly became twice as loud did Chris turn to see the cause for the elevation. The score was a perfect ten. Chris dropped to his knees as the rest of the team tackled the Californian. The announcer made official what everyone in packed Pauly Pavilion had already known.

"And the leaders after the first round, with a National Team Invitational record-breaking score of 288.45, from Knoxville, Tennessee, your Piooonneeeers!"

The team, one by one, peeled off of the pile. Meet officials tried to corral the participants and usher them off of the floor to prepare for the next session.

"Okay, fellas," said a jubilant Coach Lowery, "step one is complete. Now we need to get back to the hotel and relax."

"Relax?" said Joey. "I'm so keyed up, there's no way I can relax!"

"Really, Coach," added Patrick, "it's just one o'clock. We've got all day!"

"Well, what do you suggest, Mr. Goodman?" asked Coach.

"I don't know, but it seems like a waste of celebration time to just go back to the hotel and do nothing."

"Whatever we do," Mackee chimed in, "we ought to do something with Chris after that awesome performance."

"Here, here!" added Patrick.

"Now wait a minute, fellas," answered Chris. "I appreciate what you guys are doing, but has everyone lost track of the fact that there's nothing to celebrate yet? We're just through the first round."

"I guess that perfect score on Vault is nothing to celebrate?" asked Joey.

"Yeah," said Mackee, "you may be right about premature celebration as far as the meet is concerned, but you gotta at least let us toast a cold drink over a slice of pizza for that *awesome* set of routines you killed everybody with."

"True, and I do owe you a pizza."

"And I, the pitcher, your excellency."

"Besides," added Chris, "my routines aren't the only ones to raise an eyebrow this morning."

"Really," Patrick jumped in. "What about that Rings set from Mackee?"

"Or Joey's pig set?" added Ty.

"Face it, boys," concluded Coach Lowery, "everyone should celebrate. One person does not set a championship score record by himself. You guys were … well … *awesome!*" The Pioneers stood dumbfounded, as compliments from their coach were as rare as the routines they had displayed.

"So, the question remains," Mackee said, "where do we go to celebrate?"

"I don't know," said Patrick, "but we better figure out where on the move. It looks like they're trying to shoo us out."

As the team made its way toward the exit, a familiar group stood patiently waiting to congratulate them. Dr. Gardner, Haley, Nicole, Mrs. McClure, and other family and friends were in front of a mob of fans waiting for their new favorite gymnasts to get an autograph or just a glimpse of the new teen sensations, their Pioneers. Girls screamed, and boys shoved autograph books in their faces.

"I could get used to this!" Joey said, grabbing an autograph book from a fan.

"One of the perks, my boy, just one of the perks," said Dallas, accepting a kiss on the cheek from an overzealous fifteen-year-old girl.

"Don't get too used to it, boys," said Coach Lowery, trying to push his way through the mob. "I don't think you will get the same reaction if you fall short tomorrow."

Chris leaned over to Joey as he signed his signature in a fan's souvenir book. "All the more reason to enjoy it today, eh, Joe?"

"No kiddin'!" Joey replied as he signed another autograph.

"I'm not so sure that I like the idea of you being an teen idol, Patrick," exclaimed Nicole as Patrick accepted a kiss from another fan, this one a little closer to his age.

"What's a guy to do, Nic?" replied Patrick, defenseless as another female follower threw her arms around the Pioneer captain.

The Pioneer supporters helped escort the team through the sea of arms and autograph books.

"So, where are we goin'?" asked Mackee, bursting through the doors of the pavilion.

"I know a perfect place!" exclaimed Chris.

"Where's Joey?" asked Haley, noticing that the group was one short. The team looked around. Indeed, Joey was not with them. Chris darted back to the exit doors of the pavilion and soon emerged with the youngest Pioneer, by the scruff of his neck, his arms still reaching back toward the crowd of good-looking, well-wishing female fans.

"You know, that was not at all necessary, Chris," pleaded Joey. "I was coming right along."

"Sure you were, Joey. Sure you were."

THIRTY

▼

"THIRTY- TO FORTY-FIVE-MINUTE wait!" Joey called as he emerged from the crowd waiting to get into the resturant.

"Don't worry," answered Chris. "It's well worth the wait. In the meanwhile, check out the view." Chris walked arm in arm with Haley and his mother as they headed back down the pier that led from the shore to the resturant he had chosen.

"Good choice, son," Chris's mother replied.

"I thought you'd enjoy it, Mom," said Chris with a slight grin.

"Haley, this is where Chris's father and I used to bring Chris after watching the college gymnastics meets."

"I think the wait used to be longer," said Chris.

"No, the wait was about the same. It just seemed longer for a little boy with a bundle of energy and a man's appetite. It was so funny to watch Chris out here. While we were waiting for a seat, Chris would entertain the other patrons by tumbling up and down the pier. Why, I remember—"

"I think Haley's heard enough, Mom."

"No, this is great. Go on," urged Haley.

"Well, Chris was eight or nine years old. We had come out on a Saturday afternoon. We had the usual wait, and Chris's father and I were sitting at one of the benches while Chris was bouncing all over the place, as usual. The pier had cleared out enough that Chris had room to run into a round off and started a series of back handsprings. He had done about four or so, with no sign of slowing down—"

"When I plowed into a group of nuns who were walking toward the resturaunt. Man, was I embarrassed."

"Was anyone hurt?" asked Haley.

"Oh, no. They just slowed him down a little."

"I don't think I ever saw you and Dad laugh so hard."

"There was much to laugh about in those days." Mrs. McClure's expresion quickly changed from happy to sullen at the thought of what transpired in the following weeks.

"It wasn't long after that that Dad got sick." Chris stopped short.

"Yes, son. It had only been a couple of days before that a routine physical showed evidence of the aneurysm," An uneasy silence fell upon the trio.

"I miss Dad."

"Me too, son."

"Hey, y'all," cried Joey, approaching the group, "our table is ready. Let's eat."

As the three rose from the bench and began making their way toward the resturaunt, Chris's puzzled face was evident.

"What's the matter, son?"

Chris struggled to put his thoughts into words. "Mom, I know I've lived a little reckless, and if I ever caused you one moment of—"

"Don't you worry one bit, son," reassured Chris's mother. "I look at you with envy. I wish I were brave enough to live my life with the same energy that you have. I have never had one moment of worry or regret with you. You've always made me proud to be your mother. There are many roads you could have taken, especially in the environment you were raised in, and especially after your father was gone. I just wish there were some way that I could have made your life easier."

"You just did. I love you, Mom."

"I love you, too, son." They embraced.

After a hearty lunch, Coach Lowery stood from his chair at the end of the table and tapped his glass with his fork to get everyone's attention.

"I would like to propose a toast." Everyone at the table raised a glass.

"Regardless of what happens from here on out, I would like to take this time to congratulate each and every guy on this team. Although it is a team effort that has gotten us this far, each of you is why we are here today. Without even one of you, this could not have happened. When it is all said and done, I will have been known as the coach of one of the best teams this sport has ever seen, but I know that this result had much less to do with my ability to coach as it did with the desire, passion, and dedication that came from seven of the best athletes, teammates, and men that I am proud and privileged to call my friends. Ladies and gentlemen, I give you, *my* Pioneers!"

"Pioneers!" everyone shouted as they toasted each other. Once everyone had taken a drink, Patrick rose to his feet.

"As the captain of the team, I guess it falls on my shoulders to speak for the team as best I can. First and foremost, to Coach Lowery. He doesn't give himself quite the credit he deserves. It is through his eyes that the Pioneer spirit shines brightest. Had it not been for his dream, his vision, and his guidance, we would have never become the team we are. It is because of your hard work, tireless effort, and never-ending support that we have become the team we have. And second, I know that I speak for the rest of the team when I say that there is one more person to thank. I know that you may have found it hard to feel a part of this team, only having joined us last August, Chris, but you have shown us, each of us, what it truly means to be a Pioneer. Not only have you shown us what gymnastics can be with your awesome talent, but also the courage that you've shown us on a daily basis is beyond what any of us could imagine, and it sets a standard for each of us to reach for. Our team, our lives, will never be the same, and I know that my life has been blessed in ways that I can't even describe just for having known you. Thank you, Christopher T. McClure, for being a part of our team and a part of our lives."

"Here, here!" chimed Mackee.

Each of the Pioneers set their glasses down and rose to their feet, clapping and cheering for the Californian who had made such a difference in their lives. Chris fought hard to hide his feelings as his eyes welled. With Haley on one side and his mother on the other, Chris was enveloped with hugs and kisses.

"Speech, speech!" called the team amid claps, whistles, and cheers.

Chris dried his eyes with a napkin and tried to compose himself, then rose to his feet as the others sat. Chris took a drink of water to clear his throat and organize his thoughts.

"All my life, I had considered myself something of a loner," he began. "I knew I was a little different from other kids. After my dad died, I withdrew into my own little shell. When I found out that I had the same problem, I knew that there was no way I could get close to anyone else because I did not want to cause anyone the pain that I felt when I lost the most important person in my world. Since then, I have been on a quest. I wanted to prove to my dad, wherever he was, that I could make him proud of me, be the best at what I did. I worked harder and harder for the approval that I knew I could never get. Before I came to east Tennessee, that was all I could think about. But now, I look at what has happened to me since, and I realize just how lucky I am. My mother, who has worked way too hard to make sure that I had everything I needed, including unconditional love; Haley, who has made me realize that it is not how long you live your life that's important, but how well you live your life for others that matters; and you guys. When I first came here, I really wasn't all that interested in helping a team accomplish its goal.

All I wanted to do was what I had always done, my own thing. But you guys somehow made it important to me to see the value of a team. It seemed the more I tried to think about myself, I couldn't help but feel that what you guys did was more important. Helping Joey realize his worth to the team, tryin' to get Patrick to overcome his fear of his own talent, and showing Dallas that life is way too short to put fences between yourself and your friends. What we could do together as a team became more important to me than anything I was trying to accomplish on my own. In the process, I learned that the value of one's life is not measured by personal accomplishments, but rather by the quality of your relationship with those around you. 'Cause it doesn't matter how exciting or how many experiences you have in your life; it's the people you share them with that give them value.

"I'm very thankful for the friends and family I have, and most of all, I'm proud to be a Pioneer." Chris raised his glass, joined by everyone at the table. "The people who matter most to me are all here with me. Thank you, one and all, for being here and for making this the best moment of my life. Pioneers!" Chris chanted as he hoisted his drink.

"Pioneers!" returned the group, joining the toast.

Once each had returned his glass to the table, a moment of quiet followed as each looked at Chris and then to each other, for the first time not seeing each as individuals, but rather a family, each a priceless part of something much, much greater than the sum of the parts.

Following lunch, the group strolled along the pier, enjoying the surroundings: the waves of the ocean crashing against the shore, the gulls hovering just off the side waiting for the morsels tossed to them by children, and the panoramic view of the skyline pressed against the mountains.

"Well, I don't know about you guys," said Coach Lowery, "but I think I'm headed back to the gym to see how the other teams look."

"Weak compared to us, Coach," said Joey confidently.

"Just the same, I'm going back over to the meet. Anyone want to join me?"

"Sure, Coach," said Mackee. "Come on, guys. Let's go check out the rest of the meet."

"You guys go on ahead," said Chris. "I think I'll just hang around here for a while."

"I think I'm gonna stay behind, too, Coach," said Patrick. "I've seen enough gymnastics for one day."

"I have to head back to the office for a while," Dr. Gardner said. "Chris, call me if you need me."

"Sure thing, Rick."

The rest of the team accompanied Coach Lowery back to the meet while Chris, his mother, Haley, and Patrick stayed on the pier. The group leaned on the railing of the pier to watch the birds. Chris, with Haley on his left, his mother on the right, and Patrick on the other side of Haley, tossed crumbs to the birds.

"I see what you mean, Chris," said Patrick, looking out across the water.

"What do you mean?"

"I'm looking at everything: the ocean, the mountains, everything. I'm committing them all to memory, every nuance, every subtlety. When I think back on this weekend, I want to recall everything with as vivid a memory as if I'm right here."

"Well, I hope the rest of the weekend offers you as pleasant a memory."

"What is that supposed to mean?"

"I can feel it, Pat. It's not far off."

"Naw, you're just paranoid. You and Dr. Gardner have this thing under control."

"I wish it was just paranoia, but I'm losing some control, and I haven't had feeling in my feet or fingertips since the competition ended."

"Have you talked to Rick?"

"Yeah, there's not much else he can do. All that's left is to wait."

"Wow," Patrick exclaimed, dumbfounded.

"Hey, cheer up, pal. I'm not dead yet. There's still work to be done. Besides, that's not why I let you in on how things are goin'. I've got a favor to ask."

"Sure, Chris, what do you need?"

"I need for you to remember you made a promise."

"What do you mean?"

Chris turned to look Patrick in the eye. "You know what I mean. If something happens to me before this weekend is over, I don't want to be responsible for the team doing something stupid, like not finishing the meet."

"You know that's an awful lot to ask, pal. I can't control whether these guys will finish this meet or not. If something were to happen to you, I don't know that I would want to finish."

"You have to!" Chris exclaimed, getting in Patrick's face. "Don't you know that that was the reason I came back?"

"Yes, but what good are we without you?"

"You know the answer to that question as well as I do. Besides, I don't want to be the reason why you guys don't win this thing."

"Crap, Chris," Patrick turned to face the water as a tear was forming in his eye, "I ... I don't know if I can ... "

"Don't make me say it, Patrick."

"Say what?"

"Come on, Patrick!" said an agonizing Haley.

"Consider it a dying man's last request." Chris finally said what he had hoped he wouldn't have to say.

Patrick stood stunned. "Since you put it that way. ... But what are you gonna do tomorrow?"

"What I can. I'm gonna try to compete as long as I can."

"Are you sure that's wise, son?" asked Chris's mother.

"I have to, Mom. This is all I've been able to think about since my bike crash. If I'm gonna go out, this is how I want it to be." Chris turned back to Patrick. "So, pal, what's it gonna be?"

Patrick thought for only a second. "Anything you want, Chris." Patrick extended his hand to Chris to confirm the deal. Chris accepted Patrick's handshake and pulled him close to give him a hug.

"I love you, plowboy."

"I love you, too, Chris," Patrick returned the hug, which was soon joined by Haley and Chris's mother.

"I don't mean to be a party pooper," said Chris, "but there are a few places around here I'd like Haley to see."

"That's fine, son," replied Chris's mother. "Why don't you use the rental car?"

"Thanks for the offer, Mom, but I think I'd like to see the town once more from two wheels. Why don't you give Patrick a ride back to the pavilion, or the hotel, or wherever he's goin'."

"Where are you gonna find a motorcycle?" asked Patrick.

"Remember, plowboy, I still have friends around here. Just a couple of phone calls is all it'll take."

"Well, you take care, son. We'll see the two of you back at the hotel."

"Thanks, Mom. You're the greatest." Chris gave his mother a peck on the cheek.

"Don't do anything stupid," said Patrick, shaking Chris's hand, "like get yourselves killed. You know what LA traffic can be like."

"Right," replied Chris with a touch of sarcasm.

The two pairs parted company at the end of the pier.

"I guess it's just you and me, Mrs. M!" stated Patrick, putting his arm around Chris's mother as they headed toward the car.

"Hold on!" Chris shouted over the roar of the borrowed Kawasaki Vulcan as he leaned into the sharp turn going up Mulholland Drive. Haley responded by squeezing Chris's waist tighter, burying the side of her face deeper into his back. Chris continued up the winding road, leaning and accelerating into the turns.

Haley looked from her position behind Chris to see the sun setting off the coast, casting the sky and the objects below in an orange haze. She couldn't remember seeing anything quite so beautiful. Just as Haley was starting to enjoy the view, the motorcycle started to downshift, signaling that Chris had found the location he had sought.

Chris pulled the motorcycle off of the road and came to a stop at an overlook near the top of the drive. As the two worked to remove a blanket from where it had been tied down on the seat of the bike, Haley couldn't help but notice the beauty of the view as she looked over the twilight of the city below.

"Chris, this is beautiful!" she gasped.

"Yeah, I know. This is one of my favorite places. This is where I used to go when I felt really bad about myself," Chris said, taking a seat on the blanket and pulling Haley down to sit in front of him, her head resting against his chest, his arms around hers.

"I can see how this would be a favorite place. I don't think I've ever seen such an awesome view! I can see how this place could make anyone feel better."

"I remember feeling lousy, whether it was over my own condition, the fact that I didn't have my dad anymore, or just some silly fight I had had with my mom. I'd come up here to try to forget my troubles. I'd look out over the city and try to imagine all of those people below and what kind of problems they could be having, and before long, I realized just how small my problems were."

"But they weren't small to you."

"Sure they were. Think about it. If you knew that you were living on borrowed time, wouldn't you feel that there just wasn't enough time to worry about petty little problems, like whether I took out the garbage or whether my mom washed my favorite jeans? Looking back, I must have been a pain to put up with. There was a time when I would go off at just the smallest thing. I acted like I had been cheated out of my life. I blamed my dad. I blamed my mom just for bringing me into this world. Somehow, I was able to find a way to blame everything and everyone for my own pain."

"How did you get over it?"

"One day, I went to the hospital to visit a teammate who had been injured during a workout. He had a pretty bad break in his leg, and it was going to require surgery. He shared a room with a seven-year-old kid who was recovering from burns he had sustained when his house caught fire after he and his brother were playing with matches. He was in pretty bad shape, burned all over the place. He was going to need skin grafts and several surgeries, but was expected to recover."

"That was lucky."

"Not so for his brother, though. He was lost in the fire. He was five. Now not only was this poor kid gonna have to go through the rest of his life without his little brother, but also the knowledge of how senseless it all was."

"That's horrible."

"It was then that I realized that life was too short to complain about things that didn't matter and weren't in my control. So many times, we find ourselves caught up in worrying about unimportant little matters and forget that life is meant to be lived, not wasted on trivial stuff. It was then that I began to figure out what was important. Worrying about what time I had left became a lot less important than making each moment count."

"That's what I love about you, Chris."

"What's that, cutie?"

"You somehow make every moment with you special and memorable."

"I'm glad I have you to share it with." Chris turned Haley to face him, and as their eyes met, so did their lips, and the couple became folded within one another in a passionate embrace. Then, Haley turned to snuggle into Chris's chest once again and the two looked out on the lights of the city below and shared in the silence.

"Chris?" asked Haley after a prolonged silence.

"Yeah."

"Are you … scared?"

"Of dying? I don't know."

"How can you not know?"

"It's like, I'm prepared to go, you know. I've gone through all of the stages: denial, rage, acceptance. I think I can handle the dying part. Rick has assured me that if I go through the prolonged version, he's got some killer drugs to manage the pain. So as far as dying goes, I think I can handle it.

"It used to bother me a lot. Waking up in the middle of the night in a cold sweat, nightmares when I did sleep, especially when I was young. Once I came to grips with the fact that I couldn't control my ultimate destiny, with the help of counseling, I learned to accept things for what they are and just do what everybody else does, live my life and hope I get one more day.

"The hard part is knowing that now that the process has started, I won't be able to do all of the things that I wanted to do. You know, see the world and stuff. No, I don't think I'm scared, more hurt, I think."

"Hurt?" Haley asked as she turned to face Chris.

"Yeah, hurt that I'm leaving people that I love, hurt that my mom is gonna have to go through the pain of losing another family member, the pain that you and my friends and teammates will go through, all because of me. I think that hurts most. Actually, in a way, I consider myself lucky."

"Lucky?"

"Sure. By knowing that my time is limited, I think I can appreciate things a little more than those who think they have forever. They're so wrong. No one has as much time as they think they do. Probably, the hardest thing to get across to people is that *everyone* is on borrowed time."

"I guess that's because the short time we do have seems so long."

"Until it's too late." Chris laid back on the blanket and stared at the stars "God, what I wouldn't give for more time."

"We're in, we're in!" shouted Joey, meeting Chris and Haley in the lobby of the hotel. "We're the number three seed!"

"Have you been waiting here long?" asked Chris, looking at his watch that had just turned 11 PM.

"Maybe an hour or so. I wanted to catch you before anyone else!"

"So, who qualified ahead of us?" asked Chris.

"Who else? Lake Erie and Texas Star."

"What did they score?"

"Lake Erie just barely edged us with a 289.2, seven-tenths ahead of . Texas Star will be tough to beat, though, they scored a friggin' 292.1!"

"Holy crap! That's over a 9.7 average!" exclaimed Haley.

"Yeah, but it'll be tough for them to be that good tomorrow," said Joey.

"Don't count on it, Joe. Danny's got that team right where he wants them. They'll be tough tomorrow, you can count on it," concluded Chris. "Where's everybody else?"

"Pretty much everybody has hit the sack."

"Then, I suggest we do the same. We have a huge day tomorrow."

"No kiddin'! We're gonna be on TV tomorrow night!" said an excited Joey.

"I wouldn't give that too much thought, Joey. It may prove to be your undoing!"

"Right, but boy, will I sleep good tonight!" Joey turned and ran toward the elevators.

"Just one more night, and it'll all be over," said Chris, pulling Haley to him, his arms encircling her hips, her arms draping around his neck.

"I hope you're only talking about the competition," said Haley.

"Actually, I meant the struggle. I feel like I've been towing a barge across dry land just trying to get through this meet."

"Just make sure there's something left for me after it's over."

"What, are you kiddin'? That's the thought that has kept me goin' this long!" The two looked long and longingly into each other's eyes.

"What are you thinking, Chris?" asked Haley, looking deep into his ice blue eyes.

"I'm memorizing every little detail of your face."

"Why, am I going somewhere?"

"No, but I want that face, those eyes, and that smile to flood my thoughts as I doze off tonight."

"I love you, Christopher."

"I love you, too, Haley." Chris pulled Haley closer to him and reached down to join his lips to hers. He could feel her lips tremble as they kissed. Chris held her even tighter, for in that moment, he shared her fear.

THIRTY-ONE

▼

JOEY EXCLAIMED, "265.75!" as he ran into the dressing room of the pavilion. "That was the high score from the first two sessions."

"At least we know that it'll be near impossible for someone in the earlier sessions to sneak into the top six," concluded Mackee.

"Don't be so sure, Mack," said Coach Lowery. "It wouldn't take very many breaks for us to drop out of the running. At least we know that no one from the previous sessions has put up a huge number. Now we can focus on just hitting. Just because no one earlier has set the bar too high, let's not get overconfident," Coach Lowery looked around the room. "We still have this little problem with five other teams that we have to compete against. Where's Chris?" Just then, Coach Lowery heard the sound of the toilet flushing as Chris emerged from the lavatory.

"Chris, aren't those different shorts than the ones you wore over here?" asked Coach Lowery.

"Uh, yeah, Coach. I, uh, had a little accident in the others."

"Is everything okay?"

"Oh, yeah. I just had a little nervous dribble, if you know what I mean."

"Okay, men. Tonight, we have our final step. Everything that we have worked for this season comes to a head out there in the next couple of hours. Everything that we have done this season has been to prepare you for this moment. I know it's gonna be tough forgetting that there'll be thousands of people out there cheering at the top of their lungs. Some will be cheering for you, some for the other teams. And, I know that having all of those TV cameras pointed at us will never be far from the front of your minds, too. It would be easy to say ignore all of that and concentrate on your routines, but I know as well as you that you just can't do that. However, when it's all said and done, there will be only one team at the top of the awards stand. There's no way of knowing who it will be. It would be nice if you boys were that team. After all, that's what has been our focus all season. But, that's also been the focus of every team that has stepped out on the competition floor this weekend, and you can bet that the thought has not escaped the other teams we will compete against tonight. This I can tell you. It will be a combination of focus, execution, desire, and a little bit of luck that will determine the winner.

"Now, we do have an advantage. We know the distractions, and we have competed in similar situations this season, and you have done well. The team that finishes on top will be the one that can focus on the job at hand and not fall into the pitfall of the distractions. Do your job and focus on your routines. Two hundred sixteen routines must be competed before we know who wins. You each only have to do six of them. Keep your head focused on your responsibilities, and we stand as good a shot as anyone of being the one who stands highest of those six. No matter what happens around you, if you can take care of your six routines, it won't matter if we win or not. We will still have had the best season in Pioneer history. I couldn't be more proud of a group of men than I am of you guys. Do your best, stay focused, and, by all means, enjoy this moment, for we may not pass this way again. All right, boys, let's get in there and show them what gymnastics can be."

The team stood together in a circle, hands joined in the center.

"Pioneers!" they shouted, throwing their hands upward.

The Pioneers were the last team to enter the arena. At the sight of the Pioneers emerging from the tunnel, the patient crowd of a packed Pauly Pavilion rose to its feet and made its favorite known with an explosion of cheers. The flashing of thousands of cameras and the attention from TV cameras all steered in the direction of the Pioneers.

"Remember, only *some* of the crowd is cheering for us," Dallas said, leaning to Mackee's right ear.

"Right. Only some," Mackee replied in awe.

"Come on, you guys," called Patrick, "get focused." Patrick led his team out to a light jog around the floor exercise carpet to start warm-up. Although the team showed no outward emotion as it made its way around the white border of the royal blue carpet, it was evident that ignoring the deafening crowd and the constant clicking of camera shutters would be no simple task.

Once the boys finished their jog, they found the only empty corner of the carpet on which to sit and stretch. While Patrick led the team through its stretching routine, Coach Lowery joined them from the coaches meeting, stuffing his rotation sheet into his back pocket.

"Luck of the draw, fellas, we compete in Olympic order. We'll start on floor and finish on pipe. You can't do better than Olympic order."

"Gentlemen, at this time, please rotate to your first event," called the announcer.

"Let's do it, fellas," called Patrick as the Pioneers made their way toward the corners of the floor.

As the Pioneers moved, all eyes were on Chris to see if he would repeat the performance of his woofus from the night before. While each of the others warmed up with conservative setup tumbling, Chris had decided to let out the stops right from the start. Chris turned his round off, back handspring and punched the floor the way he had thousands of times before. Even though he had only done the beautiful, but potentially deadly, skill only a handful of times, Chris was surprised at how mechanically simple it had become. But in that half second, Chris lost eye contact with the floor. The gasps from the crowd were punctuated by Chris's body bouncing across the floor.

"Wooofff!" exclaimed Chris as the air rushed out of his lungs. Before anyone could reach him, he got back to his feet and slowly walked off the carpet, trying not to appear hurt.

"Are you all right, Chris?" asked Coach Lowery.

"Sure, Coach. No damage."

"I think maybe for today, you need to compete a different skill."

"But, I can do it, Coach! And we need—"

"We need hit, Chris. I know that there are easier skills that are worth the same without bouncing you across the gym."

"But, Coach!"

"But nothing, Chris. Use a different skill. That's an order."

"Yes, sir," Chris said reluctantly and resumed his position at the corner of the floor exercise carpet, behind Mackee, to wait his turn.

"What was that about?" asked Mackee.

"Coach put his foot down on the woofus," answered a dejected Chris.

"It's understandable. We don't need it, anyway. Just do something easier, but still harder than the other guys. That should be easy for you."

"But you don't understand—" Chris's words were lost as Mackee had already started across the carpet for his tumbling pass.

"You okay?" asked Patrick, having finished his pass and taking his position behind Chris.

"I'm fine," Chris replied with a bite in his voice.

"Hey, no big deal, Chris. Just do something easy, for you, anyway, but still grab the crowd."

"Great," Chris replied, tired of everyone else's advice. He darted across the carpet, fueled by his disgust, and whipped over his round off, back handspring and launched a double layout with two twists in the second flip to a landing that could have easily stuck if he had cared to. Instead, Chris just made contact with the floor with his feet and simply turned and began walking to his position at the end of the line for his next turn. On his way, he passed a dumbfounded Mackee, who was still looking at the corner of the floor where Chris had just casually executed one of the most difficult tumbling passes possible.

"That works." Mackee managed to force out of his stunned face.

"Gentlemen, that concludes the warm-up period," the announcer called. "At this time, please prepare for the march-in ceremony."

The teams picked up their gym bags and headed for the dressing room. Chris bent over to pick up his bag, and everything went black. Luckily, Patrick was right behind him and was able to stand him up before he plowed his lanky frame into the judges' table.

"Chris, are you okay?" asked Patrick.

"I think so. I just blacked out bending over to get my bag."

"How many fingers do I have up?" asked Patrick, waving his open hand in front of Chris's face.

"On which hand? You're wavin' three of 'em." Chris was still visibly dazed.

"Come on, I've got to get you back to the training room." Patrick put his arm around Chris's shoulder and guided his dizzy companion back toward the entrance tunnel. On the way, he glanced into the stands to find his mother and Dr. Gardner. Both knew what it could mean, so they quickly rose to their feet and raced for the training room. By the time they arrived, the team was circled around Chris, who was sitting on a training table, an ice pack on his head.

"Chris, son, are you all right?" pleaded Mrs. McClure, taking her son's hand.

"Yeah, Mom. I'm just a little dizzy."

"Let's take a look, Chris," said Dr. Gardner, wedging his way in through the team. He took a penlight out of his pocket and examined Chris's eyes, ears, and throat. "It could be nothing, but then again, it may be something. I would need to run some tests to—"

"No!" shouted Chris. "No tests. Not now. There's no time. We've got to compete in ten minutes."

"Chris, if the doctor says you need to go—" Coach Lowery's words were cut short.

"I said *no!*" demanded Chris. "If this is nothing, it'll pass. If, on the other hand, it is the start of something else, I don't want to spend the rest of whatever time I have left on an examination table and miss this competition."

"But, if it's something that can be treated … " pleaded his mother.

"But, it can't be treated, Mom. Either it gets me, or it doesn't!"

"All the more reason to get you to a hospital, Chris," she said.

"No, Mom. All the more reason for me to compete today. Now listen," Chris quieted the group, "If I'm allowed a last request, I would like to make sure that I do what I can, the best I can, for as long as I can." Chris looked into his mother's eyes, "If it's my time to go, this is how I want to go. That's final!" Chris jumped down from the training table and pulled off his tattered T-shirt. "Gentlemen, we have six routines separating us from history. I don't know about you guys, but I'm doin' mine." Chris turned and headed for the staging area for the march-in. The remainder of the team looked at each other, then at Coach Lowery.

"Well, let's go fellas. Let's not keep destiny waiting." The guys turned and headed to join their teammate.

"Do you mind if we watch from the floor, Coach?" asked Mrs. McClure.

"I imagine as long as you stay out of the competition area, it would be fine. You might want to watch from the entrance tunnel."

"I'll get some chairs," said Dr. Gardner as he rushed out to find three chairs.

"He'll be fine, Mrs. McClure," said Coach Lowery, trying to console Chris's mother.

"No he won't, Coach, but he will be happy."

The Pioneers took their place behind the other teams marching in. Haley gave each of the boys a kiss on the cheek for luck until she reached Patrick. His kiss came squarely on the lips.

"What was that for?" asked a stunned Patrick.

"Just for being you, Pat."

Then she looked at Chris. She could see the uneasiness in his face. As they embraced, she could feel him shudder with fear, although he was doing a good job of holding it in. She then gave him a very passionate kiss.

"Is that for luck?" asked Chris.

"No, hon, that was for love." They looked deeply into each other's eyes.

"Haley, I'm—"

"We all are, baby. Last chance if you want to drop out."

"Nope. Not happenin'," Chris replied quick and sure. "This is my last chance to do well."

"Chris, you don't have to prove anything to anyone. You've done more than anyone could expect."

"You're wrong. I have something to prove to myself, that I can finish what I start. I'll not be cheated."

Haley gave him one more kiss. "I love you," she whispered in his ear.

"I love you, too."

"Ladies and gentlemen," the announcer barked, "presenting the greatest athletes in the United States. It's the National Team Invitational's final round! These are the six highest scoring teams from the thirty-six that began competition yesterday. These six will compete tonight to determine the number one gymnastics team in the country … "

"We gotta go," Chris said, trying not to release his hold on Haley.

"I'll see you when it's over."

"I hope I can do the same." Chris prepared to march out with his team. Haley returned to her seat next to Chris's mother, already in tears.

"You okay?" Patrick asked, turning his head to Chris, who was lined up behind him.

"Yeah, just some tingling in my fingers and toes," answered Chris. "Hey, Patrick, keep an eye on me out there."

"You got it, pal."

As the teams entered the competition floor, the announcer introduced each team.

"Starting on horizontal Bar from Sarasota, Florida, Gold Medal Gymnastics. Starting on Parallel Bars, from Los Angeles, California, LA Elite Gymnastics. Starting on Vault, from Denver, Colorado, Apex Gymnastics. Beginning on Rings, from Austin, Texas, Texas Star Gymnastics. Starting competition on Pommel Horse, from Cleveland, Ohio, Lake Erie Gymnastics. And starting on Floor Exercise, from Knoxville, Tennessee, Pioneeeeeer Gymnastics!" As each team entered the pavilion, it was met with the maddening roar of a standing room only crowd.

After the introduction of the judges and the playing of the national anthem, the teams marched to their first competitive event.

"Come on, Mackee!" shouted Joey. "Get us started!"

The gravity of the moment was evident as Mackee began his routine with a double back that was clearly not one of his best, stumbling on the landing. Once the first pass was out of the way, Mackee was able to relax enough to complete his routine without a major break for a decent 8.85 start score.

Ty was next. Giving away very little with good form, but not amassing much in the way of difficulty, Ty was able to manage a respectable 8.95. Joey followed with a shaky routine, showing signs that the preasure and the dramatics of the events unfolding around him were certainly playing on this freshman. Joey's 8.25 score was flashed and was followed by Joey dropping his head in disgust.

"Hey, man," called Chris, putting his arm around Joey's slumpped shoulders, "keep your chin up. We've got five more events, and we're gonna need you to be ready."

"But if I continue like this, I'll be worthless to the team, and we won't win, and it'll all be my fault."

"Whoa, whoa, hold on there, little camper. Nothing has happened that will knock us out. We've got a long meet to go yet. There's plenty of time to make up for that score. Don't think so far ahead. Just take each routine as it comes, and do what you do best," reassured Chris, with little effect.

"That's easy for you to say. You didn't just blow floor!"

Chris thought for a moment.

"All right, Joey. Remember the day that AJ got hurt, and you were trying to prove to everyone that you deserved to be here? Well, you were right. You do deserve to be here, fighting for a national championship. But, you're gonna have to find that same attitude again. You've got to be just a little bit cocky and a little bit daring and show these guys how gymnastics is supposed to be done."

"What if I blow it again?"

"So you blow it. So what? Being confident and cocky doesn't ensure anything. Even the most sure can mess up, but if you did, wouldn't you want to crash having done your absolute best?"

"I guess you're right."

"Of course I'm right. Now pick yourself up and get ready for pommels."

"Yes, sir."

Chris stood up in time to see Dallas land his dismount pass and walk off the floor with a smile on his face, his clenched fist punching over his head and greeting his coach with a strong high ten. The 9.55 flashed gave cause for Dallas to punch skyward once again.

"Come on, Patrick!" shouted Dallas, exchanging a high five with his team captain as he prepared for his routine, "Give 'em hell!"

Patrick saluted the head judge and stepped into the corner. Knowing that they would have to count a low score if he missed, Patrick first thought he would go for all of his hard tumbling, but as he raised his arms for the beginning of his first pass, he knew that it was going to be a long meet, and conservative was the right way to go. He started with his double-layout to a stuck landing, which was met with thunderous applause. He continued his routine the same as he had in the preliminary round. Standing in the corner before his dismount, Patrick weighed the merit of twisting his double back dismount, but he also knew that the tucked double back would assure him of a solid score to start. Just before starting across the floor for his dismount pass, Patrick cast a glance toward the team, *his* team. the one he had tried his entire gymnastics career to bring to another level. They were all on their feet, waiting for a finish worthy of a national champion. Through a pounding heart and a gulp stuck in his throat, Patrick sprinted across the diagonal.

"He's gonna do it!" shouted Chris.

"Do what?" added Coach Lowery.

His question was immediately answered as Patrick launched his body up off of the floor, pulling his left elbow up over the top of the flip to generate a full-twisting double back to a surprising stuck landing. Patrick raised his arms jubilantly to the applause of the crowd.

"That's the way you do it, pal!" shouted Chris over the noise.

"I figured it was high time I led by example, my friend!" Patrick had to shout to be heard over the crowd as he dashed off the floor to meet his teammates.

"I knew you could do it!" Chris replied as he turned his attention toward the judges' table to await their signal to begin. Chris closed his eyes and tilted his head upward for a quick moment of meditation. Once finished, he opened his eyes to see the green start flag waving. Chris stretched to the judges and stepped into the corner.

As he stood in the corner, he didn't notice that the other events had finished, and all eyes in the packed arena were on him, especially those of the concerned Pioneer contingent. If there was any question as to Chris's ability to perform his routines, his opening pass removed all doubt. He bolted across the spring floor and catapulted his frame skyward to execute his double-twisting double layout to a solid landing. While everyone else in the arena jumped to their feet and cheered, those who were crossing their fingers breathed a collective sigh of relief.

After a quick breath, Chris darted back across the floor for a front tumbling combination that ended with a double front with a half twist. Once again, Chris had introduced a new skill to the crowd. As he sprinted across the floor for his final pass, he could feel that he was starting to black out once again. Not now! he thought. The remainder of the pass was done by reflex alone. Chris fought to stay conscious and opted for a full-twisting double tuck, something he felt he could land reasonably safe. With no way to find the ground, Chris over-rotated his landing, taking a huge step backward just to stay on the spring floor. In amazement, the stunned crowd jumped to their feet. Chris stumbled around until he could salute in the general direction of the judges before collapsing in the arms of his teammates, who had rushed out to his aid.

"What did you score, Patrick?" asked an exhausted Chris.

"Nine-seven, thanks to you, Chris."

"What do you mean thanks to me?"

"You pushed me to try. Thanks."

"Just keep it up, plowboy. We're gonna need more of that. What did I score, Joey?" asked Chris.

"It hasn't come up yet," replied Joey.

"That's not important now, Chris," said Coach Lowery. "I think you'd better stop. You almost passed out in the middle of your dismount!"

"No!" yelled Chris, thrashing his arms side to side to shake off the aid of his teammates. "I'll say when I'm finished, and I'm not finished!"

"Chris, you're gonna hurt yourself." said Coach Lowery.

"Believe me, Coach, anything that can happen to me trying to finish this meet is minor compared to what I'm gonna feel two hours from now. I can get through this. If I collapse into a coma, I'll still find a way to finish." The team looked from Chris to Coach Lowery, knowing that he alone had the power to stop Chris or allow him to carry out what could prove to be his final request.

"Coach, please," pleaded Chris.

"Okay, Chris, you can continue. But, if you want to finish this, you better think about pulling some of your difficulty. If you black out again, it might be in the middle of something that you can't safely get out of."

"Okay, Coach, I will," conceded Chris.

"You're gonna ease back your difficulty?" inquired Coach Lowery.

"I'll think about it. I'll be careful, Coach. Right now, I just want to help get you guys onto that awards stand."

"Then what?" asked Dallas, posing the magic question. Everyone looked at Chris for the answer he could not give.

"Look, Chris!" shouted Joey, looking at the scoreboard. "You still scored a 9.65!"

"Gentlemen, at this time, please rotate to your second competitive event," called the announcer. "The standings after the first event: in third place, with a 45.3, Lake Erie Gymnastics. In second place, with a 45.85, Texas Star Gymnastics, and your leaders after the first event, with a 46.7, Pioneeeer Gymnastics!"

"We're in front?" asked Joey in disbelief. "The other teams must've had a rough first event."

"Who didn't?" replied Patrick. "Lake Erie had to count two falls on pommels. We can't afford to give up anything."

Coach Lowery marched his troops to their next event. "Boys, this could be a make-or-break event. Any mental errors on pommel horse could make for a long day."

Although Pommel Horse had been the most difficult event to get going, the Pioneers had very little trouble warming up. Even Mackee, who was always sure to have several misses, was swinging as though it were his favorite event. With each turn, confidence was building for the team. If they could all hit pommels, they thought, they would be the team to beat.

Then it happened.

SMACK! Chris's legs hit the pommels during a complex combination, putting him immediately on his backside on the landing mat.

"You okay, man?" asked Patrick.

"Oh, yeah, as soon as the feeling returns to my legs!" Chris dragged himself off of the mat so the next guy could go. Mackee noticed a trickle of blood soaking through Chris's white competition pants.

"Hey, pal, you really did smack those pommels. You better clean that up."

Chris reached into his bag and pulled out a small hand towel, rolled up his pant leg, and blotted up the blood on his legs while his teammates continued to warm up.

"Chris, you gonna jump in here, bud?" asked Joey.

"Yeah, just a sec." Chris continued to blot the blood that wouldn't seem to clot.

"Are you okay, Chris?" asked Coach Lowery, noticing that Chris had missed two turns.

"I think so, Coach. I just can't get this to stop bleeding. I think it's from the blood thinner that Rick has me on."

"Well, let's get a dressing on there before you bleed all over the place." Coach Lowery motioned for a trainer to attend to the senior's knees. By the time the trainer could dress the scrapes on Chris's shins, time had run out in the warm-up, and it was time to rotate to the competition gym.

"I don't mean to be rude, dude," said Chris, "but I've got a meet to get ready for. I don't suppose you can wrap things up, you know what I mean?"

"Sorry, just had to put a couple butterflies on there. There, you're good as gold," the trainer replied as he finished his dressing.

"Let's hope you're right." Chris jumped up and joined the others.

"You gonna make it?" asked Patrick.

"Don't blame me," answered Chris. "Is it my fault Dr. Kildare was trying to earn his merit badge on my legs? Don't worry, I'll be fine."

Mackee looked at the judges knowing that no one was counting on his score to help the team. Although, a hit leadoff set would be a good momentum builder.

But, as it happened, his salute to the judges was the best part of his routine, as he proceeded to have four falls and a dismal 6.85 score.

"Don't let it get you, Mack," said Patrick, patting the shoulder of his dejected pal as he returned to the seating area. "Shake it off. We'll pick up your slack. I know you'll be picking ours up on Rings." Patrick's words, although well-intended, did little to boost Mackee's spirits.

Ty's routine quickly brought smiles to the faces of the Pioneers as the Kennedy junior gave his best Pommel Horse performance of the season to score a 9.1. His routine was just the fuel that the Pioneers needed, as Dallas picked up where his teammate had left off, hitting a strong, aggressive routine to post a 9.45.

"Keep it goin', Joey!" yelled Chris from the bench, "We need a score!"

Joey closed his eyes and visualized the same routine he had seen time and time again in his head. He opened his eyes to see the head judge's start signal. He raised his arm and turned his focus to the horse. Joey jumped into his mount and began to swing his body in counterclockwise circles, moving across and back, counter-rotating his torso opposite of his circle direction and placing his hands firmly first on leather, then on the wooden pommels. With each circle, Joey could hear Chris's voice in his head. Making his final turn around the pommels, Joey pushed up quickly to an effortless handstand pirouette before dropping to the vinyl surface. He threw his arms upward, halfway to salute the judges and half in jubilation of having, once again, conquered "the beast." The rest of the team were on their feet to meet Joey, except Patrick, who was at the chalk bucket preparing for his routine, and Chris, who was still sitting at the bench, resting before his turn. After the congratulations, Joey went to the bench to share his success with Chris.

"Heard the crowd. You must've done well," Chris said, his head still down.

"Okay, I guess. It felt good. The score is just now coming up," Joey jumped from his seat next to Chris when the 9.55 score was flashed. "Waaa-hooo!" he shouted. Chris gave him a pat on the back.

"Good job, Joey," said Chris.

"Come on, Chris, let's watch Patrick."

"I can't."

"What?"

"I can't see."

"At all?"

"Just fuzz. Everything's kinda blurry. I can make out light and dark, but not much else."

"Have you told Coach?"

"No. He would take me out."

"How do you intend to do routines?"

"By feel, I guess."

"And dismount?"

"Luck. I figure I can get through most of my routines. I only have one problem."

"What's that?"

"Can you point me to the horse?"

Joey now became Chris's eyes. Trying hard not to give away his handicap, Joey guided Chris to the chalk bucket for the rest of Patrick's routine.

"Patrick just hit his set," said Joey.

"I could tell by the cheers."

"Tear 'em up, Chris!" shouted Patrick as he gave Joey a high five on the way back to the rest of the team.

"Okay, Joey, it's showtime." Joey led Chris to the edge of the pommel horse mat, making gestures along the way to give the appearance that he was merely giving Chris last-minute strategy and not leading a sightless teammate.

"You got it from here?" asked Joey.

"Just watch," replied Chris standing stoically at the edge of the mat. Joey gave him a pat on the back and backed away. The head judge waved the start signal for Chris, but Chris made no move to acknowledge the signal.

"Crap!" Joey said under his breath, "he can't see the flag. Go, Chris!" Joey shouted to get Chris's attention. The move worked, as Chris raised his right arm in the air and stepped up on the mat. Chris reached out for the leather surface and ran both hands across the top of the horse and both pommels before coming to a starting point at the end of the horse. He then dropped his head for a second to visualize his routine once more. The crowd noise had settled for a moment in anticipation of Chris's routine, completely unaware that he was going by feel alone. Chris raised his head in hazy gaze across the horse and blew out a breath. Chris stepped to his left, raised his right arm and looked upward as if to wind up for the start of his routine. He jumped up and began to swing some of the fastest circles in his life, traveling across the body of the horse and back. Perhaps it was habit that he tried to look at the horse while he was swinging, or maybe he hoped his vision would magically return.

Either way, by the third circle of his routine, Chris realized that he would be better off simply closing his eyes and relying on his instinct and reflexes to get him through his routine.

"Come on Chris, stay strong!" shouted Joey from the bench.

Amazingly, Chris managed to get through his routine. At the end of his set, Chris swung his legs up to an effortless handstand and reached for the mat with his feet. He still had his right hand on the leather body of the horse to maintain his balance, then quickly raised his arms in triumph. He saluted in the general direction of the judges' panel, turned away from the horse, and began walking toward the sound of his team. A small stumble at the edge of the mat was a quick cue for Joey to intercept his friend before something more obvious gave away Chris's condition.

"So, how'd I do?" asked Chris as Joey grabbed his arm.

"Believe it or not, you looked better than when your eyes worked!" No sooner did Joey's words leave his lips, the rest of the team swarmed the Californian.

"What did Patrick score?" asked Chris.

"Nine-six-five. Your score just came up … 9.7!" replied Mackee.

"What was that caressing the horse before your set for?" asked Coach Lowery.

"Uh … I … just wanted to make my last routine on the horse memorable, Coach."

"If I didn't know any better," said Dallas, "I'd swear you did that set with your eyes closed."

"If anybody could pull it off, Dallas, my money would be on Chris," said Patrick.

The announcer called the standings. "Gentlemen, please rotate to your third competitive event. The standings after two events: in third place, with a 92.75, Lake Erie Gymnastics. In second place, with a 93.15, Texas Star Gymnastics. And your leaders after two events, with a score of 94.15, Pioneeeer Gymnastics!"

"Holy smokes, Chris!" shouted Joey. "We've got a full-point lead after two events!"

"We're gonna need it, plus some, Joe," replied Chris.

"But we're through the tough events."

"Yeah, but there's no way I'll be able to finish."

"I never thought I'd hear that come out of you, Chris."

"I never thought I'd lose my sight. Thanks for playing guide dog for me. Just walk shoulder-to-shoulder with me over to Rings."

"You got it. Just stick by me."

With Joey's help, Chris managed to get through warm-up without giving away his impediment.

As was the case with the other teams that had already competed on Rings, Ty found it difficult to keep the cables from swinging, which in turn made handstands and static strength parts difficult to do. When Ty finally landed, he was obviously displeased.

"Keep your chin up, Ty," said Coach Lowery. "We're counting on you for Vault."

Ty quickly unstrapped his grips, threw them in the general area of his gym bag, and sat down in a huff next to Chris.

"Rough go, eh, Ty?" inquired Chris.

"Didn't you see? I missed every hold part and swung back and forth like a trapeze!" Chris tilted his head toward Joey to give Ty his reply.

"No he didn't see you, Ty. Chris can't see."

"Holy crap! That explains the stuff at the beginning of your Pommel Horse routine."

"Yeah, don't tell Coach. He'll make me stop."

"Are you gonna do Rings?" asked Ty.

"I plan to, as long as nothing else happens."

"What about Vault, Chris?" asked Joey.

"I haven't thought that far ahead. I hope my score won't be needed."

"And if it is?" asked Ty.

"Joey will just have to point me toward the board, and I'll take my chances."

"What are you guys doin' here?" demanded Dallas, having just finished his routine. "Johnson, you're next! You might ought to get ready."

Joey jumped up and ran to the chalk bucket, quickly applied the chalk, and jogged up to his position under the ring tower.

"Nice of you to join us, Joey," said Coach Lowery. "We sure could use a good set here."

"Got one I've been saving up just for you, Coach." Joey looked to the judges' table to wait for the signal flag to begin his routine. Once waved, Joey returned a salute and turned forward to jump up to the rings. After helping Joey adjust his grips, Coach Lowery stepped back to his spotting position beside the tower.

Joey's routine was not packed with the strength of the top dogs, but what he had learned in his first year as a Pioneer was how to swing to make up for his lack of strength. With double-front combinations ending in solid handstands, Joey proved that he did not have to be a muscle head to achieve a good score. He finished his routine with a solid full-twisting tucked double back dismount.

"Way to go, Joe!" shouted the team.

Joey jogged back to the seating area, looking over his shoulder to see the score posted on the electronic scoreboard. Joey clenched his fist and pumped it back and forth several times in joy.

"How'd it go, Joey?" asked Chris upon Joey's return to the seating area. "From the sound of the crowd, it must've been pretty good."

"Yeah, 9.4!" Joey replied. "Come on Chris, we need to get you ready. You're up after Patrick." Chris rose to his feet and extended his hands to Joey.

"Joey, are my grips on the right hands?" Joey looked at his hands.

"Right hands, wrong grips!"

"What?" cried Chris.

"You have your High Bar grips on. We're on Rings!"

"Are you kidding?"

"Yeah, I'm kidding. You're fine, Chris. Just relax. Patrick is just going up." Chris responded to Joey's prank by swinging at what he thought was the back of Joey's head. Joey read his intentions and easily ducked out of the way.

"Very funny, Joey. Just tell me how Patrick does."

Joey led Chris to the chalk stand, describing Patrick's routine while they walked, including an opinionated commentary on Patrick's amplitude of swing, as well as duration and quality of his hold parts. Joey's voice rose in pitch with each skill, and he was nearly out of breath by the time Patrick climaxed his set with his stuck full twisting double layout dismount, punctuated by the roar of the crowd.

"Waaa-hooo!" shouted Joey as Patrick hit the dismount mat.

"I take it he did well," said Chris. "What do we need?"

"We need a score to cancel Ty's 7.6."

"I think I can manage."

"How do you feel?" asked Joey as he walked with Chris to the edge of the mat.

"Like crap. I feel a little dizzy, and your face is just a blur."

"Give it your best."

"I always do," replied Chris. "Now, just point me toward Coach."

"Step up twelve inches, walk straight ahead five steps, and you're there."

Chris stepped up on the mat and counted off five paces and turned around where he thought was directly below the rings.

"Chris, are you okay?" asked Coach Lowery.

"Sure, Coach. Why do you ask?"

"Because you need to step back about two feet to be under the rings."

"Oh," Chris backed up two steps to position himself in front of his coach. "Coach, I have something to tell you."

"You're blind."

"How'd you guess?"

"*I'd* have to be blind to miss that, the way you've stumbled around since Pommel Horse."

"You're not gonna pull me out?"

"Can you get through a routine safely?"

"My dismount won't be that great, but I'll give you a score you can count."

"But can you land safely?"

"My equilibrium isn't too bad. I can get to my feet," Chris replied with confidence.

"Then give it your best shot, son."

"Thanks, Coach."

"And you better salute. The judge has been waving his flag for about five seconds."

Chris turned in the general direction of the judges' table and raised his right arm. He then tilted his head back and jumped toward the blur that was the rings. Coach Lowery held him up until his grips were properly set, then lowered him to a dead hang before stepping back to watch the routine of the most gallant man he'd ever known.

Chris lowered his head for a second, then lifted it to gaze straight ahead as if to set his final bearings on the gym. He then pulled effortlessly through a butterfly cross. After rotating through his famous Maltese cross to inverted cross combinaton, Chris lowered back down to a back-lever and bounced up to iron cross. Determined to make a statement for what he knew would be the last Rings routine of his life, Chris rolled from his cross position to an inverted hang, then immediately pulled upward to execute something new—an inverted butterfly cross to inverted cross! Without hesitation, he swung forward to another Maltese cross before pressing his body back up to a motionless handstand. He then decided to show everyone that he was not just a strength specialist. From the handstand, Chris dropped into a tucked double back dislocate, to a piked double back, to a layout double back right back to where he started in another rock-solid handstand.

Coach Lowery, who had been standing at the ready, looked up from his position on the landing mat. It was then that he saw what immediately sent a chill down his spine. A trickle of blood was starting to fall from Chris's nose. Chris bailed from his handstand to a very easy layed-out double back. Although he staggered upon his landing, it was nonetheless good enough to count and was punctuated with the thunderous applause of the crowd.

Chris raised his arms to salute the judges and turned to his coach. "How's that, Coach?" he asked as Coach Lowery could see the strength draining rapidly from his star gymnast. "Don't let 'em …quit, Coach … " Chris said faintly as his body went limp and dropped to the mat.

"Chris!" shouted Coach Lowery as he reached to catch him, only to have him slip through his fingers and collapse. The capacity crowd rose to its feet and heaved a collective gasp. The rest of the Pioneers rushed to his side. Before he hit the mat, Mrs. McClure, Haley, and Dr. Gardner had leapt from their chairs and darted to the ring tower.

"Out of my way!" shouted Dr. Gardner as he pushed his way through the crowd with a stretcher in tow, dropping to his side and putting his ear on Chris's massive chest. He examined Chris for vital signs. "He's all right," he announced, "but he's unconscious. Patrick, Mackee, Dallas, help me get him on the stretcher. Be careful!" The four took great care lifting Chris onto the stretcher. The quiet calm of concern from the crowd became applause as the stretcher moved toward the exit.

As the stretcher moved off of the competition floor and toward a waiting ambulance, Chris regained consciousness.

"What happened?" Chris called out as his eyes opened and stared at the haze of the fluorescent bulbs in the arena hallway.

"You blacked out, Chris," said Dr. Gardner, "but you appear to be stable for now. But, your part of the competition is over."

"Patrick," he called faintly while extending his hand. Patrick quickly rushed to his side.

"I'm right here, pal," he called, grasping Chris's outstretched hand.

"Don't let 'em quit, plowboy," he said faintly.

"Don't worry about a thing, Chris. We're gonna finish it strong, just like you. You just rest and let the Rick take care of you. We'll take it from here."

"Rick," Chris called

"I'm here, Chris."

"Don't take me out yet. I want to stay here with my team 'til they finish," Chris pleaded.

"Chris, we've got to get you to the hospital. There's nothing here to help you if your situation degrades any further," answered Dr. Gardner.

"We all know my situation is gonna degrade further, Rick. At least give me one more minute."

"Okay, Chris," said Dr. Gardrer, stopping the gurney, "one minute."

"Thanks, Rick. Now, Patrick, you guys go out and finish what you started. Remember, the only way to control is to let go."

Patrick tightened his grip on Chris's hand.

"Not to worry, Chris. You were right. We can do this."

"No, Patrick, You were right."

"What do you mean?"

"You said it the first day I was a Pioneer. We were cruisin' on the boulevard and you summed it up."

"Golly, Chris, what did I say?"

"It's not where we're going that's important, it's how we get there…"

"…and in our case it's with class…" Patrick remembered.

"…and in style!" Chris finished the phrase.

"I remember now." Patrick recalled the silly incident with a wry smile.

"Now you guys go out there and finish this meet and show them what it is to be a Pioneer."

"You should know, Chris, you've shown us all how. Don't worry. We'll wrap this puppy up and be down to see you in a jiff."

"No rush, plowboy. I won't be there."

"What?" exclaimed Patrick.

"I'm gonna be right here, every step. My body may be hangin' on at the hospital, but my spirit, my heart, will be right here with you guys."

"Don't worry, Chris, we won't let you down," said a teary-eyed Joey.

"No chance, pal," echoed Patrick.

"Time to go, Chris," said Dr. Gardner, pulling the gurney toward the ambulance. Only then did Patrick and Chris release their grip.

"We'll be waitin' for you guys at the hospital," Haley said through her tear-drenched handkerchief.

"We'll be there right after the last dismount hits the ground."

Patrick watched as the the gurney disappeared into the tunnel.

Patrick pulled the team together to huddle. "Okay, guys, we knew this could happen. We're on our own from here on out. We just have to remember to keep our heads and compete strong. We can still finish this on top."

"Forget that noise!" shouted Joey. "I'm goin' to the hospital to be with Chris."

"Joey, we need you here. Believe me, I'd love nothing better than to dump this meet and be with Chris, too."

"Then let's go, Pat!" said Mackee, echoing Joey's desire.

"Chris made me promise, guys. He knew this might happen, and he made me promise that I would make you guys finish."

"What made him think you could make us finish?" insisted Dallas.

"He knew I couldn't, but he knew that if you guys knew that it was his … dying wish above all that you guys finish the meet, he knew that would be enough."

The team looked at each other for a gut check.

"I guess we better make it worth the effort!" said Mackee.

Patrick placed his hand in the middle of the group, soon to be followed by all of the team, their hands stacked one on top of the other.

"This is for Chris!" shouted Patrick.

"Pioneers!" shouted Joey. The team did their standing back tucks and headed back toward the ring tower.

"What would you do, Patrick?" asked Joey.

"What do you mean?" asked Patrick, puzzled.

"If this were your last chance."

Nothing else need to be said. Everyone knew just what Joey meant.

"I guess I had better do a Ring set," said Mackee, knowing that he would be the first to test his resolve.

As the Pioneers re-emerged from the tunnel, the crowd cheered, but their cheers were tempered, knowing one was missing from the fold.

Mackee approached the chalk bucket defiantly. After applying just the right amount of chalk on his hands and grips, he reached into the chalk dish to grasp one of the only chunks of chalk not pulverized into powder. Mackee used the small chunk of the magnesium carbonate compound to draw the letters "CM" on his left bicep. He then punctuated his mission by clapping his chalky hands together and marching toward the ring tower.

"Are you ready, Mack?" asked Coach Lowery, poised to assist him.

"What, are you kidding? This is gonna rock your world, Coach." Mackee saluted the head judge and jumped up to the wooden rings, gripping them as though he were choking the life out of them. Coach Lowery stepped aside to watch the show.

Mackee first paid his respects to Chris by repeating the opening sequence that Chris had done. The crowd rose to its feet to see Mackee show exceptional control through the seemingly endless strength combination of butterfly cross, Maltese cross, inverted cross, back-lever bounce cross. Mackee pulled from his cross position upward to an L seat, rolling to his inverted cross, and pressing to a rock-solid handstand. From the handstand, Mackee dropped to a double front tucked, double front piked, swing-to-handstand combination. Mackee could see his coach out of the corner of his left eye.

"Bring it home, Mack," said Coach Lowery with the clap of his hands.

Mackee took a quick breath before dropping from his handstand and swinging into an enormous triple back that he was able to kick out of to a stuck landing. Mackee thrust both fists into the chalky air, then pointed toward the sky. Coach Lowery gave Mackee a bear hug. Mackee walked sternly toward his team to accept high fives.

"All right, guys," said Mackee, "no celebrations until this thing is won, got it?" Mackee extended his fist into the center of the group, joined by all of the Pioneers.

"For Chris!" shouted Joey.

"For Chris!" repeated the team, and six fists swung into the air as the Pioneers turned and headed toward their next event.

The announcer gave the positions. "At the halfway mark, here are your standings: in third place, with a score of 140.95, Lake Erie Gymnastics; in second place, with a score of 141.2, Texas Star Gymnastics; and your leaders with three events to go, with a score of 141.35, Piooneeer Gymnastics!"

"Let's go, Joey," called Coach Lowery, "you're first up on Vault."

"Me?" Joey asked, confused.

"Yeah, you. With Chris out and Mackee still recovering from his Rings routine, I need a good vault to set our pace."

"I'll go first, Coach," said Dallas.

"Okay, Dallas. You go first, and Johnson, you'll follow Dallas."

"Thanks, Coach," replied Dallas, pulling off his warm-up jacket. He then turned to Joey. "This'll be a no-brainer, Joey. You just psych up and get ready to launch a gem, junior."

"You got it."

Dallas grabbed a chunk of chalk to dry his hands. He then took what was left of the chunk and repeated what Mackee had done on the previous event and marked Chris's initials on his left arm. He looked for his mark on the runway, took his position beside it, and looked down the eighty feet to the other end to see the start signal. Dallas raised his arm in readiness and stepped onto the runway. Dallas stretched both arms over his head and took a deep breath. He sprinted down the carpeted surface, increasing his speed with each step. The Pioneer senior made solid contact with the board and, after blocking the end of the table, catapulted his slender frame skyward. Dallas located his landing point with plenty of time to prepare for his landing, which came with ease and no extra movement.

Dallas punched the sky in jubilation and, after saluting the judges, marched defiantly back to his team.

"That's what I'm talkin' about!" shouted Mackee as his hands went up to meet Dallas' in triumph.

"All right, Johnson," said Dallas to Joey, "let's see if you can top that. McClure spent this whole season tryin' to prove to you and the rest of us that you belong here. Well, here's your chance to prove it!"

Joey slapped Dallas a high five and took his place near the runway as the score of 9.25 was flashed for Dallas' vault. The green flag raised, and Joey returned a salute to the judges' table and stepped onto the runway. He heaved a heavy sigh before taking that first step toward the board and table. With each step, he visualized what he had done hundreds of times. Run, punch, block, set. As the table grew larger, Joey's confidence increased. In his head, he could hear Chris's voice once again telling him the things he needed to do to get the best out of his vault. "Punch fast off the balls of your feet," he heard. Joey hit the board and reached up to the top of the table as fast as he could, twisting his body in such a way as to create the most torque and block. "Feel your chest rise … " He could hear Chris leading him through the vault. He soon found his body upright above the table as he had imagined thousands of times. As his rotating frame began to block his sight of the table, Joey realized he had reached the point of no return. It was time to merge his courage with his talent. "Now *twist!*" the voice said. Joey pulled his hands to his left side and turned his head. For a moment, he lost sight of the table but quickly found the royal blue surface of the landing mat, his feet sinking deeply into the eight-inch cushion Coach Lowery had placed on top of the twelve centimeter landing mat.

Joey raised his arms triumphantly, knowing that he had just nailed his first layout Tsukahara vault with a full twist. Although the team had made an oath not to celebrate early, Joey could not contain his excitment and was soon joined by his teammates, who were every bit as excited as the young freshman. The first to reach Joey was Dallas.

"Great job, squirt. I don't think my score is gonna hold up." Sure enough, the score for Joey's vault was posted. 9.75. Joey jumped into Dallas's arms.

"Good job, kid. Now get off of me before someone gets the wrong idea."

Joey could barely maintain his composure, but knowing how important it was to stay alert for the rest of the meet, he quickly cooled down. Joey looked up to the stands where his parents were seated to see his father flash a thumbs-up to his son. Joey returned the gesture with a smile and immediately turned his attention to his team.

Meanwhile, Chris, Haley, and Dr. Gardner had just arrived at the hospital. As the doors to the ambulance opened and the paramedics removed the gurney from the vehicle, Chris's mother, who had followed the ambulance in Dr. Gardner's car, met the group.

"How is he?" asked Chris's mother.

"He's weaker, Hanna," answered Dr. Gardner. "We need to get him inside."

Chris reached up from the gurney and grasped his mother's sleeve. "How … are … they … doin'?"

"They're doing fine, son. Joey just stuck his vault and scored a 9.75!"

"A layout Tsukahara isn't worth a 9.75," said Haley.

"No ... but a .. Tsuk full ... is," said Chris, a noticable smile on his face as the gurney was rolled inside into an available examination room.

"This will make you a little more comfortable, Chris," said Dr. Gardner, drawing medicine into a syringe from a bottle.

"Don't ... knock ... me ... out, Rick," demanded Chris, his words labored with the weight of exhaustion and pain. "Turn on the ... TV."

Dr. Gardner pulled the needle from the bottle and set it aside, knowing that Chris would not maintain consciousness long once injected. Haley turned on the television to the sports channel that was carrying the competiton. Chris could hear the announcer call the name of the next routine that was to perform.

"Dustin ... Hathaway. ... Haley ... "

"Yes, Chris," answered Haley as she took her place next to Chris.

"Watch this guy ... he's great!" Semiconscious, semicoherent, and in pain, Chris could still appreciate the sport.

"Holy crap!" said Joey. "Did you see that?"

"No kiddin'," said Mackee, having returned from his vault. "Hathaway just dismounted with a triple-twisting double layout off high bar."

"Not to mention the four different releases in his set," added Dallas.

"Guys, let's stay focused," said Patrick.

"We are, cap," said Dallas. "Just makin' sure we get to appreciate what all is goin' on around us as well."

Patrick was instantly reminded of his conversation with Chris at the lake, and he told the team, "If you're gonna remember it, fellas, remember it all. This will only happen once in our lives. Remember it well."

Ty returned to the team and high fives after another solid vault. Anchoring the event, Patrick took his place at the vault runway for his turn. AJ aproached him with his calculator and clipboard. "Patrick," said AJ, "with Hathaway's 9.85 on High Bar, you need a—"

"Don't tell me what I need! Just let me do this vault, and then I'll look at scores!" AJ left Patrick to do his vault. Once the judges gave Patrick the go-ahead, he started his run for the table. Patrick launched his muscular body up and over the table and into the air. He set his body into solid rotation and wrapped his arms into his chest, and in the next moment, he found himself standing on the landing mat, having stuck his own version of a full-twisting Tsukahara. Patrick didn't bother looking back for his score. He merely looked to the ceiling and thought of his best friend lying in a hospital bed.

How ironic it had all become, he thought. With the same seriousness that was keeping his best friend alive in a hospital bed fighting for his life, he and his teammates were playing like children, trying to fulfill a dying friend's wish.

The announcer chimed the end of the rotation. "Gymnasts, at this time, please rotate to your fifth competitive event. At the end of four rotations: in third place, with a score of 187.25, Lake Erie Gymnastics; in second place, with a score of 187.55, Pioneer Gymnastics; and your leaders with two events to go, with a score of 187.6, Texas Staaar Gymnastics!"

"Mom ... " Chris moaned as he struggled and lost his fight with consciousness.

"I'm here, Chris. Mommy's here!" Mrs. McClure tightened her grip on her only son's hand as his grip went limp. "Chris!" she screamed. Dr. Gardner jumped in and checked to make sure that Chris was still breathing.

"He's slipping into a coma! He's losing the ability to breathe on his own. We need to put him on a ventilator!" Haley pulled Chris's mother back from her son so medical personnel could do their job to keep Chris alive. Once he was placed on life support, Dr. Gardner explained the situation.

"Hanna, Chris has slipped into a coma. The aneurysm has grown to the point that it is causing his system to shut down. It's only a matter of time now."

"How long will you keep him on that machine?" she asked through her tears.

"He is receiving medicine to manage the pain. He's as comfortable as he can be, and as long as he has brain function, he can stay alive for quite a while or until the aneurysm ruptures. At that point, there's nothing that we can do."

"Can he hear?" asked Haley.

"Yes, I believe he can. He just can't react."

Haley walked over to the television.

"What are you doing, dear?" Mrs. McClure asked.

"The machines are too loud," Haley replied in a emotionless, monotone voice. "Chris can't hear the television."

"God, I wish Chris were here," said Joey. "We sure could use his p-bars score."

"Don't worry, Joe," said Mackee. "He's here."

The Pioneers threw inspired routines, marking handstands and nailing dismounts. With each hit routine the Pioneers could manage, the Texas Star gymnasts followed with another, slightly widening the gap between the top two teams.

"Great!" said Joey. "Hathaway just dismounted floor with a full-twisting double tuck."

"What did he score?" asked Mackee.

"Nine-seven-five." answered AJ.

"Great!" added Dallas, "Just tell me what I need to tie these jokers, Doujmovich."

AJ quickly tapped on the keys of his calculator.

"Nine-eight."

"Cool." Dallas spit into his hands. "Just watch, boys."

Dallas sauntered to the chalk dish and began the ritual of applying his chalk. The rest of the teams had finished their routines for the rotation, which meant that all eyes would be on him. That was just how Dallas wanted it. He had been upstaged by Joey on vault. Dallas would make sure that he was the focus of attention for his favorite event. Dallas approached his coach. After a moment's conversation, Coach Lowery looked over to the team and motioned for Patrick to join them. As Dallas stood at the edge of the mat, facing the middle of the bars, Coach Lowery and Patrick positioned themselves on the other side of the bars. Dallas saluted the judging panel. He then jumped into a glide, jamming his legs between his arms, and kipping up to a V support on one rail, he continued lifting his hips upward, stooping his legs out through his arms and continuing to push up to a handstand on one rail. As a salute to the Pioneer that he had clashed with on more than one occasion, Dallas dropped to imitate the sideways giant that Chris had done a day before. Once Dallas arrived in his handstand at the end of the giant, he could hear the cheers swell from the crowd. He then hopped to the other bar to drop into another giant. This time, instead of finishing back in a handstand like his first giant, or with a hop like Chris had done, Dallas released one hand as he approached the top of the bars and turned his body 180 degrees, like a blind change on high bar, and continued another quarter turn to a rock-solid handstand on both rails. He then pushed his body out and dropped for a more conventional giant, followed with another giant with a full turn on one arm, again stopping in a motionless handstand. After a back toss Diamidov, stutz handstand combinaton, Dallas drove his legs downward, then upward, thrusting his body up off of the rails into a tight piked double back dismount. With plenty of flight, Dallas easily spotted his landing surface and dug his feet into the vinyl mat.

Dallas acknowledged the deafening roar of the crowd with waves to all. He then jogged toward the seating area to prepare for the next event as if it were business as usual.

"Dallas," cried Coach Lowery, "where in the world did that set come from?"

"I knew it was there all along, Coach," he replied nonchalantly. "Like you've always said, though, I just had to apply myself." Dallas jogged back to his team and grabbed his gym bag.

As Dallas's score came up, the announcer updated the crowd with the information that the Pioneers were already aware of.

"Gymnasts, at this time, please rotate to your final competitive event. Your standings after five events: in third place, with a score of 234.5, Lake Erie Gymnastics; and going to the final event, we have a tie for the lead, with scores of 236.25, Texas Staaar and Pioonneeer Gymnastics!"

"Did you see that?" screamed Haley.

"What?" cried Chris's mother.

"That machine started goin' crazy when the score was announced! Get Dr. Gardner!" Mrs. McClure dashed out of the room and returned in an instant with Dr. Gardner.

"Look!" cried Haley. "What does this mean?"

"It shows an increase in brain activity, but it could be anything. It could be a reaction to increasing preasure on his brain, or he may be having some sort of episode ... "

"Haley said it jumped when they announced the team standings after the last event!" Mrs. McClure said.

The doctor thought for a moment, puzzled. "It's highly unlikely that he is reacting to an announcement on the television."

"But, it's not impossible, is it?" surmised Haley.

"No, not impossible, but highly unlikely."

"My boy has always been highly unlikely," replied Mrs. McClure, rushing to her son's side. "You hang in there, son. The boys are doing great, and I'm right here with you."

"Gentlemen," said Coach Lowery, gathering his team before they began their last event, "this is the last step. No matter how we finish up this event, I just want you guys to know how proud I am of each and every one of you."

"Thanks to you, Coach," said Patrick. "None of this would be possible if it hadn't been for you keeping us together."

"Thank you, Patrick," Coach Lowery put his open hand into the group that was now a team. "Now, let's go out and hit one more for Chris."

"For Chris!" the team replied.

Mackee was the first to compete on the final event, Horizontal Bar. He chalked his grips and took his place under the pipe, nine feet above the ground. He saluted the judges and jumped to the bar. His opening sequence included his only release skill, a Tkatchev. Mackee tapped his swing at the bottom of the bar and thrust his body skyward. As his body turned over, Mackee expected to see the bar between his legs, but this time felt different. For a split second, panic set into the senior. He knew he had packed his tap with a little more juice than normal, but still, the bar was not where he had expected. Instead, he was much higher than normal—and still rotating! Mackee reached for where the bar should've been but had to reach again, barely grabbing it by his fingertips. The extra gesture cost him some swing, and Mackee had to ad-lib an extra swing to get back into his routine.

"Oh no!" shouted Haley at the image on the TV screen.

"What is it, dear?" asked Chris's mother, whose attention was solely on her son.

"It's Mackee. He almost fell off the bar!"

"That's odd," said Dr. Gardner, monitoring the EEG.

"What's that, Rick?" asked Mrs. McClure.

"The meter pegged when Haley shouted."

"So, he can hear me?" said Haley, with hope.

"Not necessarily. He could be reacting to any loud noise. There's no evidence that he's able to identify the source."

"Why are you so negative?" asked Haley.

"I'm not being negative, Haley. I just don't want to raise any false hope."

"I'm thinking that any hope we can muster is better than no hope at all, Rick," insisted Chris's mother, looking at the motionless body of her son.

Mackee landed his double back dismount and saluted the judges, knowing that he had let his team down.

"Keep your chin up, Mack," insisted Coach Lowery. "It could've been a lot worse."

"Believe me, Coach, I know that it needed to be a lot better." Mackee walked back to his teammates and their attempt to keep his spirits up.

"Cheer up, Mack," said AJ, "The first two guys for Texas fell off horse twice. They'll have to count at least two falls." That was enough to renew hope for Mackee and the rest of the team.

"Come on, guys!" shouted Mackee with renewed confidence. "We're not out of this!"

Ty's routine, although only slightly more difficult than Mackee's, finished much cleaner, scoring a 9.25. With each routine, the crowd noise rose. For each routine that Texas Star hit, the Pioneers countered with another hit high bar routine. First, Joey hit an inspired routine, complete with clean releases and a stuck dismount. Texas countered with a well-composed Pommel Horse routine that outscored Joey's routine by two-tenths of a point. While the Pioneers were giving their all to stay in the hunt for the team title, AJ punched keys on his calculator as fast as he could to keep each gymnast up-to-date on the standings.

"So, how we doin', A?" asked Dallas prior to his turn.

"Well, Lake Erie is done, and the best they can do is third."

"Yeah, but what about us?"

"Hold on." AJ frantically punched the keys on his calculator. "Okay, I think I've got it. You and Patrick definitely have to hit for us to have a chance."

"A chance?"

"Yeah. Texas has two sets left, and if Hathaway hits his set, it's over."

"I guess I better put some pressure on him."

"Go get 'em, Dally."

Dallas approached the chalk dish, closed his eyes, and visualized his routine. Then, he opened his eyes and made his way to his position under the bar, where his coach stood in readiness.

"Are you ready, Dallas? This is the last routine of your career. Make it good."

"Don't speak so soon, Coach. I might just keep up this gig in college."

"Funny, I thought you couldn't wait for your career to be over."

"Perhaps I spoke a little soon, Coach. After all, the chicks dig an athlete."

"Perhaps you're right, Dallas." Coach Lowery chuckled as the head judge waved his green flag.

"This one's for you, Coach," said Dallas as Coach Lowery helped him set his grips on the bar.

Dallas wasted no time getting into the flow of his routine, snapping his body on top of the bar and using his leg kick and arm throw to accelerate his giants into his release combination. Coach Lowery noticed that Dallas was swinging unusually fast for his normal release combination, but the reason became clear when Dallas launched his body skyward to a layout Tkatchev, high above the bar, followed by his usual combination of straddled Tkatchev to Geinger. A slight feeling of anger came over Coach Lowery with Dallas' improvised routine, but he soon rationalized that Dallas was only doing what he had always wanted him to do, his very best gymnastics, no holds barred.

Dallas swung effortlessly in and out of front, back, and inverted giants. After his final pirouette, he set up for his dismount, and as much as he wanted to try double-twisting his double layout, he knew that he had done more than enough, and a safe landing would give him a better score than crashing. Dallas tapped his swing into a graceful full-twisting double back in layout position to a rock-solid landing. Dallas saluted the judges and roared as if he were the king of the jungle. His roar could not be heard over the deafening cheers of the crowd that had been on its feet since the opening routine. Dallas then turned to grasp his coach, a gesture that caught Coach Lowery off guard.

"Thank you, Coach," shouted Dallas over the frantic crowd noise. "Thanks for keeping me."

"Thanks for staying, Dallas," Coach returned.

Coach Lowery and Dallas walked back to the rest of the team while the judges tabulated the score. Both were met by the rest of the team as they stepped off of the mat.

"Where do we stand, AJ?" asked Coach Lowery.

"Hathaway's teammate just hit and went 9.5!" AJ said, out of breath with excitement.

"So why are you so excited?" asked Dallas.

"Hathaway fell off right before his dismount!" shouted Joey.

"So, what does that do for us, A?" asked Dallas.

AJ punched his keypad frantically. "Well, the team title is probably out of reach, but if Patrick can hit his set, he can win the all-around!"

"What does he need?" asked Coach Lowery.

"If my numbers are right, a 9.55 will do it."

"What about team?" asked Patrick as he covered his grips with chalk.

"Nine-eight," replied AJ. The team looked at Patrick, knowing that his routine, at best, could only score a 9.6. Patrick's look of concern soon turned into a wry smile.

"Patrick, no," said Coach Lowery. "You can be the winner. Take the good score, and walk out of here a national champion."

"We're all walkin' out of here champions, Coach!" replied the captain.

"Patrick," Coach Lowery pleaded, "don't make the same mistake I made. You've got to be *crazy*—"

"You know, Coach," Patrick replied, blowing the access chalk out of his grips, "you are exactly right. Let's go hit a set."

"Go get 'em, plowboy!" shouted the Pioneers.

"Hanna! Haley! Look at this!" shouted Dr. Gardner. "Chris's heart rate and brain activity are escalating!"

"What does that mean?" asked Chris's mother.

"It could mean a lot of things, but if I had to lay a bet, Hanna, I'd say your son is reacting to stimulus."

"What do you mean?"

"I could be wrong, but I think he can hear what's going on. Every time something happens on the television, his readings peg! None of this makes sense."

"Like I've always said, not much about my son has ever made sense." She leaned over to whisper in Chris's ear. "Hang in there, son. You're almost home." Chris's mother squeezed the hand of her son, and a tear dropped from her cheek to his, causing the meters to jump once again.

"Patrick, the judges are ready!" said Coach Lowery to his final competitor, who, for the moment, appeared oblivious to the judge's signal.

"I know, Coach. I just thought I'd send one up to Chris," Patrick closed his eyes and pointed to the sky. He opened his eyes and returned a salute to the judges' table. Coach Lowery lifted his captain to the bar and stood back to watch the show.

Patrick lifted his legs to the bar and thrust them backward to lift his body above the bar. He began to crank his body around the metal pipe for just the right timing. With each giant, Patrick's breathing became shallow, and, although the crowd noise was deafening as the entire focus of spectators, coaches, and athletes alike was on him, he had shut out everything else. It was only him and the bar. Patrick swung through the bottom of his last giant and kicked his legs upward. Patrick willed his hands to release the bar as his body rotated high above the bar. He watched the bar as long as he could, feeling his heart pounding as if at any moment it would burst right through his chest. Then came the moment of truth, and, unlike any time he had ever tried a difficult skill, an eerie calm came over him, and a familiar voice entered his head. "Twist!" said the voice, and Patrick pulled his arms into his chest to turn his body away from the bar. What came in an instant felt like a lifetime. By instinct alone, Patrick extended his arms to find what he could not yet see. Then, at once, there it was. SLAP! His hands hit the bar, his fingers wrapped around the hot metal, and without skipping a beat, Patrick swung through the bottom of his swing, turned his legs over and released once more to flip, half turn, and regrasp the bar once again. By now, Patrick could hear the crowd noise, and although he just wanted to hurry and get off the bar, he also wanted to make the moment last forever. Patrick sailed through the rest of his routine, using unusual flair and dynamics to punctuate every position. As all good things must come to an end, Patrick found himself setting up his dismount and catapulted a gigantic double full-twisting double layout, leaving him plenty of time to seek out the vinyl landing surface.

Once his feet darted into the landing mat, the crowd that had seemingly done every skill with him, burst into a deafening roar. Patrick barely took the time to salute the judges and acknowledge the crowd.

"Let's go, Coach," he said to his mentor, and the two headed toward the rest of the team. They had gathered their belongings, ready to depart for the hospital, but paused for a moment to cheer their captain. While Patrick put on his shoes, Coach Lowery quickly dialed his cell phone.

"Mrs. McClure, *look!*" cried Haley. Chris's mother raised her head from her son's chest to see what Haley saw. A tear was rolling down the side of Chris's face, and his mouth, which had been motionless with the rest of his body for better than an hour, had formed a smile.

"Wheeeee!" screamed the heart monitor.

"He's coding!" shouted Dr. Gardner, "Get the crash cart ready. Starting CPR, now—" before he could jump up on the bed, he was restrained by Chris's mother.

"No, Rick, it's time to let him go" she said with a calm voice and a tear in her eye. She stepped over to the bed where her son lay, losing his fight with life. "Good job, son. I love you. Say hello to your father for me. I'll see you both soon." She brushed Chris's blonde hair back and kissed him on the forehead.

The room phone rang. Haley answered it with tears in her eyes. "Hi, Coach ... no ... he's gone," she said through tears. "He lasted through to the end, though. ... Yes, we had the meet on the television the whole time. ... Okay ... we'll see you guys later."

Patrick pounded his left foot into his shoe and stood quickly. "Okay, let's hustle, fellas." He led his team toward the exit but was met halfway by a sorrowful Coach Lowery.

"It's ... it's too late, Patrick. He's gone." At that moment, Patrick could feel the color drain from his face.

"I knew we should've gone to the hospital," said Dallas.

"No, that would've been a waste," said Patrick.

"What do you mean?" demanded Joey. "How can you say that?"

"We would've been there, Joey, but we would only have watched Chris's last wish go with him."

"You sure you're not just thinking about yourself, Pat?" said Dallas.

"No, Dallas," added Mackee. "I'm sure we all would have much rather been with Chris, but he wanted us here, more than anything."

"More than life," added Joey with a note of sadness.

"They're right, Dallas," Coach interjected. "As much as you boys wanted to be with Chris, he wanted to be here with you. You guys should be proud. It was not an easy thing to finish this competition, but we all knew that this is what Chris wanted, and you guys did yourselves proud. Haley said that

Chris lasted as long as he could. And he was still alive when you dismounted, Patrick. So, as far as we know, Chris was here in spirit, which is exactly where he wanted to be if he couldn't be here in body."

Each of the Pioneers looked to the others, and each bowed his head for a moment of reflection, each saying good-bye in his own way.

"Okay, gentlemen," said Coach Lowery, "if Chris is looking down on you, I think he'd like to see you boys standing on the awards stand. Let's go out there and see how we ended up."

As the team emerged from the tunnel, the crowd noise level jumped once again. In their haste to leave the pavilion, no one had taken the time to see what Patrick had scored.

"Patrick, *look*!" exclaimed Joey, spinning his team captain around to see the electronic result that had not changed since Patrick's High Bar score had been posted. Patrick turned to see what he had never thought he would see.

"It's a 9.9!" shouted Mackee, hugging his pal. "We won! We won!" The team, one by one, mobbed its leader until Patrick could not be seen beneath the mound of jubilant Pioneers.

The Pioneers made their way around the pavilion floor, seeking out friends, family, and well-wishers, waving and shaking hands to those who could reach down from the seating area. Patrick sought out the green eyes of Nicole. Once their eyes met, Nicole knew that what she had feared had happened. She leaned over the railing. "Chris?" she asked, knowing the answer. Patrick nodded and shed a tear, confirming her suspicion. She, too, broke into tears. He reached up to take her hand.

"Gentlemen," called the announcer, "please report to the staging area to prepare for the awards ceremony."

"You need to go now," she said. Patrick reluctantly released her hand and started toward the tunnel. Patrick looked for his teammates. They had all scattered throughout the floor, waving and acknowledging the crowd that had supported them. He reached Mackee first.

"Let's go, Mack. We gotta get ready for awards."

"Right," he replied, caught up in the elation. "Man, I wish Chris was here."

"He is, Mack. Trust me, he's here." Patrick and Mackee gathered the rest of the team and made their way back to the tunnel for the staging of the awards ceremony. When they arrived in the tunnel, all of the teams were already there to offer congratulations and condolences. Marty Reynolds and Danny Diego met Patrick as he came back.

Danny put his arm around Patrick's shoulder. "Words can't do it for us, Patrick."

"You guys heard?"

"Well, we suspected," said Marty. "We saw you guys dash out. We figured he was okay. Then, we saw you guys come back. We figured the only way you guys would still be here is if there was nothing more to do."

"So, you guys knew about his problem?"

"We're probably the only ones," said Danny. "He wasn't the type to wear it on his sleeve."

"That was the great thing about him," added Marty. "He certainly didn't behave like someone who was living on borrowed time."

"No disrespect, Marty," said Patrick. "He actually *did* act like he was on borrowed time."

"You're right, Patrick," added Danny. "If anything, he acted like every day was his last."

"That's probably not a bad way to approach life," surmised Patrick.

While the three considered what they had just said, the staging coordinator interrupted them to line them up for awards. The first awards were for the all-around. Once they lined up, the music sounded, and the group was led out to the edge of the floor exercise carpet. The awards platform was centered on the carpet. Patrick looked at the tallest spot on the platform, which was reserved for the champion. Knowing that he would be on that spot in a moment's time, he turned to look at his team, who would soon be there as well. There, he saw Dallas with his arm around Joey's shoulder. Joey was holding his left arm up, his index finger extended. Mackee had two fingers of each hand in his mouth, helping him create a high-pitched whistle that cut through the rest of the deafening crowd noise. Coach Lowery had his arms wrapped around the shoulders of AJ and Ty, an unwrapped cigar in his mouth.

"Ladies and gentlemen," called the announcer, "presenting your National Team Invitational national all-around champion, with a score of 58.25, from Pioneer Gymnastics, Patrick Gooodmaan!"

Patrick waved his arms and walked around to the front of the awards stand. He was presented with flowers by a young lady, and the gold medal, with a red, white, and blue ribbon, was draped over his head by the mayor of Los Angeles. Patrick then ascended to the top of the awards stand to the cheers of the entire arena, everyone on their feet.

Patrick looked back to his team, then to Nicole, and finally to the roof of the pavilion to try to find the face of his dear friend. "Thanks, Chris," he said softly with a smile. Patrick then looked out at the crowd and raised his arms over his head just before the flood of tears streamed down his face.

After the thunderous ovations, the other two medal winners were announced. As Marty Reynolds stepped onto the second-place position to accept his silver medal, he extended his hand to congratulate Patrick.

"Great job, Patrick. That was one helluva High Bar set. Chris would've been proud."

"Thanks, Marty. I'm sure he is," Patrick replied as he firmly shook Marty's hand.

Then, it was Danny's turn, waving to the crowd and accepting his bronze medal.

"Way to go, Patrick. Where are you gonna be this fall?" The question had caught Patrick off guard. Until that moment, competing beyond NTI's hadn't crossed his mind.

"I don't know," was all he could think to say.

"You gotta be kiddin' me." added Marty. "See me after all this. I gotta introduce you to somebody."

"Me, too, Patrick," Danny jumped in. "There's no way you're not gonna help somebody next season!"

The announcer broke the conversation with the introduction of the medal winners:

"Ladies and gentlemen, introducing your National Team Invitational all-around champions!"

The three raised their arms to the cheers of the hoarse, yet jubilant, gymnastics fans. Patrick felt as though his heart would pound right through his chest. He had run the entire spectrum of emotions and was now looking forward to sharing the platform with his friends and teammates.

The trio was led off of the podium and back to the staging area, where Patrick was greeted with hugs and high fives by the other Pioneers. Before Patrick had a chance to recover from the reception from his teammates, it was time to march out once again, this time with his comrades.

"So, Patrick," asked Joey as they lined up for the march out, "what's it like out there?"

"A rush, Joey. It's a pure rush," For the first time, Patrick had come to understand what the total experience was about.

Patrick looked to his left and saw AJ standing by. "What are you doin', A? Get in line!"

"But I didn't compete," said AJ sadly.

"But you are a part of this team. Now get in line," Patrick commanded, and AJ jumped in at the end of the line.

"What are you doing?" demanded the staff worker in charge of lining up the teams, pulling AJ out of the line. "He didn't compete with you guys."

"He marches out, or none of us march out!" demanded Mackee, the team echoing his words. The staffer gave in, and AJ jumped back in line.

As the teams marched out, Joey was so overwhelmed by the experience that he forgot to step up on the floor exercise carpet, tripping instead, nearly knocking the entire team over.

"Sorry, guys," Joey exclaimed, righting himself.

"Don't sweat it, Joe," said Mackee. "We're all having a tough time walking right now."

"Ladies and gentlemen," called the announcer, "presenting your National Team Invitational team champions, with a score of 283.55, from Knoxville, Tennessee, Piooneeeeer Gymnaastics!"

The team marched around to the front of the awards stand, led by their captain, waving to thirteen thousand of their newest, closest friends. As the gold medals were draped over their heads, one by one, the Pioneers took their place on the stand.

"Ladies and gentlemen, your National Team Invitational team champions!"

Although Patrick was the first, it didn't take the rest of the team long to catch on to his gesture. One by one, each of the Pioneers removed his medal and raised it to the sky in tribute to their friend.

"To Chris!" Patrick shouted.

"To Chris!" the team shouted. The ovations from the crowd became puctuated by tears.

"Ladies and gentlemen, presenting the coach from Pioneer Gymnastics, Mr. James Lowery." Coach Lowery wiped the tears from his eyes and cleared his throat as he made his way to the announcer's microphone.

"Ladies and gentlemen, coaches, officials, honored guests, and of course, gymnasts, it is with mixed feelings that I stand before you. As any coach can tell you, it's not easy getting to this point. You not only have to be blessed with a team of talented, dedicated gymnasts, but also there has to be a chemistry between them, something that helps each of the gymnasts to push harder to be their best and pick them up on those not so good days.

"For me, the job has been relatively easy. This team over the past season has pushed each other, pulled for each other, and even fought with each other, but no matter what the obstacle, these guys stuck together because they had a common goal, to be standing where they are right now." Coach Lowery's words were broken off by the thunderous applause of the crowd. "As you can see, we are missing a couple of vital parts. AJ Doujmovich was injured during workouts last week, and I'm sure many of you noticed the disappearance of one of our seniors who competed earlier today. For those of you who do not already know, Chris McClure ... lost his battle with a brain aneurysm at the medical center toward the end of competition.

"Chris came to us at the end of the summer last year and, in that short period of time, impacted all of our lives. As much as I would like to say about Chris, I think it would be best if you heard it from the person that was closest to him on the team. At this time, I would like to call to the microphone the captain of the Pioneers, Patrick Goodman."

The crowd rose to its feet as the senior Pioneer jumped down from the awards stand and made his way toward the microphone. Along the way, Patrick accepted handshakes and pats on the back from coaches, judges, and athletes. As he hit the top step of the platform where the announcer's station was located, Patrick was engulfed in his coach's arms.

"I don't know what to say, Coach," he said to his mentor.

"Sure you do. Just say what's in your heart." Coach Lowery patted his protégé on the back and stood behind him as he approached the microphone. Before beginning, Patrick wiped more tears from his eyes and tried to clear his throat with little success. Through tear-soaked eyes, he looked out over the crowd and waited for the ovations to die down.

"Before Chris McClure came to our gym, we thought we had life pretty much figured out," he said. "Then, this brash, cocky, aggressive guy showed up, and we began asking questions, like, 'How can he do the things he does?' and 'Why does nothing seem to scare this guy?' Well, over the past year, we discovered a lot of the answers and along the way answered questions about ourselves that we hadn't even asked yet.

"Many have called Chris a daredevil, a risk-taker, even a fool. However, I think the word that best described Chris is ... a pioneer. Before Chris came to our gym, I never really thought about the word *pioneer*. To me, it just meant a bunch of guys that founded uncharted land and a good name for a gymnastics program. But, having someone like Chris around helped me to find the real meaning. When you think about what it takes to be a real pioneer, you'll see what I mean. To be a pioneer, whether it's the early explorers or the men and women of the space program, they each had something in common. Each had to summon up the courage to do something no one had ever done or go somewhere that no one had ever been before. It's one thing to accept risks when you can predict the outcome. It's quite another thing when you have no idea what lurks on the other side.

"Chris had known since he was a boy that he had inherited a brain aneurysm. From that moment, he knew that regardless of how he lived his life, at some point, for no apparent reason, he would be taken from this world. Perhaps knowing that his life could end at any moment made it easier for him to live the way he did, but I don't think so. Each one of us knows that at any moment, we could be struck down in a car accident or some other circumstance, but for whatever reason, we take the time we have for granted. Perhaps Chris's situation was different, but he still had to make a conscious choice to live each day as if it were truly his last, to accept each risk as an opportunity to be his very best. Chris expected his best in everything he did. It was this expectation that made him push for his very best in everything he tried.

"Chris knew that the end was coming soon, yet his dedication to this sport and his desire to see us reach our goals came first. His last … wish … " Patrick found it more and more dificult to speak, "was for us to finish this competition, with or without him. Chris made it easy for us to accept the challenges before us, because we could see every day the challenge that he was facing. Even though Chris is … gone … his presence will be felt by all of us for the rest of our lives. So, tonight when you go to bed, be sure to drop to your knees and send one up for the greatest pioneer of all, Chris McClure… … Thank you." Patrick could hold up no longer. As the flood of tears drained from his eyes, Patrick fell into his coach's grasp. Then, the two descended the steps and made their way toward the rest of their team.

The announcer closed the ceremony and dismissed the crowd. Many of the gymnasts remained on the floor, congratulating competitors and saying good-bye to gymnasts that they would not see again until the following season. For some, it was the end of their competitive careers, and for others, it was merely "so long" until they meet again on the collegiate competition floor.

THIRTY-TWO

▼

IT HAD BEEN a week since the funeral. Coach Lowery had given the team a well-deserved break from training. For Jim Lowery, it was a time to start over again. Losing four seniors left many gaps to fill, most importantly the gymnast who would lead the next group of Pioneers. There were not many freshmen to fill the spots.

As Coach walked into his office, there was a familiar figure sitting in his chair.

"Patrick!" shouted a surprised Coach Lowery. "What are you doin' here? Aren't you supposed to be on a vacation or something?"

"Actually, I leave tomorrow for a recruiting trip."

"Really? Where?"

"Ohio. Marty Reynolds hooked me up with the coach at State, and they might be able to give me a scholarship."

"Patrick, that's great!"

"Yeah, but I might not take it."

"Why in the world not?"

"Well, Danny Diego has me set up with the head coach at Los Angeles. I go out there next week."

"It all sounds very exciting, Pat. Why do you look so glum?"

"I really think that I may just go to school here instead."

"Why? There's no gymnastics program here. And, if either of these schools gives you a scholarship, that will surely take the financial pressure off of your folks."

"But, I think I know what I'd like to do, and I need to be here."

"And what would that be?"

"You're probably going to laugh."

"Try me."

"Okay. I think I'd like to coach."

"There's nothing wrong with that, Patrick. But why do you need to be here to coach?"

"Because I can't see myself working for anyone but you, Coach."

"Patrick, I appreciate the sentiment, but don't limit your possibilities. I'm in no way the best person to teach you to coach. I've enjoyed having you here, and you've done a great job teaching classes. You've turned into quite the good coach already, but you should see what the rest of the world has to offer."

"Are you tryin' to get rid of me, Coach?" Patrick said in despair.

"No, Pat. I'd love nothing more than to have you here as a part of my staff. But, I would feel really guilty if you were to pass up a scholarship just to coach here."

"But what if this is where I want to be?"

"Listen, this place will still be here when you finish your education. You owe it to yourself to have the whole college experience."

"What do you mean?"

"Everything. Competing for a college team where everyone on the team is as good as you, getting a quality education, and everything else that college has to offer."

"What if I don't like it?"

"Oh, you'll like it. It's like nothing you've experienced before. Besides, like I said, this place will still be here when you're done. I don't plan to coach the rest of my life. I'll need someone to take over the reins someday. Someone trustworthy, intelligent, and educated. Go to these recruiting trips, and see what they have to offer. Then, pick the one that suits you. You'll see that college will prepare you for life in ways you haven't even thought of yet. And when you're done, if you still want to coach, you'll always have a position here. Just get your education first."

"I guess you're right, Coach. I am kinda looking forward to going back to California. I hear Chris's mom is moving back there."

"Of course I'm right. So, what's happening with Nicole?"

"Not much. She's staying in Memphis. With her dad on staff with the university, going to school there just makes sense. So, knowing that it would be a relationship over time and distance, we both felt that we better slow down. But who knows? Fate has a funny way of changing plans." Patrick quickly tried to change the subject. "So, what about you, Coach? Have you got any new hotshots for next year?"

"I haven't the first clue. Today is the first workout before next week's tryouts."

"Do you have any potential stars?"

"There's always potential, as you know. The trick is getting them to realize it themselves."

"Well, at least you'll have Joey, Ty, and AJ to help take up the slack."

"True, but it's going to take awhile for these guys to find their identity. Do you want to see the new crop?"

"Sure!"

Coach Lowery and Patrick walked out of the office and into the gym. The floor exercise carpet was covered with wide-eyed potential team members. The pair stepped up onto the carpet. All eyes turned toward them.

"Gentlemen," announced Coach Lowery, "this is—"

"Patrick Goodman!" shouted one of the boys. "I saw him compete on television! You're the *best*!"

"Thanks, little guy," Patrick said with a blush. "I am what I am because of this man right here. If you want to be a champion, you just listen to what Coach Lowery says, and you'll do just fine."

A team candidate sitting in the front row waved his arm excitedly to get Patrick's attention. Patrick pointed the youngster out.

"What does it take to be as good as you?" asked the boy.

Patrick blushed again. "Well, obviously it takes hard work, but it's much more than that. If you're in here for the awards or the fame, I'm afraid you may not figure it out. The real secret is just loving the idea of being in here training. If you love this sport, and all that comes with it; the long hours, the bumps and bruises, the many, many failures you have to endure before you know success, then just maybe you've got what it takes."

Patrick paused for a moment, thinking of how Chris would've answered that question.

"Oh, there is one other thing," he said. "If you have a dream, regardless of whether it's to make this team or be a national champion, you must understand the cost and be happy and willing to pay it, and pay it now. If you want that dream, you have to start chasing it today. A wise man once said, 'Dream like you'll live forever, but live like you'll die tomorrow.'"

A hush fell over the group and a tear welled in Patrick's eye.

"I'm sorry, fellas. I didn't mean to be so sappy. Just remember, this life and this crazy sport are like a rollercoaster. It's gonna have its share of ups and downs. You have to keep your goals in mind to get you through the downs to appreciate the rest. Just remember that and enjoy the ride!"

"Thank you, Patrick. Boys, Patrick is just one of the many success stories of this program. Remember, you don't have to be a national champion to be a success. If you enjoy working hard and the experience of the learning process, gymnastics can take you a long way."

A smile came over Patrick's face as he remembered that those were almost the same exact words that Coach Lowery used when he was just a rookie. He and Mackee were there together, just skinny little rug rats, not unlike the group of boys seated before him. As Coach Lowery continued to talk to the new crop of Pioneers, Patrick thought about all of the experiences and emotions he had been through as a member of the Pioneer program. He took a long look around the building, recalling a different experience at each part of the gym: the contests with his teammates, the struggles and successes, Mackee's practical jokes, and Dallas's machismo, but most of all the love and camaraderie among him and his team.

Coach Lowery put the final touch on his opening-day comments to the group. A sound from behind them caused Coach Lowery and Patrick to quickly turn around to see what the others could already see. A familiar figure, with his hair cut into a mohawk and a stud in his left ear, jammed a CD into the deck. He turned around, and to the surprise of Coach Lowery and Patrick, it was Joey.

His hand poised on the play button, Joey announced to the group, "Gentlemen, it's time to rock!"

Just then, all of the memories of Patrick's experience at Pioneer Gymnastics washed over him. Good memories, bad memories, the pain, and the payoffs. Patrick realized that, with every adversity he had experienced as a Pioneer, there was an equally joyous conclusion that made the pain worthwhile. From that moment, win or lose, up or down, success or failure, no matter how he looked at it, the feeling would always be bittersweet.